D0113300

Praise for

GUANTÁNAMO DIARY

"Extraordinary.... Certainly the most important and engaging example of prison literature to have emerged so far from the misconceived Global War on Terrorism."
—Steve Coll, *New York Review of Books*

"More than just a memoir, the book is a unique and intimate view of what happens when due process is suspended and detainees...are cast into zones of nonbeing, where they are not even recognized as human.... The manuscript raises a broader question about whether torture actually works.... Slahi gives us a rare window into the Kafkaesque dilemma faced by a tortured detainee who is assumed guilty by virtue of his very captivity. The shadowy reach of the U.S. government can be felt throughout the book."
—Chris Serres, *Minneapolis Star Tribune*

"Offers a near real-time account of early experimentation at Guantánamo—something exceptionally rare because the U.S. military has never allowed reporters to talk to its prisoners, neither those cleared to go nor those awaiting trial.... The book recounts...material that would frankly be unbearable if it weren't at times clever in Slahi's capacity to frame it with irony."
—Carol Rosenberg, *Miami Herald*

"A vision of hell, beyond Orwell, beyond Kafka: perpetual torture prescribed by the mad doctors of Washington."
—John le Carré, author of *A Delicate Truth*

"Written in the colloquial... English Slahi picked up during his captivity, its pages disfigured with thousands of pitch-black 'redactions' courtesy of the American intelligence agents who play such major parts, the work is a kind of dark masterpiece, a sometimes unbearable epic of pain, anguish, and bitter humor that the Dostoyevsky of *The House of the Dead* would have recognized and embraced.... The process, which has never been described more intimately or more convincingly, resembles nothing so much as a postmodern globalized version of the Salem witch trials.... When the suffering of the untried and unconvicted becomes nothing more than collateral damage, America has crossed a gulf. The steps that took us there were largely secret, but thanks to this and other accounts we know about them now."
— Mark Danner, *New York Times Book Review*

"Vital and stunning.... An historical watershed and a literary triumph." — Elias Isquith, *Salon*

"Slahi is a fluent, engaging, and at times eloquent writer, even in his fourth language, English.... The public record, such as it is, lends weight to Slahi's version of events.... In 2004, then-Guantánamo prosecutor Lt. Col. Stuart Couch dramatically refused to bring charges against Slahi after determining that his incriminating statements were made only as a result of torture. Slahi's descriptions of that torture are the book's most compelling, and difficult, passages. They unfortunately have the substantial ring of truth, closely consistent with descriptions in official investigations of the treatment of other U.S.-held detainees.... The diary is also leavened with vivid, idiosyncratic detail that makes it impossible to discount."
— Deborah Pearlstein, *Washington Post*

"Slahi learned English during his detention. But his prose is shot through with moving pathos and beauty....Slahi's voice is complex, wry, perceptive....The handwritten pages that are interspersed throughout the book have the chastening effect of authenticity. The pages are blotted with excisions that create a literal void, the names, details, and locations that are still classified. They also come to represent a more pervasive void: an incomplete reckoning with the unconscionable policies performed in the name of American citizens."

—John Yargo, *The Millions*

"The big surprise about Slahi's book...is that, in addition to being appalling and sad, it's funny....The diary's tone is friendly, exasperated, curious, and ironic....Slahi doesn't just humanize himself; he also humanizes his guards and interrogators. That's not to say that he excuses them. Just the opposite: he presents them as complex individuals who know kindness from cruelty and right from wrong." —Joshua Rothman, *The New Yorker*

"A riveting new book has emerged from one of the most contentious places in the world, and the U.S. government doesn't want you to read it. Apologies if this sounds like an overheated marketing tagline. The thing is, it's demonstrably true....There's still plenty we don't know about Guantánamo, a prison in which horrifying acts were carried out in the name of every American citizen." —Kevin Canfield, *San Francisco Chronicle*

"Compelling reading...chiefly for its contents but also because of the idiosyncratic command of English that Mr. Slahi picked up mainly during his confinement. He vividly describes being deprived of sleep for days on end and chained to the floor of freezing cold rooms." —*Economist*

"Anyone who reads *Guantánamo Diary*—and every American with a shred of conscience should do so, now—will be ashamed and appalled. Slahi's demand for simple justice should be our call to action. Because what's at stake in this case is not just the fate of one man who managed, against all odds, to tell his story, but the future of our democracy."

—Glenn Greenwald, author of *No Place to Hide*

"Its pages reflect an intelligent human being, befuddled, betrayed, battered unceasingly for weeks and months at a time, but still capable of humor and heart."   —Steve Paul, *Kansas City Star*

"As astonishing as the scope of the abuse is Slahi's enduring warmth, even for his torturers and jailers.... Slahi's ordeal is at the heart of *Guantánamo Diary,* but the book is about much more.... It is an account of other countries' complicity in these abuses. It is a terrible example of what happens to innocent people when the rule of law is suspended. In the words of Larry Siems, the book's editor, it is 'an epic for our times.'"

—Noa Yachot, *Huffington Post*

"Gripping.... Extraordinary.... Mr. Slahi emerges from the pages of his diary...as a curious and generous personality, observant, witty, and devout, but by no means fanatical.... *Guantánamo Diary* forces us to consider why the United States has set aside the cherished idea that a timely trial is the best way to determine who deserves to be in prison."   —Scott Shane, *New York Times*

"Despite the myriad challenges of publishing such a book, *Guantánamo Diary* stands as perhaps the most human depiction of an entire post-9/11 system."

—Omar El Akkad, *Globe and Mail*

GUANTÁNAMO DIARY

After a couple of days, I was taken to interrogation, "How are you?" said ▮▮▮ it's been long time since I saw him last, "Good!", "▮▮▮▮ were in ▮▮▮▮, when you agreed facility in GTMO in all aspects. [REDACTED]

[REDACTED]

One day in paradise, and the next in the hell. Detainees of this level are completely under the mercy of their interrogators, which was very convenient for the interrogators. [REDACTED]

[REDACTED]

I was like. what the heck is going on, I've never been in trouble with the guards, and I am answering my interrogators and cooperating with them I was chocked. But I missed that cooperation meant to tell your interrogators whatever they want to hear. I was put once more in [REDACTED] End [REDACTED] I was taken to interrogation and faced the first time a new assigned [REDACTED]

~~UNCLASSIFIED~~

GUANTÁNAMO DIARY

Restored Edition

Mohamedou Ould Slahi

EDITED BY LARRY SIEMS

BACK BAY BOOKS

Little, Brown and Company

New York Boston London

Diary, restored diary, and introduction to the restored edition
copyright © 2015, 2017 by Mohamedou Ould Slahi
Notes and introduction to the original edition copyright © 2015, 2017
by Larry Siems

Hachette Book Group supports the right to free expression and the value of
copyright. The purpose of copyright is to encourage writers and artists to
produce the creative works that enrich our culture.

The scanning, uploading, and distribution of this book without permission is
a theft of the author's intellectual property. If you would like permission to
use material from the book (other than for review purposes), please contact
permissions@hbgusa.com. Thank you for your support of the author's rights.

Originally published in hardcover by Little, Brown and Company, January 2015
First Back Bay trade paperback edition, December 2015
Restored edition, October 2017

Back Bay is an imprint of Little, Brown and Company, a division of Hachette
Book Group, Inc. The Back Bay Books name and logo are trademarks of
Hachette Book Group, Inc.

The publisher is not responsible for websites (or their content)
that are not owned by the publisher.

The Hachette Speakers Bureau provides a wide range of authors for speaking events.
To find out more, go to hachettespeakersbureau.com or call (866) 376-6591.

ISBN 978-0-316-32868-5 (hc) / 978-0-316-38925-9 (pb) / 978-0-316-51788-1
(restored edition)
Library of Congress Control Number 2014954412
10 9 8 7 6 5 4 3 2 1

LSC-C

Printed in the United States of America

To my late mother, Maryem Mint El Wadia

~~UNCLASSIFIED~~
76

you keep me in jail so why should I cooperate?
I said so not knowing that Americans use torture
to facilitate interrogation. Of course, I was very
tired from being taken to interrogation
every day. My back was just conspiring against
me. I sought Medical help, "You're not
allowed to sit for so long time" said the ███████
█████ physiotherapist, "Pls, tell my interrogators
so b/c they make sit for long hours almost every
day", "I will ~~write~~ a note but I can not
sure whether it will have effect" she replied.
Feb 03 ████ washed his hands off me "I am
going to leave but if you're ready to talk
about ~~my~~ your telephone conversations request
me. I'll come back" he said, "~~Be sure~~ I
assure you that I am not going to ~~talk about~~
anything unless you answer my question - why I
am here?", ████ asked me to dedicate an
English copy of Koran to him, which I
happily did, and off he went. I never heard
about ███████████ after that, ████ and I
to "not" working ~~together~~ but he was an over-
baring person. I don't think in a megative way.
████ just had tons of reports with all kind
of evil theories. The ~~o~~ mis-mash of what-ifs
was mainly fueled with prejudices, ~~and~~
hatered, and ignorance toward the Islamic
Religion. "I am working on showing you

~~UNCLASSIFIED~~

Contents

80

I hungrily started to read the letter but soon I got chocked. The letter was a cheap ~~forgery~~, it was not from my ~~family~~. It was the production of the Intel community. "Dear brothers, what I received no letter, I am sorry!", "Bastards, they have done so with other detainees" said a detainee. But the forgery was so clumzy and unprofessional that no ~~fool~~ would fall ~~for~~ it. First, I have no brother of mine with that ~~name~~, second, my name was misspelled, third my ~~family~~ doesn't live where the correspondent mention but close enough, ~~forth~~ I know not only the hand-writing of every single member of my ~~family~~, I also know every phrases his ideas. The letter was kind of a sermon, "Be patient like your ancestors, and have ~~faith~~ that Allah is going to reward you". I was so mad at this attempt to ~~fraud~~ me, and play with my emotions. Next day, ▮3▮ ~~too~~ pulled me for interrogation. "How is your ~~family~~ doing?", "I hope they're doing well", "I've ~~been~~ working to get you the letter!", "Thank you very much, ~~but~~ good effort, but if you guys want ~~you~~ to forge a mail let me give some advices", "What are you talking about?", I smiled "~~it~~ don't really know is okay, but it was cheap to forge a message and make me believe I have in fact with my dear ~~family~~!" I said handing him

~~UNCLASSIFIED~~

A Timeline of Detention

January 2000	After spending twelve years studying, living, and working overseas, primarily in Germany and briefly in Canada, Mohamedou Ould Slahi decides to return to his home country of Mauritania. En route, he is detained twice at the behest of the United States — first by Senegalese police and then by Mauritanian authorities — and questioned by American FBI agents in connection with the so-called Millennium Plot to bomb LAX. Concluding that there is no basis to believe he was involved in the plot, authorities release him on February 19, 2000.
2000–fall 2001	Mohamedou lives with his family and works as an electrical engineer in Nouakchott, Mauritania.
September 29, 2001	Mohamedou is detained and held for two weeks by Mauritanian authorities and again questioned by FBI agents about the Millennium Plot. He is again released, with Mauritanian authorities publicly affirming his innocence.
November 20, 2001	Mauritanian police come to Mohamedou's home and ask him to accompany them for further questioning. He voluntarily complies, driving his own car to the police station.
November 28, 2001	A CIA rendition plane transports Mohamedou from Mauritania to a prison in Amman, Jordan, where he is interrogated for seven and a half months by Jordanian intelligence services.

July 19, 2002	Another CIA rendition plane retrieves Mohamedou from Amman; he is stripped, blindfolded, diapered, shackled, and flown to the U.S. military's Bagram Air Base in Afghanistan. The events recounted in *Guantánamo Diary* begin with this scene.
August 4, 2002	After two weeks of interrogation in Bagram, Mohamedou is bundled onto a military transport with thirty-four other prisoners and flown to Guantánamo. The group arrives and is processed into the facility on August 5, 2002.
2003–2004	U.S. military interrogators subject Mohamedou to a "special interrogation plan" that is personally approved by Defense Secretary Donald Rumsfeld. Mohamedou's torture includes months of extreme isolation; a litany of physical, psychological, and sexual humiliations; death threats; threats to his family; and a mock kidnapping and rendition.
March 3, 2005	Mohamedou handwrites his petition for a writ of habeas corpus.
Summer 2005	Mohamedou handwrites the 466 pages that would become this book in his segregation cell in Guantánamo.
June 12, 2008	The U.S. Supreme Court rules 5–4 in *Boumediene v. Bush* that Guantánamo detainees have a right to challenge their detention through habeas corpus.
August–December 2009	U.S. District Court Judge James Robertson hears Mohamedou's habeas corpus petition.
March 22, 2010	Judge Robertson grants Mohamedou's habeas corpus petition and orders his release.
March 26, 2010	The Obama administration files a notice of appeal.
November 5, 2010	The DC Circuit Court of Appeals sends Mohamedou's habeas corpus case back to U.S. district court for rehearing. It languishes there for years.
January 20, 2015	*Guantánamo Diary* is published in the United States, the United Kingdom, and seven other countries. Publishers in nineteen more countries will release translations of the book in the next two years.

June 2, 2016	Mohamedou appears before a Periodic Review Board in Guantánamo.
July 14, 2016	The Periodic Review Board concludes Mohamedou's imprisonment in Guantánamo "is no longer necessary to protect against a continuing significant threat to the security of the United States."
October 16, 2016	Mohamedou is released from Guantánamo. As he was on the flight to Guantánamo fourteen years before, he is shackled and wears a blindfold and earmuffs on the U.S. military transport throughout the flight.
October 17, 2016	The military transport lands at the airport in Nouakchott, Mauritania, around 2 p.m. A few hours later, Mohamedou is reunited with his family.

SECRET//NOFORN

103

PROTECTED

comfort items, except for a thin iso-mat and
a very thin, small, and worn-out blanket. I was
deprived from my books, which I owned. I was
deprived from my Koran. I was deprived
from my soap. I was deprived from my
toothpaste - maybe -, I was deprived from
the roll of toilet paper I had. The cell -
better the box - was cooled down that I was
shaking most of the time. I was forbidden
from seeing the light of the day. Every
once in a while they gave me a rec-time in
the night to keep me from seeing or interacting
with any detainees. I was living litterally in
tenor, I don't remember having slept one
night quietly, and that if they gave me a break,
which was rarely. For the next seventy days
to come I hadn't known the sweetness of
sleeping. Interrogation for 24-hours, three,
and some times four shifts a day. I rarely
got a day-off, "If you start to cooperate you will have some sleep, and hot
meals" ▮ used to tell me repeatedly.
The last visit of ICRC: After a couple days of
my tranfer ▮ from ICRC showed up at
my cell and asked me whether I wanted to write
a teller, "yes!" I said, ▮ handed a
paper and I wrote, "Mama I love you, I
just wanted to tell you that I love you!"

SECRET//NOFORN

PROTECTED

Note on the Text and Annotations of the Restored Edition

At the end of my Notes on the Text, Redactions, and Annotations for the first published edition of *Guantánamo Diary*, I wrote,

> *So many of the editing challenges associated with bringing this remarkable work to print result directly from the fact that the U.S. government continues to hold the work's author, with no satisfactory explanation to date, under a censorship regime that prevents him from participating in the editorial process. I look forward to the day when Mohamedou Ould Slahi is free and we can read this work in its entirety, as he would have it published.*

This is that day, and that edition.

On October 16, 2016, 5,445 days after he drove himself to Mauritania's national police for questioning and was forcibly disappeared, Mohamedou was released from Guantánamo and returned to his home city of Nouakchott, Mauritania. Within hours we were video chatting—the first time we had ever spoken—and within a few weeks we were meeting face-to-face in the baggage claim area of the Nouakchott airport.

Since then, in one of the most unexpected and extraordinary pleasures of my life, we have been in contact almost every day, by e-mail, WhatsApp, Skype, and text. Much of that time has been spent working on this new edition of *Guantánamo Diary,* which realizes the aspiration I expressed in my Notes to the first edition, and which fulfills what Mohamedou has described from the moment of his release, with straightforward clarity, as a responsibility to his readers: to free the text from the restraints of U.S. government censorship.

As Mohamedou explains in his Introduction to this new edition, we came to see this process as one of restoration and reparation, as of an ancient building or damaged painting.

Had we been allowed access to the still classified original uncensored manuscript, this might have seemed a simple matter of "filling in" the redactions with the deleted text. But even that would have required some editing beyond the redactions, since sometimes the redactions froze in place phrases and text that might otherwise have been edited, and sometimes my sense of the phrasing or the content beneath the redactions was incorrect.

As it was, we carried out this process of reparation in phases, working from short redactions of nouns and pronouns to longer descriptive passages and ultimately to the three multipage erasures in the original edition, two that described polygraph examinations and one that contained a poem Mohamedou had written. It was impossible to replicate the exact text that appeared in these longer passages a decade after they were written. Instead, our commitment was to reconstruct the scenes that the censored text obscured as faithfully and accurately as possible, with Mohamedou re-creating these scenes in text and then the two of us revising and editing these passages together. Our aim was always to stay as closely as possible within the textual spaces and narrative structure of the first edition. In one case, however, this process necessitated moving a block of text that originally appeared near the beginning of chapter 5 to the end of the first chapter to correct the chronology of interrogation sessions.

In this new edition, the lightly shaded text indicates areas of restoration and reparation, for anyone wishing to compare this version with the first published edition.

Not so indicated, but easily discernible in a side-by-side comparison with the first published edition, are several revisions to my footnotes. As first published, these annotations served two purposes: first and foremost, to refer readers to government documents and other publicly available information that corroborate Mohamedou's narrative; and second, to offer occasional speculations, based on my own close reading of the text and these corroborating materials, on what might be hidden beneath the redactions. Happily there is no longer any need for these speculations, and so several of my original footnotes have been eliminated. The footnotes that remain, and a few new ones that have been added, now refer entirely to the resources available to readers interested in exploring the extensive documentary record of Mohamedou's ordeal.

Five years after I was first handed a disk with the censored version of Mohamedou's handwritten manuscript, I still struggle to fathom the scope and intensity of that ordeal, and what it says about my country's commitment to the core human rights values of due process and freedom of expression. But every day I have lived with that manuscript, and now, to my great fortune, with the living presence of its author, I have understood *Guantánamo Diary* as a profound gesture of reconstruction and of hope.

One evening during my visit to Nouakchott a few weeks after his release, Mohamedou stood at the back gate of his family's weathered home on the edge of the Sahara reenacting the events of the evening of November 20, 2001, when he said goodbye to his mother and aunt, assured them he would be home in a few hours, and climbed into his car and started toward the police station. By sheer, unnerving accident, we realized as we were standing there that it was fifteen years to the hour since his fateful odyssey began. Time telescoped; I saw him both at the beginning and the end of his journey, and I recognized, in the slightest slump of his shoulders, its enormous weight.

I have felt that weight many times since, as we worked our way through this new edition. Mohamedou is home now, and with this edition, his long quest to tell this story is complete. Speaking not as an editor but as an American citizen, I see other reparations work that remains to be done. But Mohamedou has done his part. The rest is up to us.

The End of the Story, and an Introduction to the New Edition

by Mohamedou Ould Slahi

1.

Every time we had a hurricane warning in Guantánamo Bay, I had the same daydream. I imagined the prison camp wiped away and all of us, detainees and captors alike, fighting side by side to survive. In some versions I saved many lives, in others I was saved, but somehow we all managed to escape, unharmed and free.

This is what I was imagining on October 7, 2016, when Hurricane Matthew was building in the Caribbean. The forecast was predicting a direct hit on Guantánamo, so the camp command decided to move all the detainees, about seventy of us, to Camp 6, the safest facility in GTMO. I was told that my belongings might not survive the hurricane, so I took my family pictures, my Koran, and two DVDs of the TV sitcom *Two and a Half Men*. The NCO in charge, a sympathetic Hispanic sergeant first class in his forties, arranged for another detainee to lend me his portable DVD player, but the machine died within minutes.

Outside my cell, an argument broke out between one of the detainees and the guards over the temperature in the block, an argument we all knew was futile, but the detainee had started and now couldn't stop.

"You Americans, even if I treat you as human beings, you don't respect me," he was yelling.

"We can do this the easy way or the hard way," the guards were yelling back. I did my best to tune them out, and I spent the night listening for the sound of the heavy wind battering the cell, daydreaming another dramatic escape.

The structure was so strong that I never even heard the storm. But in the morning the camp was buzzing with rumors about detainees who were going to leave. One rumor said that there was a comprehensive plan that I was going be resettled along with Abdul Latif Nasir, a Moroccan detainee, and Soufiane Barhoumi from Algeria. We had all heard so many rumors over the years that turned out to be just that, rumors, that we knew not to celebrate; this would prove to be another.

For me, though, the real news came that afternoon. The bearer was our brand-new officer in charge. She had just taken over and I had not even met her yet, but now this army captain was sticking her head through my bin hole and giving me the broadest smile I'd seen in many years.

"Do you know that you're going to leave soon?" she said. It was the best introduction to a new OIC ever: I'm taking over, and you're going home.

I was moved to a different cellblock. I met with representatives from the International Committee of the Red Cross, who officially informed me that I was to be transferred. The U.S. government dreads the mention of detainees being freed, so it uses its own vocabulary of "transfer" and "resettlement," as if we were cargo or refugees. Yazan, a Jordanian representative I knew from previous ICRC delegations, asked if I would accept resettlement to my home country of Mauritania. I told him I would take any transfer I was offered, quoting the title of a Chris Cagle country song: "Anywhere but Here." The next day, my attorneys Nancy Hollander and Theresa Duncan called me from the United States to confirm the news. Only then I could say to myself, *Now it's official: I'm leaving this prison after so many years of pain and humiliation.*

"You have the Gold Meeting tomorrow," the new OIC told me when I got back to my cell after the call. Her smile still hadn't faded.

The "Gold Meeting" takes place in Gold Building, a structure that was built for interrogation. At first, the interrogations there were not so bad by Guantánamo standards. We answered all kinds of questions from FBI, CIA, and military intelligence officers, as well as investigators who came from around the world at the invitation of their American colleagues. But the building was given a face-lift in 2003 and then was used along with the so-called Brown and Yellow buildings for torture sessions. It was in this same Gold Building that I spent many sleepless and cold nights that year, shivering in my shackles, eating countless tasteless MREs, and listening to "Oh say can you see, by the dawn's early light" in an endless, repeating loop. Now the bushes around the building were growing out of control, and the old Delta Three camp next door looked like a graveyard. Romeo block, where I spent my last days before I was dragged into a boat in a fake kidnapping, existed only in bits and pieces. Everything was old and rusted and dirty. It looked like a scene after one of my hurricane daydreams.

Inside Gold Building, though, nothing had changed. Its rooms were now assigned for FBI and Army Forensics, for phone calls to lawyers, and for meetings with the ICRC. But they were still set up the same way, with their one-way mirrors and the adjacent control rooms where a bunch of idle Joint Task Force (JTF) personnel would sit chewing on their cold cheeseburgers, watching me, and asking themselves how I'd ended up in this place. Even the smell was the same: at the first hint of it, I was hearing the sound my heavy chains made the day I was dragged down the corridor to a room where I would meet Sergeant Mary, one of the main interrogators on my so-called Special Projects team.

One night in August 2003, I sat shackled in one of those rooms listening to a phone conversation one of my interpreters was having. She was calling her family back in the United States, and she had forgotten to close the door behind her. English seemed like her first language, but she was speaking to her family in Arabic, with a soft Lebanese or Syrian accent. To hear her casually sharing mundane stories about life in GTMO, very relaxed, completely oblivious to the man suffering next to her, was surreal, but it was just what I needed on that cold, unfriendly evening. I wished her soothing, musical conversation wouldn't end: she was my surrogate, doing for me what I couldn't do for myself. I saw in her a physical and spiritual conduit to my own family, and I told myself that if her family was doing well, my family must be doing well, too. That I was mitigating my loneliness by listening to someone else's intimate, personal conversation posed a moral dilemma for me: I needed to survive, but I also wanted to keep my dignity and respect the dignity of others. To this day I am sorry for eavesdropping, and I can only hope she would forgive my unintentional transgression.

Now, for the "Gold Meeting," my interpreter was a small brown Arab-American in his early thirties, with short, receding black hair.

"Are you from West Africa?" he asked in Arabic as I was led into a room and shackled to the floor. My ankle chains provided a musical backdrop to our conversation, echoing throughout Gold Building. *What do other people think about us being shackled?* I always wondered in these situations. *Do they find it normal to interact with a restrained human being? Do they feel bad for us? Do they feel safer?*

"Yes, Mauritania," I answered in Arabic, smiling.

"Do you understand when I speak?" The room was packed with people I didn't know, mostly high-ranking military officers, and he seemed eager to show how essential he was to the proceedings.

My escort team pushed the desk close enough that I could lean on it and hide my shackled feet underneath, giving the impression of a relaxed, free man. A recent picture of me adorned the door.

We waited. Like everywhere on earth, the big boss did not need to show up on time. Finally the voice of a service member, shouting as if an assault was under way, roused the room to its feet.

"Colonel Gabavics, JDG Commander, on site." The door opened and there he stood, in the flesh. It was the first and last time this man would speak to me.

"You will be transferred to your country in one week. Do you have any questions?" Because I could hardly imagine life outside Guantánamo after so many years of incarceration, I had no idea what questions to ask. I made a request instead. I told the colonel that I wished to bring my manuscripts with me—I wrote four in addition to *Guantánamo Diary* during my imprisonment—and some other writing and paintings I had made in classes I took in GTMO. I said I would also like to take several chessboards, books, and other presents I had received from his predecessors and from some of my guards and interrogators, gifts that had great sentimental value. I named those who had given me these presents, hoping he would honor my request for the sake of his friends.

"I'll talk to the people in charge," he said. "If it's okay, we will send them with you." I thanked him, smiling, wanting the meeting to end on that good note and not to screw things up by saying things I wasn't supposed to say.

The colonel disappeared as quickly as he came. The escort team took me to the room across the hall, where I found two women in uniform. A skinny brunette Army sergeant sat in front of an old Dell desktop that was running Windows 7. She kept smiling, even though her computer was a classic recipe for frustration; she typed everything at least twice, and the PC kept passing out on her. On her right sat a woman who seemed to be her boss, at least by rank, a short blond Navy lieutenant with a neat ponytail. She was friendly, too, and even asked my escort team to remove all my shackles.

There followed a photo shoot that had me posing five different ways: face the camera, face right, face left, and forty-five degrees to both sides. I had to give my fingerprints in about a dozen ways on an electronic pad. They recorded my voice as I read a page written in English: "My name is fill in the blank. I'm from fill in the blank. I love my country," and the like. That was as literary as it got. I must have been nervous, because I passed this voice recognition test only on the second try. Through it all, the sergeant struggled to save my biometric data into the old computer.

My escorts restrained me again and took me to another room, this one with an FBI team.

"If you promise to behave, I'll let them take off your restraints," a Turkish-American agent said with an honest smile. The FBI team fingerprinted me, using the old method of sticking my fingers in ink and pressing them on a paper. It was a long, tedious process, which gave me time to try out my Turkish with the agent. As we talked, his finger slipped and made its own print on the paper. He freaked out, grabbed a fresh paper, and we started again.

"I hope this will be the last time you ever have to do this," he said, laughing and handing me some sandy soap to clean my fingers. There were four other standard-issue FBI agents in the room, two middle-aged women and two other men. The whole team was having a good time with me.

"You don't need to hope," I assured him. "You can bet your last penny."

I was taken to my new home, the transfer camp. I had seen this camp a million times: it was right next to the Camp Echo isolation hut, where I lived for twelve years. If I believed in conspiracy theories, I would have said that the government purposely put the transfer camp right next to my cell for all those years to make me suffer even more. So many detainees were transferred out during those years, and I would be the last one to bid them farewell. We would speak to each other through the fence that separates the two camps. It was comforting to see innocent men finally being freed, and I was happy for every detainee who passed through the transfer camp, but it stung to watch them leave. Now that detainee was me, and I couldn't help but feel guilty. It hurt to think of leaving other innocent detainees behind, their fates in the hand of a system that has failed so badly in matters of justice.

"We missed you, 760," one of my old regular Camp Echo guards greeted me as I was unstrapped from the seat of the transport van. As we walked through the camp, a small, blond female sergeant with a southern accent went over the new rules.

"You can go anywhere you like in the camp, but you're not supposed to cross that red line. Honestly, I don't care if you do, but don't hang out long, because if they see you on the camera, we could get in trouble," she told me as she led me to my new home. "We push the food cart all the way to the white line," she went on, going over procedures I would be hearing for the last time. In one of the strange tricks of Guantánamo, the sergeant and I walked and conversed like old friends, completely overlooking the fact that I was shackled.

Because of the hurricane, many of the mesh sniper screens on the windows had been removed from the Camp Echo huts, and the contractors—mostly so-called Third Country Nationals, who make very low wages and struggle to maintain the facilities—had not finished putting them back up. From my cell, I saw a whole world that had been surrounding me for many years, so close but so elusive: the maze of interrogation rooms; Camp Legal, where detainees meet their lawyers; the hut where the translators and teachers watched TV, waiting for their next encounter with detainees; and the two buildings where detainees come to call and Skype with their families. In a parking lot nearby, people parked their big American vans and climbed out of them, looking bored and sick of their tedious jobs. Through the fence that separates my old Camp Echo Special hut from the transfer camp, I could see that my garden was gone, except for the untended grass and the few trees whose resilience is matched by those of us detainees who had managed to remain in one piece.

For the next several days, JTF staff kept pouring in to brief me about what was happening with my transfer. The news was coming thick and fast, from guards, from the OIC, the NCO in charge, from an officer from the Behavior Health Unit, and from the senior medical officer. Everyone brought good news. I was told that my items were packed and had been sent to the transport people and that they would be loaded onto the plane with me. An Air Force captain from the BHU said that she had been planning to see me the following Monday, but she now doubted

I would still be here. The senior medical officer, a Navy captain, came in person to hand me malaria medication, a sure sign that my departure was imminent. In between these visits, I spent most of my time talking with the guards about what kinds of electronic gadgets I would need to acquire when I got out, and the best ways to watch all the movies I had been forbidden to watch in GTMO. They taught me about streaming sites like Netflix and Putlocker, and even about illegal downloading.

And then the day came: Sunday, October 16, 2016. All day, people in uniform kept coming and going, most saying little, if anything at all. It was surreal—as if the whole base now had only one detainee to worry about. My new favorite OIC showed up again and again with her broad smile. My night shift didn't show up at all.

"Where's the other shift?" I asked one of the guards, a guy who had been tutoring me on how to deal with the new technologies that were waiting to overwhelm me.

"I would love it if they let me be the one leading you out of here, and the last one to say goodbye to you," he said. The specialist's prayer was answered; he would put the shackles on me for the last time.

He grew less talkative as the afternoon wore on. Everyone seemed solemn, and a complete and utter silence descended when the smiling captain came to me and said, "You have two hours left. We're going to lock you down."

"Now it's for real," I told myself. I went inside the cell and heard one of my guards trying to lock the door manually, a very familiar sound. Whenever civilians like teachers or contractors would come from outside the camp, we would be locked like this inside our cells. I took a shower and shaved. I dressed in the new detainee uniform I had been given. My old clothes, like all my belongings in the cell, had to be left behind. I tried to watch TV, then read a book, but I could do neither. I just kept pacing inside my room, praying and singing quietly. It was the longest two hours of my entire life.

"Are you ready?" the captain finally said as she looked through my bin hole.

"Yes."

"Can you stick your hands outside the bin hole?" one of the guards asked.

I offered my hands, and the guards put the shackles on my wrists, gently yet firmly, asking whether the cuffs were too tight. I shook my head. After my hands were restrained, the guards opened the door to finish my upper body and my legs. I was shocked to see how many people could fit in that small place. I saw people in uniform everywhere I looked, including the overeager translator from my meeting with the colonel. But this time he watched and said nothing. The only place I'd ever seen such solemnity was when I attended funerals. I hardly spoke, just nodding when someone asked a question.

The female captain was guiding the guards, telling them what to do next.

"Take him to the red line."

The red line was about sixty steps away from my door. I felt as though I could hear people's hearts beating as clearly as the Black Eyed Peas' "Boom Boom Pow." My escort team seemed nervous, and they went too far. The captain had to shout at them, "Do not cross the red line. Step back. Step back." The guards obeyed, leading me backward and stopping just in front of the line.

A huge gate opened, and a new escort team emerged. They quietly took control of me from my guards. They did not do the usual inspection of my restraints; they did not say anything as they led me outside the gate.

Another group was gathered there, including the senior medical officer and a very tall white man in uniform who was wearing a backpack and whose rank I couldn't see. It was dark outside, but I could see that he was holding a printout with a recent picture of me. He placed the picture beside my face, looked back and forth, and shouted, "Identity confirmed." The whole team looked as if they'd just arrived from a long trip. They all seemed sleepy, even the small black woman who'd been pointing her video camera at me from the moment I left my cell. A skinny blondish specialist would join her in the bus that transported us to the airport, and they would take turns on the camera all the way to Nouakchott.

"Do you have any complaints?" the senior medical officer asked.

I shook my head. "No."

A slight smile broke across his face, and he almost shouted, "760, I declare you fit to fly."

We passed through two more gates. We boarded a bus that drove onto a ferry, and the bus danced like a dervish in a trance as the ferry crossed the bay. We pulled out onto the airstrip and up to the back door of a cargo plane big enough to drive a truck inside. The engines were roaring, and everyone had to shout to convey the simplest message. I was led up a long cargo ramp. As soon as we stepped inside the plane I was earmuffed and blindfolded, just as I had been when I was taken from Bagram Air Base to Guantánamo Bay. This time, though, there was no beating, harassment, or degradation. I was strapped into a hard seat that was set nearly at a right angle and that did not recline. I didn't dare to complain for fear someone would change his mind and take me back to the camp. I lost track of time during the flight, fighting against the pain that began in my back, spread to my ears and head, and soon overwhelmed me from all directions.

The plane landed with a heavy thump, and I felt someone peeling off my blindfold and my earmuffs. The first thing I saw was a digital clock on the wall of the plane in front of me—a little past 14:00, it read—and a bunch of half-asleep recruits who looked like they had not had their best night. I felt gentle hands playing with my shackles, starting from the middle and working up and down.

"Did we arrive? I asked tentatively, barely in a whisper.

"Yes," a guard beside me said.

"Is this the local time?"

"Yes."

There was no mistaking the Mauritanian weather. It was a good day, not too hot—just the right, warm welcome I needed. I was escorted, unshackled, down the ramp and onto the tarmac, where several Mauritanian government officials and an American official waited. We exchanged casual greetings, and my U.S. service member escorts went directly to stand in formation near their countryman. After a few pleasantries, the American started toward his car.

"Who's that?" I asked one of the Mauritanians.

"The U.S. ambassador," he said.

"Can I say hello to him?" I asked.

He dispatched a man standing near him. The ambassador came back to me and we shook hands.

"Welcome home," he said.

2.

As a child, I always wanted to write and teach. My role models were my teachers. When I came home from school, I would gather the kids from my neighborhood who either couldn't afford school or whose parents didn't see it as necessary, and offer them classes for free, re-creating the lessons I had received earlier in the day. I used walls as my blackboard, and charcoal when I ran out of the chalk I scavenged from school. My mother didn't like the whole setup, and the general unruliness of the kids who were my students did not help in winning her approval.

I also developed a minor compulsion for writing. I would write things down anywhere and everywhere, random things I sometimes wouldn't even remember writing. More than once I was embarrassed when friends found my intimate ideas scribbled in my notebooks and even in the margins of my schoolbooks. This compulsion, it turned out, didn't even require a pen: it got so I would trace my thoughts with my finger on my thigh or in the air by my side. In Guantánamo, this drove my interrogators crazy; they did everything to stop me from writing with my finger on my body. Little did they know that most of the time I wasn't even aware that I was doing it. I wanted to comply, but I just couldn't. Their solution was to chain my hands tightly at my sides, making it impossible for me to write on my legs. But my finger kept moving anyway. Even if you succeed in shutting me up, I go on writing.

When I landed in GTMO, I was angry. As soon as I was told I could borrow a pen to write letters to my family, I decided to steal some of the paper and started to write my story in Arabic, mainly for myself. The pen was challenging, a highly bendable piece of plastic, more like a flimsy ink filler than a pen. Writing with it was like trying to get a straight answer out of a corrupt politician. I had to shake it over and over to keep the ink flowing, so it was both writing and a workout at the same time. I was supposed to give the pen back when I finished, but I managed to keep it hidden in my cell. I wrote letters to my family as well, but it didn't take a genius to figure out they would never be mailed. They were just another part of the feverish intelligence-gathering campaign in the camp. I didn't mind though. I happily obliged, drafting letters that I addressed in my mind to JTF staff members, in care of the Slahi family.

It was on Mike Block in Camp Delta that I first started writing my diaries, in Arabic, in the spring of 2003. I kept the pages hidden inside a library book, but they were confiscated when I was moved in June 2003 to total isolation in India Block. And it wasn't just my diaries. I had also been writing out English lessons for myself, copying down things I heard from my English-speaking co-detainees and that I read in books, along with Arabic poems I remembered and little interesting bits of general knowledge. These, too, were taken. For about five months, I was allowed no paper or pen at all, and then only when Mr. X gave me his pen to write "my story" for him, or to write false confessions for my interrogators. By the time the beginning pages of my diary and my other notes were finally returned to me, I had lived through many new chapters of abuse, but I could not pick up the thread. What I had been trying to write about my captivity was not meant for the intelligence community, but rather as a kind of self-advocacy addressed to readers outside of Guantánamo. Now I knew for sure that anything I wrote would only reach my interrogators, and what happens in GTMO stays in GTMO, absolutely. Even with my chains off, my hands remained shackled to my sides.

In 2004, three years after Guantánamo opened, the U.S. Supreme Court finally decided a question whose answer should have been obvious from the start: that GTMO prisoners must have some way to challenge the government's claims that they are dangerous terrorists. The government's first solution was to create the so-called Combatant Status Review Tribunals (CSRTs), where prisoners could finally contest their designation as "enemy combatants." I had never been an enemy of, or fought against, the United States, and I liked my chances when I first heard I would have a CSRT hearing. But that little rush of optimism faded when the serviceman who was to be my "personal representative" for the hearing came to see me in an empty building in Echo Special, accompanied by the woman who was my lead interrogator in the final pages of this book, a military intelligence noncommissioned officer who called herself Amy.

The PR was a young white Air Force captain in his midthirties. He was quiet, almost disinterested, and straight to the point. His demeanor spoke volumes about the kind of process that awaited me—he obviously didn't think it was going anywhere. Most of the meeting concentrated on establishing the fact that he wasn't on my side. The PR was supposed to be acting as my lawyer, in effect, but he explained that the board could pick and choose the information they would share even with him about my case. And then he informed me that he could share anything I might tell him in private with the board if he thought it had important intelligence value. Meanwhile, Amy seemed to be the one with a plan. She was encouraging me to admit to anything the board would throw at me, suggesting that this would make my life easier.

But for some reason I rebelled against the idea that I should throw in the towel. I found that somewhere, deep down, the hope of getting my freedom back had never left me. I could see the process was only for show, but I thought even if my PR and interrogator weren't as zealous as one might hope, the officers on the bench might still listen and surprise everyone. I just couldn't believe that a democratic government with more than two hundred years of experience in upholding the rule of law could really rig trials, with everyone on board.

I asked to confer with Amy. The captain thought I was an idiot. How could I seek advice from someone who wanted me locked up as long as possible, an interrogator whose job depended on keeping me in custody? But I wanted to put her on the spot; after all, she knew by then that I hadn't done anything against her country. I asked her to repeat for me the kinds of things that I should say at the hearing.

"I'm not a lawyer," she said, sweating.

The hearing started badly. I was so nervous I even made the comedy-routine mistake during the swearing in of repeating "I," then "State your name." Everyone in the room was laughing. From then on, though, I just tried to listen to the allegations and debunk them, one by one. Because detainees weren't allowed to attend tribunal sessions where the so-called secret evidence was presented—how something can be "secret" and "evident" at the same time I still don't understand—it felt as though I was defending myself against an invisible army of attorneys. But a member of the tribunal had asked Amy to leave the room during the proceedings, which I took as permission not to follow her instructions, and soon I was just concentrating on presenting the facts of my life as clearly and plainly as I could, in my rather poor English.

The result of the CSRT hearing was no shock; just about everyone got a negative result. But I was emboldened. Defending myself hadn't hurt me. It was clear that Amy had access to the transcript afterward, but she never scolded me. And more important, some of my guards openly supported me. One of my escort guards, a corporal everyone called "Marine," was making fun of the allegations after the tribunal, and he and a colleague I knew as "Big G" told me I won the argument in the CSRT. I gained credibility among the guards as an innocent man. I was recovering my voice. I began to think again about my story reaching someone outside of Guantánamo.

That opportunity came thanks to the landmark decision of

the U.S. Supreme Court in favor of the British citizen Shafiq Rasul, in which the court first ruled GTMO detainees can challenge their detention in habeas corpus proceedings in courts in the United States. Finally, we would be able to present our cases and be judged by Americans who were not in the military or intelligence services.

My first meeting with my attorneys was in mid-June 2005. I prepared for it by writing a summary for them of the full story of my detentions. One of the guards gave me a green spiral notebook that I used for that purpose, filling it with dates, names, and detailed notes about my life and five years' worth of interrogations. I handed it to Nancy Hollander and Sylvia Royce at our meeting. I consider myself very lucky: detainees had no choice in who their lawyers would be, and for some it took years to build trust with their attorneys. But I could tell right away that my team would listen to me. They took the notebook with them and asked me to write more.

I began again, this time writing the full narrative. To ensure my manuscript would not be seized or destroyed, I wrote it in chunks, as a series of letters to my lawyers. This meant what I wrote became protected attorney-client material that my interrogators couldn't read. I would finish a section, ask for an envelope, wrap the papers as tightly as I could and send them off. The letter would be delivered to a secure facility just outside Washington, D.C., where all GTMO's protected attorney-client materials are held. I wrote day and night in the isolation hut that I shared with my guard team in Camp Echo, bombarding my lawyers with writing.

I knew my story, but I didn't know all the words to express it. So I often sat with my guards, playing cards or drinking tea and writing at the same time. If I got stuck on a word or an expression, I'd simply ask them.

"How do you say in English that someone suddenly starts to cry loudly?"

"Burst into tears," a guard who was a Navy petty officer told me.

"What do you call the person who speaks on the radio?" I asked. I was remembering the woman I heard on the radio when I was being transported from the Amman airport to the Jordanian intelligence prison. I could hear her sleepy voice through my earmuffs; she kept interrupting the wonderful music with comments about the day's weather. When the Jordanian rendition team realized I could hear the radio, they jumped to turn it off and played a tape instead.

"Presenter?" one would say.

"I don't know. When they play music?"

"DJ?" one would volunteer.

"What do you call the things they put on your ears?"

"Earmuffs?"

"When you cook, when you put something on your hands to protect them from the heat?"

"Mittens?"

"Oh, yeah!"

I wrote section after section, keeping track of page numbering so that my attorneys could assemble the whole manuscript in the secret facility. I had in my head everything I wanted to write: just the truth as I remembered it, without embellishing. I came to understand that you can convey everything in your head in any language, as long as you have the will and people around you who speak the language, and you are not afraid to ask questions or make mistakes. I wrote until I was finished, and on September 28, 2005, I simply wrote, "The End."

When I began those pages, I thought I was writing for my lawyers, so they could know my story and defend me properly.

But I soon saw I was writing for different readers, ones who could never set foot in Guantánamo. For way too many years, the U.S. government had shut me up and done the talking for both of us. It told the public false stories connecting me to terrorist plots, and it kept the public from hearing anything from me about my life and how I had been treated. Writing became my way of fighting the U.S. government's narrative. I considered humanity my jury; I wanted to bring my case directly to the people and take my chances. I wasn't sure if the pages I wrote and gave to my lawyers would ever become a book. But I believed in books, and in the people who read them; I always had, since I held my first book as a child. I thought of what it would mean if someone outside that prison was holding a book I had written.

Nine years would pass before that happened. But just writing those pages empowered me. Now when Amy encouraged me to report my mistreatment, I agreed. She notified her boss, a Marine lieutenant colonel named Forest. They sat with me and questioned me about my yearlong, secret "Special Projects" interrogation and told me they were filing formal reports. Late in 2005, when I appeared again before another board assigned to review our cases, I felt safe and confident enough to tell the board many of the things I had written in the manuscript and reported to Amy. It's strange to me today to realize that in those days I may actually have been more interested in getting my story out than in getting out of GTMO. I told the board I had written a book about everything I was telling them, suggesting they should read it. They listened to me for hours, asking many questions. Only at the end of the session did I learn that the board had no power to decide my case. And still later, when my lawyers were allowed to get a transcript of this Administrative Review Board hearing, we discovered that much of what

I had told them about the mistreatment was missing. Exactly when I started to describe the worst abuses, the government claimed, the recording equipment "malfunctioned."

Any hope for justice from the GTMO system faded again, and I again doubted whether my story would ever get past the U.S. government censors. But my lawyers kept working. Because my manuscript had been sent confidentially to them, the power to clear it for public release rested with the so-called Privilege Team, a group of mostly retired intelligence officers and government employees who were granted access to view correspondence between lawyers and detainees. But the Privilege Team refused to clear the letters that made up the manuscript. Instead, it suggested that my lawyers send everything back to me in GTMO and have me try to send it to them through regular mail. I had learned from trying to send letters to my family that putting something in the mail was about as effective as throwing it away, or at least sealing it inside a time capsule. And we knew that, like those letters, anything I tried sending through regular mail would be open to the U.S. government to read and to use against me in any way it chose.

My lawyers filed secret motions in the court in Washington, D.C., to force the Privilege Team to clear the manuscript for release. Everything happened behind closed doors between my lawyers, the government's representatives, and the judge. I was not allowed to attend these sessions, or even know what was being said about my manuscript. The litigation dragged on over five years, and in the end came to nothing. My lawyers could not even tell me why the Privilege Team was insisting it could not clear the manuscript or why, in the end, our motions failed.

So my lawyers and I decided to do what the Privilege Team suggested: send the manuscript back to GTMO and give up the attorney-client privilege. Now my writings were open to the government to use against me in my own habeas corpus case and in any proceedings it might decide to bring against me. But that still was not enough for the U.S. government. The government officially declassified the manuscript, but continued to call it "protected," meaning it was still classified in effect, and could not be publicly released. Our frustration continued: we had not been fighting all those years so the government could tell my lawyers, "Now just you and your lawyer friends can read the manuscript." My lawyers prepared to take this to the secret court again. Finally, the government decided not just to declassify but to "unprotect" the manuscript—a process that included adding all the redactions it considered necessary for it to be publicly released.

This whole process took almost seven years.

I remained for all that time in my isolation hut in Camp Echo Special. There were times when my faith that I would someday be released was severely tested. In late 2006 or early 2007, two FBI agents from Minnesota came to visit me and ask me about a young Arab man whom I was told was from Minneapolis. I could not possibly have known him, and everything I thought I knew about that part of the world came from a Chris Rock standup routine. According to him, no African Americans live in Minnesota, and so, by way of extrapolation, I had concluded that there must not be any Arabs or Arab Americans in Minnesota, either. But apparently I was wrong. The two men spent hours grilling me about this young man. In the end, they pulled one of my interrogators aside and told him that the way I talked to them meant I would never leave GTMO, or so my interrogator told me after they left the base. It was one of many, many days when I felt that I would never see freedom.

But there were some very hopeful days, too. One was in January 2009, the day after President Obama's inauguration, when he signed the executive order to close Guantánamo. I don't know how the outside world received this news, but in GTMO everyone took it very seriously. The Joint Task Force gave each detainee a copy of the President's order. Very high-ranking officers toured the camp and spoke with many detainees. An Air Force captain in his jumpsuit and a four-star Navy admiral actually sat and talked to me. With them were several JTF staff members, including Paul Rester, GTMO's director of intelligence. This delegation wanted to make sure inhumane practices were no longer on the menu at the camp.

I was elated. I cleaned the whole compound and took extra care of my garden. One of my guards was telling me not to bother, since I was going home. But remembering the history of Guantánamo, and thinking it might once again be used for refugees, I wanted the camp to look as good as possible for those who might be sent there after me. Everybody in GTMO—detainees, interrogators, and guards alike—truly believed that Obama would make good on his promise to close the place. We knew some of the detainees were going to be transferred to the United States for trial, but by then everyone knew that I had done nothing, so I was sure that this would not be me. Paul Rester even told me that I was going to be released, to Belgium or to Germany, he predicted.

That did not happen. But that same year my habeas corpus case was heard by District Court Judge James Robertson in Washington, D.C. A little over a year after Obama's promise, Judge Robertson issued his decision, which ended, "The petition for habeas corpus is granted. Salahi must be released from custody. It is SO ORDERED." Again I briefly believed I would be going home. And then I learned that the Obama administration was appealing several habeas corpus decisions, including mine, and I knew once again I wasn't going anywhere. But in preparing for the habeas corpus case, I learned how much information the U.S. government itself had released about my treatment in GTMO, and Judge Robertson's opinion showed the world that the government's version of who I was and what I had supposedly done was not true. It had become impossible for the government to argue that my own version of my story must stay classified.

When my lawyers finally received the censored public version of my manuscript, they contacted Larry Siems, and he chose some excerpts and wrote about my ordeal for *Slate* magazine. I was shaken when I learned that parts of the manuscript were now in print. I was dying to read it, but it had been eight years since I had seen any part of it, and I didn't want to wake up memories I had been doing everything to forget. I was also afraid that I would embarrass myself with my unpolished English. But my fears soon faded. Of course there were painful moments in the excerpts; I read them like the wide-awake sleeping wolf in the Arabic proverb, with one eye open and one eye shut. But I also found myself reliving scenes that made me laugh.

And then, at long last, I saw my book...on TV.

It was January 20, 2015, a Tuesday, around 10 a.m. I was having a Spanish class with an Egyptian American JTF contractor who calls himself Ahmed—a random pseudonym, because contractors weren't allowed to share their names with the detainees. Ahmed's Spanish, as he had confessed to me, was extremely basic, but I welcomed any opportunity GTMO offered to learn languages, in casual conversations or classes. Since I was his only student, our class took place in my cell. That morning, I turned the TV on to make a little more noise and give some life to the class, and both of us froze: the Russian channel I had tuned into, RT, was running a long piece on my book, including a live interview with Nancy Hollander and Larry Siems in RT's London studio. At one point, my picture filled the screen.

"You know this guy?" said Ahmed, joking.

For the first time, I felt what it's like to be free inside a prison, that moment of total freedom that comes when you take back some of your lost dignity. I thought of Tim Robbins in *The Shawshank Redemption,* and the smile on his face when he offers his fellow prisoners drinks, the drinks he earned for doing his guards' tax returns. My cell expanded, the lights became brighter, colors more colorful, the sun shone warmer and gentler, and everyone around me looked friendlier; even the small, short-haired female sergeant who seemed to be on an open-ended fast from smiling smiled that day, not once but many times. Now my family and the whole world would know my side of the story. That was liberation.

About fourteen months after *Guantánamo Diary* was published, I learned that I was scheduled for a hearing before the Periodic Review Board (PRB). President Obama set up the review boards in 2011, but it took years for them to get going, and when they did, I watched for months as other detainees had their hearings. It seemed like no one wanted to touch my file. Finally, in the summer of 2016, almost fourteen years after I was brought to GTMO and six months before President Obama's second term would end, I would have my chance to be cleared for release.

As with earlier versions of review boards, I was assigned personal representatives. This time, though, the PRs really seemed to have the interests of the men they represented at heart. When I first met with my PRs, a Navy commander and an Air Force lieutenant colonel, they expressed frustration that some of the other detainees had hurt their chances during the PRB hearing because they were too thirsty to tell their stories. In fact, they explained, the Periodic Review Board was not a forum for detainees to tell their stories. This was not a court that was supposed to decide facts about the past; instead, like a parole board, the review board was supposed to weigh whether the detainee would presently pose a threat to the United States if he was released.

But when they were preparing for their hearings, my PRs told me, many of the men would write. A lot. They kept writing and writing, *I'm so and so, and I went to so and so, and I did this and this, and I'm a good man,* trying to tell their whole story. Their representatives would give their papers back to them and tell them, "We can't say this in the hearing. This hearing is very limited, very formal." But the detainees insisted. "No, it's my life, it's my decision, I want to say this." It is the burning desire of an innocent man: *I want to register an injustice, I want the world to know I did nothing wrong, I am not a bad person.* Some had lost their hearings because of this basic need.

The personal representatives told me this, and I was smiling. "You won't have this problem with me," I told them. *I've already told my story,* I was thinking. *I'm past that.* I'd had my closure. The world had my versions of events, and I was happy.

3.

But my book, as it was originally published, was broken goods.

The first I saw of the published version was a few months after publication day, when Nancy Hollander brought me a photocopy my publisher had made. She could not bring me the actual published book, because the U.S. government would not allow me to see the introduction and footnotes that Larry Siems had contributed, on the grounds that they sometimes referred to documents the government still called "Classified"—even though those documents can easily be found online. The photocopy was just my text, with all the government's redactions.

As I read through the text, my mind automatically filled in what was missing; it took me a while to realize that what I was reading and what my readers were seeing were often two different things. It wasn't just that the readers were without certain details or information. It was that they would have in their minds the idea that what was missing was something that the U.S. government considered threatening.

To be honest, I do not know why many of the things I wrote were censored, and I cannot follow the logic of many of the redactions. Why on earth would the U.S. government censor a poem I wrote for my interrogator as a parody of a well-known literary classic? Why would it censor the fake names that a group of my guards gave themselves when they decided to take on the roles of characters from *Star Wars*? Why would it censor the names of people I was being questioned about during interrogations, when it did everything it could to link me publicly to these same people? All of this supposedly had something to do with "national security," but I wasn't convinced. I had been delivered to Jordan, then to Bagram, then to Guantánamo because of "national security." I was abused in Jordan and Bagram and tortured in GTMO because of "national security." And I would always think, *Could we be a little more specific about what we mean by "national security"?*

I grew up under a military dictatorship, not as brutal as some, but undemocratic nonetheless. I remember my mother telling my older brothers not to discuss politics, for fear the walls would hear. In my country, we're used to censorship in the name of national security. What shocks people here in Mauritania is that the censorship in *Guantánamo Diary* isn't just in the Arabic edition; it comes directly from the American original, which means the information is being kept from the American people.

I wonder what would America's founders think of this censorship. I like to think it's the same thing they would think of my entire story: after all, one of the complaints against the British king listed in their Declaration of Independence was "for transporting us beyond Seas to be tried for pretended Offences." I like to believe they would have been on my side in a discussion in Guantánamo I remember with an FBI agent named William. He was explaining my legal situation to me, and how I couldn't be treated as a U.S. citizen. Understood, I said, but how can I be without protection from anywhere? Of course I was protected—by U.S. law, as American courts would later confirm, but also by the laws of Mauritania, where I was born, and by international law, because the rights the United States was violating were not just American rights, but human rights. But this was something William would not or could not see.

When I was young, I memorized a poem by the Iraqi poet Ahmed Matar called "Prison Guard." It begins,

I stood in my cell
Wondering about my situation
Am I the prisoner, or is that guard standing nearby?
Between me and him stood a wall
In the wall, there was a hole
Through which I see light, and he sees darkness
Just like me he has a wife, kids, a house
Just like me he came here on orders from above

I wasn't exactly enlightened all of my time in Guantánamo. I was often confused and angry, and still young in my thinking.

But I think it was easier for me to see the people who were guarding and interrogating me than it was for them to see me.

In the summer of 2003, after a very long day of abuse that was part of my "Special Projects" interrogation, a female sergeant bragged to me about how knowledgeable Americans are in sexual matters, and how backward "Yemenis" like me are in that department. Nothing in that long day of torments hurt me more than to be confused with someone from Yemen. I admire the Yemeni people enormously; they represent all that is decent and honorable, in my experience. But here I was, being tortured slowly, and the woman on whom the job fell that day did not even know who I was. Not even close. If she had said Moroccan, Algerian, Malian, Senegalese, even Tunisian, I could maybe understand the geographical confusion. But Sanaa is four thousand miles and a continent away from Nouakchott.

I was shocked and hurt by her ignorance, but in a way she wasn't too far off when she threw the Yemenis and me in the same pot. In Guantánamo it mattered where you were from, and early on detainees were divided into those with some entity backing them, usually an important American ally country, and those without. Those who remained in GTMO the longest were almost all from the latter group. Our individuality didn't matter as much as the fact that we were poor and from countries that lacked the political will to stand up for us and demand our release.

The interrogator who said this to me appears twice in *Guantánamo Diary*—or I should say "appears," because the U.S. government blacked out both passages so she is very difficult to see. Readers can't see any of her features; they can't even see that I refer to her as "she." I did not use her name because she did not bother even to make up a name for me. In the United States, if the FBI or the police show up on your doorstep, they say my name is so-and-so, and show you their identification. The same is true for the police and intelligence services in Mauritania, Germany, and Canada. One of the aspects of Guantánamo that I found most disrespectful and insolent to us as human beings was the way they came to us nameless, sometimes even faceless, and said, "I'm here to interrogate you and ask you questions and you don't know who I am. I can do anything to you without your being able to identify me." They were so busy hiding themselves they couldn't see the most basic things about the men that they were questioning.

Writing the manuscript for *Guantánamo Diary* was in a way a reaction to this. I first and foremost wanted to tell my side of the story, to say, "What those people are saying about me is not correct, it's wrong, and here I am: Come and test me, ask me any questions yourself. When I was nineteen and twenty I went to Afghanistan for a couple of months. That's it. I came back. I'm not a killer. I'm not a bloodthirsty person. I'm very peaceful. I love people. This is who I am." But I also meant my story to be breaking news. I wanted the world to know what was happening in Guantánamo. For over seven years, the U.S. government kept that breaking news under lock and key, until it was not news anymore. And then it still said it could be released only in censored, broken form.

I will be forever grateful to my publishers in the United States, the United Kingdom, and around the world who were kind enough to publish these broken goods, and so very, very grateful to all who read the book in its broken form. I owe my freedom to my attorneys, who wrestled my manuscript into the light, and to all of you for sharing and reading it. And I believe I owe us all this repaired version. I never meant my story to be blacked out and redacted, and since I returned home, every person I have spoken with who read this book has asked me if she or he will now be able to read it in an uncensored version.

I tried to do this in the most direct, correct way, by asking the U.S. government to give me back my original, uncensored manuscript. The government refused repeatedly, and so I have worked with my editor Larry Siems on what we came to call this "repair," because it often felt like we were trying to restore a very ancient building.

I thought at first this would be easy, a matter of reinstalling missing bricks to their proper places. I did a small section, and because the redactions were all little bricks of fact—names, places, sometimes dates—they slipped right in. But things quickly became complicated when it wasn't just a few words that were missing, but sentences and paragraphs, full pages even. I began with the obsession of replacing what was taken out brick for brick, tit for tat, as a kind of revenge for the censorship. But revenge is always problematic—it ends up imprisoning you. In the longer censored passages, I knew the action that was being described, but not the phrasing or the order of the sentences, or even the exact aspects of the person or the experience I had described.

I worked in a copy of the book, making notes above the redactions and in the margins, and then I would take a break, go home, eat lunch, and remember even more. I found myself writing and remembering, beyond the boundaries of what I was supposed to be filling in. But it was by doing this, and not trying to confine myself to the government's prescribed blacked-out spaces, that I felt myself recovering the feeling of the original pages. And then Larry and I did what we were denied the opportunity to do the first time *Guantánamo Diary* was published: we worked together to edit these censored sections.

The result, like the original uncensored manuscript, is as close as I can come to the truth as I experienced it and understand it, in the best form I can express it.

I am publishing this new, repaired edition in the same spirit in which I sent a censored version that I had not even been allowed to see into the world in 2015. This is especially true with respect to the men and women I have described in these pages. Except for senior officials who have been named publicly in U.S. government reports or the press, I have chosen in this restored edition to refer to my captors, interrogators, and guards with the names and nicknames I knew them by in prison. To all of them, I wish to renew the invitation that I delivered through my attorneys in my Author's Note for the first, censored edition. In that Note, I said that I bear no grudge against anyone for my ordeal and treatment, and I invited all of the women and men who appear in the book to read it and correct any errors. I said that I dreamed of one day sitting down with all of them for a cup of tea, having learned so much from one another. I mean this still, and most sincerely, as every day teaches me even more about forgiveness.

Repairing this broken text has been about seeing things that someone wanted hidden. Sometimes that someone was me. When I received the photocopy of my book in Guantánamo I stayed up all night reading it, afraid that I wrote something I would regret. And yes, there were things that embarrassed me. I was especially ashamed of my habit, when I was young, of making up sarcastic nicknames for people I met. The Jordanian intelligence agent who oversaw my rendition operation was not "Satan"; he is a human being, as Ahmed Matar pointed out, with a full life and a family. That kind of name-calling is someone I was, not someone I am now. In that sense, reading what I'd written ten years before really was like reading an old diary. Sometimes I laughed, and sometimes I got very upset. But mostly I just smiled at my own silliness and learned more about who I was, and also who I am. Seeing myself this way gives me confidence for the future.

I am thankful for this confidence most of all. It comes from all the characters portrayed here, mainly government employees from around the world, whose human actions were the raw material for this book, and whose complicated humanity challenged me to be truthful, above all with myself.

It comes from everyone who helped in bringing my diaries to light, because without them there would be no book at all, and I would probably still be shouting in the dark: from Nancy Hollander and Theresa Duncan, who fought for nearly eight years to get the approval for a redacted version of my manuscript to be released; from my editor Larry Siems, who worked through the maze of that manuscript and found the book I hoped it would be; and from Rachel Vogel, Geoff Shandler, Asya Muchnick, Jamie Byng, and all those who published and promoted *Guantánamo Diary* around the world.

And it comes from my heroes, my readers, who in my darkest hours I dreamed were out there and who inspired and encouraged me from the start. This new edition is for you.

~~SECRET//NOFORN~~ |04   ~~PROTECTED~~

After that visits I never saw the ICRC for more
than a year. They tried to see me but in vain.
" you started **GUANTÁNAMO** ou don't know
how much I c **DIARY** tend up killing me
I said when ▨ un ▨ pulled me for
interrogation, " We do recommend things, but we
don't have 'the final decision'" ▨ said, "I just
want to warn you, I am suffering b/c of the
harsh conditions ∅ you expose me to. I already
have sciatic nerve ~~crisis~~ attack. And torture
will not make me more cooperative." "According
to my experience, you will cooperate. We are stronger
than you, and have more resources" ▨ said.
▨ never wanted me to know his name, but he got
busted, when mistakenly one of his colleague called
him with his name. He doesn't know that I know
his name, but well I do. ▨ grew worse with
every day passing by. He started to lay me out my case —
He started with the story of ▨, and me having
recruit him for sep 11 attack, "why should he lie
to us" ▨ said, "I don't know". "All you have
to say is, I don't remember, I don't know, I have
done nothing. You Think you are going to impress an
American jury with these word. ∅ In the eyes of
Americans, you are doomed. Just looking at you in
orange suits, chains, being muslim, and Arabic
is enough to convict you" ▨ said "That is
injust", "We know that you are criminal"

~~SECRET//NOFORN~~   ~~PROTECTED~~

SECRET//NOFORN 111 PROTECTED

. I have a great body." Every once in a
while ███ offered me "the other side of the coin,"
If you start to cooperate, I am gonna stop harassing
you? otherwise I will be doing the same with you
and worse every day. I am ███████ and that why
my gov't designated me to this job. I've been always
successful. Having sex with somebody is not a considered
as torture" ███ was leading the monolog ██████.
Every now and then the ███████ entered the room, and
try to make me speak, "you cannot defeat us, we have
so many people, and we keep humilate you with America
██████", "I have a ███████ friend, I'm gonna
bring tomorrow to help me" ███ said, "At least,
cooperate" said ███████ wryly. ███ didn't undress me
but ███ was touching my private parts with ███ body.
In the late afternoon, an other torture squad started
with other poor detainee. I could hear loud music
playing. "Do you want me to send you to that team
or are you gonna cooperate" said ███████, but I didn't
answer. The guards wryly used to call
████████ b/c the most of the torture
took place in those buildings, and in the nights. When
the darkness started to cover the sorry camp, ███
██████ sent me back to my cell. "Today is just
the begin, what's coming is worse and that is
every day" ███ Doctor Routine check: In
order ██ to see how much a detainee [torture]

SECRET//NOFORN PROTECTED

ONE

Jordan–Afghanistan–GTMO

July 2002–February 2003

The American Team Takes Over... Arrival at Bagram...
Bagram to GTMO... GTMO, the New Home... One
Day in Paradise, the Next in Hell

Amman airport, July 19, 2002, 10 p.m.★

The music was off. The conversations of the guards faded
away. The truck emptied.

I felt alone in the hearse truck.

The waiting didn't last: I felt the presence of new people, a
silent team. I don't remember a single word during the whole
rendition to follow.

★ A Council of Europe investigation confirms that a CIA-leased Gulf-
stream jet with the tail number N379P departed Amman, Jordan, at 11:15
p.m. on July 19, 2002, for Kabul, Afghanistan. An addendum to that 2006
report listing the flight records is available at http://assembly.coe.int/
CommitteeDocs/2006/20060614_Ejdoc162006PartII-Appendix.pdf.

EDITOR'S NOTE ON THE FOOTNOTES: None of Mohamedou
Ould Slahi's attorneys holding security clearances has reviewed the
footnotes in this book, contributed to them in any way, or confirmed or
denied my speculations contained in them. Nor has anyone else with access
to the unredacted manuscript reviewed the footnotes, contributed to them
in any way, or confirmed or denied my speculations contained in them.

A person was undoing the chains on my wrists. He undid the first hand, and another guy grabbed that hand and bent it while a third person was putting on the new, firmer and heavier shackles. Now my hands were shackled in front of me.

Somebody started to rip my clothes with something like a scissors. I was like, What the heck is going on? I started to worry about the trip I neither wanted nor initiated. Somebody else was deciding everything for me; I had all worries in the world but making a decision. Many thoughts went quickly through my head. The optimistic thoughts suggested, Maybe you're in the hands of Americans, but don't worry, they just want to take you home, and to make sure that everything goes in secrecy. The pessimistic ones went, You screwed up! The Americans managed to pin some shit on you, and they're taking you to U.S. prisons for the rest of your life.

I was stripped naked. It was humiliating, but the blindfold helped me miss the nasty look of my naked body. During the whole procedure, the only prayer I could remember was the crisis prayer, *Ya hayyu! Ya kayyum!* and I was mumbling it all the time. Whenever I came to be in a similar situation, I would forget all my prayers except the crisis prayer, which I learned from life of our Prophet, Peace be upon him.

One of the team wrapped a diaper around my private parts. Only then was I dead sure that the plane was heading to the U.S. Now I started to convince myself that "everything's gonna be alright." My only worry was about my family seeing me on TV in such a degrading situation. I was so skinny. I've been always, but never *that* skinny: my street clothes had become so loose that I looked like a small cat in a big bag.

When the U.S. team finished putting me in the clothes they tailored for me, a guy removed my blindfold for a moment. I couldn't see much because he directed the flashlight into my eyes. He was wrapped from hair to toe in a black uniform. He opened his mouth and stuck his tongue out, gesturing for me to do the same, a kind of AHH test which I took without resistance. I saw part of his very pale, blond-haired arm, which cemented my theory of being in Uncle Sam's hands.

The blindfold was pushed down. The whole time I was listening to loud plane engines; I very much believe that some planes were landing and others taking off. I felt my "special" plane approaching, or the truck approaching the plane, I don't recall anymore. But I do recall that when the escort grabbed me from the truck, there was no space between the truck and the airplane stairs. I was so exhausted, sick, and tired that I couldn't walk, which compelled the escort to pull me up the steps like a dead body.

Inside the plane it was very cold. I was laid on a sofa and the guards shackled me, mostly likely to the floor. I felt a blanket put over me; though very thin, it comforted me.

I relaxed and gave myself to my dreams. I was thinking about different members of my family I would never see again. How sad would they be! I was crying silently and without tears; for some reason, I gave all my tears at the beginning of the expedition, which was like the boundary between death and life. I wished I were better to people. I wished I were better to my family. I regretted every mistake I made in my life, toward God, toward my family, toward anybody!

I was thinking about life in an American prison. I was thinking about documentaries I had seen about their prisons, and the harshness with which they treat their prisoners. I wished I were blind or had some kind of handicap, so they would put me in isolation and give me some kind of humane treatment and protection. I was thinking, What will the first hearing with the judge be like? Do I have a chance to get due process in a country so full of hatred against Muslims? Am I really already convicted, even before I get the chance to defend myself?

I drowned in these painful dreams in the warmth of the blanket. Every once in a while the pain of the urine urge pinched me. The diaper didn't work with me: I could not convince my brain to give the signal to my bladder. The harder I tried, the firmer my brain became. The guard beside me kept pouring water bottle caps in my mouth, which worsened my situation. There was no refusing it, either you swallow or you choke. Lying on one side was killing me beyond belief, but every attempt to change my position ended in failure, for a strong hand pushed me back to the same position.

I could tell that the plane was a big jet, which led me to believe that flight was direct to the U.S. But after about five hours, the plane started to lose altitude and smoothly hit the runway. I realized the U.S. is a little bit farther than that. Where are we? In Ramstein, Germany? Yes! Ramstein it is: in Ramstein there's a U.S. military airport for transiting planes from the middle east; we're going to stop here for fuel. But as soon as the plane landed, the guards started to change my metal chains for plastic ones that cut my ankles painfully on the short walk to a helicopter. One of the guards, while pulling me out of the plane, tapped me on the shoulder as if to say, "you're gonna be alright." As in agony as I was, that gesture gave me hope that there were still some human beings among the people who were dealing with me.

When the sun hit me, the question popped up again: Where am I? Yes, Germany it is: it was July and the sun rises early. But why Germany? I had done no crimes in Germany! What shit did they pull on me? And yet the German legal system was by far a better choice for me; I know the procedures and speak the language. Moreover, the German system is somewhat transparent, and there are no two and three hundred years sentences. I had little to worry about: a German judge will face me and show me whatever the government has brought against me, and then I'm going to be sent to a temporary jail until my case is decided. I won't be subject to torture, and I won't have to see the evil faces of interrogators.

After about ten minutes the helicopter landed and I was taken into a truck, with a guard on either side. The chauffeur and his neighbor were talking in a language I had never heard before. I thought, What the heck are they speaking, maybe Filipino? I thought of the Philippines because I'm aware of the huge U.S. military presence there. Oh, yes, Philippines it is: *they conspired* with the U.S. and pulled some shit on me. What would the questions of *their* judge be? By now, though, I just wanted to arrive and take a pee, and after that they can do whatever they please. Please let me arrive! I thought; After that you may kill me!

The guards pulled me out of the truck after a five-minute drive, and it felt as if they put me in a hall. They forced me to kneel and bend my head down: I should remain in that position until they grabbed me. They yelled, "Do not move." Before worrying about anything else, I took my most remarkable urine since I was born. It was such a relief; I felt I was released and sent back home. All of a sudden my worries faded away, and I smiled inside. Nobody noticed what I did.

About a quarter of an hour later, some guards pulled me and towed me to a room where they obviously had "processed" many detainees. Once I entered the room, the guards took the gear off my head. Oh, my ears ached so badly, and so did my head; actually my whole body was conspiring against me. I could barely stand. The guards started to deprive me of my clothes, and soon I stood there as naked as my mother bore me. I stood there for the first time in front of U.S. soldiers, not on TV, this was for real. I had the most common reaction, covering my private parts with my hands. I also quietly started to recite quietly the crisis prayer, *Ya hayyu! Ya kayyum!* Nobody stopped me from praying; however, one of the MPs was staring at me with his eyes full of hatred. Later on he would order me to stop looking around in the room.

A medic, a tall white corpsman in his early twenties, gave me a quick medical check, after which I was wrapped in Afghani cloths. Yes, Afghani clothes in the Philippines! Of course I was chained, hands and feet tied to my waist. My hands, moreover, were put in mittens. Now I'm ready for action! What action? No clue!

The escort team pulled me blindfolded to a neighboring interrogation room. As soon as I entered the room, several people started to shout and throw heavy things against the wall. In the melee, I could distinguish the following questions:

"Where is Mullah Omar?"

"Where is Osama bin Laden?"

"Where is Jalaluddin Haqqani?"

A very quick analysis went through my brain: the individuals in those questions were leading a country, and now they're a bunch of fugitives! The interrogators missed a couple of things. First, they had just briefed me about the latest news: Afghanistan is taken over, but the high level people have not been captured. Second, I turned myself in about the time when the war against terrorism started, and since then I have been in a Jordanian prison, literally cut off from the rest of the world. So how am I supposed to know about the U.S. taking over Afghanistan, let alone about its leaders having fled? Not to mention where they are now.

I humbly replied, "I don't know!"

"You're a liar!" shouted one of them in broken Arabic.

"No, I'm not lying, I was captured so and so, and I only know Abu Hafs…" I said, in a quick summary of my whole story.*

"We should interrogate these motherfuckers like the Israelis do."

"What do they do?" asked another.

"They strip them naked and interrogate them!"

"Maybe we should!" suggested another. Chairs still were flying around and hitting the walls and the floor. I knew it was only a show of force, and the establishment of fear and anxiety. I went with the flow and even shook myself more than necessary. I didn't believe that Americans torture, even though I had always considered it a remote possibility,

"I am gonna interrogate you later on," said one, and the U.S. interpreter repeated the same in Arabic.

"Take him to the hotel," suggested the interrogator. This time the interpreter didn't translate.

And so was the first interrogation done. Before the escort grabbed me, in my terrorizing fear, I tried to connect with the interpreter.

"Where did you learn such good Arabic?" I asked.

---

* Abu Hafs is MOS's cousin and former brother-in-law. His full name is Mahfouz Ould al-Walid, and he is also known as Abu Hafs al-Mauritani. Abu Hafs married the sister of MOS's former wife. He was a prominent member of al-Qaeda's Shura Council, the group's main advisory body, in the 1990s and up until the September 11, 2001, terrorist attacks in the United States. It has been widely reported that Abu Hafs opposed those attacks; the 9/11 Commission recorded that "Abu Hafs the Mauritanian reportedly even wrote Bin Ladin a message basing opposition to the attacks on the Qur'an." Abu Hafs left Afghanistan after the 9/11 attacks and spent the next decade under house arrest in Iran. In April 2012 he was extradited to Mauritania, where he was held briefly and then released. He is now a free man. The relevant section of the 9/11 Commission report is available at http://govinfo.library.unt.edu/911/report/911Report_Ch7.pdf.

"In the U.S.!" he replied, sounding flattered. In fact, he didn't speak good Arabic; I just was trying to make some friends.

The escort team led me away. "You speak English," one of them said in a thick Asian accent.

"A little bit," I replied. He laughed, and so did his colleague. I felt like a human being leading a casual conversation. I said to myself, Look how friendly the Americans are: they're gonna put you in a Hotel, interrogate you for a couple of days, and then fly you home safely. There's no place for worry. The U.S. just wants to check everything, and since you're innocent, they're gonna find that out. For Pete's sake, you're on a base in Philippines; even though it's a place at the edge of legality, it's just temporary. The fact that one of the guards sounded Asian strengthened my wrong theory of being in the Philippines.

I soon arrived, not at a hotel but at a wooden cell with neither a bathroom nor a sink. From the modest furniture—a weathered, thin mattress and an old blanket—you could tell there had been somebody here. I was kind of happy for having left Jordan, the place of randomness, but I was worried about the prayers I could not perform, and I wanted to know how many prayers I missed on the trip. The guard of the cell was a small, skinny white female, a fact which gave me more comfort: for the last eight months I had been dealt with solely by big, muscular males.

I asked her about the time, and she told me it was about eleven, if I remember correctly. I had one more question.

"What day is it?"

"I don't know, every day here is the same," she replied. I realized I had asked too much; she wasn't even supposed to tell me the time, as I would learn later.

I found a Koran gently placed on some water bottles. I realized I was not alone in the jail, which was surely not a Hotel.

As it turned out, I was delivered to the wrong cell. Suddenly,

I saw the weathered feet of a detainee whose face I couldn't see because it was covered with a black bag. Black bags, I soon would learn, were put on everybody's heads to blindfold them and make them unrecognizable, including the writer. Honestly, I didn't want to see the face of the detainee, just in case he was in pain or suffering, because I hate to see people suffering; it drives me crazy. I'll never forget the moans and cries of the poor detainees in Jordan when they were suffering torture. I remember putting my hands over my ears to stop myself from hearing the cries, but no matter how hard I tried, I was still able to hear the suffering. It was awful, even worse than torture.

The female guard at my door stopped the escort team and organized my transfer to another cell. It was the same as the one I was just in, but in the facing wall. In the room there was a half-full water bottle, the label of which was written in Russian; I wished I had learned Russian. I said to myself, a U.S. base in the Philippines, with water bottles from Russia? The U.S. doesn't need supplies from Russia, and besides, geographically it makes no sense. Where *am* I? Maybe in a former Russian Republic, like Tajikistan? All I know is that I don't know!

The cell had no facility to take care of the natural business. Washing for prayer was impossible and forbidden. There was no clue as to the *Kibla,* the direction of Mecca. I did what I could. My next door neighbor was mentally sick; he was shouting in a language with which I was not familiar. I later learned that he was a Taliban leader.

Later on that day, July 20, 2002, the guards pulled me for routine police work, fingerprints, height, weight, etcetera. I was offered a female interpreter. It was obvious that Arabic was not her first language. She taught me the rules: no speaking, no praying loudly, no washing for prayer, and a bunch of other nos in that direction. The guard asked me whether I wanted to use the bathroom. I thought he meant a place where you can shower; "Yes," I said. The bathroom was a barrel filled with human waste. It was the most disgusting bathroom I ever saw. The guards had to watch you while you were taking care of business. I couldn't eat the food—the food in Jordan was, by far, better than the cold MREs I got in Bagram—so I didn't really have to use the bathroom. To pee, I would use the empty water bottles I had in my room. The hygienic situation was not exactly perfect; sometimes when the bottle got filled, I continued on the floor, making sure that it didn't go all the way to the door.

For the next several nights in isolation, I got a funny guard who was trying to convert me to Christianity. I enjoyed the conversations, though my English was very basic. My dialogue partner was young, religious, and energetic. He liked Bush ("the true religious leader," according to him); he hated Bill Clinton ("the Infidel"). He loved the dollar and hated the Euro. He had his copy of the Bible on him all the time, and whenever the opportunity arose he read me stories, most of which were from the Old Testament. I wouldn't have been able to understand them if I hadn't read the Bible in Arabic several times—not to mention that the versions of the stories are not that far from the ones in the Koran. I had studied the Bible in the Jordanian prison; I asked for a copy, and they offered me one. It was very helpful in understanding Western societies, even though many of them deny being influenced by religious scriptures.

I didn't try to argue with him: I was happy to have somebody to talk to. He and I were unanimous that the religious scriptures, including the Koran, must have come from the same source. As it turned out, the hot-tempered soldier's knowledge about his religion was very shallow. Nonetheless I enjoyed him being my guard. He gave me more time on the bathroom, and he even looked away when I used the barrel.

I asked him about my situation. "You're not a criminal, because they put the criminals in the other side," he told me, gesturing with his hand. I thought about those "criminals" and pictured a bunch of young Muslims, and how hard their situation could be. I felt bad. As it turned out, later on I was transferred to these "criminals," and became a "high priority criminal." I was kind of ashamed when the same guard saw me later with the "criminals," after he had told me that I was going to be released at most after three days. He acted normally, but he didn't have that much freedom to talk to me about religion there because of his numerous colleagues. Other detainees told me that he was not bad toward them, either.

The second or the third night an agent named William pulled me out of my cell himself and led me to an interrogation, where the same female Arabic interpreter already had taken a seat. William was a Japanese American who worked with the CIA, as his colleague later informed me; his specialty was in brutalizing detainees who were considered important, but not valuable enough to get them tickets to the secret CIA prisons. You could tell he was the right man for the job: he was the kind of man who wouldn't mind doing the dirty work. The detainees back in Bagram used to call him William the Torturer; he reportedly was responsible for torturing even innocent individuals the government released.*

---

* At his December 15, 2005, Administrative Review Board (ARB) hearing, MOS described a U.S. interrogator in Bagram who was Japanese American and whom Bagram prisoners referred to as "William the Torturer." ARB transcript, 23. MOS's 2005 ARB hearing transcript is available at https://www.nytimes.com/interactive/projects/guantanamo/detainees/760-mohamedou-ould-slahi/documents/2.

William didn't need to shackle me because I was in shackles 24 hours a day. I slept, ate, used the bathroom while completely shackled, hand to feet. He opened a file in his hand and started by means of the female Arabic interpreter. He was asking me general questions about my life and my background. When he asked me, "What languages do you speak?" he didn't believe me; he laughed along with the interpreter, saying, "Haha, you speak German? Wait, we're gonna check."

Suddenly a tall white man wearing shorts and an oversized badge around his neck entered the room. He introduced himself as Michael, which he pronounced in the German way, *MeeShaEel*. There was no mistaking it, he was the one in charge. He scanned the room quickly, saying something to his colleagues I didn't understand, then switched languages immediately.

"Sprichst du Deutsch?" he blurted.

"Ja Wohl," I replied. Michael was not completely fluent, but his German was fairly acceptable, given that he was born and lived his whole life in the United States. He later told me that he studied German as a foreign language to further his CIA career and connect better to his German roots. He confirmed to his colleague that my German was "better than his."

Both looked at me with some respect after that, though the respect was not enough to save me from William's wrath. William asked me where I learned to speak German, and said that he was going to interrogate me again later.

Michael faced me and said, "Wahrheit macht frei, the truth sets you free."

When I heard him say that, I knew the truth wouldn't set me free, because "Arbeit" didn't set the Jews free. Hitler's propaganda machinery used to lure Jewish detainees with the slogan, "Arbeit macht frei," Work sets you free. But work set nobody free.

Michael took a note in his small notebook and left the room. William sent me back to my room and apologized to the female interpreter.

"I am sorry for keeping you awake for so long,"

"No problem!" she replied.

After several days in isolation I was transferred to the general population, but I could only look at them because I was put in the narrow barbed-wire corridor between the cells. I felt like I was out of jail, though, and I cried and thanked God. After eight months of total isolation, I saw fellow detainees more or less in my situation. "Bad" detainees like me were shackled 24 hours a day and put in the corridor, where every passing guard or detainee stepped on them. The place was so narrow that the barbed wire kept pinching me for the next ten days. I saw Omar Deghayes being force-fed; he was on a forty-five day hunger strike. The guards were yelling at him, and he was bouncing a dry piece of bread between his hands. All the detainees looked so worn out, as if they had been buried and after several days resurrected, but Omar was a completely different story: he was bones without meat. It reminded me of the pictures you see in documentaries about WWII prisoners.*

Detainees were not allowed to talk to each other, but we enjoyed looking at each other. The punishment for talking was hanging the detainee by the hands with his feet barely touching the ground. I saw an Afghani detainee who passed out a couple of times while hanging from his hands. The medics "fixed" him and hung him back up. Other detainees were luckier: they were hung for a certain time and then released. Most of the detainees

---

* Omar Deghayes was released and returned to the United Kingdom, his country of residence, on December 18, 2007.

tried to talk while they were hanging, which made the guards double their punishment. There was a very old Afghani fellow who reportedly was arrested to turn over his son. The guy was mentally sick; he couldn't stop talking because he didn't know where he was, nor why. I don't think he understood his environment, but the guards kept dutifully hanging him. It was so pitiful. One day one of the guards threw him on his face, and he was crying like a baby.

We were put in about six or seven big barbed-wire cells named after operations performed against the U.S: Nairobi, U.S.S. Cole, Dar-Es-Salam, and so on. In each cell there was a detainee called English, who benevolently served as an interpreter to translate the orders to his co-detainees. Our English was a gentleman from Sudan named Abu Mohamed. His English was very basic, and so he asked me secretly whether I spoke English. "No," I replied—but as it turned out I was a Shakespeare compared to him. My brethren thought that I was denying them my services, but I just didn't know how bad the situation was.

Now I was sitting in front of bunch of dead regular U.S. citizens. My first impression, when I saw them chewing without a break, was, What's wrong with these guys, do they have to eat so much? Most of the guards were tall, and overweight. Some of them were friendly and some very hostile. Whenever I realized that a guard was mean I pretended that I understood no English. I remember one cowboy coming to me with an ugly frown on his face:

"You speak English?" he asked.

"No English," I replied.

"We don't like you to speak English. We want you to die slowly," he said.

"No English," I kept replying. I didn't want to give him the satisfaction that his message arrived. People with hatred always have something to get off their chests, but I wasn't ready to be that drain.

Prayer in groups wasn't allowed. Everybody prayed on his own, and so did I. Detainees had no clues about prayer time. We would just imitate: when a detainee started to pray, we assumed it was time and followed. The Koran was available to detainees who asked for one. I don't remember asking myself, because the handling by the guards was just disrespectful; they threw it to each other like a water bottle when they passed the holy book through. I didn't want to be a reason for humiliating God's word. Moreover, thank God, I know the Koran by heart. As far as I recall, one of the detainees secretly passed me a copy that nobody was using in the cell.

After a couple of days, William the Torturer pulled me to interrogate me. The same female acted as an interpreter.

"Tell me your story," William asked.

"My name is, I graduated in 1988, I got a scholarship to Germany...." I replied in very boring detail, none of which seemed to interest or impress William. He grew tired and started to yawn. I knew exactly what he wanted to hear, but I couldn't help him.

He interrupted me. "My country highly values the truth. Now I'm gonna ask you some questions, and if you answer truthfully, you're gonna be released and sent safely to your family. But if you fail, you're gonna be imprisoned indefinitely. A small note in my agenda book is enough to destroy your life. What terrorist organizations are you part of?"

"None," I replied.

"You're not a man, and you don't deserve respect. Kneel, cross your hands, and put them behind your neck."

I obeyed the rules and he put a bag over my head. My back

was hurting bad lately and that position was so painful; William was working on my sciatic problem.⋆ He brought two projectors and adjusted them on my face. I couldn't see, but the heat overwhelmed me and I started to sweat.

"You're gonna be sent to a U.S. facility, where you'll spend the rest of your life," he threatened. "You'll never see your family again. Your family will be f★★cked by another man. In American jails, terrorists like you get raped by multiple men at the same time. The guards in my country do their job very well, but being raped is inevitable. But if you tell me the truth, you're gonna be released immediately."

I was old enough to know that he was a rotten liar and a man with no honor, but he was in charge, so I had to listen to his bullshit again and again. I just wished that the agencies would start to hire smart people. Did he really think that anybody would believe his nonsense? Somebody would have to be stupid: was he stupid, or did he think I was stupid? I would have respected him more had he told me, "Look, if you don't tell me what I want to hear, I'm gonna torture you."

Anyway, I said, "Of course I will be truthful!"

"What terrorist organizations are you part of?"

"None!" I replied. He put back the bag on my head and started a long discourse of humiliation, cursing, lies, and threats. I don't really remember it all, nor am I ready to sift in my memory for such bullshit. I was so tired and hurt, and tried to sit but he forced me back. I cried from the pain. Yes, a man my age cried silently. I just couldn't bear the agony.

After a couple of hours William sent me back to my cell, promising me more torture. "This was only the start," as he put it. I was

---

⋆ At his 2005 ARB hearing, MOS indicated that an interrogator nicknamed "William the Torturer" made him kneel for "very long hours" to aggravate his sciatic nerve pain and later threatened him. ARB transcript, 23.

returned to my cell, terrorized and worn out. I prayed to Allah to save me from him. I lived the days to follow in horror: whenever William went past our cell I looked away, avoiding seeing him so he wouldn't "see" me, exactly like an ostrich. He was checking on everybody, day and night, and giving the guards the recipe for every detainee. I saw him torturing this other detainee. I don't want to recount what I heard about him; I just want to tell what I saw with my eyes. It was an Afghani teenager, I would say 16 or 17. William made him stand for about three days, sleepless. I felt so bad for him. Whenever he fell down the guards came to him, shouting "no sleep for terrorists," and made him stand again. I remember sleeping and waking up, and he stood there like a tree.

Whenever I saw William around, my heart started to pound, and he was often around. One day he sent the female interpreter to me to pass me a message.

"William is gonna kick your ass."

I didn't respond, but inside me I said, May Allah stop you! But in fact William didn't kick my rear end; instead Michael pulled me for interrogation. He was a nice guy; maybe he felt he could relate to me because of the language. And why not? Even some of the guards used to come to me and practice their German when they learned that I spoke it.

Anyway, he recounted a long story to me. "I'm not like William. He's young and hot-tempered. I don't use inhumane methods; I have my own methods. I want to tell something about American history, and the whole war against terrorism."

Michael was straightforward and enlightening. He started with American history and the Puritans, who punished even the innocents by drowning them, and ended with the war against terrorism. "There is no innocent detainee in this campaign: either you cooperate with us and I am going to get you the best deal, or we are going to send you to Cuba."

"What? *Cuba?*" I exclaimed. "I don't even speak Spanish, and you guys *hate* Cuba."

"Yes, but we have an American territory in Guantánamo," he said, and told me about Teddy Roosevelt and things like that. I knew that I was going to be sent further from home, which I hated.

"Why would you send me to Cuba?"

"We have other options, like Egypt and Algeria, but we only send them the very bad people. I hate sending people over there, because they'll experience painful torture."

"Just send me to Egypt."

"You sure do not want that. In Cuba they treat detainees humanely, and they have two Imams. The camp is run by the DOJ, not the military."*

"But I've done no crimes against your country."

"I'm sorry if you haven't. Just think of it as if you had cancer!"

"Am I going to be sent to court?"

"Not in the near future. Maybe in three years or so, when my people forget about September 11." Michael went on to tell me about his private life, but I don't want to put it down here.

I had a couple more sessions with Michael after that. He asked me some questions and tried to trick me, saying things like, "He said he knows you!" for people I had never heard of. He took my email addresses and passwords. He also asked the German intelligence agents who were present in Bagram to interrogate me, but they refused, saying that German law forbids them from interrogating aliens outside the country.† He was trying the whole time to

---

★ Department of Justice. This is not true, of course. The Guantánamo Bay detention camp is located on the Guantánamo Bay Naval Base and is run by a U.S. military joint task force under the command of the U.S. Southern Command.

† Press accounts indicate that MOS was eventually interrogated by both German and Canadian intelligence agents in Guantánamo; later in the manuscript, in the scene where he meets with what appear to be BND

convince me to cooperate so he could save me from the trip to Cuba. To be honest, I preferred to go to Cuba than to stay in Bagram.

"Let it be," I told him. "I don't think I can change anything."

Somehow I liked Michael. Don't get me wrong, he was a sneaky interrogator, but at least he spoke to me according to the level of my intellect. I asked Michael to put me inside the cell with the rest of the population, and showed him the injuries I had suffered from the barbed wire. He approved: in Bagram, interrogators could do anything with you; they had overall control, and the MPs were at their service. Sometimes Michael gave me a drink, which I appreciated, especially with the kind of diet I received, cold MREs and dry bread in every meal. I secretly passed my meals to other detainees.

One night Michael introduced two military interrogators who asked me about the Millennium Plot. They spoke broken Arabic and were very hostile to me; they didn't allow me to sit and threatened me with all kind of things. But Michael hated them, and told me in German, "If you want to cooperate, do so with me. These MI guys are nothing." I felt myself under auction to whichever agency bids more.

In the population we always broke the rules and spoke to our neighbors. I had three direct neighbors. One was an Afghani teenager who was kidnapped on his way to Emirates; he used to work there, which was why he spoke Arabic with a Gulf accent. He was very funny, and he made me laugh; over the past nine months I had almost forgotten how. He was spending

interrogators in GTMO, MOS specifically references such a prohibition on external interrogations. See footnote on page 49; see also http://www .spiegel.de/international/world/from-germany-to-guantanamo-the -career-of-prisoner-no-760-a-583193-3.html; and http://www.thestar .com/news/canada/2008/07/27/csis_grilled_trio_in_cuba.html.

holidays with his family in Afghanistan and went to Iran; from there he headed to the Emirates in a boat, but the boat was hijacked by the U.S. and the passengers were arrested.

My second neighbor was a twenty-year-old Mauritanian guy who was born in Nigeria and moved to Saudi Arabia. He'd never been in Mauritania, nor did he speak the Mauritanian dialect; if he didn't introduce himself, you would say he was a Saudi.

My third neighbor was a Palestinian from Jordan named Ibrahim. He was captured and tortured by an Afghani tribal leader for about seven months. His kidnapper wanted money from Ibrahim's family or else he would turn him over to the Americans, though the latter option was the least promising because the U.S. was only paying $5,000 per head, unless it was a big head. The bandit arranged everything with the family regarding the ransom, but Ibrahim managed to flee from captivity in Kabul. He made it to Jalalabad, where he easily stuck out as an Arab mujahid and was captured and sold to the Americans. I told Ibrahim that I'd been in Jordan, and he seemed to be knowledgeable about their intelligence services. He knew all the interrogators who dealt with me, as he himself spent 50 days in the same prison where I had been.

When we spoke, we covered our heads so guards thought we were asleep, and talked until we got tired. My neighbors told me that we were in Bagram, in Afghanistan, and I informed them that we were going to be transferred to Cuba. But they didn't believe me.

Around 10 a.m. on August 4, 2002 a Military unit, some armed with guns, appeared from nowhere. The armed MPs were pointing their guns at us from upstairs, and the others were shouting at the same time, "Stan' up, Stan' up..." I was so scared. Even though I expected to be transferred to Cuba some time that day, I had never seen this kind of show.

We stood up. The guards kept giving other orders. "No talking...Do not move...Ima fucking kill yo'...I'm serious!" I hated it when Ibrahim from Palestine asked to use the bathroom and the guards refused. "Don't move." I was like, Can't you just keep it till the situation is over? But the problem with Ibrahim was that he had dysentery, and he couldn't hold it; he had been subjected to torture and malnutrition in Kabul during his detention by the Northern Alliance tribal leader. Ibrahim told me that he was going to use the bathroom anyway, which he did, ignoring the shouting guards. I expected every second a bullet to be released toward him, but that didn't happen. The bathroom inside our shared cells was also an open barrel, which detainees in punishment cleaned every day for every cell. It was very disgusting and smelled so bad. Being from a third world country, I have seen many unclean bathrooms, but none of them could hold a candle to Bagram's.

I started to shake from fear. One MP approached the gate of our cell and started to call the names, or rather the numbers, of those who were going to be transferred. All the numbers called in my cell were Arabs, which was a bad sign. The brothers didn't believe me when I told them we were going to be transferred to Cuba. But now I felt myself confirmed, and we looked at each other and smiled. Several guards came to the gate with a bunch of chains, bags, and other materials. They started to call us one by one, asking each detainee to approach the gate, where he got chained.

One of the guards shouted my number. I proceeded to the gate like a sheep being led to her butcher. At the gate, a guard yelled, "Turn around!" which I did, and "Both hands behind!"

When I slid my hands through the bin hole behind my back, one of the guards grabbed my thumb and bent my wrist. "When you fuckin' move, I'm gonna break your hand." Another guard chained my hands and my feet with two separate chains. Then a bag was put over my head to blindfold me. The gate was opened, and I was roughly pushed and thrown over the back of another detainee in a row. Although I was physically hurt, I was solaced when I felt the warmth of another human being in front of me suffering the same. The solace increased when Ibrahim was thrown over my back. Many detainees didn't exactly understand what the guards wanted from them, and so got hurt worse. I felt lucky to have been blindfolded, for one, because I missed a lot bad things that were happening around me, and for two, because the blindfold helped me in my daydreaming about better circumstances. Thank ALLAH, I have the ability to ignore my surroundings and daydream about anything I want.

We were supposed to be very close to each other. Breathing was very hard. We were 34 detainees, all of whom were Arab except for one Afghani and one from the Maldives.* When we were put in a row, we were tied together with a rope around our upper arms. The rope was so tight that the circulation stopped, numbing my whole arm.

We were ordered to stand up, and were pulled to a place where the "processing" continued. I hated it because Ibrahim kept stepping on my chain, which hurt badly. I tried my best

---

* In-processing height and weight records indicate that thirty-five detainees arrived in Guantánamo on August 5, 2002. The records of that group are available at http://humanrights.ucdavis.edu/reports/heights-and-weights-files/ISN_680-ISN_838.pdf. An official list of Guantánamo detainees that the Pentagon released in May 2006 is available at http://archive.defense.gov/news/May2006/d20060515%20List.pdf.

not to step on the chain of the man in front of me. Thank God the trip was short: somewhere in the same building we were set down next to each other on long benches. I had the feeling that the benches made a circle.

The party started with dressing the passengers. I got a headset that prevented me from hearing. It gave me such a painful headache; the set was so tight that I had the top of my ears bleeding for a couple of days. My hands were now tied to my waist in the front, and connected with a chain all the way to my feet. They connected my wrists with a six-inch hard plastic piece, and made me wear thick mittens. It was funny, I tried to find a way to free my fingers, but the guards hit my hands to stop moving them. We grew tired; people started to moan. Every once in a while one of the guards took out one of my ear plugs and whispered a discouraging phrase:

"You know, you didn't make any mistake: your mom and dad made the mistake when they produced you."

"You gonna enjoy the ride to the Caribbean paradise...." I didn't answer any provocation, pretending not to understand what he said. Other detainees told me about having been subject to such humiliation, too, but they were luckier; they understood no English.

My flipflops were taken away, and I got some made-in-China tennis shoes. Over my eyes they put really ugly, thick, blind-folding glasses, which were tied around my head and over my ears. They were similar to swimming goggles. To get an idea about the pain, put some old goggles around your hand and tie them tight, and stay that way for a couple of hours; I am sure you will remove them. Now imagine that you have those same goggles tied around your head for more than forty hours. To seal the dressing, a sticky pad was placed behind my ear.

Sometime during the processing we got a cavity search, to the laughter and comments of the guards. I hated that day when I started to learn my miserable English vocabulary. In such situations you're just better off if you don't understand English. The majority of the detainees wouldn't speak about the cavity searches we were subject to, and they would get angry when you started to talk about them. I personally wasn't ashamed; I think the people who did these searches without good reason should be ashamed of themselves.

I grew sick, tired, frustrated, hungry, nauseous, and all other bad adjectives in the dictionary. I am sure I wasn't the only one. We got new plastic bracelets carrying a number. My number turned out to be 760, and my next, with ISN 761, was Ibrahim. You could say my group was the 700 series.*

Ibrahim used the bathroom a couple of times, but I tried not to use it. I finally went in the afternoon, maybe around 2 p.m.

"Do you like music?" the guard who was escorting me there asked when we were alone.

"Yes, I do!"

"What kind?"

"Good music!"

"Rock and Roll? Country?" I wasn't really familiar with these types he mentioned. Every once in a while I used to listen to German radio with different kinds of Western music, but I couldn't tell which one was which.

"Any good music," I replied. The good conversation paid off in the form that he took my blindfold off so that I could take care of my business. It was very tricky, since I had chains all around my body. The guard placed me gently back on the

---

* Ibrahim Mahdi Achmed Zeidan was released from Guantánamo on November 7, 2007.

bench, and for the next couple of hours waiting was the order. We were deprived from the right of performing our daily prayers for the next forty-eight hours.

Around four p.m., the transport to the airport started. By then, I was a "living dead." My legs weren't able to carry me anymore; for the time to come, the guards had to drag me all the way from Bagram to GTMO.

We were loaded in a truck that brought us to the airport. It took five to ten minutes to get there. I was happy for every move, just to have the opportunity to alter my body, for my back was killing me. We were crowded in the truck shoulder-to-shoulder and thigh-to-thigh. Unluckily I was placed facing the back of the vehicle, which I really hate because it gives me nausea. The vehicle was equipped with hard benches so that the detainees sat back to back and the guards sat at the very end shouting, "No talking!" I have no idea how many people were in the truck; all I know is that one detainee sat on my right, and one on my left, and another against my back. It is always good to feel the warmth of your co-detainees, somehow it's solacing.

The arrival at the airport was obvious because of the whining of the engines, which easily went through the earplugs. The truck backed up until it touched the plane. The guards started to shout loudly in a language I could not differentiate. I started to hear human bodies hitting the floor. Two guards grabbed a detainee and threw him toward two other guards on the plane, shouting "Code"; the receiving guards shouted back confirming receipt of the package. When my turn came, two guards grabbed me by the hands and feet and threw me toward the reception team. I don't remember whether I hit the floor or was caught by the other guards. I had started to lose feeling and it would have made no difference anyway.

Another team inside the plane dragged me and fastened me on a small and straight seat. The belt was so tight I could not breathe. The air conditioning hit me, and one of the MPs was shouting, "Do not move, Do not talk," while locking my feet to the floor. I didn't know how to say "tight" in English. I was calling, "MP, MP, belt..." Nobody came to help me. I almost got smothered. I had a mask over my mouth and my nose, plus the bag covering my head and my face, not to mention the tight belt around my stomach: breathing was impossible. I kept saying, "MP, Sir, I cannot breathe!...MP, SIR, please." But it seemed like my pleas for help got lost in a vast desert.

After a couple minutes, Ibrahim was dropped beside me on my right. I wasn't sure it was him, but he told me later he felt my presence beside him. Every once in a while, if one of the guards adjusted my goggles, I saw a little. I saw the cockpit, which was in front of me. I saw the green camo-uniforms of the escorting guards. I saw the ghosts of my fellow detainees on my left and my right. "Mister, please, my belt...hurt...," I called. When the shoutings of the guards faded away, I knew that the detainees were all on board. "Mister, please...belt...." A guard responded, but he not only didn't help me, he tightened the belt even more around my abdomen.

Now I couldn't endure the pain; I felt I was going to die. I couldn't help asking for help louder. "Mister, I cannot breathe..." One of the soldiers came and untightened the belt, not very comfortably but better than nothing.

"It's still tight..." I had learned the word when he asked me, "Is it tight?"

"That's all you get." I gave up asking for relief from the belt.

"I cannot breathe!" I said, gesturing to my nose. A guard appeared and took the mask off my nose. I took a deep breath and felt really relieved. But to my dismay, the guard put the mask back on my nose and my mouth. "Sir, I cannot breathe... MP....MP." The same guy showed up once more, but instead of taking the mask off my nose, he took the plug out of my ear and said, "Forget about it!" and immediately put the ear plug back. It was harsh, but it was the only way not to smother. I was panicking, I had just enough air, but the only way to survive was to convince the brain to be satisfied with the tiny bit of air it got.

The plane was in the air. A guard shouted in my ear, "Ima gonna give you some medication, you get sick." He made me take a bunch of tablets and gave me an apple and a peanut butter sandwich, our only meal since the transfer procedure began. I've hated peanut butter since then. I had no appetite for anything, but I pretended I was eating the sandwich so the guards don't hurt me. I always tried to avoid contact with those violent guards unless it was extremely necessary. I took a bite of the sandwich and kept the rest in my hand till the guards collected the trash. As to the apple, the eating was tricky, since my hands were tied to my waist and I wore mittens. I squeezed the apple between my hands and bent my head to my waist like an acrobat to bite at it. One slip and the apple is gone. I tried to sleep, but as tired as I was, every attempt to take a nap ended in failure. The seat was as straight as an arrow, and as hard as a stone.

After about five hours, the plane landed and our ghosts were transferred to another, maybe bigger plane. It was stable in the air. I was happy with every change, any change, hoping for the betterment of my situation. But I was wrong, the new plane wasn't better. I knew that Cuba was quite far, but I never thought it to be that far, given the U.S.'s high speed airplanes. At some point, I thought that the government wanted to blow up the plane over the Atlantic and declare it an accident, since all the detainees had been interrogated over and over and over. But this crazy plan was the least of my worries; was I really worried about a little death pain, after which I would hopefully enter paradise with God's mercy? Living under God's mercy would be better than living under the U.S.'s mercy.

The plane seemed to be heading to the kingdom of far, far away. Feeling lessened with every minute going by; my body numbed. I remember asking for the bathroom once. The guards dragged me to the place, pushed inside a small room, and pulled down my pants. I couldn't take care of my business because of the presence of others. But I think I managed with a lot of effort to squeeze some water. I just wanted to arrive, no matter where! Any place would be better than this plane.

After I don't know how many hours, the plane landed in Cuba. The guards started to pull us out of the plane. "Walk! . . . Stop!" I couldn't walk, for my feet were unable to carry me. And now I noticed that at some point I had lost one of my shoes. After a thorough search outside the plane, the guards shouted, "Walk! Do not talk! Head down! Step!" I only understood "Do not talk," but the guards were dragging me anyway. Inside the truck, the guards shouted "Sit down!" Cross your legs!" I didn't understand the last part but they crossed my legs anyway. "Head down!" one shouted, pushing my head against the rear end of another detainee like a chicken. A female voice was shouting all the way to the camp, "No Talking," and a male voice, "Do not talk," and an Arabic translator who dutifully but clumsily tried to keep up with his angry American colleagues, struggling with their curses and dirty words. "Keep your head down." I was completely annoyed by the American way of talking; I stayed that way for a long time, until I got cured by meeting other good Americans. At the same time, I was thinking about how they gave the same order two different ways: "Do not talk" and "No talking." That was interesting.

By now the chains on my ankles were cutting off the blood to my feet. My feet became numb. I heard only the moaning and crying of other detainees. Beating was the order of the trip. I was not spared: the guard kept hitting me on my head and squeezing my neck against the rear end of the other detainee. But I don't blame him as much as I do that poor and painful detainee, who was crying and kept moving, and so kept raising my head. Other detainees told me that we took a ferry ride during the trip, but I didn't notice.

After about an hour we were finally at the promised land. As much pain as I suffered, I was very happy to have the trip behind me. A Prophet's saying states, "Travel is a piece of torture." This trip was certainly a piece of torture. Now I was only worried about how I was going to stand up if they asked me to. I was just paralyzed. Two guards grabbed me and shouted "Stan' up." I tried to jump but nothing happened; instead they dragged me and threw me outside the truck.

The warm Cuban sun hit me gracefully. It was such a good feeling. The trip started in Bagram on August 4, 2002 at 10 a.m., and we arrived in Cuba around 12:00 or 1:00 p.m. on August 5th, which meant we spent more than thirty hours in an ice-cold airplane.* I was luckier than a Sudanese brother

---

* A 2008 investigation by the British human rights organization Reprieve found that transfers of prisoners from Bagram to Guantánamo typically involved a stop at the U.S. air base in Incirlik, Turkey, and the Rendition Project has found that a C-17 military transport plane, flight number RCH233Y, flew from Incirlik to Guantánamo on August 5, 2002, carrying thirty-five prisoners. See http://humanrights.ucdavis.edu/projects/the -guantanamo-testimonials-project/testimonies/testimony-of-other -physicians/journey_of_death.pdf; and http://www.therenditionproject.org .uk/pdf/PDF%20154%20[Flight%20data.%20Portuguese%20flight%20 logs%20to%20GTMO,%20collected%20by%20Ana%20Gomes].pdf.

who froze totally. He happened to ask the guard to turn down the A/C on the plane. The guard not only refused to meet his wish, but he kept soaking him with water drops all the way to Cuba. The medics had to put him in a room and treat him with a blazing fire.

"When they started the fire, I said to myself, here you go, now they start the torture!" he told us. I laughed when he recounted his story in Camp Delta's Oscar Block the next morning.

I could tell they had changed the guard team for a better one. The old team used to say "Wader"; the new team says "Water." The old team used to say, "Stan' up"; the new team, "Stand up." The old team was simply too loud.

I could also tell the detainees had reached their pain limit. All I heard was moaning. Next to me was an Afghani who was crying very loudly and pleading for help, but each time he rose up the MPs pounded him back down to the ground. He was speaking in Arabic, "Sir, how could you do this to me? Please, relieve my pain, Gentlemen!" But nobody even bothered to check on him. The fellow was sick back in Bagram. I saw him in the cell next to ours; he was vomiting all the time. I felt so bad for him. At the same time, I laughed. Can you believe it, I stupidly laughed! Not at him; I laughed at the situation. First, he addressed them in Arabic, which no guards understood. Second, he called them Gentlemen, which they were most certainly not.

In the beginning I enjoyed the sunbath, but the sun grew hotter with every minute that went by. I started to sweat, and grew very tired of the kneeling position I had to remain in for about six hours. Every once in a while a guard shouted, "Need water!" I don't remember asking for water, but it's likely that I did. I was still stuck with the blindfold, but my excitement about being in a new correctional facility with other human beings I could socialize with, in a place where there would be no torture or even interrogation, overwhelmed my pain; that and the fact that I didn't know how long the detention was going to last. And so I didn't open my mouth with any complaints or moans, while many brothers around me were moaning and even crying. I think that my pain limit had been reached a long time before.

I was dead last to be "processed"; people who got hurt on the plane probably had priority, such as the Sudanese man. Finally two escorting guards dragged me into the clinic. They stripped me naked and pushed me into an open shower. I took a shower in my chains under the eyes of everybody, my brethren, the medics, and the Army. The other brothers who preceeded me were still stark naked. It was ugly, and although the shower was soothing, I couldn't enjoy it. I was ashamed and I did the old ostrich trick: I looked down to my feet. The guards dried me and took me to the next step. Basically the detainees went through a medical check, where they took note of everybody's biological description, height, weight, scars, and experienced the first interrogation inside the clinic. It was like a car production line. I followed the steps of the detainee who preceded me, and he followed somebody else's steps, and so on and so forth.

"Do you have any known diseases?" asked the young nurse.

"Yes, sciatic nerve and hypotension."

"Anything else?"

"No."

"Where did they capture you?"

"I don't understand," I replied. The doctor repeated the nurse's question, but I still didn't understand. He spoke too quickly.

"Never mind!" the doctor said. One of my guards gestured to me, putting one of his hands over the other. Only then did I understand the doctor's question.

"In my country!"

"Where are you from?"

"Mauritania," I replied as the guards were dragging me to the next step. Medics are not supposed to interrogate detainees, but they do anyway. Personally I enjoy conversations with everybody and I couldn't care less about them breaking the rules.

It was cool and crowded inside the hospital. I was solaced by the fact that I saw detainees who were in the same situation as me, especially after they wrapped us in the orange uniform. Interrogators were disguised among the Medics to gather information.

"Do you speak Russian?" an old civilian, an Intel wreck of the cold war, asked me. He interrogated me a couple of times later on, and told me that he once worked with Gulbuddin Hekmatyar, a Mujahideen leader in Afghanistan during the war with the Soviets who supposedly used to turn over Russian detainees to the U.S. "I interrogated them. They're now U.S. citizens, and among my best friends," he told me. He claimed to be responsible for a section of the GTMO Task Force. Interrogators like him were sneaking around, trying to converse "innocently" with the detainees. However, interrogators have a hard time mixing in with other people. They're simply very clumsy.

The escort led me to a room with many detainees and interrogators at work. "What's your name? Where are you from? Are you married?"

"Yes!"

"What's the name of your wife?" I forgot the name of my wife and several members of my family as well because of the persistent state of depression I had been in now for the last nine months. Since I knew that nobody was going to buy such a thing, I went, "Zeinebou," just a name that came to my mind.

"What languages do you speak?"

"Arabic, French, German."

"Sprechen Sie Deutsch?" asked a male interrogator in uniform who was helping his black female colleague typing in laptop.

"Bist du so-and-so?" I asked, using a German name I had been given in Afghanistan. The guy's nametag said Graham, and so he was shocked when I mentioned his name. The black woman stared at him in confusion.

"Who told you about me?"

"Michael, from Bagram!" I said, explaining that in Bagram Michael told me about him, in case I needed a German translator in GTMO.

"We'll keep the conversation in English, but very simple," he said. Michael's CIA colleague avoided me for the rest of his time in GTMO.

I was listening to the interrogation of a Tunisian fellow detainee.

"Did you train in Afghanistan?"

"No."

"You know if you lie, we're gonna get the information from Tunisia!"

"I am not lying!"

The medical check resumed. A black female corpsman took a thousand and one tubes of blood off me. I thought I was going to pass out or even die. A blood pressure check showed 110 over 50, which is very low. The doctor immediately put me on small red tablets to increase my blood pressure. Pictures were taken. I hated the fact that my privacy was being disrespected in every way. I was totally under the mercy of somebody I didn't trust and who might be ruthless. Many detainees would smile for the camera. I personally never smiled, and I don't think that on that day, August 5th, 2002, any detainee did.

After the endless processing, the escort team took me out of the clinic. "Keep your head down!" It was already dark outside but I couldn't tell what time it was. The weather was nice. "Sit down." I sat outside for about thirty minutes before the escort team picked me up and put me in a room and locked me to the floor. I didn't notice the lock, nor had I ever been subject to it before. I thought the room was to be my future home.

The room was bare but for a couple of chairs and a desk. There was no sign of life. "Where are the other detainees?" I said to myself. I grew impatient and decided to go outside the room and try to find other fellow detainees, but as soon as I tried to stand up the chains pulled me down hard. Only then did I know that something was wrong with my assumptions. As it turned out, I was in the interrogation booth in Brown Building, a building with history.

All of a sudden three men entered the room: the older guy who spoke to me earlier in the clinic, an FBI agent who introduced himself as William, and a young Moroccan man who served as an interpreter.*

---

* The FBI led MOS's interrogations for his first several months in Guantánamo, waging a well-documented struggle to keep him out of the hands of military interrogators. The protracted interagency conflict between the FBI

"Comment vous vous appelez?" asked William in a thick accent.

"Je m'appelle......," I answered, and that was the end of William's French. Interrogators always tend to bring the factor of surprise as a technique.

I glimpsed one of the guy's watches. It was nearly 1 a.m. I was in a state where my system had gotten messed up; I was wide awake in spite of more than forty-eight hours of sleeplessness. The interrogators wanted to use that weakness to facilitate the interrogation. I was offered nothing such as water or food. William led the interrogation, and the Moroccan man was a good translator. The other guy didn't get the chance to ask questions, he just took notes, William didn't really come up with a miracle: all he did was ask me some questions I had been asked uninterruptedly for the past three years. He spoke a very clear English, and I almost didn't need the translator. He seemed to be smart and experienced. When the night grew late, William thanked me for my cooperation.

"I believe that you are very open," he said. "The next time we'll untie your hands and bring you something to eat. We will not torture you, nor will we extradite you to another country."

---

and the Pentagon's Defense Intelligence Agency over the military's interrogation methods has been widely documented and reported, most notably in a May 2008 report by the U.S. Department of Justice's Inspector General titled *A Review of the FBI's Involvement in and Observations of Detainee Interrogations in Guantanamo Bay, Afghanistan, and Iraq* (hereafter cited as DOJ IG). The report, which is available at http://www.justice.gov/oig/special/s0805/final.pdf, includes substantial sections devoted specifically to MOS's interrogation. "The FBI sought to interview Slahi immediately after he arrived at GTMO," the DOJ Inspector General reported in one of those sections. "FBI and task force agents interviewed Slahi over the next few months, utilizing rapport building techniques." At his 2005 ARB hearing, MOS described an "FBI guy" who interrogated him shortly after his arrival and told him, "We don't beat people, we don't torture people, it's not allowed." DOJ IG, 122, ARB transcript 23.

I was happy with William's assurances, and encouraged in my cooperation. As it turned out, he was either misleading me or he was unknowledgeable about the plans of his government.

The three men left the room and sent the escort team to me, which led me to my cell. It was in Oscar Block, a block designed for isolation.★ I was the only detainee who had been picked for interrogation from our entire group of thirty-four detainees. There was no sign of life inside the block, which made me think that I was the only one around. When the guard dropped me in the frozen-cold box I almost panicked behind the heavy metal door. I tried to convince myself, It's only a temporary place, in the morning they're going to transfer me to the community. This place cannot be for more than the rest of the night! In fact, I spent one whole month in Oscar Block.

It was around 2 a.m. when the guard handed me an MRE. I tried to eat what I could, but I had no appetite. When I checked my stuff I saw a brand new Koran, which made me happy. I kissed the Koran and soon fell asleep. I slept deeper than I ever had.

The shoutings of my fellow detainees woke me up in the early morning. Life was suddenly blown into that dark Oscar Block. When I arrived earlier that morning, I never thought that human beings could be possibly stored in a bunch of cold boxes;

★ The March 3, 2003, Camp Delta Standard Operating Procedures instructed that arriving prisoners be processed and held for four weeks in a maximum security isolation block "to enhance and exploit the disorientation and disorganization felt by a newly arrived detainee in the interrogation process" and "to [foster] dependence of the detainee on his interrogator." The document is available at http://www.comw.org/warreport/fulltext/gitmo-sop.pdf (hereafter cited as SOP).

I thought I was the only one, but I was wrong, my fellow detainees were only knocked out due to the harsh punishment trip they had behind them. While the guards were serving the food, we were introducing us to ourselves. We couldn't see each other due to the design of the block but we could hear each other.

"Salam Alaikum!"

"Waalaikum Salam."

"Who are you?

"I am from Mauritania... Palestine... Syria... Saudi Arabia...!"

"How was the trip?"

"I almost froze to death," shouted one guy.

"I slept the whole trip," replied Ibrahim.

"Why did they put the patch beneath my ear?" said a third.

"Who was in front of me in the truck?" I asked. "He kept moving, which made the guards beat me all the way from the airport to the camp."

"Me, too," another detainee answered.

We called each other with the ISN numbers we were assigned in Bagram. My number was 760. In the cell on my left was 706, Mohammed al-Amin from Mauritania. He was about twenty years old, and had been captured in Pakistan and sold to the Americans. Though Mauritanian, he had never really been in the country; I could tell because of his Saudi accent. On my right was the guy from the Maldives, whose number was 730. He spoke poor Arabic, and claimed to have been captured in Karachi, where he attends the University. In front of my cell they put the Sudanese, next to each other.*

---

* Mohammed al-Amin was born in Mauritania but moved to Saudi Arabia for religious studies. He was released and transferred to Mauritania

Breakfast was modest: one boiled egg, a hard piece of bread, and something else I don't know the name of. It was my first hot meal since I left Jordan. Oh, the tea was soothing! I like tea better than any food, and for as long as I can remember I've been drinking it. Tea is a crucial part of the diet of people from warmer regions; it sounds contradictory but it is true.

People were shouting all over the place in indistinct conversations. It was just a good feeling when everybody started to recount his story. Many detainees suffered, some more and some less. I didn't consider myself the worst, nor the luckiest. Some people were captured with their friends and their friends disappeared from the face of the earth; they most likely were sent to other allied countries to facilitate their interrogation by torture, such as the detainees who were sent to Egypt and Jordan. I considered the arrival to Cuba a blessing, and so I told the brothers, "Since you guys are not involved in crimes, you need to fear nothing. I personally am going to cooperate, since nobody is going to torture me. I don't want any of you to suffer what I suffered in Jordan. In Jordan, they hardly appreciate your cooperation."

I wrongly believed that the worst was over, and so I cared less about the time it would take the Americans to figure out that I was not the guy they are looking for. I trusted the American justice system too much, and shared that trust with the detainees from European countries. We all had an idea about how the democratic system works. Other detainees, for instance those from the Middle East, didn't believe it for a second and trust the American system. Their argument lay on the growing hostility of extremist Americans against Muslims and the Arabs. With every day going by, the optimists lost ground. The interrogation

---

on September 26, 2007. Ibrahim Fauzee, who is from the Maldives, was released on March 11, 2005.

methods worsened considerably as time went by, and as you shall see, those responsible for GTMO broke all the principles upon which the U.S. was built and compromised every great principle such as Ben Franklin's "They that give up essential liberty to obtain a little temporary safety deserve neither liberty nor safety."

All of us wanted to make up for months of forced silence, we wanted to get every anger and agony off our chests, and we listened to each other's amazing stories for the next thirty days to come, which was our time in Oscar Block. When we later got transferred to a different block, many fellow detainees cried for being separated from their new friends. I cried, too.

The interrogation escort team showed up at my cell.

"Reservation!" said one of the MPs, holding the long chains in his hands. Reservation is the code word for being taken to interrogation. Although I didn't understand where I was going, I prudently followed their orders until they delivered me to the interrogator. His name was Hamza, or at least that was what he was called, and he was wearing a U.S. Army uniform. He was an intelligence officer in the Kentucky National Guard, a man with all the paradoxes you may imagine. He spoke Arabic decently, with a Jordanian accent; you could tell he grew up among Arabic-speaking friends.*

---

* Around this time, FBI-led interrogation teams often included members of the military's Criminal Investigation Task Force (CITF) and military intelligence agents. The DOJ Inspector General's report records that "in May 2002, the military and the FBI adopted the 'Tiger Team' concept for interrogating detainees. According to the first GTMO case agent, these teams consisted of an FBI agent, an analyst, a contract linguist, two CITF investigators, and a military intelligence interrogator." The IG found that "the FBI withdrew from participation in the Tiger Teams in the fall of 2002

I was terrified when I stepped into the room in Brown Building because of the CamelBak on Hamza's back, from which he was sipping. I never saw a thing like that before. I thought it was a kind of tool to hook on me as a part of my interrogation. I really don't know why I was scared, but the fact that I never saw Hamza nor his CamelBak, nor did I expect an Army guy, all these factors contributed to my fear.

The older gentleman who interrogated me the night before entered the room with some candies and introduced Hamza to me, "I chose Hamza because he speaks your language. We're going to ask you detailed questions about your cousin Abu Hafs. As to me, I am going to leave soon, but my replacement will take care of you. See you later." He stepped out of the room leaving me and Hamza to work.

Hamza was a friendly guy. He was a reserve officer in the U.S. Army who believed himself to be lucky in life. Hamza wanted me to repeat to him my whole story, which I've been repeating for the last three years over and over. I got used to interrogators asking me the same things. Before the interrogator even moved his lips I knew his questions, and as soon as he or she started to talk, I turned my "tape" on. But when I came to the part about Jordan, he felt very sorry!

"Those countries don't respect human rights. They even torture people," he said. I was comforted: if Hamza criticized cruel interrogation methods, it meant that the Americans wouldn't do something like that. Yes, they were not exactly following

---

after disagreements arose between the FBI and military intelligence over interrogation tactics. Several FBI agents told the OIG that while they continued to have a good relationship with CITF, their relationship with the military intelligence entities greatly deteriorated over the course of time, primarily due to the FBI's opposition to the military intelligence approach to interrogating detainees." DOJ IG, 34.

the law in Bagram, but that was in Afghanistan, and now we are in a U.S. controlled territory.

After Hamza finished his interrogation, he sent me back and promised to come back should new questions arise. During the session with Hamza, I asked him to use the bathroom. "No. 1 or No. 2?" he asked. It was the first time I heard the human private business coded in numbers. In the countries I've been in, it isn't customary to ask people about their intention in the bathroom, nor do they have a code.

I never saw Hamza in an interrogation again. The FBI's William resumed his work a couple of days later, only the FBI team was now reinforced by José, a Hispanic American who spoke unaccented English and fluent Spanish. José was another friendly guy. He and William worked very well together. For some reason, the FBI was interested in taking my case in hand. Although a military interrogator came with the team a couple of times and asked some questions, you could tell that William had the upper hand.★

The team worked on my case for over a month, on almost a daily basis. They asked me all kind of questions, and we spoke about other political topics beside the interrogation. Nobody ever threatened me or tried to torture me, and from my side I was cooperating with the team very well. "Our job is to take your statements and send them to the analysts in D.C. Even if you lie to us, we can't really tell right away until more information comes in," said William.

The team could see very clearly how sick I was; the prints of Jordan and Bagram were more than obvious. I looked like a ghost.

"You're getting better," said the Army guy when he saw me

★ As the DOJ IG report makes clear, the FBI maintained overall control of the interrogation of MOS throughout 2002 and early 2003. DOJ IG, 122.

three weeks after my arrival in GTMO. On my second or third day in GTMO I had collapsed in my cell. I was just driven to my extremes; the MREs didn't appeal to me. The Medics took me out of my cell and I tried to walk the way to the hospital, but as soon as I left Oscar Block I collapsed once more, which made the Medics carry me to the clinic. I threw up so much that I was completely dehydrated. I received first aid and got an IV. The IV was terrible; they must have put some medication in it that I have an allergy to. My mouth dried up completely and my tongue became so heavy that I couldn't ask for help. I gestured with my hands to the corpsmen to stop dripping the fluid into my body, which they did.

Later that night the guards brought me back to my cell. I was so sick I couldn't climb on my bed; I slept on the floor for the rest of the month. The doctor prescribed Ensure and some hypotension medicine, and every time I got my sciatic nerve crisis the corpsmen gave me Motrin.

Although I was physically very weak, the interrogation didn't stop. But I was nonetheless in good spirits. In the Block we were singing, joking, and recounting stories to each other. I also got the opportunity to learn about the star detainees, such as his excellence Mallah Zaeef, the former Taliban ambassador to Pakistan, who fed us with the latest news and rumors from camp, and the Jordanian Abu Huzaifa, who had been transferred to Oscar Block due to his "behavior."★

Abu Huzaifa told us how he was tortured in Kandahar with

★ Mullah Abdul Salam Zaeef was the Afghan ambassador to Pakistan before the U.S. invasion of Afghanistan in October 2001. After the invasion he was seized by Pakistani authorities and turned over to the U.S. He was held in Guantánamo until his release in 2005. Abu Huzaifa, known formally as Ahmed Hassan Jamil Suleyman, was released from Guantánamo on December 2, 2007.

other detainees. "They put us under the sun for a long time, we got beaten, but brothers don't worry, here in Cuba there is no torture. The rooms are air-conditioned, and some brothers even refuse to talk unless offered food," he said.

"I cried when I saw detainees blindfolded and taken to Cuba on TV. The American Defense Secretary spoke on TV and claimed these detainees are the most evil people on the face of the earth. I never thought that I would be one of these 'evil people,'" said Ibrahim, the Sudanese who suffered hypothermia during the flight to Guantánamo.

Ibrahim had been working as an Arabic teacher for a Kuwaiti relief organization, helping to educate Afghani refugees. He was captured with four other colleagues of his in his domicile in Peshawar after midnight under the cries of his children; he was pried off his kids and his wife. The same thing exactly happened to his friends, who confirmed his story. I heard tons of such stories and every story made me forget the last one. I couldn't tell whose story was more saddening. It even started to undermine my story, but the detainees were unanimous that my story was the saddest. I personally don't know. The German proverb says: "Wenn das Militar sich bewegt, bleibt die Wahrheit auf der Strecke." When the Military sets itself in motion, the truth is too slow to keep up, so it stays behind.

The law of war is harsh. If there's anything good at all in a war, it's that it brings the best and the worst out of people: some people try to use the lawlessness to hurt others, and some try to reduce the suffering to the minimum.

On September 4, 2002, I was transferred to Delta Block, and so the interrogators ended the isolation and put me in with general population. On the one hand, it was hard for me to leave the friends I'd just made, and on the other hand I was excited about going to a dead normal Block, and being a dead average detainee. I was tired of being a "special" detainee, riding all over the world against my will.

I arrived in Delta Block before sunset. For the first time in more than nine months, I was put in a cell where I could see the plain. And for the first time I was able to talk to my fellow detainees while seeing them. I was put in cell number 5, between two Saudis from the South. Both were very friendly and entertaining. They had both been captured by the Pakistanis and sold to the U.S. When the prisoners tried to free themselves from the Pakistani Army, which was working on behalf of the U.S., one of them, an Algerian, grabbed the AK47 of a Pakistani guard and shot him. In the melee, the other captured detainees asserted control of the transport bus; the guards fled, and the detainees fled too—just as far as where another army, a U.S. division, was awaiting them, and they were captured again. The bus escape attempt caused many casualties and injuries. I saw an Algerian detainee who was completely disabled due to the amount of bullets he had taken.

I had a good time in Delta Block at the beginning, but things started to get ugly when some interrogators started to practice torture methods on some detainees, though shyly. As far as I heard and saw, the only method practiced at first was the cold room, all night. I know a young Saudi man who was taken to interrogation every night and put back in his cell in the morning. I don't know the details of what exactly happened to him because he was very quiet, but my neighbors told me that he refused to talk to his interrogators. One of my neighbors also told me that he was also put in the cold room two nights in a row because he refused to cooperate.

Most of the detainees by then were refusing to cooperate after they felt they had provided everything relevant to their cases. People were desperate and growing tired of being interrogated all the time, without hope of an end. I personally was relatively new and wanted to take my chances: maybe my fellow detainees were wrong! But I ended up bumping into the same brick wall as anybody else. Detainees grew worried about their situation and the absence of a due process of law, and things started to get worse with the use of painful methods to extract information from detainees.

Around mid-September, 2002, not long after my transfer to Delta Block, a new team with two agents with rhyming names, John and Don, pulled me to interrogation and introduced themselves as the team that was going to assess me for the next two months.

"How long am I going to be interrogated?"

"As long as the government has questions for you!"

"How long is that?"

"I can only tell you that you will not spend more than five years here," said John. The team was communicating with me through an Arabic interpreter who looked like he was in his late forties.

"I'm not ready to be asked the same questions again and again!"

"No, we have some new questions." But as it turned out they were asking me the very same questions I had been asked for the last three years. Even so, I was reluctantly cooperating. I honestly didn't see any advantages in cooperating, I just wanted to see how far things were going to go.

Around the same time another interrogator, a CIA agent who called himself Peter, pulled me to interrogation. He was a very tall, skinny white man in his early forties. He had an organized goatee, and spoke perfect Arabic with a distinct Tunisian accent. Peter possessed the kind of confidence and authority his job required. He was straightforward with me, and even shared with me what the U.S. government was saying about other detainees and about me. He was talking, and talking, and talking some more: he was interested in getting me to work for him, as he had tried with other North African Arabs.*

"Next Thursday, I've arranged a meeting with the Germans. Are you going to talk to them?"

"Yes, I am." That was the first lie I detected, because the FBI's William had told me, "No foreign government is going to talk to you here, only us Americans!" In fact, I heard about many detainees meeting with non–American interrogators, such as the Uighur detainees from China. Agents from Chinese intelligence services came to GTMO and were helping the U.S. to extract information from the Uighur detainees. These foreign interrogators threatened some of their interviewees with torture when they got back home.

"I hope I see you in another place," said the Chinese interrogator to one of the Uighur detainees. "If we see each other in Turkistan, you're gonna talk a lot!"†

---

* In 2013, the Associated Press reported that between 2002 and 2005, CIA agents in GTMO sought to recruit detainees to serve as informants and double agents for the United States. The CIA also helped facilitate interrogations by foreign intelligence agents in Guantánamo. Adam Goldman and Matt Apuzzo, "Penny Lane, GITMO's Other Secret CIA Facility," Associated Press, November 26, 2013, http://bigstory.ap.org/article/penny-lane-gitmos-other-secret-cia-facility.

† The interrogations of ethnic Uighur detainees by Chinese intelligence agents in GTMO, which were reportedly preceded by periods of sleep deprivation and temperature manipulation, were first revealed in the May 2008 DOJ Inspector General's report, *A Review of the FBI's Involvement in and Observations of Detainee Interrogations in Guantanamo Bay, Afghanistan, and Iraq.* McClatchy Newspapers reported that the interrogations took place

But I was not afraid of talking to anyone. I had done no crimes against anybody. I even wanted to talk to prove my innocence, since the American motto was "GTMO detainees are guilty until proven innocent." I knew what was awaiting me when it came to foreign interrogators, and I wanted to get things out off my chest.

The day came and the guards pulled me and took me to a building called Orange Trailer, where detainees usually met CIA and foreign intelligence agents. Two German gentlemen were sitting on the other side of the table, and I was looking at them, locked on the floor. The older man was quieter than the younger one, who played the bad guy role during the interrogation. Neither introduced himself, which was completely against the German customs and laws; they just stood in front of me like ghosts, the same as the rest of the secret interrogators.*

"Do you speak German, or do we need an interpreter?" asked the younger agent.

"I am afraid we don't," I replied.

"Well, you understand the seriousness of the matter. We've come from Germany to talk to you.

"People have been killed," continued the older man.

I smiled. "Since when are you allowed to interrogate people outside Germany?"

---

over a day and a half in September 2002. See http://www.mcclatchydc .com/2009/07/16/72000/uighur-detainees-us-helped-chinese.html.

* In 2008, *Der Spiegel* reported that in September 2002, two members of the Bundesnachrichtendienst (BND) and one member of the Office for the Protection of the Constitution, Germany's foreign and domestic intelligence agencies, interviewed MOS for ninety minutes in Guantánamo. John Goetz, Marcel Rosenbach, Britta Sandberg, and Holger Stark, "From Germany to Guantanamo: The Career of Prisoner No. 760," *Der Spiegel,* October 9, 2008, http://www.spiegel.de/international/world/from -germany-to-guantanamo-the-career-of-prisoner-no-760-a-583193.html.

"We are not here to discuss the judicial grounds of our questioning!"

"I might, sometime in the future, be able to talk to the press and give you away," I said. "Though I don't know your names, I'll recognize your pictures, no matter how long it takes!"

"You can say whatever you want, you're not gonna hurt us! We know what we're doing," he said.

"So clearly you guys are using the lawlessness of this place to extract information out of me?"

The younger agent jumped in. "Herr Salahi, if we wanted to, we could ask the guards to hang you on the wall and kick your ass!"★ When he mentioned the crooked way he was thinking, my heart started to pound, because I was trying to express myself carefully and at the same time avoid torture.

"You can't scare me, you're not talking to a child. If you continue speaking to me with this tone, you can pack your luggage and go back to Germany."

"We are not here to prosecute you or scare you, we would just be grateful if you would answer a couple of questions we have," said the older agent.

"Look, I've been in your country, and you know that I was never involved in any kind of crimes. Plus, what are you worried about? Your country isn't even threatened. I've been living peacefully in your country and never abused your hospitality. I am very grateful for all that your country helped me with; I don't stab in the back. So what theater are you trying to play on me?"

The younger agent adjusted his tone. "Herr Salahi, we know that you are innocent, but we did not capture you, the Ameri-

---

★ "Salahi" is a variant spelling of MOS's last name that is generally used in court documents in the United States.

cans did. We are not here on behalf of the U.S. We work for the German government, and lately we stopped some bad plots. We know you cannot possibly know about these things. However, we only want to ask you about two individuals, Christian Ganczarski and Karim Mehdi, and we would be grateful if you would answer our questions about them."*

"It's just funny that you've come all the way from Germany to ask about your own people! Those two individuals are good friends of mine. We attended the same mosques, but I don't know them to be involved in any terrorist operations."

The session didn't last much longer than that. They asked me how I was doing and about the life in the camp and bid me farewell. I never saw the Germans after that.

Meanwhile, the team with Agents John and Don kept questioning me.

"Do you know this guy, Ramzi bin al-Shibh?" asked John.

"No, I don't," I honestly answered.

"But he knows you!"

"I am afraid you have another file than mine!"

"No, I read your file very thoroughly."

"Can you show me his picture?"

"Yes. I'm going to show it to you tomorrow."

"Good. I might know him by another name!"

---

* Karim Mehdi was born in Morocco and lived in Germany, and traveled with MOS to Afghanistan in 1992. Mehdi was arrested at Charles de Gaulle airport in Paris on June 3, 2003. Christian Ganczarski, a Polish-born German citizen, was arrested at the same airport the following day. Mehdi was tried and sentenced to nine years in prison for plotting a bombing on Reunion Island, and Ganczarski was tried and sentenced to eighteen years in prison in connection with the bombing of a tourist bus in Tunisia in April 2002. Both are discussed in Judge James Robertson's habeas corpus opinion. See https://www.aclu.org/files/assets/2010-4-9-Slahi-Order.pdf. See also http://articles.latimes.com/print/2003/jun/07/world/fg-terror7; and http://news.bbc.co.uk/2/hi/africa/6088540.stm.

"Do you know about the American bases in Germany?"

"Why do you ask me about that? I didn't go to Germany to study the American bases, nor am I interested in them in any way!" I angrily replied.

"My people respect detainees who tell the truth!" the skinny agent said, while his colleague Agent Don took notes. I took the hint that he was calling me a liar in a stupid way. The session was terminated.

The next day John and Don reserved me in the interrogation booth and showed me two pictures. The first one turned out to be that of Ramzi bin al-Shibh, who was suspected of having participated in the September 11 attack and who was captured in Karachi in a joint operation exactly one year later. The second picture was of Mohamed Atta, one of the September 11 hijackers. As to Mohamed Atta, I had never heard of him or saw him, and as to Ramzi bin al-Shibh, I figured I've seen the guy, but where and when? I had no clue! But I also figured that the guy must be very important because the agencies were running fast together to find my link with him.★ Under the circumstances, I denied having seen the guy. Look at it, how would it have looked had I said I'd seen this guy, but I don't know when and where? What interrogator would buy something like that? Not one! And to be honest with you, I was as scared as hell.

The FBI team reserved me again the next day and showed me the picture of Ramzi bin al-Shibh, and I denied that I knew

---

★ Ramzi bin al-Shibh was captured in a shoot-out in a suburb of Karachi, Pakistan on September 11, 2002. At his 2005 ARB hearing, MOS told the panel, "September 11th, 2002, America arrested a man by the name of Ramzi Bin al Shibh, who is said to be the key guy in the September 11th attacks. It was exactly one year after 9/11, and since his capture my life has changed drastically." ARB transcript, 23.

him, the same way I had the day before. My denial that I knew a man that I don't really know, I just saw him for a very short time once or twice and had no association whatsoever with him, gave fuel to all kind of wild theories linking me to the September 11 attack. The investigators were just drowning and were looking for any straw to grab, and I personally didn't exactly want to be that straw.

"We'd like you to take a polygraph test," said John.

"It's not compulsory," his partner added. But I knew that refusing to take the test would be seen as a clear indication that I was guilty, though there had been no discussion of what crime I was supposed to be guilty of. The agents explained the polygraph process to me through an interpreter, and I agreed to take the test. I asked when the test would happen.

"In the next few days!"

In the meantime I was transferred to Lima Block, where I met an Algerian-Bosnian man named Mustafa Ait Idir for the first time. He was another one of the star detainees. Mustafa heard about my story, and like any other curious person, he wanted to have more information. On my side, I also wanted to converse with cultured people. As far as I could tell, Mustafa was a decent guy; I had a hard time picturing him as a criminal.*

Lima Block was filled with European and North African detainees. For the first time I got to know the Algerians, Moroccans, and Tunisians, and the Danish, Swedish, French, and Bosnian detainees as well. I was happy to be with the detainees from the Maghreb; being from the region, I could understand their jokes much better and quicker than the amazing ones from

---

* Mustafa Ait Idir won his habeas corpus petition in U.S. federal court and was released from Guantánamo on December 16, 2008.

detainees from the Arab peninsula, and they got my jokes, too. The other Mauritanian on the block and I tried to get to know each other, but we weren't allowed. Our only contact was when he and I felt sick and were transferred to the Navy hospital in the same truck, but we couldn't talk much. On the way, he and our Syrian translator got into a heated debate about the job of translators in GTMO, and I used the distraction to look outside through the clumsily blinded window. I saw a woman jogging, and a bunch of water supply pipes. I was reminded that there's a life outside GTMO, and I suddenly felt very afraid. Grimly, I realized that I felt safer shackled in a truck surrounded by guards who were given firearms as soon as we left the camp's gate.

The day of the polygraph came, and the escort team led me silently to Gold Building. I always wanted to know where I was going and why. I remember one time when the escorting team refused to tell me where I was going: I thought they were taking me to my execution.*

When I entered the room where the test was supposed to take place, I expected to see a huge machine. I had told my neighbors in Lima Block about the upcoming polygraph test, and my neighbor Jabir Jubran Al Fayfi, who had been an MP in the

---

* At his 2005 ARB hearing, as he is describing his FBI interrogations through the winter of 2002, MOS said, "Then I took a polygraph and [Ramzi bin al-Shibh] refused to take a polygraph for many reasons. It turns out he is very contradictory and he lies. They said that to me themselves. They said my credibility is high because I took the polygraph." After his capture on September 11, 2002, Ramzi bin al-Shibh was held and interrogated at several CIA black sites. News reports suggest that bin al-Shibh was interrogated in a CIA-run facility near Rabat, Morocco, in late September and through the fall of 2002, and in 2010 the U.S. government acknowledged it possessed videotapes of bin al-Shibh's 2002 interrogation in Morocco. See, e.g., http://www.nytimes.com/2010/08/18/world/18tapes.html; and http://hosted.ap.org/specials/interactives/wdc/binalshibh/content.swf.

Saudi army, told me he had taken one before. His description of the test was not exactly comforting. Adding to that, an Egyptian novel fell into my hands a few days before the test that dramatically described an Egyptian double agent undergoing a lie detector test that was given by the Israeli Mossad. If I believed in conspiracies, I would have assumed the interrogators sent the librarian to deliver me that particular book, but I couldn't tell if it was to scare me or encourage me, or what the lesson was supposed to be. In the novel, after much sweating and panting, the Egyptian emerged victorious; the moral seemed to be that you could lie and pass the test, but if you are telling the truth, you can still fail.*

From the book and from Jabir I somehow imagined the lie detector as a big, elliptical-like machine I would climb onto and be wired everywhere. Then I would start running and sweating as interrogators beside me threw random questions at me and recorded my vital signs, which would indicate my truthfulness or lack thereof. I expected a great deal of shouting and intimidation, like in the Egyptian novel. But when I entered the room, I found a big table with a laptop, a blood pressure cuff, a big belt, a small printer, and many thin cables and other stuff I didn't understand. I was relieved because the equipment looked much less intimidating than I'd imagined. American genius never stopped impressing me: with such a small device they can decide whether or not you are lying!

The guards sat me in a chair next to the empty table and left me alone. The tester was watching me from the next room to see how I behaved. When he decided to end his self-imprisonment behind the mirror he entered the room, accompanied by an

---

* Jabir Jubran Al Fayfi was released from Guantánamo and repatriated to Saudi Arabia in December 2006.

interpreter whose Arabic was very weak. It was entertaining to watch the exchange between them as the interpreter struggled to keep up with his sermon.

He started with stories of his great achievements, naming many high-profile people suspected of heinous acts of violence whom he had saved and sent home. The stories in the *Thousand and One Nights* paled in comparison to his imagination. He walked me through the technological part briefly, mostly to scare me and convince me to tell him the truth, as Abu Zubaydah and others supposedly had when he tested them. He ran a belt around my abdomen and another one around my rib cage to measure the pattern of my breathing. He placed a cuff around my upper arm to measure the changes in my blood pressure, and wrapped a sensor around the tip of my index finger, explaining that if I lied I would sweat and thus drive down the temperature on my finger. Then he hit the real meat, conducting a comprehensive and thorough interrogation.*

---

* Abu Zubaydah is Zayn al-Abidin Muhammad Husayn, the first man to be detained in a secret CIA prison and subjected to its so-called Enhanced Interrogation Techniques. Abu Zubaydah was wounded and captured in a shootout in Faisalabad, Pakistan, on March 28, 2002, and transferred to a secret CIA interrogation facility in Thailand. There, FBI agents and CIA personnel clashed over how Abu Zubaydah was to be interrogated. The CIA prevailed, winning Bush administration approval to subject him to ten abusive interrogation techniques including confinement in small boxes and waterboarding. In December 2002, the CIA closed the secret facility in Thailand and transferred Abu Zubaydah to another black site in Poland. He was held there and in other secret prisons until he was transferred, along with thirteen other so-called high value detainees who had been held and interrogated in CIA black sites, to Guantánamo on September 6, 2006. A full, if partially redacted, account of Abu Zubaydah's torture in CIA custody is provided in the Executive Summary of the Senate Select Committee on Intelligence's 2014 *Study of the Central Intelligence Agency's Detention and Interrogation Program,* available at https://fas.org/irp/congress/2014_rpt/ssci-rdi.pdf. He remains in Guantánamo.

He laid out pictures of some of the suspected 9/11 hijackers and planners and asked me whether I knew or ever met them. I couldn't understand his logic, because he kept showing me more than one picture at a time and asking questions about them, as if they were joined and did everything together. Why didn't he take them one by one? I told the tester that I never met or talked to any one of them, even though I remembered seeing Ramzi bin al-Shibh once. But I couldn't remember where, so I decided to skip that information because I was too scared, especially because I could see the FBI and the tester clearly suspected him of being a 9/11 co-conspirator.

The tester told me the results of the test were "inconclusive." He seemed to notice his mistake of not separating the guys and asking about them individually, but his attempts to convince me to take the test one more time fell on deaf ears. I was tired like never before, and I told him that I didn't really need freedom that badly. The whole process was tedious and long, "comme un jour sans pain," as the French say, except it really was a day without bread. I was sent back to my cell, sure they were now planning on me staying for the long haul.

After a couple of days, I was taken to interrogation.

"How are you?" said John. It had been a long time since I'd seen him.

"Good!"

John and his colleague talked about the polygraph and tried to get me to agree to take it again, but I refused. I really couldn't see what good it would do. They also tried to gather intels from me about other detainees. The Joint Task Force was starting to turn up the heat against the detainees. Treatment in the interrogation rooms was getting worse and worse, and visits from the so-called IRF team to pick up "non-compliant detainees" were commonplace. One time, the whole unit was deployed to search detainees at the same time. It was in the dead of night when I was pulled out of my cell and searched by the guards, with the TV camera on me and contractors watching the whole show. I wasn't the only one; the whole block of forty-eight detainees was searched. The relationship between the Joint Detention Group and the detainees was becoming very tense, and there was nothing much detainees could do to change their situation: the deck was stacked against us, and JDG held all the cards.*

In Major General Dunlavey's era, there were many issues, most of which were initiated by the desperation of the detainees. Endless interrogation. Disrespect of the Holy Koran by some of the guards. Torturing detainees by making them spend the night in a cold room (though this method was not practiced nearly as much as it would be in General Geoffrey Miller's time). So we decided to go on a hunger strike; many detainees took part, including me. But I could only strike for four days, after which I was a ghost.†

---

* In November 2002, two military Joint Task Forces, JTF 160, which ran the prison operations of the Guantánamo Bay detention camp, and JTF-170, which handled interrogation operations, were merged to form Joint Task Force Guantánamo (JTF-GTMO), under the command of General Geoffrey Miller. The Joint Detention Group (JDG) is the component of the JTF-GTMO responsible for guarding prisoners and maintaining camp security. Guantánamo's Initial Response Force (IRF) teams are described in the 2003 Camp Delta Standard Operating Procedures as five-man units equipped with riot gear and "specializing in the extraction of a detainee who is combative, resistive, or if the possibility of a weapon is in the cell at the time of the extraction." SOP 24.2.

† Later in the manuscript, MOS writes that he participated in a hunger strike in September 2002, and news reports document a hunger strike in late September and October of that year (see, e.g., http://america.aljazeera.com/articles/multimedia/guantanamo-hungerstriketimeline.html, quoting an FBI document attributing that protest to anger over treatment by guards and the ongoing detention without trial or legal process). That hunger strike occurred toward the end of the tenure of Major General

"Don't break, you're gonna weaken the group," said my Saudi neighbor.

"I told you guys I'm gonna hunger strike, not that I'm gonna commit suicide. I'm gonna break," I replied.

The situation grew even worse when General Miller took over. He was a hardworking man, the kind of man to be picked for the dirtiest job, when many others had failed. General Miller was a very radical hater. He completely changed the detention policies in GTMO in all aspects. He used to tour the blocks nonstop, giving guards and interrogators instructions for what to do with us. I personally don't know what he told them, but as someone on the receiving end of his orders, I definitely felt the pain.

General Miller was responsible for a kind of class society he created in the camp. Blocks were defined by their levels, and there were five levels. The best was Level One, for so-called highly compliant detainees. Level Four was for isolation as a disciplinary measure, and Level Five was reserved for people who were considered of high intelligence value. Detainees of this level are completely under the mercy of their interrogators, which was very convenient for the interrogators. The system

Michael E. Dunlavey, who was the commander of JTF-170, the intelligence operations in Guantánamo, from February through October 2002. He was succeeded by Major General Geoffrey D. Miller, who became commander of JTF-GTMO, which encompassed all Guantánamo operations, in November 2002.The Senate Armed Services Committee has documented at length the trend toward more abusive interrogations in October and November 2002, which included the development of the military's first "Special Interrogation Plan" for Mohammed al-Qahtani. On December 2, 2002, Secretary of Defense Donald Rumsfeld signed a memo authorizing interrogation methods including nudity, forced standing and stress positions, and twenty-hour interrogations. U.S. Senate Armed Services Committee, "Inquiry in the Treatment of Detainees in U.S. Custody," November 20, 2008, http://www.armed-services.senate.gov/imo/media/doc/Detainee-Report-Final_April-22-2009.pdf (hereafter cited as SASC).

was designed to keep us on edge all the time: One day in paradise, and the next in hell.

In the beginning, when we were informed about the new system, it was a given to me that I was Level One. But to my dismay, I was put with the pariah block, the supposed worst of the worst. I was like, what the heck is going on, I've never been in trouble with the guards, and I am answering my interrogators and cooperating with them. But I missed that cooperation meant telling your interrogators whatever they want to hear.

I was put once more in Oscar Block toward the end of 2002.

An escort team appeared in front of my cell.

"760 reservation!" they said.

"OK, just give me a second!" I put my clothes on and washed my face. My heart started to pound. I hated interrogation; I had gotten tired of being terrified all the time, living in constant fear day-in and day-out for the last thirteen months.

"Allah be with you! Keep your head on! They work for Satan!" yelled my fellow detainees to keep me together, as we always did when somebody got pulled for interrogation. I hated the sounds of the heavy metal chains; I could hardly carry them when they were given to me. People were always getting taken from the block, and every time I heard the chains I thought it would be me. You never know what's going to happen in the interrogation; people sometimes never came back to the block, they just disappeared. It happened to a Moroccan fellow detainee, and it would happen to me, as you're going to learn, God willing.

When I entered the room in Brown Building, it was crowded with another new FBI-led team. William introduced me to an

FBI agent named Robert and someone from the New York Police Department he called Tom; with them was a military intelligence officer and a young Moroccan man who they explained was a French, not an Arabic, interpreter.*

"Hi!"

"Hi!" they said, almost in unison.

"I've chosen Robert and Tom based on their experience and maturity," William said. "They'll be assessing your case from now on. There are a couple of things that need to be completed in your case. For instance, you didn't tell us everything about Raouf Hannachi. He's a very important guy."†

"First, I told you what I know about Raouf Hannachi, even though I don't need to be providing you information about anybody. We're talking here about me. Second, in order to continue my cooperation with you, I need you to answer me one question: WHY AM I HERE? If you don't give me the answer, you can consider me a non-existent detainee." Later on I learned from my great lawyers Nancy Hollander, Sylvia Royce, and Theresa Duncan that the magic formulation of my request is a Petition for a Writ of Habeas Corpus. Obviously that phrase makes no sense to the average, mortal man like me. The average person would just say, "Why the hell are you locking me up?" I'm not a lawyer, but common sense dictates that after three years of interrogating me and depriving me of my liberty, the

---

* The 2008 DOJ Inspector General's report identifies the two FBI agents who interview MOS from this point until he is turned over to the JTF-GTMO task force in May 2003 by the pseudonyms "Poulson" and "Santiago." According to the DOJ IG report, the team at this time also included a detective from the New York Police Department's Joint Terrorism Task Force, who interrogated Slahi with "Poulson" in January 2003. DOJ IG, 295–99.

† Raouf Hannachi is a Tunisian-born Canadian citizen who lived in Montreal in 2000. See footnote on page 290.

government at least owes me an explanation why it's doing so. What exactly is my crime?

"It makes no sense: It's like somebody who quits a 10-mile trip after traveling nine miles," said William. It would have been more accurate had he said "a million mile trip after traveling one mile."

"Look, it's as simple as ABC: answer me the question and I'll cooperate with you fully!"

"I have no answer!" William said.

"Neither do I!" I replied.

"It says in the Koran somebody who kills one soul is considered to have killed all of humanity," said the French translator, trying to reach a breakthrough. I looked at him disrespectfully with the side of my face.

"I am not the guy you're looking for!" I said in French, and I repeated it in plain English.

Tom, the NYPD officer, started. "I am sure you're against killing people. We're not looking for you. We're looking for those guys who are out there trying to hurt innocents." He said this while showing me a bunch of ghostly pictures. I refused to look at them, and whenever he tried to put them under my sight I looked somewhere else. I didn't even want to give him the satisfaction of having taken a look at them.

"Look, Ahmed Ressam is cooperating, and he has a good chance of getting his sentence reduced to twenty-seven years— and Ressam is really a bad person. Somebody like you needs only to talk for five minutes, and you're a free man," said Robert. He was everything but reasonable. When I contemplated his statement, I was like, God, a guy who is cooperating is gonna be locked up for 27 more years, after which he won't be able to enjoy any kind of life. What kind of harsh country is that?" I am sorry to say that Robert's statement wasn't worth an answer. He and William tried to reason with the help of the MI guy, but there was no convincing me to talk.*

You could tell that the interrogators were getting used to detainees who refused to cooperate after having cooperated for a while. Just as I was learning from other detainees how not to cooperate, the interrogators were learning from each other how to deal with non-cooperating detainees. The session was closed and I was sent back to my cell. I was satisfied with myself, since I now officially belonged to the majority, the non-cooperating detainees. I minded less being locked up unjustly for the rest of my life; what drove me crazy was to be expected to cooperate, too. You lock me up, I give you no information. And we both are cool.

---

* Ahmed Ressam was arrested as he tried to enter the United States from Canada in a car laden with explosives on December 14, 2000; he was convicted the following year of planning to bomb Los Angeles International Airport on New Year's Day 2001 as part of what became known as the Millennium Plot. In May 2001, after entering a guilty plea and before sentencing, Ressam began cooperating with U.S. authorities in exchange for assurances of a reduced sentence. A U.S. Court of Appeals later wrote that "Ressam continued cooperating until early 2003. Over the course of his two-year cooperation, he provided 65 hours of trial and deposition testimony, and 205 hours of proffers and debriefings. Ressam provided information to the governments of seven different countries and testified in two trials, both of which ended in convictions of the defendants. He provided names of at least 150 people involved in terrorism and described many others. He also provided information about explosives that potentially saved the lives of law enforcement agents, and extensive information about the mechanics of global terrorism operations." As MOS indicates here, Ressam never named or implicated him in any way in all those sessions. Ressam later recanted some of his testimony implicating others in the Millennium Plot. He originally received a twenty-two-year sentence with five years' supervision after his release. In 2010 the Ninth Circuit Court of Appeals ruled that that sentence was too lenient and violated mandatory sentencing guidelines, and remanded the case to a federal judge for resentencing. The court's opinion is available at http://cdn.ca9.uscourts.gov/datastore/opinions/2010/02/02/09-30000.pdf.

The sessions continued with the new team. William rarely attended the sessions; "I won't come as long as you don't give us every piece of information you have," he once said. "Still, because we're Americans we treat you guys according to our high standards. Look at ISN 207, we're offering him the latest medical technology." The detainee he mentioned, a young Saudi named Mishal Alhabiri, had been gravely injured in detention, and the JTF people said that he tried to commit suicide. Interrogators brought up his situation a couple of times to showcase that the U.S. was treating detainees humanely.*

"You want just to keep him alive because he might have some Intels, and if he dies, they're gonna die with him!" I responded. U.S. interrogators always tended to mention free food and free medical treatment for detainees. I don't really understand what other alternatives they have! I personally have been detained in non-Democratic countries, and the medical treatment was the highest priority. Common sense dictates that if a detainee goes badly ill there will be no Intels, and he'll probably die.

We spent almost two months of argumentation. "Bring me to the court, and I'll answer all your questions," I would tell the team.

"There will be no court!" they would answer.

"Are you a Mafia? You kidnap people, lock them up, and blackmail them," I said.

"You guys are a law enforcement problem," said Tom. "We cannot apply the conventional law to you. We need only circumstantial evidence to fry you."

---

* Mishal Awad Sayaf Alhabiri suffered a significant brain injury while in Guantánamo. The U.S. government asserted that the injury was the result of oxygen loss during a suicide attempt, but other prisoners have alleged the injury occurred during a beating by an Initial Reaction Force (IRF) team. Alhabiri was repatriated to Saudi Arabia on July 20, 2005.

"I've done nothing against your country, have I?"

"You're a part of the big conspiracy against the U.S.!" Tom said.

"You can pull this charge on anybody! What have I done?"

"I don't know, you tell me!"

"Look, you kidnap me from my home in Mauritania, not from a battlefield in Afghanistan, because you suspected me of having been part of the Millennium Plot—which I am not, as you know by now. So what's the next charge? It looks to me as if you want to pull any shit on me."

"I don't want to pull any shit on you. I just wish you had access to the same reports as I do!" said Robert.

"I don't care what the reports say. I'd just like you to take a look at the reports from January 2000 linking me to the Millennium Plot. And you now know that I'm not a part of it, after the cooperation of Ahmed Ressam.

"I don't think that you are a part of it, nor do I believe that you know Ahmed Ressam," Robert said. "But I do know that you know people who know Ressam."

"I don't know, but I don't see the problem if it is the case," I replied, "Knowing somebody is not a crime, no matter who he is."

A young Egyptian who was serving as interpreter that day tried to convince me to cooperate. Like almost every other interpreter in GTMO, he called himself Mohamed. "Look, I have come here sacrificing my time to help you guys, and the only way to help yourself is to talk," he said.

"Aren't you ashamed to work for these evil people, who arrest your brothers in faith for no reason than being Muslim?" I asked him. "Mohamed, I am older than you are, speak more languages, I have a higher college grade, and I've been in many more countries than you have. I understand you're here to help yourself and make money. If you're trying to fool anybody, it's only yourself!" I was just so mad because he talked to me as if I were a child. Robert and Tom were just staring.

These conversations took place again and again in different sessions. I kept saying, "You tell why I am here, I'll cooperate; you don't tell me, I'm not gonna cooperate. But we can talk about anything else beside interrogation."

Robert welcomed that idea. He assured me that he was going to ask his boss to provide him the cause of my arrest, because he didn't know it himself. In the meantime he taught me a lot about American culture and history, the U.S. and Islam, and the U.S. and the Arab world. The team started to bring movies in; I saw *The Civil War*, Muslims in the U.S., and several other *Frontline* broadcasts regarding terrorism. "All of this shit happens because of hatred," he would say. "Hatred is the reason for all disasters."

"I am gonna show you the evidence bit by bit," said Robert one day. "There is a big al Qaeda guy who told us that you are involved."*

"I guess you shouldn't ask me questions then, since you have a witness. Just take me to court and roast me," I said. "What have I done, according to your witness?"

"He said you are a part of the conspiracy." I grew tired of the words Big Conspiracy against the U.S. Robert could not give me anything to grab onto, no matter how much I argued with him.

---

* Because redactions sometimes obscured the chronology of scenes, these eight paragraphs (beginning here with " 'I am gonna show you the evidence bit by bit' " and continuing through "when it comes to the harsh justice of the U.S. during war") appeared in Chapter Five, pages 196–198, of the original redacted edition. They have been moved here to their correct position.

As to Tom from the NYPD, he was not an argumentative guy; "If the government believes that you're involved in bad things, they're gonna send you to Iraq or back to Afghanistan," he said.★

"So if you guys torture me, I'm gonna tell you everything you want to hear?"

"No, look: if a mom asks her kid whether he's done something wrong, he might lie. But if she hits him, he's gonna admit it," replied Tom. I had no answer to this analogy. Anyway, the "big al Qaeda" guy who testified against me turned out to be Ramzi bin al-Shibh. Ramzi was said to have said that I helped him to go to Chechnya with two other guys who were among the hijackers, which I hadn't done. Though I had seen him once or twice in Germany, I didn't even know his name. Even if I had helped them to go to Chechnya, that would be no crime at all, but I just hadn't.

By then I knew about the horrible torture that Ramzi bin al Shibh had suffered after his arrest in Karachi. Eyewitnesses who were captured with him in Karachi said, "We thought he was dead. We heard his cries and moans day and night until he was separated from us." We had even heard even rumors in the camp that he died under torture. Overseas torture was obviously a common practice and professionally executed; I heard so many testimonies from detainees who didn't know each other that they couldn't be lies. And as you shall see, I was subject to torture in this base of GTMO, like many other fellow detainees. May Allah reward all of us.

"I don't believe in torture," said Robert. I didn't share with

---

★ The DOJ's Inspector General reported that MOS told investigators that an agent identified in the report by the pseudonym "Santiago," whom MOS described "as a 'nice guy,'" "told Slahi he would be sent to Iraq or Afghanistan if the charges against him were proved." DOJ IG, 296.

him my knowledge about Ramzi having been tortured. But because the government has sent detainees including me, Mamdouh Habib, and Mohamed Saad Iqbal overseas to facilitate our interrogation by torture, that meant that the government believes in torture; what Robert believes in doesn't have much weight when it comes to the harsh justice of the U.S. during war.★

As for Tom, he was interested in getting information as quickly as possible using classic police methods. He offered me McDonald's one day, but I refused because I didn't want to owe him anything. "The Army are fighting to take you to a very bad place, and we don't want that to happen!" he warned me.

"Just let them take me there; I'll get used to it. You keep me in jail whether or not I cooperate, so why should I cooperate?" I said this still not knowing that Americans use torture to facilitate interrogations. I was very tired from being taken to interrogation every day. My back was just conspiring against me. I even sought Medical help.

"You're not allowed to sit for such a long time," said the female Navy physiotherapist.

"Please tell my interrogators that, because they make me sit for long hours almost every day."

★ Mamdouh Habib, a dual citizen of Egypt and Australia, was arrested in Pakistan in October 2001, interrogated by Pakistani and American intelligence, and then subjected to extraordinary rendition to Egypt for interrogation by Egyptian intelligence services. He was renditioned again from Egypt to Guantánamo in 2002 and held there until his release on January 27, 2005. Mohamed Saad Iqbal is a Pakistani national who was detained in January 2002 in Jakarta, Indonesia. He was questioned briefly by Indonesian officials and then renditioned to Egypt, where he was interrogated for four months by Egyptian intelligence. In April 2002 he was renditioned to Bagram, where he was held until he was transferred to Guantánamo in March 2003. He was released from Guantánamo on August 31, 2008.

"I'll write a note, but I'm not sure whether it will have an effect," she replied.

It didn't. Instead, in February 2003, Tom washed his hands of me.★

"I am going to leave, but if you're ready to talk about your telephone conversations, request me, I'll come back," he said.

"I assure you, I am not going to talk about anything unless you answer my question: Why am I here?"

★ The DOJ IG report indicates that the NYPD detective who was part of the interrogation team in January 2003 "told Slahi that if he did not explain certain phone calls he would be sent to a 'very bad place.'" DOJ IG, 299.

BEFORE

SECRET//NOFORN   PROTECTED

285

or crying. ~~IIII~~ Ultimately I ended up doing both. I kept
reading the short message over and over. I knew it was for
real from my mom not like the fake the one I got one year
ago. The only problem I couldn't respond the letter b/c
I was still then not allowed to see the ICRC.
was the one who handed me that historical piece of paper.
The ~~First~~ Unofficial Laughter in the ocean of Tears: ▮
▮▮▮▮▮▮▮▮▮▮ kept getting me English
litterature books I enjoyed reading, most of them
were Western. But I ~~remember~~ still remember one
book called The Catcher in The Rye that made me laugh
until my stomach hurt. I was a funny book. I ~~keep~~
tried to keep my laughter as low as possible and
pushing it down, but the guards felt something - "Are
you crying?" asked me one of them - " No, I am alright!"
I responded. And since interrogators are not professional
come dians, most of the humour they, some tris, came up
with ~~with~~ a bunch of lame jokes that really didn't
make me laugh, but I forced myself to always to an
official smile. ▮
▮▮▮▮▮▮▮▮▮ came on Sunday morning
and waited outside the building. ▮▮▮▮ appeared
before my cell ▮▮▮▮▮▮. I didn't recognize
him. I thought he was a new interrogator. But
he spoke I knew it was him. "Are ▮▮▮▮▮▮▮" -
" Don't worry. Your interrogator is waiting outside
on you". - I was overwhelmed and terrified at
the same time. It was too much for me. ~~took~~
▮▮▮▮▮ led me outside the building where

TWO

Senegal-Mauritania

January 21, 2000–February 19, 2000

The First Arrest in Senegal...An Escorted Home-
coming...The First Interrogation in Mauritania...
Getting Stuck in a Cul-de-Sac...The U.S. Dramatizes
the Matter

A Mauritanian folktale tells us about a rooster-phobe who
would almost lose his mind whenever he encountered a
rooster.

"Why are you so afraid of the rooster?" the psychiatrist
asks him.

"The rooster thinks I'm corn."

"You're not corn. You are a very big man. Nobody can mistake you for a tiny ear of corn," the psychiatrist said.

"I know that, Doctor. But the rooster doesn't. Your job is to
go to him and convince him that I am not corn."

The man was never healed, since talking with a rooster is
impossible. End of story.

For years I've been trying to convince the U.S. government
that I am not corn.

It started in January 2000, when I was returning to Mauritania after living twelve years overseas. At 8 p.m. on January

21, 2000, my friends Ahmed Laabidi and the librarian of the al Sunnah mosque dropped me off at Dorval Airport in Montreal. I took the night Sabena flight to Brussels and was continuing to Dakar the next afternoon. I arrived in Brussels in the morning, sleepy and worn out. After collecting my luggage, I collapsed on one of the benches in the International area, using my bag as a pillow. One thing was sure: anybody could have stolen my bag, I was so tired. I slept for one or two hours, and when I woke up, I looked for a toilet where I could wash and a place to pray.

The airport was small, neat, and clean, with restaurants, duty-free shops, phone booths, Internet PCs, a mosque, a church, a synagogue, and a psych consulting bureau for atheists. I checked out all the God's houses, and was impressed. I thought, This country could be a place I'd want to live. Why don't I just go and ask for asylum? I'd have no problem; I speak the language and have adequate qualifications to get a job in the heart of Europe. I had actually been in Brussels, and I liked the multicultural life and the multiple faces of the city.

I left Canada mainly because the U.S. had pitted their security services on me, but they didn't arrest me, they just started to watch me. Being watched is better than being put in jail, I realize now; ultimately, they would have figured out that I am not a criminal. "I never learn," as my mom always put it. I never believed that the U.S. was evilly trying to get me in a place where the law has nothing to say.

The border was inches away. Had I crossed that border, I would never have written this book.

Instead, in the small mosque, I performed the ritual wash and prayed. It was very quiet; the peacefulness was dominating. I felt so tired that I lay down in the mosque and read the Koran for some time and fell asleep.

I woke up to the movements of another guy who came to pray. He seemed to know the place and to have transited through this airport many times. He was tall and thin, in his late thirties or early forties, and very friendly. We greeted each other after he finished his prayer.

"What are you doing here?" he asked me.

"I'm transiting. I came from Canada, and am heading for Dakar."

"Where are you from?"

"Mauritania. What about you?'

"I'm from Senegal. I'm a merchant between my country and the Emirates. I'm waiting on the same flight as you."

"Good!" I said.

"Let's go rest. I'm a member of Club Such-and-Such," he suggested, I don't recall the name. We went to the club, and it was just amazing: TV, coffee, tea, cookies, a comfortable couch, newspapers. I was overwhelmed, and I spent most of the time sleeping on a couch. At some point, my new Senegalese friend wanted to have lunch, and woke me up to do the same. I was concerned I wouldn't be able to come back because I had no club card and they had just let me in because my Senegalese friend flashed his membership card. However, my stomach's call was louder, and I decided to go outside and have some food. I went to the Sabena Airlines counter and asked for a free meal card, and found a restaurant. Most of the food was mixed with pork, so I decided on a vegetarian meal.

I went back to the club and waited until my friend and I were called to our flight, Sabena #502 to Dakar. I had chosen Dakar because it was by far cheaper than flying directly to Nouak-chott, Mauritania. Dakar is only about 300 miles from Nouak-chott, and I arranged with my family to pick me up there. So far so good; people do it all the time.

During the flight, I was full of energy because I had had some quality sleep in Brussels airport. Next to me was a young French girl who lived in Dakar but was studying medicine in Brussels. I was thinking that my brothers might not make it to the airport on time, so I would have to spend some time in a hotel. The French girl benevolently enlightened me about the prices in Dakar, and how the Senegalese people try to overcharge strangers, especially the taxi drivers.

The flight took about five hours. We arrived around 11 p.m., and the whole formalities thing took about thirty minutes. When I took my bag from the baggage claim, I bumped into my Senegalese friend, and we bid each other farewell. As soon as I turned away carrying my bag, I saw my brother Hamoud smiling; he obviously had seen me before I saw him. Hamoud was accompanied by my other brother Mohamed Salem and two friends of theirs I didn't know.

Mohamed Salem grabbed my bag and we headed toward the parking lot. I liked the warm night weather that embraced me as soon as I left the gate. We were talking, asking each other excitedly how things were going. As we crossed the road, I honestly cannot describe what happened to me. All I know is that in less than a second my hands were shackled behind my back and I was encircled by a bunch of ghosts who cut me off from the rest of my company. At first I thought it was an armed robbery, but as it turned out it was a robbery of another kind.

"We arrest you in the Name of the Law," said the special agent while locking the chains around my hands.

"I'm arrested!" I called to the brothers I couldn't see anymore. I figured if they missed me all of a sudden it would be painful for them. I didn't know whether they heard me or not, but as it turned out, they had heard me indeed because my

brother Mohamed Salem kept mocking me later and claiming
that I am not courageous since I called for help. Maybe I'm not,
but that's what happened. What I didn't know was that my two
brothers and their two friends were arrested at the same time.
Yes, their two friends, one who came with my brothers all the
way from Nouakchott, and the other, his brother who lives in
Dakar and just happened to ride with them to the airport, just
in time to be arrested as a part of a "gang": What luck!

I honestly was not prepared for this injustice. Had I known
the U.S. investigators were really so full of it, I wouldn't have
left Canada, or even Belgium when I was transiting through.
Why didn't the U.S. have me arrested in Germany? Germany
is one of the closest allies of the U.S. Why didn't the U.S. have
me arrested in Canada? Canada and the U.S. are almost the
same country. The U.S. interrogators and investigators claimed
that I fled Canada out of fear that I was going to be arrested,
but that doesn't really make any sense. First of all, I left using
my passport with my real name, after going through all formalities including all kinds of registrations. Secondly, is it better to
be arrested in Canada or Mauritania? Of course in Canada! Or
why didn't the U.S. have me arrested in Belgium, where I spent
almost twelve hours?

I understand the anger and frustration of the U.S. about terrorist attacks. But jumping on innocent individuals and making
them suffer, looking for fake confessions, doesn't help anybody.
It rather complicates the problem. I would always tell the U.S.
agents, "Guys! Cool down! Think before you act! Just put a
small percentage on the possibility that you might be wrong
before you irreparably injure somebody!" But when something
bad happens, people start to freak out and lose their composure.
I've been interrogated throughout the last six years by over a
hundred interrogators from different countries, and they have

one thing in common: confusion. Maybe the government wants them to be that way, who knows?

Anyhow, the local police at the airport intervened when they saw the mêlée—the Special Forces were dressed in civilian suits, so there really was no differentiating them from a bunch of bandits trying to rob somebody—but the guy behind me flashed a magic badge, which immediately made the policemen retreat. All five of us were thrown in a cattle truck, and soon we got another friend, the guy I had met in Brussels, just because we bid each other farewell at the luggage carousel.

The guards got in with us. The leader of the group sat up front in the passenger seat, but he could see and hear us because the glass that usually separates the driver from the cattle wasn't there anymore. The truck took off like in a Hollywood chase scene. "You're killing us," one of the guards must have said, because the driver slowed down a little bit. The local guy who came to the airport with my brothers was losing his mind; every once in a while he spat some indistinct words conveying his worries and unhappiness. As it turned out the guy thought that I was a drug dealer and he was relieved when the suspicion turned out to be terrorism! Since I was the starring actor, I felt bad for causing so much trouble for so many people. My only solace was that I didn't mean to—and also, at that moment, the fear in my heart overwhelmed the rest of my emotions.

When I sat down on the rough floor, I felt better surrounded by the warmth of the company, including the Special Forces agents. I started to recite the Koran.

"Shut up!" said the boss in the front. I didn't shut up; I lowered my voice, but not enough for the boss. "Shut up!" he said, this time raising his baton to hit me. "You're trying to bewitch us out!" I knew he was serious, and so I prayed in my heart. I hadn't tried to bewitch anybody out, nor do I know how to do it, but Africans are some of the most gullible folks I ever knew.

The trip took between fifteen and twenty minutes, so it was shortly after midnight when we arrived at the Commissariat de Police. The masterminds of the operation stood behind the truck and got involved in a discussion with my Brussels friend. I didn't understand anything; they were speaking in Wolof, the local language. After a short discussion, the guy took his heavy bags, and off he went. When I later asked my brothers, who speak Wolof, what he told the police, they told me that he said he had seen me in Brussels and never before, and that he didn't know that I was a terrorist.

Now we were five persons jailed in the truck. It was very dark outside, but I could tell that people were coming and going. We waited between forty minutes and an hour in the truck. I grew more nervous and afraid, especially when the guy in the passenger seat said, "I hate working with the Whites," or rather he used the word 'Moors,' which made me believe that they were waiting on a Mauritanian team. I started to have nausea, my heart was a feather, and I shrank so small to hold myself together. I thought about all the kinds of torture I had heard of, and how much I could take tonight. I grew blind, a thick cloud built in front of my eyes, I couldn't see anything. I grew deaf; after that statement all I could hear was indistinct whispers. I lost the feeling of my brothers being with me in the same truck. I figured only God can help my situation. God never fails.

"Get out," shouted the guy impatiently. I fought my way through and one of the guards helped me jump down the step. We were led into a small room that was already occupied by mosquitoes, just in time for them to start their feast. They didn't even wait until we slept; they went right away about their business, tearing us apart. The funny thing about mosquitoes is that they're shy in small groups and rude in big ones. In small groups, they wait until you fall asleep, unlike in big groups, where they start to tease you right away, as if to say: "What can you do about it?" And in fact, nothing. The toilet was filthy as it could be, which made it an ideal environment for breeding mosquitoes.

I was the only chained person. "Did I beat you?" asked the guy while taking off the handcuffs.

"No, you didn't." When I looked I noticed I already had scars around my wrists. The interrogators started to pull us one by one for interrogation, starting with the strangers. It was a very long, scary, dark and bleak night.

My turn came shortly before the first daylight.

In the interrogation room there were two women, a white American who was most likely a U.S. intelligence officer based in Senegal and the local Senegalese police chief, and two men, a Senegalese interrogator and his recorder. The female Police Chief was in charge of the police station, but she was not part of the interrogation; she looked so tired that she fell asleep several times out of boredom. The American woman was taking notes, and sometimes she passed notes to the interrogator. The interrogator was a quiet, skinny, smart, rather religious and deep thinking man.

"We have very heavy allegations against you," he said, pulling a thick stack of papers out of a bright yellow envelope. Before he had them halfway out, you could tell he had been reading the stuff many times. And I already knew what he was talking about, because the Canadians had already interviewed me.

"I have done nothing. The U.S. wants to dirty Islam by pinning such horrible things on Muslims."

"Do you know Ahmed Ressam?"

"No, I don't. I even think his whole story was a fake, to unlock the terrorism budget and hurt the Muslims." I was really honest about what I said. Back then I didn't know a whole lot of things that I do now. I believed excessively in Conspiracy Theories—though maybe not as much as the U.S. government does.

The interrogator also asked me about a bunch of other people, most of whom I didn't know. The people I did know were not involved in any crimes whatsoever, as far as I knew. Lastly, the Senegalese asked me about my position toward the U.S., and why I had transited through his country. I really didn't understand why my position toward the U.S government should matter to anybody. I am not a U.S. citizen, nor did I ever apply to enter the U.S., nor am I working with the U.N. Besides, I could always lie. Or let's say I love the U.S., or I hate it, it doesn't really matter as long as I haven't done any crimes against the U.S. I explained all this to the Senegalese interrogator with a clarity that left no doubt at all about my circumstances.

"You seem very tired! I suggest you go and have some sleep. I know it's hard," he said. Of course I was dead tired, and hungry and thirsty. The guards led me back to the small room where my brothers and the other two guys were lying on the floor, fighting against the most efficient Senegalese Air Force Mosquitoes. I was no luckier than the rest. Did we sleep? Not really.

The interrogator and his assistant showed up early in the morning. They released the two guys, and took me and my brothers to the headquarters of the Ministère de L'Intérieur.

The interrogator, who turned out to be a very high-level person in the Senegalese government, took me to his office and made a call to the Minister of Internal Affairs.

"The guy in front of me is not the head of a terrorist organization," he said. I couldn't hear what the minister said. "When it comes to me, I have no interest in keeping this guy in jail— nor do I have a reason," the interrogator continued. The telephone call was short and straightforward. In the meantime, my brothers made themselves comfortable, bought some stuff, and started to make tea. Tea is the only thing that keeps the Mauritanian person alive, with God's help. It had been a long time since any of us had eaten or drunk anything, but the first thing that came to mind was tea.

I was happy because the one-ton stack of paper the U.S. government had provided the Senegalese about me didn't seem to impress them; it didn't take my interrogator a whole lot of time to understand the situation. My two brothers started a conversation with him in Wolof. I asked my brothers what the conversation was about, and they said that the Senegalese government was not interested in holding me, but the U.S. was the one that was going to call the shots. Nobody was happy with that, because we had an idea of what the U.S. call would be like.

"We're waiting on some people from the U.S. embassy to show up," said the interrogator. Around eleven o'clock a black American woman showed up. She took pictures, fingerprints, and the report the recorder had typed earlier that morning. My brothers felt more comfortable around the black woman than the white woman from last night. People feel comfortable with the looks they are used to, and since about 50 percent of Mauritanians are black, my brothers could relate to them more. But that was a very naïve approach: in either case, black or white, she would just be a messenger.

After finishing her work, the American woman made a couple of calls, pulled the interrogator aside and spoke to him briefly, and then she was gone. The inspector informed us that my brothers were free to go and that I was going to be held in contempt for some time.

"Do you think we can wait on him until he gets released?" my brother asked.

"I would suggest you guys go home. If he gets released, he will find his way." My brothers left and I felt abandoned and lonely, though I believe my brothers did the right thing.

For the next couple of days, the Senegalese kept interrogating me about the same things; the U.S. investigators sent them the questions. That was all. The Senegalese didn't hurt me in any way, nor did they threaten me. Since the food in jail was horrible, my brothers arranged with a family they knew in Dakar to bring me one meal a day, which they consistently did.

My concern, as I say, was and still is to convince the U.S. government that I am not a corn. My only fellow detainee in the Senegalese jail had a different concern: to smuggle himself to Europe or America. We definitely had different Juliets. The young man from Ivory Coast was determined to leave Africa.

"I don't like Africa," he told me. "Many friends of mine have died. Everybody is very poor. I want to go to Europe or America. I tried twice. The first time I managed to sneak into Brazil when I outsmarted the port officials, but one African guy betrayed us to the Brazilian authorities, who put us in jail until they deported back to Africa. Brazil is a very beautiful country, with very beautiful women," he added.

"How can you say so? You were in jail the whole time!" I interrupted him.

"Yes, but every once in a while the guards escorted us to look around, then took us back to jail," he smiled.

"You know, brother, the second time I almost made it to Ireland," he went on. "But the ruthless captain kept me in the ship and made customs take me."

Sounds Columbus-y, I thought. "How did you get on board in the first place?" I wondered.

"It's very easy, brother. I bribed some of the workers at the port. Those people smuggled me onto a ship heading to Europe or America. It didn't really matter. I hid in the containers section for about a week until my provisions were gone. At that point, I came up and mingled with the crew. At first, they got very mad. The captain of the ship headed to Ireland was so mad that he wanted to drown me."

"What an animal!" I interrupted, but my friend kept going.

"But after some time the crew accepted me, gave me food, and made me work."

"How did they catch you this time?"

"My smugglers betrayed me. They said the ship was heading nonstop to Europe. But we made a stop in Dakar and customs took me off of the ship, and here I am!"

"What's your next plan?"

"I'm gonna work, save some money, and try again." My fellow detainee was determined to leave Africa at any cost. Moreover, he was confident that one day he was going to put his feet in the promised land.

"Man, what you see on TV is not how real life looks like in Europe," I said.

"No!" he answered. "My friends have been successfully smuggled into Europe, and they have good lives. Good looking women and a lot of money. Africa is bad."

"You might as easily end up in jail in Europe."

"I don't care. Jail in Europe is good. Africa is bad."

I figured the guy was completely blinded by the rich world that deliberately shows us poor Africans a "paradise" we cannot enter, though he had a point. In Mauritania, the majority of the young people want to emigrate to Europe or the U.S. If the politics in African countries don't change radically for the better, we are going to experience a catastrophe that will affect the whole world.

His cell was catastrophic. Mine was a little better. I had a very thin worn-out mattress, but he had nothing but a piece of carton he slept on. I used to give him my food because when I get anxious I can't eat. Besides, I got good food from outside, and he got the bad food of the jail. The guards let us be together during the day and locked him up nights. My cell was always open. The day before I was extradited to Mauritania, the ambassador of Ivory Coast came to confirm the identity of my fellow detainee. Of course he had no papers whatsoever.

"We are releasing you!" the recorder who had been interrogating me for the last several days said happily.

"Thank you!" I interrupted him, looking in the direction of Mecca, and prostrating myself to thank God for being free.

"However, we have to turn you over to your country."

"No, I know the way, I'll do it on my own," I said innocently, thinking I didn't really want to go back to Mauritania, but maybe to Canada or somewhere else. My heart had been teased enough.

"I am sorry, we have to turn you over ourselves!" My whole happiness turned into agony, fear, nervousness, helplessness, confusion and other things I cannot describe. "Gather your stuff!" the guy said. "We're leaving."

I started to gather my few belongings, heartbroken. The inspector grabbed my bigger bag and I carried my small brief-case. During my arrest, the Americans had copied every single piece of paper I had and sent it all to Washington for analysis.

It was around 5 p.m. when we left the gate of the Commis-sariat de Police. Out front stood a Mitsubishi SUV. The inspec-tor put my bags in the trunk, and we got into the back seat. On my left sat a guard I had never seen before, older and big boned. He was quiet and rather laid back; he looked straight ahead most of the time, only rarely scanning me quickly with the side of his eye. I hated it when guards would keep staring at me as if they had never seen a mammal before. On my right was the inspector who had been the recorder. In the passenger's seat sat the lead interrogator.

The driver was a white American in his mid-forties, around five foot eight. He was the one giving the marching orders to both the Senegalese and the Mauritanians. From his tan you could tell he had spent some time in a warm place, but not in Senegal because the interrogator kept guiding him to the air-port. Or maybe he was looking for best way, I couldn't tell. He spoke French with a heavy accent, though he was stingy in his conversation; he limited himself exactly within the necessary. He never looked at or addressed me. The other two interroga-tors tried to talk to me, but I didn't answer, I kept reading my Koran silently. Out of respect, the Senegalese didn't confiscate my Koran, unlike the Mauritanians, Jordanians, and Americans.

It took about 25 minutes to the airport. The traffic was quiet around and inside the terminal. The white driver quickly found a parking place. We got out of the truck, the guards carrying my luggage, and we all passed through the diplomatic way to the waiting room. It was the first time that I shortcut the civilian formalities while leaving one country to another. It was a treat, but I didn't enjoy it. Everybody seemed to be prepared in the airport. In front of the group the interrogator and the white guy kept flashing their magic badges, taking everybody with them. You could clearly tell that the country had no sovereignty: this was still colonization in its ugliest face. In the so-called free world, the politicians preach things such as sponsoring democracy, freedom, peace, and human rights: What hypocrisy! Still, many people believe this propaganda garbage.

The waiting room was empty. Everybody took a seat, and one of the Senegalese took my passport and went back and stamped it. I thought I was going to take the regular Air Afrique flight that was scheduled to Nouakchott that afternoon. But it didn't take very long to realize I had my own plane to myself. As soon as the guy returned with my stamped passport, all five of us stepped toward the runway, where a very small white plane was already running its engines. The American man gestured for us to stay behind and he had a quick talk with the pilot. Maybe the interrogator was with him, too, I can't remember. I was too scared to memorize everything.

Soon enough we were told to get in. The plane was as small as it could be. We were four, and barely managed to squeeze ourselves inside the butterfly with heads down and backs bent. The pilot had the most comfortable place. She was a French lady, you could tell from her accent. She was very talkative, and rather on the older side, skinny and blond. She didn't talk to me, but she exchanged some words with the inspector during the trip. As it turned out, I later learned she told her friends in Nouakchott about the secret package she delivered from Dakar. The bigger guard and I squeezed ourselves, knees-on-faces, in the back seat, facing the inspector, who had a little better seat in front of us. The plane was obviously overloaded.

The interrogator and the American man waited until they made sure that the plane took off. I wasn't paying attention to the conversations between the pilot and the inspector, but I heard her at one point telling him that the trip was only 300 miles, and would take between 45 minutes and an hour, depending on the wind direction. That sounded so medieval. The inspector tried to talk to me, but there was nothing to talk about; to me everything was already said and done. I figured he had nothing to say to help me, so why should I talk to him?

I hate traveling in small planes because they're shaky and I always think the wind is going to blow the plane away. But this time was different, I was not afraid. In fact I wanted the plane to crash, and only me to survive. I would know my way: it was my country, I was born here, and anybody would give me food and shelter. I was drowned in my dreams, but the plane didn't crash; instead it was getting closer and closer to its destination. The wind was in its favor. I was thinking about all my innocent brothers who were and still are being rendered to strange places and countries, and I felt solaced and not alone anymore. I felt the spirits of unjustly mistreated people with me. I had heard so many stories about brothers being passed back and forth like a soccer ball just because they have been once in Afghanistan, or Bosnia, or Chechnya. That's screwed up! Thousands of miles away, I felt the warm breath of these other unjustly treated individuals comforting me. I stuck all the time to my Koran, ignoring my environment.

My company seemed to have a good time checking the weather and enjoying the beach we had been flying along the whole time. I don't think that the plane had any type of navigation technologies because the pilot kept a ridiculously low altitude and oriented us with the beach. Through the window I started to see the sand-covered small villages around Nouakchott, as bleak as their prospects. There definitely had been a sandstorm earlier that day; People were just gradually daring to go outside. The suburbs of Nouakchott appeared more miserable than ever, crowded, poor, dirty, and free of any of life's crucial infrastructures. It was the Kebba ghetto I knew, only worse. The plane flew so low I could tell who was who among the people who were moving, seemingly disoriented, everywhere.

It had been a long time since I had seen my country last—since August 1993, in fact. I was coming back, but this time as a terrorism suspect who was going to be hidden in some secret hole. I wanted to cry out loud to my people, "Here I am! I am not a criminal! I'm innocent! I am just the guy you knew, I'm no different!" But my voice was oppressed, just like in a nightmare. I couldn't really recognize anything, the city plan had changed so radically.

I finally realized the plane was not going to crash, and I was not going to have the chance to talk to my people. It's amazing how hard it can be for someone to accept his miserable situation. The key to surviving any given situation is to realize that you are in it. Whether I wanted it or not, I was going to be delivered to the very people I didn't want to see.

"Can you do me a favor?" I asked the Inspector.

"Sure!"

"I'd like you to inform my family that I'm in the country."

"OK. Do you have the phone number?"

"Yes, I do." The inspector, against my expectation, indeed called my family and told them about my reality. Moreover, the Senegalese made an official press declaration stating that they turned me over to my country. Both the Mauritanians and Americans were pissed off about that.

"What did you tell the inspector?" the Mauritanian DSE, the Directeur de la Sûreté de l'État, asked me later.*

"Nothing."

"You're lying. You told him to call your family." It didn't really take David Copperfield to figure out that the telephone call was intercepted.

The handover was quick. We landed near the back door of the airport, where two men were waiting, the Mauritanian inspector and another freakin' big black guy, most likely brought to take care of business—just in case!

"Where is the Airport Police Chief?" the inspector wondered, looking at his black colleague. I knew the Airport Police Chief: he had once been in Germany, and I gave him shelter and helped him buy a Mercedes-Benz. I hoped he would show up, so he could see me and put in a good word for me. But he never showed. Nor would he have put in a good word for me: Mauritanian Intelligence is by far the highest law enforcement authority. But I felt like I was drowning, and I would have grabbed any straw I encountered.

"You will be escorted to the hotel to spend the rest of the night," said the inspector to his guests.

"How are you?" he said ungenuinely, looking at me.

"I'm fine."

"Is that all he has?" he asked.

"Yes that's it." I was watching all my belongings on earth being passed around as if I'd already died.

"Let's go!" the inspector said to me. The black guy, who never took his eyes off me, carried the luggage and pushed me

---

* The Directeur de la Sûreté de l'État, abbreviated as DSE, is the director of the Mauritanian intelligence service.

before him toward a dirty small room at the secret gate of the airport. In the room, the black dude unfolded his dirty black 100 year-old turban.

"Mask your face thoroughly with this turban," said the Inspector. Typically Mauritanian: the Bedouin spirit still dominates. The inspector should have foreseen that he would need a Turban to wrap my head, but in Mauritania organization is almost non-existent; everything is left to whim and chance. It was tricky, but I hadn't forgotten yet how to fold a turban around my head. It is something people from the desert must learn. The turban smelled of piled-up sweat. It was just disgusting to have it around your mouth and nose. But I obediently complied with the orders and held my breath.

"Don't look around," the inspector said when the three of us stepped out of the room toward the parked Secret Police car, a Renault Twelve. I sat in the passenger's seat, the inspector drove, and the black guy sat in the back seat, without saying a word. It was about sunset, but you couldn't tell exactly because the cloud of sand was covering the horizon. The streets were empty. I illegally looked around whenever the chance arose, but I could hardly recognize anything.

The trip was short, about ten minutes to the Security Police building. We stepped out of the car and entered the building, where another guard was waiting on us. The environment was an ideal place for mosquitoes, human beings are the strangers in that place: filthy toilet, dirty floor and walls, holes connecting all the rooms, ants, spiders, flies.

"Search him thoroughly," the inspector told the guard, whose name was Yacoub.

"Give me everything you have," Yacoub respectfully asked me, wanting to avoid searching me. I gave him everything I

had except for my pocket Koran. The inspector must have realized I would have one, so he sent Yacoub again, who came back
and said, "Do you have a Koran?"

"Yes, I do."

"Give it to me! I told you to give me everything." By now
the guard was growing afraid of being sent back again, so he
searched me gently, but he didn't find anything but my pocket
Koran. I was so sad, tired, and terrorized that I couldn't sit up
straight. Instead I put my jacket on my face and fell on the inch-
thick, worn-out 100 year-old mattress, the only object that
existed in that room. I wanted to sleep, lose my mind, and not
wake up until every bad thing was over. How much pain can
I take? I asked myself. Can my family intervene and save me?
Do they use electricity? I had read stories about people who
were tortured to death. How could they bear it? I'd read about
Muslim heroes who faced the death penalty, head up. How did
they do it? I didn't know. All I knew was that I felt so small
before all the big names I knew, and that I was scared to death.

Although the mosquitoes were tearing me apart, I fell asleep.
Every once in a while I woke up and asked myself, Why don't
they interrogate me right now, and do with me whatever they
want, and everything will be over? I hate waiting on torture;
an Arabic proverb says, "Waiting on torture is worse than torture." I can only confirm this proverb. I managed to perform
my prayers, how I don't know.

Sometime around midnight I woke up to people moving
around, opening and closing doors in an extraordinary manner.
When the guard opened the door to my room, I glimpsed the
face of a Mauritanian friend who happened to be with me a

long time ago when I visited Afghanistan in 1992 during the struggle against communism. He looked sad and weathered, and must have gone through painful torture, I thought. I almost lost my mind, knowing for sure I was going to suffer at least as much as he had, given his close relationship with the Mauritanian president and the power of his family—qualities I don't have. I thought, The guy surely must have spoken about me, and that is the reason why they brought him here.

"Get up!" said the guards. "Put on your turban." I put on the dirty turban, gathered my last strength, and followed the guards to the interrogation room like a sheep being driven to its last destination, the slaughterhouse.

When I was driven past the guy I had seen earlier, I realized he was just a screwed-up guard who failed to keep his uniform the way it should be. He was sleepy and drowsy: they must have called him in the midst of his sleep, and he hadn't yet washed his face. It was not the friend I thought it was; anxiety, terror, and fear were dominating my mind. Lord have mercy! I was somewhat relieved. Did I commit a crime? No. Did my friend commit a crime? No. Did we conspire to committing a crime? No. The only thing we had done together was make a trip to Afghanistan in February 1992 to help the people fighting against communism. And as far as I was concerned that was not a crime, at least in Mauritania.

So why was I so scared? Because crime is something relative; it's something the government defines and re-defines whenever it pleases. The majority of people don't know, really, where the line is that separates breaking the law from not breaking it. If you get arrested, the situation worsens, because most people trust the government to have a good reason for the arrest. On top of that, if I personally had to suffer, I didn't want anybody to suffer with me. I thought they arrested my friend in connection with the Millennium Plot, if only because he had been in Afghanistan once.

I entered the interrogation room, which was the office of the DSE. The room was large and well-furnished: leather couch, two love-seats, coffee table, closet, one big desk, one leather chair, a couple of other chairs for unimportant guests, and, as always, the picture of the president conveying the weakness of the law and the strength of the government. I wished they had turned me over to the U.S.: at least there are things I could refer to there, such as the law. Of course, in the U.S. the government and politics are gaining more and more ground lately at the cost of the law. The government is very smart; it evokes terror in the hearts of people to convince them to give up their freedom and privacy. Still, it might take some time until the U.S. government overthrows the law completely, like in the third world and the communist regimes. But really that is none of my concern, and thank God my government doesn't possess the technology to track Bedouins in the vast desert.

There were three guys in the interrogation room: the DSE, his assistant, and his recorder. The DSE asked them to bring my stuff in. They thoroughly searched everything I had; no stone remained unturned. They didn't speak to me, they only spoke with each other, mostly in whispers, just to annoy the hell out of me. At the end of the search, they sorted out my papers and put aside the ones they thought interesting. Later on, they asked me about every single word in those papers.

"I am going to interrogate you. I just want to tell you as a forewarning that you better tell me the whole truth," the DSE said firmly, making a big effort to take a break from smoking his pipe, which he never took off his lips.

"I sure will," I answered.

"Take him back," the DSE dryly ordered the guards.

"Listen, I want you to tell me about your whole life, and how you joined the Islamic movement," said the DSE when the guards dragged my skeleton away from the mosquitoes and back into the interrogation room.

If you get arrested for the first time, chances are that you're not going to be forthcoming, and that's OK; even though you know you haven't done any crimes, it seems sensible. You're very confused, and you'd like to make yourself appear as innocent as possible. You assume you are arrested more or less on a reasonable suspicion, and you don't want to cement that suspicion. Moreover, questioning involves a lot of stuff nobody wants to talk about, like your friends and your private life. Especially when the suspicions are about things like terrorism, the government is very rude. In the interrogation you always avoid talking about your friends and your private, intimate life. And finally, you are so frustrated because of your arrest, and you really don't owe your interrogators anything. On the contrary, they owe you to show you the true cause of your detention, and it should be entirely up to you to comment then or to leave them be. If this cause is enough to hold you, you can seek professional representation; if not, well you shouldn't be arrested in the first place. That's how the civilized world works, and everything else is dictatorship. Dictatorship is governed by chaos.

To be honest with you, I acted like any average person: I tried to make myself look as innocent as a baby. I tried to protect the identities of every single person I knew, unless he or she was too well known to the police. The interrogations continued in this manner, but when they opened the Canadian file, things soured decidedly.

The U.S. government saw in my arrest and my rendition to

Mauritania a once-in-a-blue-moon opportunity to unveil the plan of Ahmed Ressam, who back then was refusing to cooperate with the U.S. authorities. Furthermore, the U.S. wanted to learn in detail about my friends in both Canada and Germany, and even outside those countries. After all my cousin and brother Mahfouz Ould al-Walid was already wanted with a reward of US $5 million.* The U.S. also wanted to learn more about the whole Jihadi issue in Afghanistan, Bosnia, and Chechnya. Expertise for free. For the aforementioned, and for other reasons I don't know, the U.S. drove my case as far as it could be driven. They labeled me "Mastermind of the Millennium Plot." They asked all countries to provide any tiny bit of information they possessed about me, especially Canada and Germany. And since I am already a "bad" guy, force must be applied to roast me.

To the dismay of the U.S. government, things were not really as they seemed, nor did the government achieve what it wanted. No matter how smart somebody plans, God's plan always works. I felt like 2Pac's "Me Against the World." And here's why.

All the Canadians could come up with was, "We have seen him with x and y, and they're bad people." "We've seen him in this and that mosque." "We have intercepted his telephone conversations, but there's nothing really!" The Americans asked the Canadians to provide them the transcripts of my conversations, but after they edited them. Of course it doesn't make sense to

---

* MOS's cousin and former brother-in-law, Mahfouz Ould al-Walid, also known as Abu Hafs al-Mauritani, was wanted in connection with al-Qaeda attacks in the 1990s, with a $5 million reward under the FBI's Rewards for Justice Program. The reward for senior al-Qaeda figures increased to $25 million after the September 11, 2001, terrorist attacks. See, e.g., U.S. State Department, "Patterns of Global Terrorism," appendix D, May 21, 2002, http://www.state.gov/documents/organization/20121.pdf.

selectively take different passages from a whole conversation and try to make sense of them. I think the Canadians should have done one of two things: either refused to provide the Americans any private conversation that took place in their country, or provided them the whole conversation in its original form, not even translated.

Instead, out of the words the Canadians chose to share with their U.S. colleagues, U.S. interrogators magically stuck with two words for more than four years: Tea and Sugar.

"What do you mean by tea and sugar?"

"I mean tea and sugar." I cannot tell you how many times the U.S. asked me, and made other people ask me, this question. Another Mauritanian folktale recounts about a man who was born blind and who had one chance to get a glimpse of the world. All he saw was a rat. After that, whenever anybody tried to explain anything to the guy, he always asked, "Compare it with the rat: Is it bigger? smaller?"

Canadian intelligence wished I were a criminal, so they could make up for their failure when Ahmed Ressam slipped from their country to the U.S. carrying explosives. The U.S. blamed Canada for being a preparation ground for terrorist attacks against the U.S., and that's why Canadian Intel freaked out. They really completely lost their composure, trying everything to calm the rage of their big brother, the U.S. They began watching the people they believed to be bad, including me. I remember after the failed Millennium Plot, the Canadians tried to implant two cameras, one in my room, one in my roommate's. I used to be a very heavy sleeper. I heard voices but I couldn't tell what it was—or let's say I was too lazy to wake up and check on them. My roommate Mourad was different; he woke up and followed the noise. He laid low and watched until the tiny hole was through. The guy in the other room blew through the hole, and when he checked with his eye, he made eye contact with Mourad.

My roommate woke me up and told me the story.

"Mourad, I heard the same voices in my room." I said to him. "Let's check!" Our short investigation was successful: we found a tiny twin hole in my room.

"What should we do?" Mourad asked.

"We call the police," I said.

"Well, call them!" he said. I purposely didn't use our telephone; instead, I went out and used a public phone, dialing 911. Two cops showed up, and I explained to them that our neighbor, without our consent, drilled two holes in our house, and we wanted him to be held for his illegal action toward us. Basically, we asked for a fair relief.

"Put some caulk inside the holes and the problem is solved," said one of the cops.

"Really? I didn't know that. Are you a carpenter?" I said. "Look! I didn't call you to give me advice on how to fix my house. There's an obvious crime behind this, trespassing and violation of our privacy. If you don't take care of us, we'll take care of ourselves. And by the way: I need you guys' business cards," I said. Each one silently produced a business card with the other cop's name and contact on the back of it. Obviously, those cops were following some idiot directions in order to deceive us, but for the Canadian Intel it was too late. For days to come we were just sitting and making fun of the plan.

The irony was that I lived in Germany for twelve years and they never provided any incriminating information about me, which was accurate. I stayed less than two months in Canada, and yet the Americans claimed that the Canadians provided tons of information about me. The Canadians don't even know me! But since all Intel work is based on what ifs, Mauritania and the U.S. started to interpret the information as they pleased, in order to confirm the theory that I was the mastermind of Millennium Plot.

The interrogation didn't seem to develop in my favor. I kept repeating my Afghanistan Jihad story of 1991 and early 1992, which didn't seem to impress the Mauritanian interrogator. Mauritania doesn't give a damn about a trip to Afghanistan; they understand it very well. If you try to make trouble inside the country, however, you're going to be arrested, regardless of whether or not you've been in Afghanistan. On the other hand, to the American government a bare visit to Afghanistan, Bosnia, or Chechnya is worth watching you for the rest of your life and trying to lock you up. All the Arabic countries have the same approach as Mauritania, except the communist ones. I even think the communist Arab countries are at least fairer than the U.S. government in this regard, because they forbid their citizens to go to Jihad in the first place. Meanwhile, the U.S. government prosecutes people based on an unwritten law.

My Mauritanian interrogator was interested in my activities in Canada, which are non-existent in the criminal sense, but nobody was willing to believe me. All my answers to the question, "Have you done this or that while in Canada?" were, "No, No, No, No." And there we got completely stuck. I think I looked guilty because I didn't tell my whole story about Afghanistan, and I figured I had to fill that gap in order to make my case stronger. The interrogator had brought film equipment with him that day. As soon as I saw it, I started to shake: I knew that I would be made to confess and that they were going to broadcast me on the National TV, just like in October 1994, when the Mauritanian government arrested Islamists, made them confess, and broadcast their confessions.* I was so scared my feet couldn't carry my body. You could tell there was a lot of pressure on my government.

"I've been very patient with you, boy," the interrogator said. "You got to admit, or I am going to pass you the special team." I knew he meant the torture team. "Reports keep coming every day from everywhere," he said. In the days before this talk I couldn't sleep. Doors kept getting opened and closed. Every move around me hit my heart so bad. My room was next to the archive, and through a small hole I could see some of the files and their labels; I started to hallucinate and read papers about me that didn't exist. I couldn't take anything anymore. And torture? No way.

"Look, Director! I have not been completely truthful with you, and I would like to share my whole story." I told him. "However, I don't want you to share the Afghanistan story with the U.S. government, because they don't understand this whole Jihad recipe, and I am not willing to put gas on the fire."

"Of course I won't," the DSE said. Interrogators are used to

---

* Mauritanian President Maaouya Ould Sid'Ahmed Taya came to power in a military coup in 1984 and became president in 1992. During his long tenure as head of state, Ould Taya carried out several waves of arrests of political opponents and Islamists like the one described here, in which more than ninety people, including a former government minister and ten religious leaders, were arrested and then amnestied after publicly confessing to membership in illegal organizations. A crackdown on Islamists in the army and education system led to a failed coup attempt in 2003, and Ould Taya was ultimately deposed in a successful coup in 2005. By that time, in part because of his close cooperation with U.S. antiterrorism policies, which included allowing the rendition of MOS, and his aggressive campaign against Islamists in Mauritania, Ould Taya had lost much of his public support. See http://www.nytimes.com/2005/08/08/international/africa/08mauritania.html?fta=y&_r=0; http://www.csmonitor.com/2005/0809/p07s02-woaf.html; and http://www.ft.com/cms/s/0/23ab7cfc-0e0f-11da-aa67-00000e2511c8.html#axzz2vwtOwdNb.

lying to people; the interrogator's whole job is about lying, outsmarting, and deception. "I can even send my recorder and my assistant away, if you'd like," he continued.

"No, I don't mind them around." The DSE called his driver and sent him to buy some food. He brought chicken salad, which I liked. It was my first meal since I left Senegal; it was now February 12, 2000.

"Is that all you're gonna eat?" wondered the DSE.

"Yes, I'm full."

"You don't really eat."

"That's the way I am." I started to recount my whole Jihad story in the most boring detail. "And as to Canada or an attack against the U.S., I have nothing to do with it," I finished. In the days that followed I got, by far, better treatment and better food, and all the questions he asked me and all my answers were consistent in themselves and with the information he already knew from other sources. When the DSE knew that I was telling him the truth, he quit believing the U.S. reports to be the Gospel truth, and very much put them aside, if not in the garbage.

On February 14, 2000, an FBI team from the United States showed up to interrogate me. There were three of them, two FBI agents named Jack and Michael, and someone they said was from the Justice Department. Evidently the Mauritanian authorities had shared all of my interviews with the FBI team, so that U.S. agents and the Mauritanians were at the same level of information.*

---

* MOS told the Administrative Review Board panel in 2005 that an American team consisting of two FBI agents and a third man from the Justice Department interrogated him over a two-day period near the end of his detention in Mauritania. His detention for questioning at the behest of the

When the team arrived they were hosted at the Halima Hotel, where it turned out they were spotted by the local press. Deddahi Ould Abdallahi, the DSE, gave me a forewarning the day they came to interrogate me.

"Mohamedou, we have nothing on you. When it comes to us, you are a free man," he told me. "However, those people want to interrogate you. I'd like you to be strong, and to be honest with them."

"How can you allow foreigners to interrogate me?"

"It's not my decision, but it's just a formality," he said. I was very afraid, because I had never met American interrogators, though I anticipated that they would not use torture to coerce information. But the whole environmental setup made me very skeptical toward the honesty and humanity of the U.S. interrogators. It was kind of like, "We ain't gonna beat you ourselves, but you know where you are!" So I knew the FBI wanted to interrogate me under the pressure and threat of a non-democratic country.

The atmosphere was prepared. I was told what to wear and what to say. I never had the chance to take a shower or to wash my clothes, so I wore some of my dirty clothes. I must have smelled terribly. I was so skinny from my confinement that my clothes didn't fit; I looked like a teenager in baggy pants. But as much as I was pissed, I tried to look as comfortable, friendly, and normal as I could.

The FBI team arrived around 8 p.m., and the interrogation room was cleaned for them. I entered the room smiling. After

United States in early 2000 was widely reported in the local and international press; in a BBC report, Mauritanian officials confirmed that he was questioned in mid-February 2000 by the FBI. The *New York Times* reported that MOS was released from Mauritanian custody on February 19, 2000. ARB transcript, 17; http://news.bbc.co.uk/2/hi/africa/649672.stm; http://www.nytimes.com/2000/02/21/world/terrorist-suspect-is-released-by-mauritania.html.

diplomatic greetings and introductions I sat down on a hard chair, trying to discover my new world.

The leader of the team, Special Agent Jack, started to talk. "We have come from the States to ask you some questions. You have the right to remain calm. You may also answer some questions and leave others. Were we in the U.S., we would have provided you with a lawyer free of charge."

I almost interrupted his nonsense and said, "Cut the crap, and ask me the questions!" I was like, "What a civilized world!" In the room, there were only the FBI interrogators with an Arabic interpreter. The Mauritanian interrogators stepped outside.

"Oh, thank you very much. I don't need any lawyer," I said.

"However, we would like you to answer our questions."

"Of course I will," I said. They started to ask me about my trip to Afghanistan during the war against communism, showed me a bunch of pictures, asked me questions about Canada, and hardly any questions about Germany. As to the pictures and Canada, I was completely truthful, but I deliberately withheld some parts of my two Afghanistan trips in January 1991 and February 1992. You know why? Because it is none of the U.S. government's business what I had done to help my Afghani brothers against the communists. For Pete's sake, the U.S. was supposedly on our side! When that war was done I resumed my regular life; I hadn't broken any Mauritanian or German laws. I legally went to Afghanistan and came back. As for the U.S., I am not a U.S. citizen, nor have I been in the U.S.—so what law have I possibly broken? I understand that if I enter the U.S. and they arrest me for a reasonable suspicion, then I completely have to explain to them my position. And Canada? Well, they made a big deal out of me being in Canada, because some Arab guy had tried to attack them from Canada. I explained with definite evidence that I was not a part of it. Now F★ck off and leave me alone.

The FBI interrogators told me that I wasn't truthful.

"No, I was," I lied. The good thing was that I didn't give a damn about what they thought. Special Agent Michael kept writing my answers and looking at me at the same time. I wondered, how could he do both? But later I learned that FBI interrogators study your body language while you're speaking, which is nothing but bullshit.* There are many factors involved in an interrogation, and they differ from one culture to another. Since the United States knows my entire case now, I suggest that Agent Michael should go back and check where he marked me as lying, just to check his competence. The U.S. interrogators also went outside their assignment and did what any interrogator would have done: they fished, asking me about Sudan, Nairobi, and Dar Es Salaam. How am I supposed to know about those countries, unless I have multiple doppelgängers?

Special Agent Jack offered to have me work with them. I think the offer was futile unless they were dead sure that I was a criminal. I'm not a cop, but I understand how criminals can repent—but I personally had done nothing to repent for. The next day, about the same time, the FBI team showed up once more, trying to get at least the same amount of information I had shared with the Mauritanians, but there was no persuading me. After all the Mauritanian authorities duly shared everything with them. The FBI team didn't push me in any uncivilized way; they acted rather friendly. The chief of the team said, "We're done. We're going back home," exactly like Umm 'Amr

---

* The FBI lists body language among possible deception clues in material posted on its website, and former FBI agents have written and spoken publicly on the subject. See, e.g., https://leb.fbi.gov/2011/june/evaluating -truthfulness-and-detecting-deception; and http://cjonline.com/news/ local/2010-11-26/no_lie_ex_fbi_agent_spots_fibbers.

and her donkey.* The FBI team left Nouakchott, and I was released on February 19, 2000.

"Those guys have no evidence whatsoever," the DSE said sadly. He felt completely misused. The Mauritanians didn't want me delivered to them in the first place, because it was a no-win situation: if they found me guilty and they delivered me to the U.S., they were going to feel the wrath of the public; if not, they would feel the wrath of the U.S. government. In either case, the President was going to lose his office.

So in the end, something like this must have happened under the table:

"We found nothing on him, and you guys didn't provide us any evidence," the Senegalese must have said. "Under these circumstances, we can't hold him. But if you want him, take him."

"No, we can't take him, because we've got to get evidence on him first," answered the U.S. government.

"Well, we don't want to have anything to do with him," said the Senegalese.

"Turn him over to the Mauritanians," the U.S. government suggested.

"No, we don't want him, just take him!" cried the Mauritanian government.

"You got to," said the U.S. government, giving the Mauritanians no choice. But the Mauritanian government always prefers keeping peace between the people and the government. They don't want any trouble.

"You are free to go," said the DSE.

"Should I give him everything?"

"Yes, everything," the DSE answered. He even asked me to

* The reference is to a pre-Islamic proverb about a cursed woman who is expelled from her tribe; the sense is of an unwanted person who goes away and is not seen again.

double-check on my belongings, but I was so excited I didn't
check on anything. I felt as if the ghoul of fear had flown from
my chest.

"Thank you very much," I said. The DSE ordered his assistant and recorder to drive me home. It was about 2 p.m. when
we took off toward my home.

"You'd better not talk with journalists," said the inspector.

"No, I won't." And indeed, I never disclosed the scandal of
foreign interrogators violating the sovereignty of my country
to journalists. I felt so bad about lying to them.

"Come on, we have seen the FBI guys at the Hotel Halima,"
a reporter told me after my release. God, those journalists are
wizards.

"Maybe they were listening to my interrogation," I said
unconvincingly.

I tried to recognize the way to my home, but believe me, I
didn't recognize anything until the police car parked in front
of our house and dropped me there. It had been almost seven
years since I saw my family last.* Everything had changed.
Children had become men and women, young people had
become older. My strong mom had become weak. Nonetheless
everybody was happy. My sister Nejah and my former wife had
hardly slept nights, praying to God to relieve my pains and suf-
ferings. May God reward everybody who stood on my side.

Everybody was around, my aunt, the in-laws, friends. My
family kept generously feeding the visitors, some of whom came
just to congratulate me, some to interview me, some just to get

---

* MOS left Mauritania in 1988 to study in Germany. He testified at his
2004 Combatant Status Review Tribunal (CSRT) hearing that he visited his
family in Mauritania for two or three weeks in 1993. The CSRT transcript
is available at http://online.wsj.com/public/resources/documents/couch
-slahihearing-03312007.pdf. CSRT transcript, 5.

to know the man who had made news for the last month. After the first few days, my family and I were making plans for my future. To make a long story short, my family wanted me to stay in the country, if only to see me every day and enjoy my company. I said to myself, Screw it, went out, found a job, and was enjoying looking into the pretty face of my mom every morning. But no joy is forever

THREE

Mauritania

September 29, 2001–November 28, 2001

A Wedding and a Party...I Turn Myself In...Release
from Custody...The Camel Rests in Two Steps...The
Secret Police Show Up at My House..."Independence
Day"...A Flight to Jordan

September 29, 2001, was a very busy day: for one, I was involved
in organizing the wedding of my lovely niece Zeinebou Mint
Elmamy, and for two, I was invited to attend a big dinner organized by a very important man in my tribe named Ahmed Ould
El Moctar Ould Khattary. This man had unluckily been
involved in a terrible car accident, and had recently come back
after spending some time in the U.S. for medical treatment.
Ould Khattary enjoys a high respect among the people from
the South, and the dinner was to aid what we call The Cadres
of Trarza.*

In the morning I asked my boss to give me some money to

---

* Trarza is the region of southern Mauritania that extends from the
Senegalese border north to the capital. It was also the name of a precolonial
emirate in the same region. The Cadres of Trarza is a community
organization.

help my sister with the wedding.* In Mauritania we have the bad habit of organizing everything on the whim, a heritage of rural life that all Mauritanians still deal with today. My job was to help transport the invited guests to the site where the wedding was taking place.

Weddings in the Islamic, Arabic world are not only different from one country to another, but within the same country there are all kinds of different customs. My niece's wedding followed the customs that are practiced by average prestigious families in southern Mauritania.

Most of the work is usually done by the guy. He investigates the would-be wife's background by unleashing the female relatives he trusts the most. The report of this "committee" will produce an assessment of the technical data of the girl, her attitude, her intellect, and the like; sometimes this investigation step can be skipped when the girl already has a good reputation.

The next step is dating, though that is different than the American model. The interested guy dates his would-be wife in her family's house, usually in the presence of other family members. The goal of these dates is for both to get to know each other. The dating can take between a couple of months

---

* When MOS returned to Mauritania in 2000 he worked as an electronics and computer specialist, first for a medical equipment supply company and then, starting in July 2001, for a company named Aman Pêche in Nouakchott. "This is a French word for fish," he explained at his CSRT hearing. "This company was a company of people from my tribe, and they gave me more money to join them. They wanted to develop the business and to use me; I was just setting up at my office, because they didn't know what to do with me at first. They had many electronic devices they wanted me to take care of. I had just set up my office and installed the AC, and September 11th happened. Then America went crazy looking for leads; and I was the cousin of the right hand of Osama bin Laden, and oh, get him." CSRT transcript, 8; ARB transcript, 18.

and a couple of years, depending on the man and the girl. Some girls don't want to start a family before graduating from school, and some do — or let's say family pressure and the man compel her to start the family right away. On the other hand, most guys aren't ready for marriage; they just want to "reserve" the girl and go about their business until they are financially ready. The groom is usually older than the bride, sometimes even much older, but in a few cases the bride happens to be older, and sometimes much older. Mauritanians are relatively tolerant when it comes to age differences.

Before the guy officially asks for the hand of the girl, he secretly sends a good friend to the girl to ask her whether she might consider him. When that is established, the decisive step comes next: the guy asks the girl's mom whether she would accept him as the husband of her daughter. Guys only ask for the hand of a girl if they know they will more than likely be accepted, so sometimes the guy sends a trusted third person in order to avoid the embarrassment of being turned down. Only the mother of the girl can decide; most fathers have little say.

This step, though not official, is binding for both. Everybody now knows that the couple is engaged. Premarital sex is not tolerated in Mauritania, and not only for religious reasons: many guys mistrust any girl who accepts having sex with them. They assume, if she accepts having sex with me, she would accept another man, and another man, in an endless sexual adventure. Although the Islamic religion treats males and females the same way in this regard, the society tends to accept premarital sex from men much more than women. You can compare it with cheating in the U.S.: the society tolerates it more if a man cheats than if a woman does. I never met an American man who would forgive cheating, but I did meet many American women who would.

There is no party or engagement ring, but the fiancé is now entitled to give his wife-to-be presents. Before the engagement, a lady would not accept presents from a stranger.

The last step is the actual wedding, the date of which is set by agreement of both; each party can take as much as time as he or she needs, as long as it is reasonable. The man is expected to produce a dowry as a necessary formality, but it is not appropriate for the girl's family to ask for any sum; the whole thing must be left to the man and his financial possibilities. So dowries vary from a very modest to a relatively sinfully high amount. Once the man produces whatever his possibilities and judgment allow, many families will only take a small, symbolic amount and send the rest to the man's family, at least half of the dowry

The wedding party traditionally takes place in the girl's family house, but lately some people have found a lucrative business in professionally organizing weddings in club-like houses. The party begins with the *Akd,* the marriage agreement, which can be performed by any Imam or respected Sheikh. Mauritanians don't believe in governmental formalities, and so hardly anybody declares his marriage at a government institution unless it is for financial advantages, which rarely exist.

The wedding party equally drains both the groom's and bride's family. Traditionally, Mauritanians would party for seven full days, but the punishments of modern life cut those seven days back to one single night. Only the friends of the groom from his generation are allowed to attend the wedding, unlike women, who can be all different ages. At the party women don't mingle directly with men, though they can be in the same hall; each sex respects the spot of the other. However, all the attendants talk to each other and enjoy the same entertainment that takes place in the middle of the hall, such as sketches, music, and poetry. When I was a child, women and men used to pass coded messages back and forth targeting a particular individual who certainly understood the message; the messages usually unfolded a funny situation that could happen to anybody and that is somewhat embarrassing. The person's friends would laugh at him or her, and he or she would have to fight back targeting the anonymous person who sent the message. People don't do this teasing entertainment anymore.

During the wedding food and drinks are generously served. The party traditionally closes with what they call the *Taweez-Pillage,* which doesn't have anything to do with the literal meaning of the words. It just describes the plot by the women to kidnap the bride, and the brothers' efforts to prevent the act. The bride's female friends are allowed to conspire and kidnap the bride and hide her; it is the job of the groom and his friends to prevent this event, and should the men fail in preventing the abduction, it is their duty to find the bride and deliver her to her husband. The bride must cooperate with her female friends, and she usually does, otherwise she'll be branded with all kinds of bad adjectives. It sometimes takes many days for the males to find the bride.

When the man succeeds in getting the bride the party is over, and the bride is given to the groom. Both get escorted by their closest friends in a long rally leading to the house of the new family, while the rest of the attendants retreat to their own homes.

The wedding of my beloved niece Zeinebou Mint Elmamy would have gone more or less like this. I wasn't supposed to attend the party because I was way older than the groom, and in any case I didn't have time. I had another interesting party waiting on me. When I finished delivering the guests I checked with my mom on the situation. Everything seemed to be alright; my services no longer were required as far as I could see. The atmosphere of wedding was clearly going to take over.

When I got to the party, which was in the beautiful villa of Ahmed Ould El Moctar Ould Khattary in Tevrlegh Zeina, the warmth of companionship hit me gracefully. I didn't know the majority of the guests, but I spotted my beloved cousin and dear friend Dr. Ibrahim Ould N'taghri drowned in the middle of the crowd. I right away fought through the crowd and sat beside him.

He was happy to see me, and introduced me to the most remarkable guests. We retreated to the margin of the party with a few of his friends, and Ibrahim introduced me to a friend of his, a young lawyer. The lawyer asked Ibrahim and me whether he could defend our cousin Mahfouz, who now was wanted by the U.S. authorities with a $25 million reward.*

"What are you going to do for him? Reduce his sentence from 500 to 400 years?" I asked wryly. People in the other parts of the free world like Europe have problems understanding the draconian punishments in the U.S. Mauritania is not a country of law, so we don't have a problem understanding whatever the government does; even so, the Mauritanian legal code, when it is followed, is much more humane than the American. Why sentence somebody to 300 years when he is not going to live that long?

We were just talking like that, and enjoying the food that was generously served, when my cell phone rang. I pulled it out of my pocket and stepped aside. The display read the phone number of the DSE, the Directeur de la Sûreté de l'État.

"Hi," I answered.

"Mohamedou, where are you?" he said.

"Don't worry! Where are you?"

"I'm outside of my front door! I'd like to see you."

---

* In the wake of the 9/11 attacks, Mahfouz Ould al-Walid (Abu Hafs) was now the subject of a $25 million bounty (see footnote on p. 96).

"Fine. Just hold on, I'm on my way!" I said. I took my cousin Ibrahim aside.

"Look, Deddahi called me, and I'm going to see him."

"As soon as he releases you, give me a buzz."

"Alright," I said.

The DSE was waiting in front of his house, but he was not alone: his assistant stood beside him, which was not a good sign.

"Salam Alaikum," I said, stepping outside my car.

"Waalaikum Assalam. You're gonna ride with me, and somebody else is going to drive your car."

"Fine." The Inspector and I rode with the DSE and headed toward the secret, well-known jail.

"Look, those people told us to arrest you."

"Why?"

"I don't know, but I hope you'll be free soon. This whole 9/11 attack thing is screwing up everybody." I didn't say a thing. I just let him and his assistant make small talk, to which I paid no attention. The DSE had already called and interrogated me twice in the two and a half weeks since the 9/11 attack, but obviously the American government was not satisfied with a yard; they wanted a mile at first, and then the whole Autobahn, as it turned out in the end.

They put me in the same room I had been in one and a half years ago. The Inspector went out to brief the guards, which gave me the opportunity to give a quick call to my cousin Ibrahim.

"I'm arrested," I whispered, and hung up without even waiting on his answer. Then I erased my whole phone book. Not that I had any hot numbers—all I had were some numbers of business partners in Mauritania and Germany—but I didn't want the U.S. government harassing those peaceful people just because I had their numbers in my phone. The funniest record I deleted read "PC Laden," which means computer store; the

word for "store" in German just happens to be "Laden." I knew
no matter how hard I would have tried to explain that, the U.S.
interrogators would not have believed me. For Pete's sake, they
always tried to pin things on me that I had nothing to do with!

"Give me your cell phone," the Inspector said when he
returned. Among the belongings the Americans took back
home with them later was that old, funny looking cell phone,
but there were no numbers to check. As to my arrest, it was
sort of like political drug-dealing: the FBI asked the U.S. president to intervene and have me arrested; in turn George W.
Bush asked the vanishing Mauritanian president for a favor; on
receiving the U.S. president's request, his Mauritanian colleague
moved his police forces to arrest me.

"I really have no questions for you, because I know your
case," the DSE said. Both the DSE and his assistant left, leaving
me with the guards and oodles of mosquitoes.

After several days in the prison, the DSE came to my cell.

"Look! Those people want to know about Mehdi and Ganczarski, and they said you were a part of Millennium Plot."

"Well, Mehdi and Ganczarski are my friends in Germany,
and as to the Millennium Plot, I had nothing to do with it."

"I'll give you a pen and paper, and you write whatever you
know."

After two weeks of incarceration in the Mauritanian prison, two
white U.S. interrogators, Mr. Lee and his German interpreter,
Mr. Grant, came to the jail late one afternoon to interrogate me.*

---

* In his 2005 ARB testimony, MOS dates this interrogation as October
13, 2001, and speculates that these two interrogators are FBI, though "they
are American, they may be anything." ARB transcript, 18.

Before the two-man U.S. team met me, they asked the police to storm my house and office and confiscate anything that could give leads to my "criminal" activities. A special security team took me home, searched my house, and seized everything they thought might be relevant for the Americans. When the team arrived my wife was asleep, and they scared the hell out of her: she had never seen police searching somebody's house. Neither had I, for that matter, but I had no problem with the search except that it bothered my family. My neighbors didn't care much, first because they know me, and second because they know that the Mauritanian police are unjust. In a separate operation, another team searched the company where I worked. As it turned out, the Americans were not interested in any of the garbage except my work computer and the cellphone.

When I entered the interrogation room, the two Americans were sitting on the leather sofa, looking extremely angry. They must have been FBI, because the stuff they confiscated ended up in FBI's hands back in the States.

"Hi," I said, reaching out my hand. But both my hand and my "Hi" remained hanging in the air. Agent Lee seemed to be the leader. He pushed an old metal chair toward me.

"Do you see the picture on the wall?" Agent Lee said, pointing at the President's picture, with Agent Grant translating into German.

"Yes," I answered.

"Your president promised our president that you are going to cooperate with us," Agent Lee said. I thought, How cheap! I personally don't give a damn about either president; to me both are unjust and evil.

"Oh, yes! I surely will," I said, reaching for a drink on a table filled with all kinds of drinks and sweets. Agent Lee jerked the drink out of my hand.

"We are not here for a party," he said. "Look, I am here to find the truth about you. I'm not here to detain you."

"OK! You ask and I'll answer."

In the midst of this discourse, the tea guy surged into the room, trying to accommodate his angry guests. "Fuck off!" said Agent Lee. He was very disrespectful toward poor people, an idiot, and a racist who had one of the lowest self-esteems in the world. For my part, I ignored all the curses he addressed me with and just stayed cool, though very thirsty, because the session lasted the whole night.

"Before 9/11 you called your younger brother in Germany and told him, 'Concentrate on your school.' What did you mean with this code?"

"I didn't use any code. I always advise my brother to concentrate on his school."

"Why did you call a satellite company in the U.S.?"

"Because we have our Internet connection from the U.S., and I needed support."

"Why did you call this hotel in Germany?"

"My boss asked me to make a reservation for one of his cousins."

"How many computers do you have?"

"Only my work computer."

"You're lying! You have a laptop."

"That's my ex-wife's."

"Where is your ex-wife living?"

"The DSE knows."

"OK, let's check this lie out." Agent Lee disappeared for several minutes, asking the DSE to search my ex-wife's house and seize the laptop.

"What if you're lying?"

"I am not."

"But what if?"

"I'm not."

Of course he threatened me with all kinds of painful torture should it turn out I was lying. "You know we have some black motherfuckers who have no mercy on terrorists like you," he said, and as he proceeded, racial references kept flying out of his mouth. "I myself hate the Jews"—I didn't comment—"but you guys come and hit our building with planes," he continued.

"That's between you and the people who did it. You must resolve your problem with them; I have nothing to do with it."

Every once in a while Agent Lee received a call, obviously from a lady. During that time the other German-speaking idiot came up with the most stupid questions.

"Check this out. This is a German newspaper writing about you guys," he said. I scanned a newspaper article about the extremist presence in Germany.

"Well, Mr. Grant, that's none of my problem. As you can see, I'm in Mauritania."

"Where is Abu Hafs? Where is Noumane?" Agent Lee asked angrily.★

"I am not in Afghanistan, I'm in Mauritania—in prison. How can I possibly know their whereabouts?"

★ "Noumane" is Noumane Ould Ahmed Ould Boullahy. A footnote to Judge James Robertson's opinion granting MOS's habeas corpus petition notes, "The government asserts that Salahi swore the oath to Osama bin Laden, and did so at the same time as Noumane Ould Ahmed Ould Boullahy, who went on to become one of bin Laden's bodyguards. There is no evidence that Salahi maintained, or that he ever had, any relationship with Boullahy." The opinion is available at https://www.aclu.org/files/assets/2010-4-9-Slahi-Order.pdf.

"You're hiding him," he said. I was going to say, "Check up my sleeves," but I realized my situation didn't allow it.

"Ahmed Ressam said that he knew you!"

"I don't know Ahmed Ressam. There is nothing to change about that fact." In the meantime, the DSE and his assistant came back with my ex-wife's laptop. They weren't allowed into the interrogation room; they knocked at the door and Agent Lee stepped outside. I looked with the side of my eyes and recognized the laptop bag. I was happy that they found the "big secret."

Agent Lee returned. "What if I told you that they didn't find the laptop," he said, trying to be smarter than he is.

"All I can tell you is that I have no laptop," I said, letting him believe that I hadn't seen the case. He didn't ask anymore about the laptop after that. They mirrored all the hard disks and took them home, just to waste four years popping their eyes out of their heads looking for non-existent treasure. Tough luck!

"We have invaded Afghanistan and are killing everybody. Do you think that's OK?" Agent Lee asked.

"You know best what you're doing," I said.

"Do you know Hauoari?"★

"No!"

"The Canadians said that they saw him with you. Either I am lying to you or they lied to me—or you're lying."

"I don't know him, but in the mosque, and in the café beneath it, I was always around many people I don't know."

"Why do you think we picked you up out of more than two million Mauritanians?"

★ Mokhtar Hauoari, an Algerian-Canadian, was convicted and sentenced to twenty-four years in prison in connection with the Millennium Plot.

"I don't know why. All I know is I haven't done anything against you."

"Write your name in Arabic." I wrote my name. For some reason, he kept taking pictures during the session. He really confused the hell out of me.

"Why did you call the UAE?"

"I didn't."

"So you think I am lying to you?"

"No, but I don't remember calling the UAE." As it turned out he did lie, but maybe unintentionally. I didn't call the UAE, but I did receive a call from a female friend of mine, Dr. Eeman from Saudi Arabia, who tried desperately to bring me and my ex-wife back together. I couldn't remember this during the session, I was so nervous. But when I was released, my family helped me remember, so I went to the police on my own and explained the call to them, and another call my cousin Ibrahim, who is a radiologist, made to France to contact his medicine supplier in Paris. In real life, if I give my phone to somebody I trust, I don't ask him about the details of his call. But if you get arrested, you have to lay out your whole life, and something like "I don't remember" doesn't work.

During the session, Agent Lee called my family and me all kind of names, and forbade me to drink from the goods that my people paid for—it was, after all, our taxes that made the U.S. guests comfortable. At the end of the session, when I was about to dehydrate, Agent Lee hit me in the face with 1.5-liter water bottle and left the room. I didn't even feel the pain from a blow that almost broke my nose because of the relief of Agent Lee and his translator leaving. Agent Lee didn't write anything, which struck me as strange because interrogators always want to write, but I believe that they recorded the session. Mr. Grant tried his best to repeat the curses that Agent Lee was generously producing. I think that Mr. Grant was worthless to Mr. Lee; he just brought him along as a translator.

The Americans left Mauritania, and the next day, the Mauritanian government released me without any charges. Furthermore, the DSE went to the Media Center and informed them that I was innocent and acquitted of every charge. The DSE's boss, the Directeur Général de la Sûreté Nationale,* offered me a loan in case I had any problems getting back to my job, and at the same time, the DSE called the President and Director General of my company and assured him that I am innocent and must resume my work.†

"We never doubted him for a second. He is welcome any time," my former boss answered. Still, the government was ordered by the U.S. to keep me under house arrest with no reason besides injustice and the misuse of power. I wasn't worried about getting a job after jail because I knew that Mauritanians were growing tired of Americans jumping on innocent people all around the world and trying to incriminate them. In fact, I got more job opportunities than I ever had in my life. My only worry was for my sister Nejah, who was suffering from depression and anxiety. My family of course was very happy to have me back, and so were my friends and relatives who kept coming to greet me and wish me good luck.

But the camel, as they say, rests in two steps.

Legend has it that an urban dweller rode a camel with a Bedouin. The Bedouin sat in front of the hump, and the urban dweller behind it so he could steady himself by grabbing the

---

* The Sûreté Nationale is the Mauritanian national police force; the Directeur Général de la Direction Générale de la Sûreté Nationale, abbreviated as DG, is the country's top law enforcement official.

† In the manuscript, this is abbreviated PDG, short for the French title *président-directeur général,* the equivalent of president and CEO.

Bedouin. When they arrived home, the camel bent his front legs to come to rest, and the Bedouin, caught off guard, lost his equilibrium and fell to the ground. The urban dweller couldn't help laughing at the Bedouin.

The Bedouin looked at his friend and said, "Too soon to be happy: the camel rests in two steps." And indeed, as soon as the camel bent his rear legs to come to his final rest, the urban dweller fell on his face.

As far as I can remember, I never fell off a camel; however, as soon as I resumed my life, the U.S. government started conspiring with the Mauritanian government to kidnap me.

It was around 4 p.m. when I got back from work about a month later. It had been a long day, hot, and humid: one of those days. The Islamic calendar read Ramadan 4th, and so far everybody in the family was fasting except for the kids.*

It had been a remarkable workday. My company sent me to assess a relatively big project for our small company: we had been asked to give an estimate to network the Presidential Palace for both computers and telephones. I had made an appointment with the project coordinator for early that morning, and waiting outside his office was the order of the first half of the day. There are two things all government officials have in common: they don't respect appointments, and they never start work on time.

During Ramadan, most people party nights and sleep days. I hadn't partied last night, but I had stayed up late for another reason: namely I had a little familial fight with my beloved wife. I hate fights, and so I was depressed and couldn't sleep the whole night.

---

* Ramadan 4th was Tuesday, November 20, in 2001.

As drowsy and sleepy as I was, I still managed to be on the site of my rendezvous, though not punctually, with time enough to beat the coordinator by hours. His office was closed, and there was no free chair in the corridor, and so I had to put up with squatting on the floor with my back to the wall. I fell asleep many times.

Around noon my colleague and cousin Ould Khattary showed up and took me to the Presidential Palace. I thought there would be a lot of formalities, especially for a "terrorist suspect" such as myself, but nothing like that happened. You had to give your name the day before, and when I showed the guards my ID they verified the visitors' list, where my name appeared with the appropriate clearance. I was shocked. But after all, only the Americans suspect me of terrorism, no other country. The irony is that I have never been in the States, and all the other countries I have been in kept saying, "The guy is alright."

As soon as I entered the sanctuary of the palace, I felt as if I were in another country. There was a garden inside with all kinds of flowers. Water fountains created a light drizzle. The weather was just cool and fine.

We went right to business. I went through many rooms on different floors and took some measurements, but we were stopped and advised to leave the actual palace because there was an official visit. We could stay inside the compound, and so I used that time and went to the palace's central telephone exchange to check on the infrastructure. The IT guy was the cousin of the president, and as friendly as most people from Atar. He was more of a security choice; the president trusts his own people most, which makes perfect sense. I felt depressed because the whole project needed much more work than what it said in the papers, and I needed help, professional help. I didn't want to mess around with the Presidential Palace. I would rather retreat completely than start selling them made-in-Timbuktu hi-tech equipment.

The IT guy showed us the things we needed to see and disappeared to his guests. It was late, and the project coordinator asked for another appointment to finish the measurement work and the assessment of the needed infrastructure. My cousin Ould Khattary and I left with the intention of coming back tomorrow and finishing the work. By the time we left the gate, I was already tired, and like, Get me the hell outta here. I made a call to my boss and briefed him, and I even went to the office after that and told my colleagues what happened.

On the way home, my cousin Hussein Ould Ndjoubnane called me to make sure that I would be at dinner in his house. Hussein is a government employee who studied administration and joined our bureaucracy, working his way up to the position of a Prefect. He is also an old friend of the family; I knew him and played cards with him when I was a child. Today Hussein was organizing a big dinner for his friends, including my brother, who was on vacation with us from Germany, and me. Right when Hussein called, my car had a breakdown. I hated it when my As-Old-As-My-Grandpa car did that.

"Do you need me to come to you?" Hussein asked.

"No, I can see a garage not far from me. I'm sure they'll help me."

"Don't forget our Dinner Party, and remind Seyloum!" he said.★

A mechanic from the garage found that the benzene pipe to the carburetor was broken, and fixed it. In Mauritania people fix everything; in Germany, people replace everything. The mechanic wanted me to pay him more than I thought he ought to be paid, and so I did the thing I hate the most, negotiation, and paid him the amount we agreed on. One thing I like about

---

★ Seyloum is the nickname of MOS's older brother Mohamed Salem.

Germany is that you don't need to negotiate; everything is labeled with a price. You could be mute and nonetheless be treated justly. The thing about negotiation is that most of the time somebody is going to be disadvantaged. Personally, I just want a fair price for both parties that makes each party happy.

When I arrived at my mom's home around 4 p.m., only my aunt Khadijettou, Nen as we call her, and my sister Nejah were there, and both were asleep. My mom had gone outside to gather her scattered sheep; it was feeding time. I went inside the house and put on my bathrobe. On my way to the shower, my mom and two secret police guys surged almost simultaneously into the house.

"Salahi, the Director General wants to see you!"

"Why?"

"We don't know," said one of the guys.

"OK. I'm going to take a shower and change my clothes."

"OK!" said the guy, stepping out. "We're gonna wait on you outside." The secret police respected me highly since I turned myself in a couple of weeks ago; they knew I am not a person who flees. I had basically been under house arrest since 2000 but I could have fled the country anytime; I didn't, and didn't have any reason to. I took my shower and changed. In the meantime my aunt woke up because of the noise. My sister didn't wake up, as far as I remember, and that was good, because I was only worried about her and the extreme depression she had been suffering.

"I think the police called you because you bought a new TV, and they don't want you to watch TV. Don't you think?" said my mom innocently.

I smiled and said, "I don't think so, but everything is going to be alright." My mom was referring to the new satellite antenna I installed the night before to have better TV reception. The irony is that the arresting agent, Agent Yacoub, was the one who helped me install the antenna. When I was in prison the month before, he had asked me to find a job for him because the police paid him miserably. I promised him I would, and in the meantime, I wanted to offer him an opportunity to do some work for me, so I called him to help fix my antenna, and paid him adequately. That was the only way for a man like him to survive. I helped him get some work, and we were sipping tea and joking in my house.

"I didn't bring you to my house to arrest me," I said jokingly.

"I hope you will never be arrested," Agent Yacoub said.

My mom's house is next to my brother's, with a short wall that separates them. I could simply have jumped to my brother's house, and escaped through his door that opens to a completely other street, and guess what? There would be no finding me, not only because so many people would shelter me, but also because the police agents would not have been interested in finding me. I even believe that the government would have been much happier saying to the U.S., "He fled, we couldn't find him."

You should know, Dear Reader, that a country turning over its own citizens is not an easy deal. The President wished he hadn't had to turn me over. I wonder why? After all it cost him his office afterward. I understand that if the U.S. captures me in Afghanistan and takes me to GTMO for whatever reason, my government cannot be blamed because I chose to go to Afghanistan. But kidnapping me from my house in my country and giving me to the U.S., breaking the constitution of Mauritania and the customary International Laws and treaties, that is not OK. Mauritania should have asked the U.S. to provide evidence that incriminates me, which they couldn't, because they had none. But even if the U.S. did so, Mauritania should try me according to the criminal code in Mauritania, exactly as Germany does with its citizens who are suspected of being involved in 9/11. On the other hand, if the U.S. says, "We have no evidence," then the Mauritanian response should be something like, "Fu*k you!" But no, things don't work this way. Don't get me wrong, though: I don't blame the U.S. as much as I do my own government.

The secret police agents obviously wanted me to flee, especially Agent Yacoub. But I wanted to keep it real—not to mention that the government itself assured my family that I had done nothing, and so my family always wanted to me to go to the police whenever they asked to see me. The funny thing about "Secret Police" in Arab countries is that they are more known to the commoners than the regular police forces. I think the authorities in Arabic countries should think about a new nomenclature, something like "The Most Obvious Police."

There were four of them when I stepped outside the door with my mom and my aunt. My mom kept her composure, and started to pray using her fingers. As to my aunt, that was her first time seeing somebody taken by the police, and so she got crippled and couldn't say a word. She started to sweat heavily and mumbled some prayers. Both kept their eyes staring at me. It is the taste of helplessness, when you see your beloved fading away like a dream and you cannot help him. And same for me: I would watch both my mom and my aunt praying in my rearview mirror until we took the first turn and I saw my beloved ones disappear.

"Take your car, we hope you can come back home today," one of the guys had instructed me. "The DG might just ask you some questions." Agent Yacoub occupied my passenger seat, as sad as he could be.

"Salahi, I wish I were not part of this shit," he said. I didn't respond. I kept following the police car that was heading toward the secret, well-known jail. I had been incarcerated a couple times in the same illegal prison, and knowing it didn't make me like it. I hated the compound, I hated the dark, dirty room, I hated the filthy bathroom, and I hated everything about it, especially the constant state of terror and fear.

"Earlier today the Inspector was looking for you. You know the DSE is on a trip in Spain. The Inspector asked us who has your phone number. But I didn't say anything, even though I have it," said Agent Yacoub, trying to make himself feel better. The only other guy who had my phone number was the DSE, and obviously he didn't give it to anybody.

So here we are, at the gate of the resented prison. Inspector Ismael was in his office, looking at me with his dishonest smile, which he quickly changed into a frown.

"We didn't have your phone number. The director is on a trip. He's coming in three days, and meanwhile we are going to hold you in contempt."

"Why? I'm really growing tired of being arrested for no reason. What do you want from me now? You've just released me," I said, frustrated and angry, especially since the guy who knows my case was not in the country.

"Why are you so scared? I never knew you like that," the inspector said.

"Look, you arrested me after 9/11, and the U.S. interrogators came here and interrogated me. After that you, when you realized that I'm innocent, you released me. I sort of understand the mass arrest after 9/11, but this arrest right now is not OK."

"Everything is gonna be alright. Give me your cell phone,"

the inspector lied, smiling his usual forced smile. The police inspector had about as much clue as I did about the goal of my arrest because the government wouldn't have shared anything with him. I don't think that the Mauritanian government had reached a resolution on my case; the main guy, DSE Deddahi, was on a trip, and without him a decision could hardly be made. What the inspector and I both knew back then was that the U.S. asked Mauritania's then-president to hold me; the Mauritanian president asked his Directeur Général de la Sûreté Nationale—who is now the president—to arrest me; and he in his turn ordered his people, led by the inspector, to hold me in contempt.*

However, I think that the U.S. wasn't making a secret of its wish, namely to have me in Jordan, and so at the point of my arrest on November 20, 2001, two people knew the plan: the Mauritanian president and his DG. But since the U.S. was asking so much from its ally, the Mauritanian government needed some time to digest and confer. Turning me over to Jordan involved some serious things. The Mauritanian constitution would have to be broken. The Mauritanian President was hanging onto his office by a spider's thread, and any trouble would shake him heavily. The U.S. hadn't asked the Mauritanians to turn me over to them, which would make more sense; no, they wanted me in Jordan, and that was a big disrespect to the sovereignty of Mauritania. The Mauritanian government had been asking for evidence, any evidence, and the U.S. had failed to provide anything, and so arresting me in itself was burdensome for the government, let alone sending me to Jordan. The

---

* Mauritania's Directeur Général de la Sûreté Nationale in 2001 was Ely Ould Mohamed Vall. Vall, who served as director of the national police under President Maaouya Ould Taya, seized power himself in a bloodless coup when Ould Taya was out of the country on August 3, 2005.

Mauritanian government sought incriminating evidences from the countries I had been in, Germany and Canada, and both countries provided only good conduct reports. For these and other reasons, the Mauritanian President needed his trusted guy, the DSE, before he took such a dangerous step.

I handed my cell phone to the Inspector, and he ordered the guards to take care of me and left. So I had to party with the guards instead of Hussein Ould Ndjoubnane and the rest of my cousins.

In Mauritania, the guards of secret detainees are part of the Secret Police, and as much as they might sympathize with you, they would do anything they were ordered to, even if it involved taking your life. Such people are resented in the society because they are the arms of the dictatorship; without them the dictator is crippled. They must not be trusted. And yet I didn't feel any hatred toward them, just bad for them; they had the right to be as miserable as the majority of Mauritanians. Most of them knew me from previous arrests.

"I divorced my wife!" a young guard told me.

"Why, man? You have a daughter."

"I know but I don't have enough money to rent a place for my wife and me, and my wife got fed up with living in my mom's house. They just couldn't get along."

"But divorce? Come on!"

"What would you have done in my shoes?" I couldn't find any answer, because the simple Math was against me. The guy's salary was about 40 or 50 dollars a month, and in order to have a somewhat decent life he needed at least $1,000. All my guards had something in common: they all lived way below the poverty line, and without a supplementary job none of them could make it to the end of the month. In Mauritania, the gap between leading officers and enlisted agents is just too big.

"We have seen many people who have been here and ended up occupying very high level jobs in the government. We're sure you will, too," they always teased me. I'm sure they aspired to better jobs in the government, but I personally don't believe in working with a government that's not righteous; to me, the need for the miserable wages is not an excuse for the mischief they were doing under the color and authority of an unjust regime. In my eyes, they were as guilty as anybody else, no matter what excuses they may come up with.

Nonetheless, the Mauritanian guards, without exception, all expressed their solidarity with me and wished they didn't have to be the ones who had to do the job. They showed me all kinds of sympathy and respect, and they always tried to calm me down because I was worried about being turned over to the States and sent to a Military Tribunal. By then, the U.S. President was barking about putting terrorist suspects before military tribunals, and all kinds of other threats. I knew I would have no chance to be tried justly in a foreign military tribunal. We ate, prayed, and socialized together. We shared everything, food, tea, and we had a radio receiver to hear the news. We all slept in a big room with no furniture and an oodle of mosquitoes. Since it was Ramadan, we ate nights and stayed awake for the most part, and slept during day. They were obviously directed to treat me that way; the inspector sometimes joined us to check on things.

As scheduled, the DSE came back from his trip. "Hi," he greeted me.

"Hi."

"How are you doing?"

"Fine! Why are you arresting me?"

"Be patient! It's not a fire!" he said. Why did he speak about fire? I wondered. He didn't look happy at all, and I knew it wasn't me who was causing his unhappiness. I was completely depressed and terrorized, and so I fell sick. I lost my appetite and couldn't eat anything, and my blood pressure dropped gravely. The DSE called a doctor to check on me.

"You cannot fast. You have to eat," he said, prescribing some medicine. Since I couldn't stand up I had to urinate in a water bottle, and as to anything else, I didn't need to because I hadn't eaten anything. I really got very sick, and the Mauritanian government was completely worried that the Merchandise was going to vanish before the U.S. client took it. Sometimes I tried to sit up in order to eat a little bit, but as soon as I sat straight, I started to get dizzy and fell down. All that time I drank and ate what I could while lying on a thin mattress.

I spent seven days in Mauritanian custody. I didn't get any visits from my family; as I later learned, my family was not allowed to see me, and they were denied the knowledge of my whereabouts. On the eighth day, November 28, 2001, I was informed that I was going to be shipped to Jordan.

November 28th is Mauritanian Independence Day; it marks the event when the Islamic Republic of Mauritania supposedly received its independence from the French colonists in 1960. The irony is that on this very same day in 2001, the independent and sovereign Republic of Mauritania turned over one of its own citizens on a premise. To its everlasting shame, the Mauritanian government not only broke the constitution, which forbids the extradition of Mauritanian criminals to other countries, but also extradited an innocent citizen and exposed him to the random American Justice.

The night before the multilateral deal was closed between Mauritania, the U.S., and Jordan, the prison guards allowed me to watch the parade that was coming from downtown toward the Presidential Palace, the bands escorted by schoolboys carrying lighted candles. The sight awoke childhood memories of when I took part in the same parade myself, as a schoolboy, nineteen years before. Back then I looked with innocence at the event that marked the birth of the nation I happened to be part of; I didn't know that a country is not considered sovereign if it cannot handle its issues on its own.

The Secret Service is the most important government corps in the third world, and in some countries in the so-called free world as well, and so the DSE was invited to the ceremonial colors at the Presidential Palace in the morning. It was between 10 and 11 o'clock when he finally came in, accompanied by his assistant and his recorder. He invited me to his office, where he usually interrogates people. I was surprised to see him at all because it was a holiday. Although I was sick, my blood pressure rose so much from the unexpected visit that I was able to stand and go with them to the interrogation room. But as soon as I entered the office I collapsed on the big leather black sofa. It was obvious that my hyperactivity was fake.

The DSE sent all the guards home, and so I was left with him, his recorder, and his assistant. The guards gestured to me happily as they left the building, as if to say, "Congratulations!" They and I both thought that I was going to be released, though I was skeptical: I didn't like all the movements and telephone conversations that were going on around me.

The DSE sent his assistant away, and he came back with a couple of cheap things, clothes and a bag. Meanwhile the recorder collapsed asleep in front of the door. The DSE pulled me into a room with nobody but us.

"We're going to send you to Jordan," he announced.

"Jordan!" What are you talking about?"

"Their King was subject to a failed assassination attempt."

"So what? I have nothing to do with Jordan; my problem is with Americans. If you want to send me to any country, send me to the U.S."

"No, they want you to be sent to Jordan. They say you are the accomplice of Ahmed Ressam, though I know you have nothing to do with Ressam's plot or with September 11."

"So why don't you protect me from this injustice as a Mauritanian citizen?" I asked.

"America is a country that is based on and living with injustice," was his answer.

"OK, I would like to see the President!" I said.

"No, you can't. Everything is already irreversibly decided."

"Well, I want to say good-bye to my mom," I said.

"You can't. This operation is secret."

"For how long?"

"Two days, or maximum three. And if you choose, you don't need to talk to them," he added. "I really have no problem with that." I knew that he was speaking out of his rear end, because I was destined to Jordan for a reason.

"Can you assure me of when I'll be coming back?"

"I'll try. But I hope this trip to Jordan will add another positive testimony in your favor. The Senegalese, the Canadians, the Germans, and I myself believe that you're innocent. I don't know how many witnesses the Americans need to acquit you."

The DSE took me back to his office and tried several times to call his boss, the DG. When he finally reached him, the DG could not give a precise date for my return but assured him that it would be a couple of days. I don't know for sure, but I believe that the Americans outsmarted everybody. They just asked to get me to Jordan, and then there would be another negotiation.

"I don't know exactly," the DSE told me honestly when he got off the phone. "But look: today is Wednesday. Two days for interrogation, and one day for the trip. So you will be back here Saturday or Sunday."

He opened the bag that his assistant brought and asked me to try on the new cheap clothes. I put on the complete suit: a t-shirt, a pair of pants, jacket and plastic shoes. What a sight! Nothing fit; I looked like a skeleton dressed in a new suit. But who cared? At least I didn't.

Between the time when I got the decision and the time the U.S. turned me over to the Jordanian Special Forces, I was treated like a UPS package. I cannot describe my feelings: anger, fear, powerlessness, humiliation, injustice, betrayal. . . . I had never really contemplated escaping from jail, although I had been jailed unjustly four times already. But today I was thinking about it because I never, even in my dreams, considered I would be sent to a third country that is known throughout the world as a torture-practicing regime. But that was my only bullet, and if I used it and missed I would look very bad in the eyes of my government. Not that that mattered; they obviously would still comply with the U.S. even if I was an angel in their eyes. After all, I had turned myself in.

I looked around for ways to escape. Let's say I managed to get out of the building: I would need a taxicab as soon as I reached the main road. But I had no money on me to pay a cab, and I couldn't take one to a place where somebody knew me because those are the first places they're going to look. When I checked the doors, there was only one door that I would not have any reason to approach, so I asked to use the bathroom. In the bathroom I trimmed my beard and meditated about the other door. It was glass, so I could break it, but I knew the plan of the building; that door would lead to an armed guard who might shoot me dead right away. And even if I managed to sneak past the guard, I had to go around the Ministry for Internal Affairs that neighbors the main street, where there are always guards watching people coming and going. It would be impossible to go through the gate. Maybe, just maybe there's a possibility of jumping the wall, but was I strong enough to do that? No, I wasn't. But I was ready to pull all my strength together and make the impossible possible.

All these plans and thoughts were going through my head when I was using the bathroom. I looked at the roof, but there was no way to escape there; the roof was concrete. I finished cleaning and shaving and left. Outside of the bathroom there was a hall without a roof; I thought I could maybe climb the wall and leave the compound by going from one roof to another. But there were two constraints: one, the wall was about 20 feet tall and there was nothing to grab onto in order to climb; and two, the whole compound could be encircled in a matter of minutes by the police, so that no matter where I landed I would be secure in police hands. I realized escape would remain an unrealized dream for somebody who suddenly found all doors before him closed except the door to heaven.

The DSE kept making calls to the incoming flight that carried the special mission team. "They should be here in about three hours. They're in Cyprus now!" he said. Normally he was not supposed to tell me where the plane was, or who was on the plane, or where I was going to be taken; the Americans wanted to maintain the terrorizing factors as harshly as possible. I should know nothing about what was happening to me. Being taken to an airport blindfolded, put in a plane, and taken to a country that is an eleven hour flight away together make enough horrible factors that only people with nerves of steel would survive. But the DSE didn't care about telling me everything he knew. Not because he was worried about me, but because he knew for a fact that agreeing to such a horrible operation was at the same time agreeing to give up power. The turmoil against the Mauritanian President was already there, but the DSE knew this would certainly break the camel's back. I knew the same, and so I kept praying, "Oh, Lord please don't let people spill blood in my name!"

The DSE learned from the tower that the plane was expected around 7:00 or 7:30 p.m. The recorder had been sleeping the whole time, so the DSE sent him home. It was around 6:00 p.m. when the DSE, his assistant, and I took off in the Director's luxurious Mercedes. He called the airport watch one more time to make the necessary arrangements to smuggle me securely without anybody noticing. I hoped his plan would fail and somebody would rat the government out.

The DSE headed in the opposite direction of the airport: he wanted to waste time and arrive at the airport about the same time as the Jordanian delegation. I was hoping that their plane would crash. Even though I knew it was replaceable, I wanted the plan to be postponed, like if you got news of your death and you wanted to postpone it. The DSE stopped at a grocery store and went in to buy some snacks for us to break the fast; sunset was going to catch us at the airport about the time of the unwelcome arrival. In front of the store stood a white U.N. truck. The driver had entered the store and left the engine running. I thought, with some luck I could possibly hijack it, and with some more luck I could get away, because the Benz would have little chance against the stronger body of the Toyota 4-wheel-drive truck.

But I saw some drawbacks that discouraged me from the attempt. The hijacking would involve innocent parties: in the cab sat the family of the truck driver, and I was not ready to hurt innocent people. A hijacking would also involve neutralizing the Benz, which could cost the lives of two police officers. Although I wouldn't feel guilty about them getting themselves killed while trying to unjustly and illegally arrest me, I didn't want to kill anybody. And was I really physically able to execute the operation? I wasn't sure. Thinking of the operation was sort of daydreaming to distract myself from the horrible unknown that was awaiting me.

I should mention that in Mauritania the police don't have the American's extremely paranoid and vigilant technique of blindfolding, ear-muffing, and shackling people from head to toe; in that regard Mauritanians are very laid back. As a matter of fact, I don't think anybody is as vigilant as the Americans. I was even walking free when we arrived at the airport, and I could easily have run away and reached the public terminal before anybody could catch me. I could at least have forcibly passed the message to the public, and hence to my family, that I was kidnapped. But I didn't do it, and I have no explanation for why not. Maybe, had I known what I know today, I would have attempted anything that would have defeated the injustice. I would not even have turned myself in to begin with.

After the grocery stop, we took off straight to the airport. There was hardly any traffic due to the holiday; people had retreated peacefully, as usual on this day, to their homes. It had been eight days since I last saw the outside world. It looked bleak: there must have been a dust storm during the day that was just starting to give way in favor of the ocean breeze. It was a situation I had seen a thousand and one times, and I still liked it. It's like whenever the dust storm kills the city, the ocean breeze comes at the end of the day and blows the life back into it, and slowly but surely people start to come out.

The twilight was as amazing and beautiful as it had always been. I pictured my family already having prepared the Iftar fast-breaking food, my mom mumbling her prayers while duly working the modest delicacies, everybody looking for the sun to take its last steps and hide beneath the horizon. As soon as the Muezzin declares, "God is Great" everyone would hungrily grab something to drink. My brothers prefer a quick smoke and a cup of tea before anything; my sisters would drink first. None of my sisters smoke, smoking for a lady in my culture is not appropriate. The only absent person is me, but everybody's heart is with me, everybody's prayers are for me. My family thought it would be only a matter of several days before the government released me; after all, the Mauritanian authorities told my family that I have done nothing, they were just waiting until the Americans would see the truth and let me be. How wrong was my family! How wrong was I to put my faith in a bunch of criminals and put my fate in their country! I didn't seem to have learned anything. But regret didn't seem to help either: the ship had sailed.

The Mercedes was heading soundlessly to the airport, and I was drowned in my daydreams. At the secret gate, the airport police chief was waiting on us as planned. I hated that dark gate! How many innocent souls have been led through that secret gate? I had been through it once, when the U.S. government brought me from Dakar and delivered me to my government twenty months earlier. Arriving at the gate put an end to my dreams about a savior or a miraculous sort of a superman who would stop the car, neutralize the police officers, and carry me home on his wings so I could catch my Iftar in the warmth of my mom's hut. There was no stopping God's plan, and I was complying and subduing completely to his will.

The Airport Police Chief looked rather like a camel herder. He was wearing a worn-out Boubou, the national dress, and an unbuttoned T-shirt.

"I told you I didn't want anybody to be around," said the DSE.

"Everything's alright," the chief said reluctantly. He was lazy, careless, naïve, and too traditional. I don't even think he had a clue about what was going on. He seemed to be a religious, traditional guy, but religion didn't seem to have any influence on his life, considering the wrong conspiracy he was carrying out with the government.

The Muezzin started to sing the amazing Azan declaring the end of the day, and hence the fast. "ALLAH is Great, Allah is great." "I testify there is no God but God," once, twice, and then twice, "I testify Mohamed is the messenger of God." "Come to pray, Come to pray, Come to flourish, Come to flourish," and then, twice, "God is Great" and "There is no God but God." What an amazing message! But guess what, dear Muezzin, I cannot comply with your call, nor can I break my fast. I wondered, Does this Muezzin know what injustice is taking place in this country?

There was no clean place around. All the miserable budget the government had approved for the restoration of the airport had literally been devoured by the agents the government put its trust in. Without saying anything, I went to the least dirty spot and started to perform my prayer. The DSE, his assistant, and the chief joined in. After I was done praying, the DSE offered me water and some sweet buns to break my fast; at that same moment the small business jet hit the runway. I had no appetite anyway, but the arriving plane sealed any need to eat. I knew I was not going to survive without eating, though, so I reached for the water and drank a little bit. I took a piece of the sweet bread and forced it inside my mouth, but the piece apparently landed in a cul-de-sac; my throat conspired against me and closed. I was losing my mind from terror, though I tried to act normally and regain my composure. I was shaking, and kept mumbling my prayers.

The ground crew directed the small airplane toward the Benz. It came to a stop inches away, the door opened, and a dark-skinned man in his late forties stepped down the accommodation ladder with steady steps. He was rather heavy, with one of those big bellies that no amount of tucking can do away with, and had one of those beard and mustache combinations that keeps drowning in anything they drink. Oh Lord, I wouldn't share a drink with one of those people, not even for a million dollars. As soon as I saw the guy, I gave him the name Satan.

When he hit the ground he scanned us standing before him with his fox's eyes. He had a dry, neutral smile, and the habit of tweaking his mustache, and he kept moving his eyes, one wide-opened and the other squinted. I could easily see the shock on his face because he didn't seem to find the person he was looking for, namely me. But you could tell it was not the first time he led an abduction operation: he completely maintained his composure, as if nothing big was happening.

"We've brought people here in bags," his associate Officer Rami told me later in Jordan.

"But how did they survive the trip without suffocating?"

"We make an opening for the nose to facilitate a continuous oxygen supply," Officer Rami said. I don't know about the bags story, but I do know cases of kidnapping terrorist suspects to Jordan.

Satan was expecting his prey to be shackled, blindfolded,

earmuffed. But me, standing before him in civilian clothes with eyes wide open like any human being, that struck him. No, that is not the way a terrorist looks—especially a high-level terrorist who was supposedly the brain behind the Millennium Plot.

"Hi," he said; he obviously wasn't used to the beautiful Muslim greeting, "Peace be with you!" He quickly exchanged words with the DSE, though they didn't understand each other very well. The DSE wasn't used to the Jordanian dialect, nor was the Jordanian guest used to the Mauritanian way of speaking. I had an advantage over both of them: there is hardly any Arabic dialect I don't understand because I used to have many friends from different cultural backgrounds.

"He said he needs fuel," I explained to the DSE. I was eager to let my predator know *I am, I am.* I took my bag and showed my readiness to board, and that's when Satan realized that I was the meager "terrorist" he was sent to pick up.

The DSE handed him my passport and a thin folder. At the top of the accommodation ladder there were two young men dressed in Ninja-like black suits who turned out to be the guards who were going to watch me during the longest eleven-hour trip of my life. I quickly spoke to the DSE in a manner I knew Satan wouldn't understand.

"Tell him not to torture me."

"This is a good guy; I would like you to treat him appropriately!" the DSE said vaguely.

"We're going to take good care of him," answered Satan in an ambiguous statement.

The DSE gave me some food to eat during the flight. "No need, we have enough food with us," Satan said. I was happy, because I liked the Middle Eastern cuisine.

I took the seat that was reserved for me, and the leader of the operation ordered a thorough search while the plane was rolling on the runway. All they found was my pocket Koran, which they gave back to me. I was blindfolded and earmuffed, but the blindfold was taken away to allow me to eat when the plane reached its regular altitude. As much as I knew about the basics of telecommunication tools, I was terrorized when they put on the earphone-like earmuffs: I thought it was a new U.S. method to suck intels out of your brain and send them directly to a main computer which analyzes the information. I wasn't worried about what they would suck out of my brain, but I was worried about the pain I may suffer due to electrical shocks. It was silly, but if you get scared you are not you anymore. You very much become a child again.

The plane was very small, and very noisy. It could only fly for three to three-and-a-half hours, and then it had to take fuel. "They are in Cyprus," the DSE told me several hours before their arrival in Nouakchott; I figured the return would be by the same route, because such crimes have to be perfectly coordinated with the conspiring parties.

Satan offered me a meal. It looked good, but my throat was stiff and I felt like I was trying to swallow rough stones. "Is that all?" Satan wondered.

"I am alright, Hajji," I said. Hajji literally means somebody who has performed the pilgrimage to Mecca, but in the Middle East you respectfully refer to anybody you don't know as Hajji. In Jordan they even called every detainee Hajji in order to keep the names secret.

"Eat, eat, enjoy your food!" Satan said, trying to give me some comfort to eat and stay alive.

"Thanks, Hajji, I've eaten enough."

"Are you sure?"

"Yes, Hajji," I replied. Satan looked at me, forcing the most dishonest, sardonic smile I ever saw, exactly like he did when he stepped down out of the plane back in Nouakchott airport.

The guards collected the garbage and placed the tray table in the upright position. I had two of them watching me, one right behind my neck, and the second sitting next to me. The guy behind me was staring at me the whole time; I doubt he ever blinked his eyes. He must have been through some rough training.

"In my training, I almost lost my composure," one young recruit later told me in the Jordanian prison. "During the training, we took a terrorist and slew him in front of all students. Some couldn't take it and burst out crying," he continued.

"Where did you guys train?" I asked him.

"An Arabic country, I cannot tell you which one." I felt nauseous, but tried my best to act in front of the guy as if everything were normal and he were a hero. "They want us to have no mercy with terrorists. I can kill a terrorist who is running away without wasting more than one bullet," he demonstratively claimed.

"Oh, that's great! But how do you know he is a terrorist? He might be innocent," I gauged.

"I don't care: if my boss said he is a terrorist, he is. I am not allowed to follow my personal judgment. My job is to execute." I felt so bad for my people and the level of cruelty and gruesomeness they have fallen into. Now I was standing for real before somebody who is trained to kill blindly whomever he is ordered to. I knew he wasn't lying, because I met a former Algerian soldier once who was seeking asylum in Germany, and he told me how gruesomely they dealt with the Islamists, too.

"During an ambush, we captured a sixteen-year-old teenager, and on the way to the jail our boss stopped, took him off the truck, and shot him dead. He didn't want him in jail, he wanted revenge," he told me.

I wondered why there was so much vigilance, given that I was shackled and there were two guards, two interrogators, and two pilots. Satan asked the guard who was sitting beside me to empty his seat, and he sat beside me and started to interrogate me.

"What's your name?"

"Mohamedou Ould Salahi."

"What's your nickname?"

"Abu Musab."

"What other nicknames do you have?"

"None!"

"Are you sure?"

"Yes, Hajji!" I wasn't used to an interrogator from the Sham region, and I had never heard that accent in such a scary way. I find the Sham accent one of the sweetest in the Arabic language, but Satan's accent was not sweet. He was just evil: the way he moved, spoke, looked, ate, everything. During our short conversation we were almost shouting, but we could hardly hear one another because of the extremely loud whining of the engines. I hate small planes. I always feel as if I'm on the wing of a demon when I travel in them.

"We should stop the interrogation and resume it later on," he said. Thank you, old engines! I just wanted him out of my face. I knew there was no way around him, but just for the time being.

At around midnight GMT on Wednesday, November 28, 2001, we landed in Cyprus. Was it a commercial airport or the military airport? I don't know. But Cyprus is one of the Mediterranean paradises on Earth.

The interrogators and the two pilots put their jackets on and left the plane, most likely for a break. It looked like it had been raining; the ground looked wet, and a light drizzle was caressing the ground. Every once in a while I stole a quick glimpse through the small, blurry window. The breeze outside gave away the presence of a cold winter on the island. I felt some noises that shook the small plane; it must have been the fuel cistern moving. I drowned in my daydreams.

I was thinking, Now the local police will suspect the plane, and hopefully search it. I am lucky because I'm breaking the law by transiting through a country without a transit visa, and I'll be arrested and put in jail. In the prison, I'll apply for asylum and stay in this paradise. The Jordanians can't say anything because they are guilty of trying to smuggle me. The longer the plane waits, the better my chances are to be arrested.

How wrong I was! How comforting a daydream can be! It was my only solace to help me ignore and forget the evilness that surrounded me. The plane indeed waited long enough, about an hour, but there was no searching the plane. I was nonexistent in the passengers' list that the Jordanians gave to the local authorities. I even thought I saw police in thick black uniforms coming near the plane, but I was not to be spotted because I was sandwiched between two seats and had to keep my head down, so I looked like a small bag. I might be wrong though, and just saw them because I wanted the police to come and arrest me.

Satan, his associate, and the two pilots came back and we took off. The pilots switched places. I saw the fat pilot sitting in front of Satan; he was almost as broad as he was tall. Satan started a conversation with him. Although I couldn't hear the talk, I assumed it to be a friendly discussion between two mature men, which was good. Satan grew tired like everybody else, except for the young guard who kept his never-blinking eyes pointed on me. Every once in a while he made a comment like, "Keep your head down!" and "Look down," but I kept forgetting the rules. I had the feeling that this would be my last flight, because I was certain I wouldn't make it through the torture. I thought about every member of my family, even my far nephews and nieces and my in-laws. How short is this life! In a blink of an eye, everything is gone.

I kept reading my Koran in the dim light. My heart was pounding as if it wanted to jump out of my mouth. I barely understood anything of what I was reading; I read at least 200 or 300 pages unconsciously. I was prepared to die, but I never imagined it would be this way. Lord have mercy on me! I think hardly anybody will meet death the way he or she imagined. We human beings take everything into consideration except for death; hardly anybody has death on his calendar. Did God really predestinate for me to die in Jordan at the hands of some of the most evil people in the world? But I didn't really mind being killed by bad people; before God they will have no case, I was thinking.

A fake peace dominated the trip between Cyprus and my unknown present destination. The bandits seemed to be exhausted from the previous day trip from Amman to Nouakchott, and that was a blessing for me. At around 4 a.m. GMT on Thursday, November 29, the plane started to lose altitude again, and finally landed in a place I didn't know. I think it was an Arabic country somewhere in the Middle East, because I think I spotted signs in Arabic through the small windows when I stole a quick glimpse off my guarding demon. It was still nighttime, and the weather seemed to be clear and dry; I didn't see any signs of winter.

This time I did not hope for the police to search the airplane, because Arabic countries are always conspiring with each other against their own citizens. What treason! Nonetheless, any leak of information wouldn't hurt. But I didn't give that daydream a second thought. We didn't stay long, though we went through the same procedure, Satan and his two pilots going for a short break, and the same noises of taking on fuel that I heard in Cyprus. The plane took off to its final destination, Amman, Jordan. I don't think that we made any more stops, though I kept passing out and coming to until we arrived in Jordan.

Over 90 percent of Jordanians are Muslim. For them, as for all Muslims from the Middle East, fasting during Ramadan is the most important religious service. People who don't fast are resented in the society, and so many people fast due to social pressure even though they don't believe in religion. In Mauritania, people are much more relaxed about fasting, and less relaxed about prayer.

"Take your breakfast," said the guard. I think I had fallen asleep for a moment.

"No, thanks."

"It's your last chance to eat before the fast begins."

"No, I'm OK."

"Are you sure?"

"Yes, Hajji." They started to eat their breakfast, chewing like cows; I could even hear them through my earmuffs. I kept stealing glimpses toward the small windows until I saw the first daylight prying the darkness open.

"Hajji, I'd like to perform my prayer," I said to the guard. The guard had a little conversation with Satan, who ordered him to take off one of my earmuffs.

"There is no opportunity to pray here. When we arrive, you and I are going to pray together," said Satan. I was sort of comforted, because if he prays that was a sign that he was a believer, and so he wouldn't possibly hurt his "brother" in belief. And yet he didn't seem to have knowledge about his religion. Prayer must be performed on time in the best manner you can, at least in your heart. You cannot postpone it except for the reasons explained in the Islamic scriptures. In any case, the promised prayer with Satan never took place.

FOUR

Jordan

November 29, 2001–July 19, 2002

The Hospitality of My Arab Brothers...Cat and Mouse: ICRC vs. Jordanian Intel...The Good News: I Supposedly Attempted to Kill the Mauritanian President... Bodybuilding Center: What I Know Kills Me...Unjust Justice

Thursday, November 29, 2001, around 7:00 a.m. local time.

The small plane clumsily started to fight its way through the cloudy and cold sky of Amman. We finally hit the ground and came to a standstill. Everybody was eager to get the hell out of the plane, including me.

"Stand up," said one the guards, taking off the metal handcuffs that had already built a ring around my wrists. I was relieved, and sat silently talking to myself. "Look, they're friendly. They just wanted to make sure that you didn't do anything stupid in the plane; now that we arrived, there is no need for cuffs or earmuffs." How wrong I was! They just took the handcuffs off in order to handcuff me again behind my back and put on bigger earmuffs and a bag over my head, covering my neck. My heart started to pound heavily, which raised my blood pressure and helped me to stand steadier on my feet. I started to mumble my prayers. This was the first time that I got treated this way. My pants started to slip down my legs because I was so skinny and had been virtually without food for at least a week.

Two new, energetic guards dragged me out of the plane. I twisted my feet when I reached the ladder; I couldn't see anything, nor did the stupid guards tell me anything. I fell face down, but the guards caught me before I hit the ladder.

"Watch out!" said Officer Rami, my future interrogator, to the guards. I memorized his voice, and when he later started to interrogate me, I recognized it from that day. I now knew that I had to step down the ladder until my feet hit the ground, and an ice-cold winter breeze hit my whole body. My clothes were not designed for this weather. I was wearing the worthless, made-in-a-cheap-country clothes I got from the Mauritanian authorities.

One of the guards silently helped my feet get into the truck that was parked inches away from the last step of the ladder. The guards squeezed me between them in the back seat, and off took the truck. I felt comforted; it was warm inside the truck, and the motor was quiet. The chauffeur mistakenly turned the radio on. The female DJ voice struck me with her Sham accent and her sleepy voice. The city was awakening from a long, cold night, slowly but surely. The driver kept accelerating and hitting the brakes suddenly. What a bad driver! They must have hired him just because he was stupid. I was moving back and forth like a car crash dummy.

I heard a lot of horns. It was the peak time for people who were going to work. I pictured myself at this very same time back home, getting ready for work, enjoying the new day, the morning ocean breeze through my open window, dropping my nephews off at their respective schools. Whenever you think life is going in your favor, it betrays you.

After about 40 or 45 minutes of painful driving, we took a turn, entered a gate, and stopped. The guards dragged me out of the truck. The cold breeze shook my whole body, though only for a very short time before we entered the building and I was left near a heater. I knew how the heater looked even with my eyes closed; I just sensed it was like the ones I had in Germany. Later on, I learned from the guards that the prison facility was built by a Swedish company.

"Do not move," said one of the guards before they both emptied out of the place. I stood still, though my feet could hardly carry me and my back hurt so bad. I was left there for about 15 or 20 minutes before Officer Rami grabbed me by the back of my collar, almost choking me to death. Officer Rami pushed me roughly up the stairs. I must have been on the ground floor, and he pushed me to the first.

Legend has it that Arabs are among the most hospitable folks on the face of the earth; both friends and enemies are unanimous about that. But what I would be experiencing here was another kind of hospitality. Officer Rami pushed me inside a relatively small room with a desk, a couple of chairs, and another guy sitting behind the desk and facing me. He was a heavy and lazy-looking man in his late twenties who repeated every task many times over. Like the rest of the guards, he was dressed in a Jordanian Army uniform and had a high-and-tight haircut. You could see that he had been doing this work for some time: there were no signs of humanity in his face. He hated himself more than anybody could hate him.

The first thing I saw were two pictures on the wall, the present King Abdullah and his extinguished father Hussein. Such pictures are the proof of dictatorship in the uncivilized world. In Germany I never saw anybody hang the picture of the president; the only time I saw his picture was when I was watching news, or driving around during elections, when they hang a bunch of candidates' pictures. Maybe I'm wrong, but I mistrust anybody who hangs the picture of his president, or any president who wins any elections with more than 80%. It's just ridiculous. On the other wall I read the time on a big hanging clock. It was around 7:30 a.m.

"Take your clothes off!" said the guard. I complied with his order except for my underwear. I was not going to take them off without a fight, no matter how weak it would be. But the guard just handed me a clean, light blue uniform. Jordanians are materially much more advanced and organized than Mauritanians; everything in the prison was modest, but clean and neat. It was the first time I put on a prison uniform in my life. In Mauritania there is no specific uniform, not because Mauritania is a democratic country, but maybe because the authorities are too lazy and corrupt. A uniform is a sign of backwards and communist countries. The only so-called "democratic" country that has this technique of wrapping up detainees in uniforms is the U.S.; the Jordanians have adopted a 100% American system in organizing their prisons.

The young guy behind the table was rather fat. He was acting as a clerk, but he was a horrible one.

"What's your name? What's your address in Amman?"

"I am not from Amman."

"Where the hell are you from?"

"I am from Mauritania," I answered.

"No, I mean where do you live here in Jordan?"

"Nowhere!"

"Did they capture you while transiting through the airport?"

"No, Hajji took me from my country to question me for two days and bring me back." I wanted to make it sound as harmless as possible. Besides, that's what I was told, even though I had the feeling now that I was being lied to and betrayed.

"How do you spell your name?" I spelled out my complete name, but the guy didn't seem to have gone to primary school. He wrote as if with Chinese chopsticks. He kept filling out one form after another and throwing the old ones in the garbage can.

"What have you done?"

"I've done nothing!"

Both burst out in laughter. "Oh, very convenient! You have done nothing but you are here!" I thought, What crime should I say in order to satisfy them?

I presented myself as a person who came all the way from Mauritania to provide intels about my friends. "Hajji told me he needed my help," I said. But then I thought, What a silly answer. If I were going to provide information freely, I could do so in Mauritania. The guards didn't believe me anyway; what criminal benevolently admits to his crime? I felt humiliated because my story sounded weird and untruthful.

In the bureaucratic chaos, the prison's commanding officer took the process in hand. He took my wallet and copied my personal data from my ID. He was a serious looking officer in his late thirties, light blond, Caucasian looking, with a dry face. It was obvious he was married to the cause. During my sojourn in the Dar Al Tawqif wa Tahqiq, the "House for Arrest and Interrogation,"* I kept seeing him working day and night and

---

* In its 2008 report "Double Jeopardy: CIA Renditions to Jordan," Human Rights Watch recorded that "from 2001 until at least 2004, Jordan's General Intelligence Department (GID) served as a proxy jailer for the U.S.

sleeping in the prison. Most of the guards do. They work far from home, and the guards told me their shifts could stretch for several days; during that time they rarely left the facility. I would catch him sneakily trying to look through the bin hole without me noticing him. I'm-Watching-You, as I called him, was an officer in what they call the al Jaish Al Arabi, the Arab Legion. I was thinking, What a masquerade! If this is the protector of us Arabs, we screwed up! As an Arabic saying has it, "Her protector is her assailant."

"Why do they call you guys the Arab Legion?" I asked one of the guards later.

"Because we are supposed to protect the entire Arab world," he responded.

Central Intelligence Agency (CIA), holding prisoners that the CIA apparently wanted kept out of circulation, and later handing some of them back to the CIA." Human Rights Watch reported that MOS and at least thirteen others were sent to Jordan during this period, where they were "held at the GID's main headquarters in Amman, located in the Jandawil district in Wadi Sir. The headquarters, which appear to cover nearly an acre of land, contain a large four-story detention facility that Human Rights Watch visited in August 2007."

Researchers who carried out that visit recorded that "the administrative offices and interrogation rooms are on the second floor of the building, while visiting rooms are on the ground floor. During the period that Human Rights Watch inspected the facility, all of the detainees in custody were held on the second floor. There are also many cells on the ground floor and third floor, however, as well as a small number of cells on the fourth floor, which includes a few collective cells and what the director called the 'women's section' of the facility. In addition, the facility has a basement where many prisoners have claimed that they were brought for the most violent treatment. Prisoners in GID detention at Wadi Sir are kept in single-person cells and are prohibited from speaking with one another, but some have managed to communicate via the back window of their cells. (Each cell faces onto the central courtyard, and has a window looking out on the yard.)" *Double Jeopardy*, 1, 10–11. The Human Rights Watch report is available at http://www.hrw.org/sites/default/files/reports/jordan 0408webwcover.pdf.

"Oh, that's really great," I said, thinking that we'd be just fine if they protected us from themselves.

After they had finished processing me, one of the escorting guards handcuffed me behind my back, blindfolded me, and grabbed me as usual by the back of my collar. We got in the lift and I felt it going up. We must have landed on the third floor. The guard led me through a corridor and took a couple turns before a heavy metal door opened. The guard uncuffed me and took off the blindfold.

I looked as far as my eyes could reach. It was not far: about 8 or 9 feet to a window that was small and high so detainees could not look outside. I climbed up once, but I saw nothing but the round wall of the prison. The prison was in the shape of a circle. The idea was smart, because if you succeeded in jumping out of the window, you would land in a big arena with a 30 or 40 foot concrete wall. The room looked bleak and stark, though clean. There was a wooden bed and an old blanket, a small sheet, and that was about it. The door closed loudly behind me and I was left on my own, tired and scared. What an amazing world! I enjoyed visiting other countries, but not this way.

I performed my ritual wash and tried to pray standing, but there was no way so I opted to pray sitting down. I crawled over to the bed and soon trailed off. Sleep was a torture: as soon as I closed my eyes, the friends I was potentially going to be asked about kept coming to me and talking to me. They scared the hell out of me; I woke up numerous times mumbling their names. I was in a no-win situation: if I stayed awake, I was so dead tired, and if slept I got terrorized by nightmares to the point that I screamed out loud.

Around 4:30 p.m., the guard on watch woke me up for food. Meals were served from a chariot that goes through the corridor from cell to cell, with the cook passing by again later to collect the empty plates. Detainees were allowed to keep one cup for tea and juice. When the cook showed up for my plate, he saw that I hardly ate anything.

"Is that all?" As much as I liked the food, my throat conspired against me. The depression and fear were just too much.

"Yes, thanks."

"Well, if you say so!" The cook quickly collected my plate and off he rolled. In jail it's not like at home; in jail if you don't eat, it's OK. But at home your parents and your wife do their best to persuade you. "Honey, just eat a little bit more. Or should I prepare you something else? Please, just do it for my sake. Why don't you tell me what you'd like to eat?" In both cases, though, you more than likely won't eat more—in jail because they scare the hell out of you, and at home because you're spoiled. It's the same way when you feel sick. I remember a very funny case when I was really hurting; it was either head-ache or stomach ache.

"I'm in so much pain! Can you please give me some medication?"

"Fuck you, crybaby," the guard said. I burst into laughter because I remembered how my family would be overreacting if they knew I was sick.

After giving my trash back I went back to sleep. As soon as I closed my eyes I saw my family in a dream, rescuing me from the Jordanians. In the dream I kept telling my family that it was just a dream, but they would tell me, "No, it's for real, you're home." How devastating, when I woke up and found myself in the dimly lit cell! This dream terrorized me for days. "I told you it's a dream, please hold me and don't let me go," I would say. But there was no holding me. My reality was that I was secretly detained in a Jordanian jail and my family could not even possibly know where

I was. Thank God after a while that dream disappeared, though every once in a while I would still wake up crying intensely after hugging my beloved youngest sister.

The first night is the worst; if you make it through that you're more than likely going to make it through the rest. It was Ramadan, and so we got two meals served, one at sunset and the second before the first light. The cook woke me up and served me my early meal. Suhoor is what we call this meal; it marks the beginning of our fasting, which lasts until sunset. At home, it's more than just a meal. The atmosphere matters. My older sister wakes everybody and we sit together eating and sipping the warm tea and enjoying each other's company. "I promise I will never complain about your food, Mom," I was thinking to myself.

I still hadn't adjusted to Jordanian time. I wasn't allowed to know the time or date, but later when I made friends among the guards they used to tell me what time it was. This morning I had to guess. It was around 4:30 a.m., which meant around 1:30 a.m. back home. I wondered what my family was doing. Do they know where I am?* Will God show them my place? Will I ever see them again? Only Allah knows! The chances looked very low. I didn't eat a lot, and in fact the meal was not that big; a pita bread, buttermilk, and small pieces of cucumber. But I ate more than I did the night before. I kept reading the Koran in the dim light; I wasn't able to recite because my brain was not working properly. When I thought it must be dawn I prayed, and as soon as I finished the Muezzin started to sing the

---

* In fact, it would be almost a year before MOS's family learned where he was—and only because a brother in Germany saw an article in *Der Spiegel* in October 2002 that reported MOS was in Guantánamo. See Editor's Introduction to the First Edition, page 384, and "From Germany to Guantanamo: The Career of Prisoner No. 760," *Der Spiegel*, October 29, 2008.

Azan, his heavenly, fainting, sleepy, hoarse voice awakening in me all kind of emotions. How could all those praying believers possibly accept that one of their own is buried in the Darkness of the Dar Al Tawqif wa Tahqiq.

There are actually two Azans, one to wake people to eat the last meal, and the other to stop eating and go to pray. It sounds the same; the only difference is that in the last one the Muezzin says, "Prayer is better than sleeping." I redid my prayers once more and went to bed to choose between being terrorized while awake or asleep. I kept switching between both, as if I were drunk.

That second day passed without big events. My appetite didn't change. One of the guards gave me a book to read. I didn't like it because it was about philosophical differences between all kinds of religions. I really needed a book that would give me comfort. I wished we had a little more peace in the world. I was between sleeping and waking at around 11 p.m. that evening when the guards shouted "Tahgig!" "Interrogation!" and opened the door of my cell.

"Hurry up!" I froze and my feet numbed, but my heart pumped so hard that I jumped off my bed and complied with the order of the guard. The escort guards handcuffed me behind my back and pushed me toward the unknown. Since I was blindfolded I could think about my destination undisturbed, though the pace of the escorting guard was faster than my anticipation. I felt the warmth of the room I entered. When you're afraid you need warmth.

The guard took off both the handcuffs and the blindfold. I saw a big blue machine like the ones in airports for scanning luggage, and some other object to measure height and weight. How relieved I was! They were just going about taking the traditional prisoner data like fingerprints, height, and weight.

Although I knew there was no getting around the interrogation session, I both wanted to get through it as soon as possible and was so afraid of that session. I don't know how to explain it, it might not make sense, I'm just trying to explain my feelings then the best way I can.

Another day passed. The routine was no different than the days before, though I gathered one vital piece of information: the number of my cell. After the Iftar fast-breaking meal, the guards would start calling a number, a door would open loudly, and you could hear the footsteps of the taken-away detainees. I figured they were being taken away for interrogation. I imagined I heard the guards shouting my cell number about a hundred times, and after each I went to the toilet and performed a ritual wash. I was just so paranoid. Finally, around 10 p.m. on Saturday, a guard shouted "Tahgig!" for real.* I quickly went to the bathroom. Not that I needed to, I really hadn't drunk anything and I had already urinated about half a gallon, but the urge was there. What was I going to urinate, blood?

"Hurry up, we don't have time," said the guard who stood at the opened heavy metal door. Later on, I learned that 8 p.m. to 1 a.m. was the prime time for interrogations, with the heaviest traffic of detainees being moved to and from the interrogation rooms. The sergeant handcuffed and blindfolded me, and pushed me off. We took the lift and went one floor down, took a couple of turns, and entered a new area; a door opened and I went down a step. The odor of cigarette smoke hit me. It was the interrogation area, where they smoke relentlessly, like an old train. It's disgusting when the smoke keeps adding up and dominates the odor of a house.

---

* MOS arrived in Jordan on Thursday, November 29, so it is now the evening of Saturday, December 1, 2001.

The area was remarkably quiet. The escorting guard dropped me against a wall and retreated.

"What people did you send to Chechnya?" an interrogator named Abu Raad shouted at a detainee in English.

"I ain't sent nobody," responded the detainee in broken Arabic, with an obvious Turkish accent. I right away knew the setup: This interrogation was meant for me.

"Liar," shouted Abu Raad.

"I ain't lying," the guy responded in Arabic, although Abu Raad kept speaking his loose English.

"I don't care if you have a German or American passport, you're going to tell me the truth," said Abu Raad. The setup fit perfectly, and was meant to terrorize me even more. And even though I knew right away it was a setup, it worked.

"Hi, Abdallah," said Abu Raad.

"Hi," I responded, feeling his breath right in front of my face. I was so terrorized that I hadn't realized what he was saying.

"So your name *is* Abdallah," he concluded.

"No!"

"But you responded when I called you Abdallah," he argued. I found it idiotic to tell him that I was so terrorized that I didn't realize what name he called me.

"If you look at it, we all are Abdallah," I correctly answered. Abdallah means "God's servant" in Arabic. But I actually knew how Abu Raad came up with that name. When I arrived in Montreal, Canada, on November 26, 1999, my friend Hasni introduced me to his roommate Mourad by my given name. Later on I met another Tunisian who I'd happened to see when I visited the year before. He called me Abdallah by mistake, and I responded because I found it impolite to correct him. Since then Mourad had called me Abdallah, and I found it cool. I wasn't trying to deceive Mourad or anyone; after all, Mourad had keys to our common mailbox and always collected my official mail, which obviously bore my given name.

That was the story of the name. Obviously the Americans tasked the Jordanians with investigating why I took the name Abdallah in Canada, but the Jordanians understand the recipe far more than Americans, and so they completely ignored this part of the interrogation.

"Do you know where you are?" asked Abu Raad.

"In Jordan," I responded. He was obviously shocked. I shouldn't have been informed about my destination, but the Mauritanian interrogator must have been so angry that he didn't exactly follow the orders of the Americans. The initial plan was to send me from Mauritania to Jordan blindfolded and not inform me about my destination, in order to plant as much fear and terror in my heart as possible to break me. But as soon as I answered the question, Abu Raad knew that this part of the plan was broken, and so he took off my blindfold right away and led me inside the interrogation room.

It was a small room, about 10 x 8 feet, with an old table and three weathered chairs. Abu Raad was in his late thirties or early forties, Palestinian, with a belly that had already started to give in to gravity. His assistant, Officer Rami, was a younger, taller, and probably smarter version of Abu Raad. He was obviously the type who is ready to do the dirty side of any job. He also looked Palestinian. I scanned both back and forth and wondered about these guys. The whole problem of terrorism was caused by the aggression of Israel against Palestinian civilians, and the fact that the U.S. is backing the Israeli government in its mischiefs. When the Israelis took over Palestine under the fire of the British Artillery, the invasion resulted in a mass migration of the locals. Many of them ended up in neighboring countries, and Jordan received the lion's share; more than 50 percent of Jordanians are of Palestinian origin. To me, these interrogators just didn't fit in the vests they were wearing: it didn't make sense that Palestinians would work for Americans to defeat the people who are supposedly helping them. I knew that these two interrogators standing before me didn't represent any moral values, and didn't care about human beings' lives. I found myself between two supposedly fighting parties, both of which considered me an enemy; the historical enemies were allied to roast me. It was really absurd and funny at the same time.

Abu Raad and his cohorts played a vital role in the Americans' War against Terrorism. He was charged with interrogating the kidnapped individuals the U.S. delivered to Jordan and assigning them to the different members of his team. He also personally came to GTMO to interrogate individuals on behalf of the U.S.

Abu Raad opened a medium-sized binder; it turned out to be a file on me that the U.S. had turned over to the Jordanians. He started to ask me questions that were not related to each other. It was the first time I ever experienced this technique, the goal of which is to quickly bring the liar into contradiction. But Abu Raad obviously was not briefed enough about my case and the history of my interrogation: it wouldn't have mattered whether I was lying or telling the truth, because I had been questioned so many times about the exact same things by different agencies from different countries. Should I have lied, I would have been able to lie again and again and again, because I had had enough time to straighten my lies. But I hadn't lied to him — nor did he doubt my truthfulness.

First he showed me the picture of the Turkish detainee he had been interrogating earlier, and said "If you tell me about this guy, I am going to close your case and send you home." Of course he was lying.

I looked at the photo and honestly answered, "No, I don't know him." I am sure the guy was asked the same question about me, and he must have answered the same because there was no way that he knew me.

Officer Rami was sitting on Abu Raad's left and recording my answers. "Do you drink tea?" Abu Raad asked me.

"Yes, I like tea." Abu Raad ordered the tea guy to bring me a cup, and I got a big, hot cup of tea. When the caffeine started to mix with my blood I got hyper and felt so comforted. Those interrogators know what they are doing.

"Do you know Ahmed Ressam?" asked Abu Raad. I had been asked about Ahmed Ressam a thousand and one times, and I tried everything I could to convince interrogators that I don't know that guy: if you don't know somebody, you just don't know him, and there is no changing it. Even if they torture you, they will not get any usable information. But for some reason the Americans didn't believe that I didn't know him, and they wanted the Jordanians to make me admit it.

"No, I don't know him," I answered.

"I swear to Allah you know him," he shouted.

"Don't swear," I said, although I knew that taking the Lord's name in vain is like sipping coffee for him. Abu Raad kept swearing. "Do you think I am lying to you?"

"No, I think you forgot." That was too nicely put, but the fact that the Americans didn't provide the Jordanians with any substantial evidence tied the hands of the Jordanians mightily. Yes, Jordanians practice torture on a daily basis, but they need a reasonable suspicion to do so. They don't just jump on anybody and start to torture him. "I am going to give you pen and paper, and I want you to write me your resumé and the names of all of your friends," he said, closing the session and asking the guard to take me back to my cell.

The worst was over; at least I thought so. The escorting guards were almost friendly when they handcuffed and blindfolded me. There is one common thing among prison guards, whether they are American, Mauritanian, or Jordanian: they all reflect the attitude of the interrogators. If the interrogators are happy the guards are happy, and if not, then not.

The escorting guards felt some freedom to talk to me. "Where are you from?"

"Mauritania."

"What are you doing in Jordan?"

"My country turned me over."

"Are you kidding me?"

"No, I'm serious."

"Your country is fucked up." In the Jordanian Prison, as in Mauritania and GTMO, it was extremely forbidden for the guards to interact with detainees. But hardly anybody followed the rules.

"You are starving, man, why don't you eat?" one of the escorting guards asked me. He was right. The shape of my bones was clear, and anybody could tell how serious my situation was.

"I am only going to eat if I get back home. I'm not interested in prison food. I'm interested in my mom's food," I answered.

"God willing, you're going to get out, but for the time being you got to eat." I don't want to make him look good, his type of job already defines his personality, but he felt that his country was not just. I needed any comforting word, and so far he had done a good job with me. Other guards joined us in the corridor and asked him where I'm from.

They opened the door to my stark, dark cell. I felt as though a big burden was taken off my back. "It's only a matter of days, and then they'll send me back home. The DSE was right," I thought. The Jordanians were as confused about the case the U.S. had given them as I was. The U.S. government obviously hadn't given any substantial material to help the Jordanians to do their dirty job. The painful fear started to diminish, and I started to feel like eating.

Sneaky I'm-Watching-You appeared at the bin hole of my cell and gave me thirty numbered pieces of paper. The coordination between the interrogators and guards was perfect. I immediately wrote both assignments. I was tasked by Abu Raad with writing the names of all my friends, but that was ridiculous: I had so many acquaintances that it would be impossible to include them in less than a big book. So I completed a list of my closest friends and a traditional resumé, using about ten pages. For the first time I had some relatively good sleep that night.

Some time in the next couple of days I'm-Watching-You picked up the written materials and the empty papers as well. He counted the papers thoroughly.

"Is that all you have to write?"

"Yes, Sir!" I'm-Watching-You had been working day and night, and all he was doing was checking on detainees through the bin holes. Most of the time I didn't notice him. Once he caught me having a good time with a guard and he took me and interrogated me about what we were talking about. As to the guard, he disappeared and I never saw him again.

"Put your stuff together," a guard said, waking me in the morning. I grabbed my blanket, my Koran, and the one library book I had. I was so happy because I thought I was being sent home.

The guard made me hold my stuff and blindfolded me. They didn't send me home; instead I found myself locked in the cellar, in a communal cell close to the prison kitchen. The cell there was not clean. It seemed to have been abandoned for a long time. I still wanted to believe in good intentions, and I thought this was the transfer cell for detainees before their release. I was so tired and the cell was so cold that I went to sleep.

Around 4:30 p.m. Iftar was served, and I slowly came to life. I noticed an old paper on the door with the rules of the prison. The guards had clumsily forgotten to tear it off. I wasn't supposed to read the rules, but since nobody is perfect, I had the chance to discover something. The rules stated, among other things, (1) You are only allowed to smoke if you are cooperating; (2) Talking to the guards is forbidden; (3) the ICRC visits the prison every 14 days; (4) Do not talk to the ICRC about your political case.* I was happy, because I would at least be able to send letters to my family, but I missed a vital point: I had been taken temporarily to the cellar to hide me from the ICRC in a Cat-and-Mouse game that lasted eight months, my entire stay in Jordan.

Every fourteen days, the guards would consistently move me from my cell to the cellar, where I would spend a couple of days before they brought me back to my cell. When I discovered the trick, I explicitly asked my interrogator Rami and his boss Abu Raad to see the ICRC.

"There is no ICRC here. This is a Military prison," he lied.

"I have seen the clauses of the Rules, and you're hiding me in the cellar every 14 days to prevent me from meeting the Red Cross."

---

* The ICRC is the International Committee of the Red Cross, which has a mandate under the Geneva Conventions to visit prisoners of war, civilians interned during conflicts, and others detained in situations of violence around the world. An internationally acknowledged purpose of these visits is to ensure humane treatment and deter and prevent abuse.

Officer Rami looked at me firmly. "I am protecting you! And you are not going to see the ICRC." I knew then that there was no changing their minds, and Rami himself couldn't even decide the issue. It was way above him. The conspiracy between Mauritania, the U.S., and Jordan to commit the crime was perfect. If my involvement in terrorism were cemented, I would be executed and the party would be over, and who was to know what had happened?

"I'd like to see the Mauritanian Ambassador," I asked the interrogator.

"Impossible."

"OK, what about Mauritanian Intel?" I asked.

"What do you want with them?"

"I would like to ask them about the reason for my incarceration in Jordan. At least you know that I have done nothing against your country."

"Look, your country is a good friend of ours, and they turned you over to us. We can do anything we like with you, kill you, arrest you indefinitely, or release you if you admit to your crime." Officer Rami both lied and told the truth. Arab countries are not friends. On the contrary, they hate each other. They never cooperate; all they do is conspire against each other. To Mauritania, Jordan is worthless, and vice-versa. However, in my case the U.S. compelled them both to work together.

I tried so many times to contact my family but to no avail, and then I washed my hands of the evils and I prayed to God to take care of my family and make them know where I was. In time, I noticed that I was not the only hidden package: between one and three other detainees were subject to the cellar operation at any one time, and the numbers kept changing as time went by. My whole time in Jordan, I was always in isolation, of course. But I could tell whether there were detainees in the neighboring cells, based on the movements of the food chariot, the guards, and the movement of detainees.

For a while my neighbors were two courageous boys. Although talking was forbidden, those two boys were always shouting, "God's help is coming soon. Remember, God is on our side, and Satan is on theirs!" No matter what the guards did to them, they kept solacing the other detainees and reminding them of God's inevitable relief. You could tell from the accent that they were Jordanians, which made sense, since the locals are more likely to be protected by their families than foreigners. Nonetheless, I have no doubt those boys suffered for what they did.

In that cold, dark section of the Intelligence prison, I was the only constant in my neighborhood; the cells next to me kept changing owners. At one point, my next-door neighbor happened to be a young Lebanese nitwit who kept crying and refusing to eat. His story, according to the guards, went like this: He came to Jordan from Lebanon to have some fun. When he bumped into a routine police patrol in downtown Amman, they found an AKM-47 in his trunk and arrested him. Now, having a gun on you in Lebanon is not a big deal, but in Jordan it is forbidden to carry weapons. Taken to jail, the young Lebanese suspect was losing his mind. He kept crying and refusing his food for at least two weeks until his release. Oh, what a relief for me, when they released him! I felt so bad for him. I am sure he learned his lesson, and will think twice about having a weapon in his trunk the next time he comes to Jordan.

Next came a young Jordanian. He had been sentenced to one year, and at the end of the year he went crazy. He kept shouting, "I need to see my interrogator!" When I asked the guards why he was doing this, they answered, "Because his sentence is over, but they won't let him go." Sometimes he would start to sing loudly, and sometimes he shouted at the guards, asking for a cigarette. I don't blame him: unless you have nerves of steel, chances are you'll lose your mind in Jordanian custody. And after him, my neighbor was an older Palestinian who kept coughing the whole time. "He is very old," a guard told me. "Why did they arrest him?" I wondered.

"Wrong place, wrong time," the guard answered. The older man was always asking for more food and smokes. After a couple of weeks, he was released. I was happy for everybody released from that crazy facility.

It is just amazing that the FBI trusts the Jordanians more than the other American intelligence agencies. When I turned myself in in the fall of 2001, the FBI confiscated my hard disk, and when they sent me to Jordan, they sent the contents of my hard disk to Jordan, too. The DoD has been trying for years to get that disk. It doesn't make sense that the FBI would cooperate more with foreign organizations than the domestic ones, but I do believe that the Intel industry is like any other industry: you buy the best product for the best price, regardless of the country of origin. Do the Jordanians offer the best product in this case? I'm not sure, but they understand the recipe of terrorism more than Americans. Reportedly without the Jordanians in the field, the Americans would never have achieved what they have. However, the Americans over-estimate the capability of the Jordanians by sending them people from all over the world, as if the Jordanians were some super Intel Agency.

"I am going to show you some pictures, you tell me about them," said my interrogator Rami. Lately, he and Abu Talal had been taking turns interrogating me, with Abu Raad the leader. In Jordan, they have a technique in which two interrogators or more interrogate you separately about the same thing, in order to make sure that you don't change your statements. They rarely sat together and interrogated me.

"Alright!" I said. Officer Rami started showing me pictures, and as soon as I saw the first one I knew it was from my computer, or more accurately the computer of the company I had been working for. My heart started to pound, and I felt my saliva getting extremely bitter. My face started to turn as red as an apple. My tongue got heavy and twisted. Not because I had done any crimes with my computer; there was really nothing on the hard drive but my business emails and other related data. I remember having over 1500 email messages, and a whole bunch of pictures. But there is more to it when somebody's freedom is violated.

The PC belonged to a company that trusted me, and the fact that a foreign country such as the U.S. was searching the disk and confiscating material was a big burden for the company. The PC held the financial secrets of a company, which the company wouldn't be willing to share with the rest of the world. Moreover, I worked for a family company and the family hardly drew a line between their company and their private lives, which meant that the computer also contained private familial data the family wouldn't share with the world. On top of that, in the office the PC was a shared station, and anybody in the company could and did use it, so there are a lot of data I didn't know of, though I was 100% sure there was no crime behind it, knowing my colleagues and their dedication to their work and life. I personally had emails with my friends in Germany, some of them aren't even Muslims. But I was more worried about my emails with the Muslim friends, especially any of the ones who had ever financially or spiritually helped the oppressed people in Bosnia or Afghanistan, because their messages would be interpreted evilly. Just put yourself in my shoes and imagine somebody storming your house and trying to mess with your whole private life! Would you welcome such an assault?

I started to answer him to the best of my knowledge, especially about my own pictures. He put the pictures I could identify on one side, and the rest on another side. I explained to him that the PC had been used by several colleagues, one of whom scanned all kinds of different pictures for the clients of the Internet café, including all kinds of private family pictures. I was so mad at myself, my government, the U.S., and the Jordanians because I saw how many people's private lives were being violated. I was also confronted in a later session with a couple emails I interchanged with Christian Ganczarski and Karim Mehdi. The funny thing was that Mehdi sent an email before I got arrested, and the Mauritanian government interrogated me about it and I explained to them with definite evidence that there was no evil in it. As soon as I got back to my office I wrote Mehdi the following email: "Dear Brother! Please stop sending emails, because the Intel are intercepting our emails and giving me a hard time." I openly didn't want any trouble, and so wanted to close any door that would lead in that direction.

"Why did you write Mehdi this email?" asked Officer Rami. I explained the message to him.

"No, it's because you are afraid that the government would learn about your mischiefs with your friend," he commented sillily.

"Well, this message was addressed to both Mehdi and the government. I know my emails are intercepted by the government, and I always assumed that the government got a copy of my email traffic," I said.

"You were using a code when you wrote Mehdi to stop emailing you," he said.

"Well, I am sure you have dealt with coded messages in your career, or you have specialists who help you. Go to them first, before you make up your mind."

"No, I want you to explain the code to me."

"There is no code, what you understand is what I meant." But I had another issue with the Jordanian interrogators: my original emails were in German, and the Americans translated them into English and sent them to the Jordanians, who in their turn translated the English versions into Arabic. Under these circumstances, the original text suffered and the space for evil interpretations widened with every translation.

And there was no end to evil interpretations. In the summer 2001 I was tasked by my company to technologically assist the visit of the Mauritanian President to the city of Tidjikja. The family that employed me is from Tidjikja, so it made sense that their interest lay in the well-being of the city. We installed a small media consulting center that operated over the Internet to transmit the visit of the President in real time. The company took many pictures where my colleagues and I appeared close to the president. In the closest one, the President stood behind my neck wondering at me "magically playing with the computer."

"I can tell, you were plotting to kill the President," said Officer Rami.

I couldn't help laughing. "So why didn't I kill him?"

"I don't know. You tell me," Rami said.

"Look! If I tried to kill my president in my country, it's none of your business, nor that of the Americans. Just turn me over to my country and let them deal with me." I was both angry and hopeful, angry because the U.S. wanted to pin any crime on me, no matter what, and hopeful because they were going to turn me over to my country to suffer the death penalty. The Americans couldn't possibly have dreamt of a better option. But the Jordanians were fishing on behalf of the Americans, and whenever you notice your interrogator fishing, you can be sure that he is bankrupt.

Though he was as evil as he could be, Officer Rami was sort of a reasonable interrogator, and so he never asked me again about the plot on my President, nor about the pictures in my hard disk. And yet I regretted that I didn't act on the suspicion and make myself look guilty in order to get myself extradited back to Mauritania. It was a crazy and desperate idea, and I don't think that the Mauritanians would have played along because they knew for fact I hadn't plotted against the president. But when my situation worsened in the Jordanian prison, I thought about confessing that I had an operation going on in Mauritania, and had hidden explosives. The idea was that I would try to be sent back to Mauritania.

"Don't do that! Just be patient and remember that Allah is watching," one of my guards told me when I asked him for advice. By then I had made a lot of friends among the guards; they brought me the news and taught me about Jordanian culture, the torture methods in the prison, and who's who among the interrogators.

It was categorically forbidden for the guards to interact with the detainees, but they always broke these rules. They recounted the latest jokes to me and offered me cigarettes, which I turned down because I don't smoke. They told me about the other detainees and their cases and also about their own private lives, marriage, children, and the social life in Jordan. I learned almost everything about life in Amman from speaking with them. They also brought me the best books from the library—even the Bible, which I requested because I wanted to study the book that must more or less have shaped the lives of the Americans. In Jordan they have a pretty respectable collection, though some of it is meant as propaganda for the King. The best part about the books was that detainees used them to pass messages back and forth, solacing each other by writing good things inside the book. I didn't know any detainees, but the first thing I always did was to sift through a book looking for messages. I memorized all of them.

The guards were picked mostly from the Bedouin tribes that are known for their historical loyalty to the King, and paid miserable wages, about $430 a month, give or take. Although this wage is among the best in Jordan, a guard can't start a family without another support of his own. But when a guard serves for fifteen years, he has the option of retiring with half of his current wage or continuing with that money plus his usual wage. The guards are part of Jordan's Elite Special Forces, and enjoy all kinds of training overseas. There are no females in the Special Forces.

The guards were responsible for moving detainees from one cell to another, to interrogations, to the shower, or to see their parents during the visits that took place on Fridays. I was so frustrated when I had to watch everybody seeing his family, while week after week I was deprived of that right. Lower ranking guards were responsible for the watch, and one was assigned for the grocery that took place every Saturday. The responsible grocery guard would go cell to cell with a list, writing down what each detainee wished to buy. You could buy juice, milk, candy, underwear, a towel, and that was about it; if you had enough money you would get what you ordered, and if not then not. I had about $87 on me when I was sent to Jordan, which seemed to have been enough for my modest groceries. One time, when the grocery guard was going around with his list, I spotted my name and my accusation: "Participation in Terrorist attacks."

Every other day the guards offered you a five-minute recreation time. I hardly ever took advantage of it; the fact that I had to be shackled and blindfolded was just not worth it. Every once in a while detainees got their hair cut, and every Sunday the guards gave us cleaning materials to mop our cells, and they mopped the floor outside. The jail was not dirty.

The prison was run by three individuals: the director of the prison, or the warden, who was a Bedouin, and his two assistants who used to make the rounds. They played a role similar to the one the Joint Task Force played in GTMO Bay. They are supposedly independent from the Intel community, but in practice both work together and collect Intels, each with its own methods. The director was a very big guy who dressed proudly in his Bedouin-civilian suits. He passed by every morning and asked every single detainee, "How are you doing? Need anything?" He always woke me up asking me the same question.

During my entire eight months in the Jordanian prison I asked him once for a water bottle, which he brought me. I wanted to put the ice-cold water I got from the faucet on the heater in order to warm it up so I could take care of my own hygiene. I do think that it was good thing for him to check on detainees. However, the chances were really zero that detainees were going to fix any problems with the help of a director who also was actively taking part in torture. The Director made sure that everybody got three meals a day, breakfast around 7 a.m., lunch around 1 p.m., mostly chicken and rice, and dinner, a light meal with tea.

The two assisting officers were continually patrolling through the corridor and checking on everybody, including whether the guards were following the rules. One of the officers was responsible for what they call External Operations, such as capture and house searches.

Then there were the interrogators. Jordanian interrogators have been working side-by-side with the Americans since the beginning of the operation baptized the "Global War Against Terrorism," interrogating people both inside and outside Jordan. They have agents in Afghanistan, where they profit from their average Middle Eastern looks. In the beginning the Jordanians were seen as a potential associate for doing the dirty work; the fact that Jordanians widely use torture as a means to facilitate interrogation seemed to impress the American authorities. But there was a problem: the Jordanians don't take anybody and torture him; they must have reason to practice heavy physical torture. As Americans grew hardened in their sins, they started to take the dirty job in their own hands. Nonetheless, being arrested in a Jordanian jail is an irreparable torture already.

I had three interrogators in Jordan: Abu Talal, who interrogated me only a few times; Officer Rami, who did most of the heavy lifting in my case until he told me that as far as he was concerned my case was closed; and Abu Raad, their boss. Besides leading the interrogators' team in Jordan, Abu Raad was also interrogating detainees in GTMO, and most likely in other secret places in Afghanistan and elsewhere, on behalf of the U.S. government. He seems to be widely known in Jordan, as I learned from a Jordanian detainee in GTMO. Abu Raad seemed to be pretty well experienced: he saw my file once and decided it wasn't worth wasting his "precious" time on me, and so he never bothered to see me again. Together, the three had much more knowledge about Jihadi movements than their American counterparts.

"You know, Ould Salahi, your only problem is your time in Canada. If you really haven't done nothing in Canada, you don't belong in jail," concluded Officer Rami after several sessions.

He was a specialist on Afghanistan; he himself had attended the training camps there as an undercover agent during the war against communism. When I was training in Al Farouq in '91, he was working undercover as a student in Khalden.* He questioned me thoroughly about my whole trip to Afghanistan and showed satisfaction with my answers. That was very much his whole job. In the winter of 2001 he was sent, maybe undercover, to Afghanistan and Turkey to help the U.S. capture Mujahideen, and I saw him when he came back in the summer of 2002 with a whole bunch of pictures. Part of his mission was to gather Intels about me from other detainees in Afghanistan, but he didn't seem to have come up with anything. Officer Rami showed me the pictures. I didn't recognize anybody, and felt bad for myself. Why did they show me more than 100 pictures, and I knew none of them? It didn't make sense. Usually, interrogators ask about people that are connected to you. So I decided to recognize at least one picture.

"This is Gamal Abdel Nasser," I said.

---

* MOS trained at the al-Farouq training camp near Khost, Afghanistan, for six weeks in late 1990 and early 1991. At the time, both the al-Farouq and Khalden camps were training al-Qaeda fighters for the conflict with the Soviet-backed government in Kabul. As the appellate court reviewing MOS's habeas case wrote, "When Salahi took his oath of allegiance in March 1991, al-Qaida and the United States shared a common objective: they both sought to topple Afghanistan's Communist government." See http://www.aclu.org/files/assets/2010-4-9-Slahi-Order.pdf; and http://caselaw.findlaw.com/us-dc-circuit/1543844.html.

"You are making fun of me, aren't you?" said Officer Rami angrily.

"No, no, I just thought it looks like him." Nasser is a former Egyptian president who died before I was born.

"These people are from the same gang as you are," Rami said.

"Maybe. But I don't know them," I said. He didn't say much after that; Officer Rami just spoke about his adventure in Afghanistan. "You're courageous," I remarked, to give him fuel for more talk.

"You know, the Americans are using smart weapons that follow their target based on temperature changes. Many brothers have been captured," Officer Rami recounted under the thick cloud of his cigarette smoke.

Officer Rami was aggressive but not violent, except on a few occasions. One happened right near the end of my time in Jordan.*

Boom! He slapped me across the face, and pushed my face against the wall. I was sobbing, maybe more because of frustration than pain.

"You are not a man! I am going to make you lick the dirty floor and tell me your story, beginning from the point when you got out of your mother's vagina," he continued. "You haven't seen nothing yet." He was correct, although he was the biggest liar I ever met. He lied so much that he contradicted himself because he would forget what he had said the last time

---

* At his 2005 ARB hearing, MOS said that his main interrogator in Jordan was "young" and "a very bright guy." He testified that this particular interrogator "struck me twice in the face on different occasions and pushed me against concrete many times because I refused to talk to him," and "threatened me with a lot of torture and...took me to the one room where they torture and there was this guy who was beaten so much he was crying, crying like a child." ARB transcript, 21.

about a specific topic. In order to give himself credibility, he kept swearing and taking the Lord's name in vain. I always wondered whether he thought I believed his garbage, though I always acted as if I did; he would have been angry if I called him a liar. He arrested big al Qaeda guys who talked about me being the bad guy, and he released them a thousand and one times from the prison when they told the truth. The funny thing was that he always forgot that he arrested and released them already.

"I arrested your cousin Abu Hafs and he told me the whole truth. As a matter of fact, he said 'Don't you put your hands on me, and I'm gonna tell you the truth,' and I didn't, and he did. He told me bad things about you. After that I bid him farewell and secretly sent him to Mauritania, where he was going to be interrogated for a couple of weeks and released. But you're different. You keep holding back Intels. I am going to send you to the secret political prison in the middle of the desert. Nobody is gonna give a shit about you." I had to keep listening to this same garbage over and over; the only thing he changed was the dates of arrest and release. In his dreams, he also arrested Abu Zubaydah and other individuals who had supposedly been providing information about me. Good for him; as long as he didn't beat me or attack me verbally I was cool, and would just listen carefully to his Thousand-and-One-Arabian-Nights tales.

"I've just arrived from the U.S., where I interrogated Ahmed Ressam," he obviously lied.

"Well, that's good, because he must have told you that he doesn't know me."

"No, he said he does."

"Well, that's none of your business, right? According to you, I've done crimes against the U.S., so just send me to the U.S. or tell me what have I done against your country," I remarked sharply. I was growing tired of the futile conversation with him, and of trying to convince him that I had nothing to do with Millennium Plot.

"I am not working for the Americans. Some of your friends are trying to hurt my country, and I'm asking you indirect questions as an interrogation technique," Officer Rami lied.

"Which friends of mine are trying to hurt your country?" I wondered.

"I cannot tell you!"

"Since I haven't tried to hurt your country, there's no blaming me. I am not my friends. Go and arrest them and release me." But if you are trying to make sense of things, the interrogation room is not for you. Whenever Officer Rami told me he had arrested somebody, I knew that the guy was still free.

Although he used physical violence against me only twice, he kept terrorizing me with other methods that were maybe worse than physical pain. He put a poor detainee next to my interrogation room, and his colleague started to beat him with a hard object until he burst out crying like a baby. How cheap! That was painful. I started to shake, my face got red, my saliva got as bitter as green persimmon, my tongue as heavy as metal. Those are the symptoms I always suffer when I get extremely scared, and the constant fear didn't seem to harden me. My depression reached its peak.

"Do you hear what's happening next door?"

"Yes."

"Do you want to suffer the same?" I almost said yes. It was so hard for me to helplessly listen to somebody suffering. It's not easy to make a grown-up cry like a baby.

"Why? I am talking to you!" I said, showing a fake composure. After all, the brother next door was also talking to his interrogator. Officer Rami sardonically smiled and continued to smoke his cigarette as if nothing were happening. That night I was very cooperative and quiet; the logical and argumentative human being in me disappeared all of a sudden. Rami knew what he was doing, and he had apparently been doing it for a long time.

He would make me pass through the torture row so I would hear the cries and moans and the shouting of the torturers. I was blessed because the guards kept me blindfolded so I couldn't see the detainees. I was not supposed to see them, nor was I interested in seeing a brother, or actually anybody, suffering. The Prophet Mohamed (Peace be upon him) said, "God tortures whoever tortures human beings," and as far as I understand it, the person's religion doesn't matter.

"I am going to send you to the Shark Pool," Officer Rami threatened me, when I refused to talk to him after he hit me.

"You don't know me. I swear by Almighty God I'll never talk to you. Go ahead and torture me. It will take my death to make me talk, and for your information I'm sorry for every bit of cooperation I have offered in the past," I said.

"First of all, your cooperation was achieved by force. You didn't have a choice. Nor will you in the future: I am going to make you talk," he said.

Officer Rami started to push me against the wall and hit me on the sides of my face, but I didn't feel any pain. I don't think he hit me with his whole strength; the guy looks like a bull, and one real blow from him would have cost me thirty-two teeth. As he was hitting me, he started to ask me questions. I don't remember the questions, but I do remember my answers. There was only one answer.

"*Ana Bari'a,* I am innocent." I drove him crazy, but there was no making me talk.

"I have no time right now, but you're gonna suffer heavily tomorrow, son of a . . . . ." he said, and immediately left the room.

The escort took me back to my cell. It was around midnight; I sat on my prayer mat and started reading the Koran and praying until very late. I could hardly concentrate on what I was reading. I kept thinking, What will it be like in the Shark Pool? I had heard of an electrified pool, I knew they used one in Egypt, but "Shark Pool" sounded terrible.

But the rendezvous came and went without me being taken to the torture place, one day, two days, three days! Nothing happened to me, except for no food, not because they didn't give it to me but because I had no appetite, as always when I get depressed. I learned later from the Jordanian detainee in GTMO who spent fifty days in the same prison that there is no such thing as the Shark Pool, but that they do have other painful methods of torture, like hanging detainees from their hands and feet and beating them for hours, and depriving them from sleep for days until they lose their minds.

"In Jordan they don't torture unless they have evidence," Ibrahim said. "If they knew what I do about you, they wouldn't even have bothered arresting you. The Americans told them to," he continued.

"The torture starts around midnight and finishes around dawn. Everybody takes part, the prison director, the interrogators, and the guards," Ibrahim told me in GTMO. His information was consistent with what I saw. I personally heard beatings, but I don't know whether the detainees were hung up or not when the beating happened. And I witnessed sleep deprivation more than once.

Late one night when I was talking to some of my guard friends, I kept hearing sounds as if some people were performing harsh training with loud voices to get the whole energy out of their body, like in Kung-Fu. I heard heavy bodies hitting the floor. It was just too noisy, and too close to my third-floor cell.

"Are you guys training so late?" I asked one of the guards. Before he could say a word, another guy appeared dressed in Ninja-like suit that covered him from head to toe. The guard looked at him and turned to me, smiling.

"Do you know this guy?" he asked. I forced an official smile.

"No." The new guy took his mask off, and he looked like the devil himself. Out of fear, my smile turned to laughter. "Oh, yes! We know each other," I said.

"Mohamed asks if you guys are training now?" my guard wryly asked the Ninja, mispronouncing my name.

"Yes! Do you want to train with us? We have many detainees enjoying PT," he said sardonically. I knew right away that he meant torture. My laughter faded into a smile, and my smile into fixed lips over my teeth. I didn't want to reveal my disappointment, fear, and confusion.

"No, I'm just fine," I said. The devil resumed his business, and I asked the guard, "Why do they put on the masks for this type of job?"

"They want to protect their identities. In Jordan, you can get killed for doing such things." He was right: most of the detainees were arrested because they know something, not because of crimes, and so they will be released sooner or later. I wished I hadn't known about that mischief; it was just impossible for me to sleep when was I listening to grown-ups crying like babies. I tried to put every object in my ears and around my head but nothing helped. As long as the torture lasted, I couldn't sleep. The good thing was that the torture wasn't every day, and the voices didn't always reach my cell.

In February 2002, the director of Jordan's Antiterrorism

Department was the subject of an assassination plot.* He almost gave his soul back. Somebody planted a time bomb in the chassis of the car of the biggest target of the Islamic movement in Jordan. The bomb was supposed to explode on the way between his home and his office—and it did. But what happened seemed like a miracle. On his way to work, the director felt like buying cigarettes. His driver stopped in front of a store and left to grab a pack of cigarettes. The director felt like going with his chauffeur. As soon as both left the car, the bomb exploded. Nobody was harmed, but the vehicle was history.

The investigation led to a suspect, but the secret police couldn't find him. But the King of the Fight against Terrorism cannot be messed with; suspects must be arrested and the guilty party must be found. Immediately. The Jordanian secret Agency had to have revenge for the big head. The peaceful brother of the suspect was to be taken as a pawn and tortured until his brother turned himself in. Special Forces were sent out, arrested the innocent boy in a crowded place, and beat him beyond belief. They wanted to show people the destiny of a family when one of its members tries to attack the government. The boy was taken to the prison and tortured every day by his interrogator.

"I don't care how long it takes, I am going to keep torturing you until your brother turns himself in," his interrogator said. The family of the boy was given opportunity to visit the boy, not for humane reasons, but because the interrogator wanted the family to see the miserable situation of the boy so they would turn in the suspected son. The family was devastated,

---

* Press reports document an assassination attempt like the one described here, aimed at General Ali Bourjaq, head of Jordan's antiterrorism unit, on February 20, 2002, in Amman. See, e.g., http://www.imra.org.il/story .php3?id=20580.

and soon the information leaked that the suspect was hiding in his family's house. Late that night, an operation stormed the house and arrested him. The next day his brother was released.

"What will you say if somebody asks you about the bruises and injuries I caused you?" the interrogator asked him.

"I'll say nothing!" answered the boy.

"Look, we usually keep people until they heal, but I'm releasing you. You go ahead and file anything you like against me. I did what I got to do to capture a terrorist, and you're free to go." As to his brother, he was taken care of by the director himself: he kept beating him for six straight hours. And that is not to mention what the other interrogators did to satisfy their chief. I learned all this from the guards when I noticed that the prison had become remarkably crowded. Not that I could see anybody, but the food supply shrunk decidedly; they kept moving detainees to and from their cells; whenever detainees were led past my cell the guards closed my bin hole; and I saw the different shifts of guards more frequently than usual. The situation started to improve in the summer 2002.

By then, the Jordanians were basically done with me. When Officer Rami finished my hearing, he handed me my statements. "Read the statements and sign them," he said.

"I don't need to read them, I trust you!" I lied. Why should I read something when I didn't have the option to sign or to refuse? No judge would take into consideration somebody's statements that were coerced in a prison facility such as the Jordanian Military prison.

After about a week Officer Rami took me to interrogation in a nice room. "Your case is closed. You haven't lied. And I thank you for your cooperation. When it comes to me, I am done with you, but it's the decision of my boss when you'll go home. I hope soon."

I was happy with the news; I had expected it, but not that soon.

"Would you like to work for us?" he asked me.

"I'd like to, but I really am not qualified for this type of work," I said, partly lying and partly telling the truth. He tried in a friendly way to convince me, but I, with the most friendliness I could manage, told him that I was way too much of an idiot for Intel work.

But when the Jordanians shared the result of their investigation with the U.S. and sent them the file, the U.S. took the file and slapped the Jordanians in their faces. I felt the anger of Uncle Sam thousands of miles away, when Officer Rami came back into his old skin during the last two months of my incarceration in Jordan. The interrogations resumed. I tried all I could to express myself. Sometimes I talked, sometimes I refused. I hunger-struck for days, but Officer Rami made me eat under threat of torture. I wanted to compel the Jordanians to send me back home, but I failed. Maybe I wasn't hardcore enough.

GTMO

SECRET//NOFORN 324 **PROTECTED**

They had no reason to doubt me b/c I never lied to them
and ███ made sure to get me the ███████ in GTMO. I took

███████████████████████████████████████

" Who do you think you are? I am not telling the truth b/c of
████████████, I would cooperate, to my advantage, with every
body regardless his gender or his look. Just calm down,

███████████████████████████████████████

" I am leaving " ████ said. ████ also was upset b/c I told
that ████ ~~doesn't~~ didn't have ~~experience~~ as much

SECRET//NOFORN   PROTECTED

FIVE

GTMO

February 2003–August 2003

First "Mail" and First "Evidence"...The Night of Terror...The DoD Takes Over...24 Hour Shift Interrogations...Abduction inside the Abduction...The Arabo-American Party

"The rules have changed. What was no crime is now considered a crime."

"But I've done no crimes, and no matter how harsh you guys' laws are, I have done nothing."

"But what if I show you the evidence?"

"You won't. But if you do, I'll cooperate with you."

Agent Robert showed me the worst people in GTMO. There were fifteen, and I was number 1; number 2 was Mohammed al Qahtani.*

_____

* At his 2005 ARB hearing, MOS told the panel, "Then the FBI at GTMO Bay during the time era of General Miller, they released a list of the highest priority detainees here at GTMO. It was a list of 15 people and I was, guess which number, number ONE. Then they sent a special FBI team and the leader was [redacted] and I worked with him especially for my case....I thought he was just making fun of me when he said I was number ONE in the camp, but he was not lying; he was telling the truth,

"You gotta be kidding me," I said.

"No, I'm not. Don't you understand the seriousness of your case?"

"So, you kidnapped me from my house, in my country, and sent me to Jordan for torture, and then took me from Jordan to Bagram, and I'm still worse than the people you captured with guns in their hands?"

"Yes, you are. You're very smart! To me, you meet all the criteria of a top terrorist. When I check the terrorist check list, you pass with a very high score."

I was so scared, but I always tried to suppress my fear. "And what is your FBI check list?"

"You're Arab, you're young, you went to Jihad, you speak foreign languages, you've been in many countries, you're a graduate in a technical discipline."

"And what crime is that?" I said.

"Look at the hijackers: they were the same way."

"I am not here to defend anybody but myself. Don't even mention anybody else to me. I asked you about my crime, and not about x's or y's crimes. I don't give a damn!"

"But you are part of the big conspiracy against the U.S."

"You always say that. Tell me my part in this 'big conspiracy!'"

"I am going to tell you, just *sabr,* be patient."

My sessions continued with arguments of this nature. Then one day when I entered the interrogation room in Brown Building, I saw video equipment already hooked up. To be honest, I was terrified that they were going to show me a video with me committing terrorist attacks. Not that I have done

---

as future events would prove. He stayed with me until May 22, 2003."
ARB transcript, 24.

anything like that in my life. But my fellow detainee Mustafa from Bosnia told me that his interrogators forged an American passport bearing his picture. "Look: We now have definitive evidence that you forged this passport and you were using it for terrorist purposes," they told him. Mustafa laughed wholeheartedly at the silliness of his interrogators. "You missed that I'm a computer specialist, and I know that the U.S. government would have no problem forging a passport for me," he said. The interrogators quickly took the passport back and never talked about it again.

Scenarios like that made me very paranoid about the government making up something about me. Coming from a third-world country, I know how the police wrongly pin crimes on political rivals of the government in order to neutralize them. Smuggling weapons into somebody's house is common, in order to make the court believe the victim is preparing for violence.

"Are you ready?" said Robert.

"Y-e-e-s!" I said, trying to keep myself together, though my blushing face said everything about me. Robert hit the play button and we started to watch the movie. I was ready to jump when I saw myself blowing up some U.S. facility in Timbuktu. But the tape was something completely different. It was a tape of Osama bin Laden speaking to an associate I didn't recognize about the attack of September 11. They were speaking in Arabic. I enjoyed the comfort of understanding the talk, while the interrogators had to put up with the subtitles.

After a short conversation between UBL and the other guy, a TV commentator spoke about how controversial the tape was. The quality was bad; the tape was supposedly seized by U.S. forces in a safehouse in Jalalabad.

But that was not the point. "What do I have to do with this bullshit?" I asked angrily.

"You see Osama bin Laden is behind September 11," Robert said.

"You realize I am not Osama bin Laden, don't you? This is between you and Osama bin Laden; I don't care, I'm outside of this business."

"Do you think what he did was right?"

"I don't give a damn. Get Osama bin Laden and punish him."

"How do you feel about what happened?"

"I feel that I'm not a part of it. Anything else doesn't matter in this case!" When I came back to Lima Block I was telling my friends about the masquerade of the "definitive evidence" against me. But nobody was surprised, since most of the detainees had been through such jokes.

During my conversations with Robert and his associate, I brought up an issue that I believe to be basic.

"Why are you guys banning my incoming mails?"

"I checked, but you have none!"

"You're trying to say that my family is refusing to respond to me?"

The brothers in the block felt bad for me. I was dreaming almost every night that I had received mail from my family. I always passed on my dreams to my next door neighbors, and the dream interpreters always gave me hope, but no mails came. "I dreamt that you got a letter from your family," was a common phrase I used to hear. It was so hard for me to see other detainees having pictures of their families, and having nothing— zip—myself. Not that I wished they never got letters: on the contrary, I was happy for them, I read their correspondence as if it were from my own mom. It was customary to pass newly received mails throughout the block and let everybody read them, even the most intimate ones from lovers to the beloved.

Robert was dying to get me cooperating with him, and he

knew that I had brought my issue to the detainees. So he was working with the mail people to get me something. A recipe was prepared and cooked, and around 5 p.m. the postman showed up at my cell and handed me a letter, supposedly from my brother. Even before I read the letter, I shouted to the rest of the block, "I received a letter from my family. See, my dreams have come true, didn't I tell you?" From everywhere my fellow detainees shouted back, "Congratulations, pass me the letter when you're done!"

I hungrily started to read, but I soon got a shock: the letter was a cheap forgery. It was not from my family, it was the production of the Intel community.

"Dear brothers, I received no letter, I am sorry!"

"Bastards, they have done this with other detainees," said a neighbor. But the forgery was so clumsy and unprofessional that no fool would fall for it. First, I have no brother with that name. Second, my name was misspelled. Third, my family doesn't live where the correspondent mentioned, though it was close. Fourth, I know not only the handwriting of every single member of my family, but also the way each one phrases his ideas. The letter was kind of a sermon, "Be patient like your ancestors, and have faith that Allah is going to reward you." I was so mad at this attempt to defraud me and play with my emotions.

The next day, Robert pulled me for interrogation.

"How's your family doing?"

"I hope they're doing well."

"I've been working to get you the letter!"

"Thank you very much, good effort, but if you guys want to forge mail, let me give you some advice."

"What are you talking about?"

I smiled. "If you don't really know, it's okay. But it was cheap to forge a message and make me believe I have contact with my dear family!" I said, handing the strange letter back.

"I don't do shit like that," Robert said.

"I don't know what to believe. But I believe in God, and if I don't see my family in this life, I hope to see them in the afterlife, so don't worry about it." I honestly don't have proof or disproof of whether Robert was involved in that dirty business. But I do know that the whole matter is much bigger than Robert; there are a bunch of people working behind the scene.★ The FBI was in charge of my case through Robert and his team, but I was taken for interrogation a couple of times by other intelligence agencies without his consent or even knowledge. As to letters from my family, I received my first letter, a Red Cross message, on February 14, 2004, 816 days after I was kidnapped from my house in Mauritania. The message was seven months old when it reached me.

Agent Robert finally came forth on his promise to deliver the reasons why his government was locking me up. But he didn't show me anything that was incriminating. In March 2002 CNN had broadcast a report about me claiming that I was the coordinator who facilitated the communication between the September 11 hijackers through the guestbook of my homepage. Now Robert showed me the report.†

★ People were indeed "working behind the scene." Though the FBI was still leading MOS's interrogation, the DOJ IG found that through the spring of 2003, "Military Intelligence personnel observed many of Slahi's interviews by Poulson and Santiago from an observation booth," and that MI agents were complaining about the FBI's rapport-building approach. The Senate Armed Services Committee reported that military interrogators started circulating a draft "Special Interrogation Plan" for MOS in January 2003. DOJ IG, 298, SASC, 135.

† On March 6, 2002, CNN aired a story titled "Al Qaeda Online for Terrorism." As MOS indicates here, the story suggested that he was "running a seemingly innocuous website" where al-Qaeda was secretly exchang-

"I told you that you fucked up," Robert said.

"I didn't design my homepage for al Qaeda. I just made it a long time ago and never even checked on it since early 1997. Besides, if I decided to help al Qaeda, I wouldn't use my real name. I could write a homepage in the name of John Smith." Robert wanted to know everything about my homepage and why I even wrote one. I had to answer all that bullshit about a basic right of mine, writing a homepage with my real name and with some links to my favorite sites.

In one session, Robert asked, "Why did you study microelectronics?"

"I study whatever the heck I want. I didn't know that I had to consult the U.S. government about what I should or should not study," I said wryly.

"I don't believe in the principle of black and white. I think everybody is somehow in between. Don't you think so?" Robert asked.

"I've done nothing."

"It is not a crime to help somebody to join al Qaeda and he ended up a terrorist!" Robert told me repeatedly. I understood exactly what he meant: Just admit that you are a recruiter for al Qaeda.

"Might be. I'm not familiar with U.S. laws. But anyway, I didn't recruit anybody for al Qaeda, nor did they ask me to!" I said.

As a part of his "showing me the evidences against me," Robert asked a colleague of his for help. It was Michael, one of the FBI agents who interrogated me back in Nouakchott in February

---

ing messages through the website's guestbook. The allegation that MOS ran a website that facilitated al-Qaeda communications does not appear in any of the summaries of evidence against MOS from Guantánamo. See http://transcripts.cnn.com/TRANSCRIPTS/0203/06/lt.15.html.

2000. Michael is one of those guys, when they speak you think they're angry, and they might not be.

"I am happy that you showed up, because I would like to discuss some issues with you," I said.

"Of course, Michael is here to answer your questions!" said Robert.

"Remember when you guys came to interrogate me in Mauritania?" I began. "Remember how sure you were that I was not only involved in Millennium, but that I was the brain behind it? How do you feel now, knowing that I have nothing to do with it?"

"That's not the problem," Michael answered. "The problem was that you weren't honest with us."

"I don't have to be honest to you. And here's a news flash for you: I'm not going to talk to you unless you tell me why I am here," I said.

"That's your problem," Michael said. You could tell that Michael was used to humbled detainees who probably had to cooperate due to torture. He was by then interrogating Ramzi bin al-Shibh. He spoke very arrogantly; he as much as told me, "You're gonna cooperate, even against your will, ha! ha!" I admit I was rude with him, but I was so angry since he had wrongly accused me of having been part of the Millennium Plot and now was dodging my requests to him to come clean and say he and his government were wrong.

Michael looked worn out from his trip; he was very tired that day. "I don't see why you don't cooperate," he said. "They share food with you, and speak to you in a civilized way," he said.

"Why should I cooperate with any of you? You're hurting me, locking me up for no reason."

"We didn't arrest you."

"Send me the guy who arrested me, I'd like to talk to him."

After that tense discussion, the interrogators left and sent me back to my cell.

"For these next sessions, I have asked for Agent Michael to help me in laying out your case. I want you to be polite to him," Robert said at our next session.

I turned to his colleague. "Now you're convinced that I am not a part of Millennium. What's the next shit you're gonna pull on me?"

"You know, sometimes we arrest people for the wrong thing, but it turns out they are involved in something else!" Michael said.

"And when are you going to stop playing this game on me? Every time there is a new suspicion, and when that turns out to be incorrect, I get a new one, and so on and so forth. Is there a possibility in the world that I am involved in nothing?"

"Of course; therefore you have to cooperate and defend yourself. All I am asking is for you to explain some shit to me," said Robert. When Michael arrived he had a bunch of small papers with notes, and he started to read them to me. "You called Raouf Hannachi and asked him to bring you some sugar. When you told him about Hasni being back in Germany, he said, 'Don't say this over the phone.' I wouldn't say something like that to anybody I called."

"I don't care what Raouf Hannachi says over the phone. I am not here on behalf of Raouf; go and ask him. Remember, I'm asking you what *I* have done."

"I just want you to explain these conversations to me—and there's much more," said Michael.

"No, I am not answering anything before you answer my question. What have I done?"

"I don't say you've done anything, but there are a lot of things that need to be clarified."

"I've answered those questions a thousand and one times; I told you I mean what I am saying and I'm not using any code. You're just so unjust and so paranoid. You're taking advantage of me being from a country with a dictatorship. If I were German or Canadian, you wouldn't even have the opportunity to talk to me, nor would you arrest me."

"In asking you to cooperate, we're giving you an opportunity. After we share the cause of your arrest with you, it will be too late for you!" Michael said.

"I don't need any opportunities. Just tell me why you arrested me, and let it be too late." Agent Robert knew me better than Agent Michael did; thus, he tried to calm both of us down. Michael was trying to scare me, but the more he scared me, the sharper and less cooperative I got.

The camp was locked down the whole day. Around 10 p.m. I was pulled out of my cell and taken to Brown Building. The room was extremely cold. I hate to be woken up for interrogation, and my heart was pounding: Why would they take me so late?

I don't know how long I'd been in the room, maybe two hours. I was just shaking. I made my mind up not to argue anymore with the interrogators. I'm just gonna sit there like a stone, and let them do the talking, I said to myself. Many detainees decided to do so. They were taken day after day to interrogation in order to break them. I am sure some got broken because nobody can bear agony the rest of his life.

After letting me sweat, or let's say "shake," for a couple hours, I was taken to another room in Brown Building, where Agents Robert and Michael and another FBI agent who called himself

Chris sat. This room was acceptably cold. The military people were watching and listening from another room as usual.

"We couldn't take you during day because the camp was locked down," said Robert. "We had to take you now, because Michael is leaving tomorrow."

I didn't open my mouth. Robert sent his friends out. "What's wrong with you?" he said. "Are you OK? Did anything happen to you?" But no matter how he tried, there was no making me talk.

The team decided to take me back to the cold room. Maybe it wasn't so cold for somebody wearing regular shoes, underwear, and a jacket like the interrogators, but it was definitely cold for a detainee with flip-flops and no underwear whatsoever.

"Talk to us!" Robert said. "Since you refuse to talk, Michael is going to talk to you anyway."

Michael started his lecture, "We have been giving you an opportunity, but you don't seem to want to take advantage of it. Now it's too late, because I am going to share some information with you."

Michael put down three big pictures of four individuals who are believed to be involved in the September 11 attack. "This guy is Ramzi bin al-Shibh. He was captured in Karachi on September 11, 2002, and since then I've been interrogating him. I know more about him than he knows about himself. He was forthcoming and truthful with me. What he told me goes along with what we know about him. He said that he came to your house on advice of a guy named Khalid el Masri, whom he met on a train. Ramzi bin al-Shibh wanted somebody to help him getting to Chechnya."

"That was around October 1999," he continued. "He showed up at your house with these two guys," he said, pointing at Ziad

Jarrah and Marwan al-Shehhi. "The other guy," he said, pointing at Mohamed Atta, "was not able to see you because he had a test. You advised them to travel through Afghanistan instead of Georgia, because their Arab faces would give them away and they probably would have been turned back. Furthermore, you gave them a phone contact in Quetta of a guy named Omar Abdel-Rahman. These guys traveled shortly after that meeting with you to Afghanistan, met Osama bin Laden, and swore a pledge to him. Bin Laden assigned them to the attack of September 11, and sent them back to Germany."

He went on. "When I asked Ramzi what he thinks about you, he replied that he believes you to be a senior recruiter for Osama bin Laden. That's his personal opinion. However, he said that without you, he would never have joined al Qaeda. In fact, I'd say without you September 11 would never have happened. These guys would have gone to Chechnya and died."

Agent Michael excused himself and left. I was kept the rest of the night with Robert and Agent Chris, both staring at me in an eerie silence. I was so scared. The guy made me believe I was the one behind September 11. How could that possibly have happened? I was like, Maybe he's right. And yet anybody who knew the basics about the attack, which were published and updated through time, can easily see what a swiss cheese Michael was trying to sell me. The guys he mentioned were reportedly trained in 1998, and joined al Qaeda and were assigned to the attack then. How could I possibly have sent them in October 1999 to join al Qaeda, when they not only already were al Qaeda, but had already been assigned to the attack for more than a year?

I was kept up the rest of the night and forced to see pictures of dead body parts which were taken at the site of the Pentagon after the attack. It was a nasty sight. I almost broke down, but I managed to keep myself silent and together.

"See the result of the attack?" Robert asked.

"I don't think he foresaw what these were going to do," said Agent Chris. They were talking to each other, asking and answering each other. I kept myself as the present-absent. They kept sliding those nasty pictures in front of me the whole night. At the break of dawn, they sent me back to a cell in a new block, Mike Block. I prayed and tried to sleep, but I was kidding myself. I could not get the human body parts out of my head. My new neighbors, especially David Hicks and Bisher al-Rawi, tried to help me.*

"Don't worry! Just talk to them and everything is gonna be alright," David Hicks encouraged me. Maybe his advice was prudent, and anyway I felt that things were going to get nastier. So I decided to cooperate.

Agent Robert pulled me to interrogation the next day. I was so worn out. I had no sleep last night, nor during the day.†

---

* David Hicks, an Australian citizen, was detained in Afghanistan in December 2001 and held in Guantánamo until April 2007. Bisher al-Rawi, a resident of the United Kingdom at the time he was detained in Banjul, Gambia, in November 2002, was transferred to Guantánamo in March 2003. He was released and transferred to the United Kingdom in March 2007.

† A 1956 CIA study titled "Communist Control Techniques: An Analysis of the Methods Used by Communist State Police in the Arrest, Interrogation, and Indoctrination of Persons Regarded as 'Enemies of the State'" had this to say about the effects of sleep deprivation and temperature manipulation as coercive interrogation methods: "The officer in charge has other simple and highly effective ways of applying pressure. Two of the most effective of these are fatigue and lack of sleep. The constant light in the cell and the necessity of maintaining a rigid position in bed compound the effects of anxiety and nightmares in producing sleep disturbances. If these are not enough, it is easy to have the guards awaken the prisoners at intervals. This is especially effective if the prisoner is always awakened as soon as he drops off to sleep. The guards can also shorten the hours available for sleep, or deny sleep altogether. Continued loss of sleep produces clouding

"I am ready to cooperate unconditionally," I told him. "I don't need any proof whatsoever. You just ask me questions and I'm gonna answer you." And so our relationship seemed to enter a new era.

During his time with me, Robert made a couple of trips, one to Canada and one to Europe, I believe to Germany, in order to investigate my case and gather evidence against me. In February 2003, while he was on his trip to Canada an agent from the Canadian Security Intelligence Service pulled me to interrogation.

"My name is Christian, from Canada. I came here to ask you some questions about your time in my country," said Christian while flashing his badge. He was accompanied by one female and one male who were just talking notes.*

---

of consciousness and a loss of alertness, both of which impair the victim's ability to sustain isolation. It also produces profound fatigue.

"Another simple and effective type of pressure is that of maintaining the temperature of the cell at a level which is either too hot or too cold for comfort. Continuous heat, at a level at which constant sweating is necessary in order to maintain body temperature, is enervating and fatigue producing. Sustained cold is uncomfortable and poorly tolerated....

"The Communists do not look upon these methods as 'torture.' Undoubtedly, they use the methods which they do in order to conform, in a typical legalistic manner to overt Communist principles which demand that 'no force or torture be used in extracting information from prisoners.' But these methods do, of course, constitute torture and physical coercion. All of them lead to serious disturbances of many bodily processes."

Sleep deprivation has been used specifically in the service of conditioning prisoners to make false confessions. A study by the U.S. Air Force sociologist Albert Biderman of the means by which North Korean interrogators were able to coerce captured U.S. airmen into falsely confessing to war crimes found that sleep deprivation, as a form of induced debilitation, "weakens mental and physical ability to resist." See http://www.theblackvault.com /documents/mindcontrol/comcont.pdf; and http://www2.gwu.edu/ ~nsarchiv/torturingdemocracy/documents/19570900.pdf.

  ★ The *Toronto Star* reported that CSIS agents interviewed detainees with ties to Canada in Guantánamo, including MOS, in February 2003. See

"Welcome! I'm glad that you have come because I want to clarify some reports you produced about me which are very inaccurate." I continued, "Especially since my case with the U.S. is spinning around my time in Canada, and every time I argue with the Americans they refer to you. Now I want you guys to sit with the Americans and answer one question: Why are you arresting me? What crime have I done?"

"You have done nothing," Christian said.

"So I don't belong here, do I?"

"We didn't arrest you, the U.S. did."

"That's correct, but the U.S. claims that you pitted them on me."

"We just have some questions about some bad people, and we need your help."

"I'm not helping you unless you tell the Americans in front of me that one or the other of you lied."

The agents went out and brought FBI Agent William in, who was probably watching the session through the one-way mirror in the next room.

"You are not honest, since you refuse to answer the Canadian's questions. This is your opportunity to get help from them," William said.

"Mr. William, I know this game better than you do. Stop trying to talk nonsense to me," I said. "Look, you keep telling me the Canadians say such and such. Now it's you guys' opportunity to face me with my charges," I said.

"We don't accuse you of any crime," said William.

"Then release me!"

"That's not in my hands." William tried to convince me but

Michelle Shephard, "CSIS Grilled Trio in Guantánamo," http://www .thestar.com/news/canada/2008/07/27/csis_grilled_trio_in_cuba.html.

there was no convincing me. I was sent back to my cell and taken again the next day, but I just sat there like a stone. I didn't waste a word because I had told them clearly the conditions of my cooperation. The CSIS agents also interrogated a teenager called Omar Khadr and made the Army take all his belongings. We detainees felt bad for him: he was just too young for this whole campaign.*

When Robert came back, he was pissed off because the JTF leadership had ignored him and were exposing me to whomever they wanted. Now I knew the FBI team had no control over my fate; they didn't have the ability to deal with me, and henceforth I could not really trust them. I don't like to deal to somebody who cannot keep his word. I knew then for a fact that the FBI team was nothing but a step, and the real interrogation was going to be led by the Department of Defense. If you look at the situation, it makes sense: most of the detainees were captured by DOD troops in a military operation, and they wanted to maintain the upper hand. FBI agents are only guests in GTMO, no more, no less; the facility is run by the U.S. military.

---

* In 2010 the Supreme Court of Canada found that the interrogations of Omar Khadr's by Canadian Security Intelligence Service (CSIS) and the Foreign Intelligence Division of the Department of Foreign Affairs and International Trade (DFAIT) agents in Guantánamo in February and September 2003 and March 2004 violated the Canadian Charter of Rights and Freedoms. The Supreme Court held, "The deprivation of [Khadr]'s right to liberty and security of the person is not in accordance with the principles of fundamental justice. The interrogation of a youth detained without access to counsel, to elicit statements about serious criminal charges while knowing that the youth had been subjected to sleep deprivation and while knowing that the fruits of the interrogations would be shared with the prosecutors, offends the most basic Canadian standards about the treatment of detained youth suspects." The Supreme Court's opinion is available at http://scc-csc.lexum.com/decisia-scc-csc/scc-csc/scc-csc/en/item/7842/index.do.

It happened again. When Robert went to Canada in May 2003, a team that claimed it was from the Royal Canadian Mounted Police reserved me for interrogation, and they were no luckier than their fellow citizens from CSIS. Agent Robert was completely overawed by his colleagues from the JTF command.

Robert came back from Canada. "I was ordered to quit your case and go back to the U.S. My boss believes that I'm only wasting my time. The MI will take your case," Robert told me. I wasn't happy that he was leaving, but I wasn't really that upset. Agent Robert was the guy who understood the most about my case, but he had neither power nor people who backed him up.

The next day the team organized a pretty lunch party. They bought good food as a good-bye. "You should know that your next sessions will not be as friendly as these have been," Robert said, smiling wryly. "You will not be brought food or drinks anymore." I understood the hint as rough treatment, but I still never thought that I was going to be tortured. Furthermore, I believed that Robert and his associate Agent Chris would inform the proper authorities to stop a crime if they knew one was going to happen.

"I wish you good luck, and all I can tell you is to tell the truth," Agent Robert said. We hugged, and bid each other good-bye.*

---

* MOS told the Administrative Review Board that his last interview with FBI interrogators took place on May 22, 2003; the DOJ IG report confirms that "in late May 2003 the FBI agents who were involved with Slahi left GTMO, and the military assumed control over Slahi's interrogation." ARB transcript, 25; DOJ IG, 122.

A few days after the military took over MOS's interrogation, an FBI agent circulated a report documenting FBI concerns about the military's interrogation methods in Guantánamo. According to the DOJ IG report, a month later, on July 1, 2003, the FBI's assistant general counsel, Spike Bowman, sent an e-mail to senior FBI officials, "alerting them that the military had

*　　*　　*

When I entered the room a desk was prepared with several chairs on the other side of the table. As soon as the guards locked me up to the floor, a tall female Navy Lieutenant and a tall female in civilian clothes entered the room. The Lieutenant, who said her name was Ronica, seemed to be the leader of the team. She had very long black hair and smiled most of the time, even when she was making sarcastic comments. Her associate, a blond woman in her mid-forties who called herself Sam, introduced herself to me as an agent of the FBI. You could tell they had a head start I didn't. Ronica and Samantha brought heavy binders with them, and were talking to each other.*

"When is the guy supposed to come?"

"Nine o'clock." Against interrogation customs, one of the supposed members of the team did not show up with the rest. It was a technique used to scare and irritate the detainee.

The door opened. "I am sorry, I was thinking diplomatic

---

been using techniques of 'aggressive interrogation,' including 'physically striking the detainees, stripping them and pouring cold water on them and leaving them exposed (one got hypothermia) and similar measures.' Bowman opined that: 'Beyond any doubt, what they are doing (and I don't know the extent of it) would be unlawful were these Enemy Prisoners of War (EPW). That they are not so designated cannot be license to do something that you cannot do to an EPW or criminal prisoner.' Bowman expressed concern that the FBI would be 'tarred by the same brush' and sought input on whether the FBI should refer the matter to the DoD Inspector General, stating that '[w]ere I still on active duty, there is no question in my mind that it would be a duty to do so.'" ARB transcript, 25; DOJ IG, 122, 121.

* The second female interrogator was only posing as an FBI agent. The DOJ Inspector General found that "the person who identified herself as 'Samantha' was actually an Army Sergeant." According to the IG, "On several occasions in early June 2003 an Army Sergeant on the DIA Special Projects Team at GTMO identified herself to Slahi as FBI SSA 'Samantha Martin' in an effort to persuade Slahi to cooperate with interrogators." DOJ IG, 296, 125.

time," the new arrival said. "You know, those of us not from JTF are on another time." The older looking gentleman was dying to impress. I wasn't sure how much he succeeded. He said he was from the Department of State, and acted very rushed. He even brought his McDonald's with him, but offered nothing to anybody.

"I just arrived from Washington," he commenced. "Do you know how important you are to the U.S. government?"

"I know how important I am to my dear mom, but I'm not sure when it comes to the U.S. government." The Navy Lieutenant Ronica couldn't help smiling, although she tried hard to keep her frown. I was supposed to be shown harshness.

"Are you ready to work with us? Otherwise your situation is gonna be very bad," the man continued.

"You know that I know that you know that I have done nothing," I said. "You're holding me because your country is strong enough to be unjust. And it's not the first time you have kidnapped Africans and enslaved them."

"African tribes sold their people to us," he replied.

"I wouldn't defend slavery, if I were in your shoes." I said. I could tell the Lieutenant was the one with the most power, even though the government let other agencies try their chances with detainees. It's very much like a dead camel in the desert, when all kinds of bugs start to eat it.

"If you don't cooperate with us we're gonna send you to a tribunal and you're gonna spend the rest of your life in the prison," Lieutenant Ronica said.

"Just do it!"

"You must admit to what you have done," Samantha said, gesturing to a big binder in front of her.

"What have I done?"

"You know what you've done."

"You know what, I am not impressed, but if you have questions I can answer you," I said.

"I have been working along with my colleagues Robert and Chris on your case. Robert and Chris are gone. But I'm still here to give you an opportunity."

"Keep the opportunity for yourself, I need none." The purpose of this session was to scare the hell out of me, but it takes more than that to scare me. The self-described "diplomat" disappeared for good, and I never saw him again; Lieutenant Ronica and Samantha kept interrogating me for some time, but there was nothing new. Both women were using dead-traditional methods and techniques I probably mastered better than they had.

"What is the name of your current wife?" was Samantha's favorite question. When I arrived in Cuba on August 5, 2002, I was so hurt physically and mentally that I literally forgot the name of my wife and provided a wrong one. Samantha wanted to prove that I am a liar.

"Look, you won't provide us information we don't already know. But if you keep denying and lying, we'll assume the worst," said Lieutenant Ronica. "I have interrogated some other detainees and found them innocent. I really have a problem sleeping in a comfortable room while they suffer in the block. But you're different. You're unique. There's nothing really incriminating, but there are a lot of things that make it impossible not to be involved."

"And what is the straw that broke the camel's back?"

"I don't know!" Lieutenant Ronica answered. She was a respectable lady and I very much respected her honesty. She was appointed to torture me but she ultimately failed, which led to her separation from my case. To me Samantha was an evil person. She always laughed sardonically.

"You're very rude," she once said.

"So are you!" I replied. Our sessions were not fruitful. Both Lieutenant Ronica and Samantha wanted to reach a breakthrough, but there was no breakthrough to be reached. Both wanted me to admit to being part of the Millennium Plot, which I wasn't. The only possible way to make me admit to something I haven't done is to torture me beyond my limit of pain.

"You're saying that I am lying about that? Well guess what, I have no reason not to keep lying. You don't seem any more impressive than the hundred interrogators I have had lately," I said.

"You're funny, you know that?"

"Whatever that means!"

"We're here to give you an opportunity. I've been in the block for a while, and I am leaving soon, so if you don't cooperate..." Samantha continued.

"Bon Voyage!" I said. I felt good that she was leaving because I didn't like her.

"You speak with a French accent."

"Oh, God, I thought I speak like Shakespeare," I said wryly.

"No you speak pretty well, I only mean the accent," said Samantha. But Lieutenant Ronica was a polite and honest person. "Look, we have so many reports linking you to all kinds of stuff. There is nothing incriminating, really. But there are too many little things. We will not ignore anything and just release you."

"I'm not interested in your mercy. I only want to be released if my case is completely cleared. I really am tired of being released and captured in an endless Catch-22."

"You need your freedom, and we need information. You give

us what we need and in return, you get what you need," the Lieutenant said. The three of us argued this way for days without any success.

And then the guy I call "I-AM-THE-MAN" came into play. It was around noon when an army sergeant joined the two women while they were interrogating me.

"This Sergeant First Class will be joining us in your case," the Navy Lieutenant said, gesturing to the new arrival.

"This sergeant is working for me. He is going to be seeing you often, among others who are working for me. But you're gonna see me also," Lieutenant Ronica continued. Sergeant Shally sat there like a stone; he didn't greet me or anything. He was writing his notes and hardly looked at me, while the other women were asking questions. "Don't make jokes, just answer her questions," he said at one point. I was like, Oops. He expected me to be completely subdued, given my circumstances, and he was very disturbed at the defiant way I was addressing his colleagues. It soon became clear that Sergeant Shally was chosen with some others to do the dirty work. He had experience in MI; he had interrogated Iraqis who were captured during Operation Desert Storm. He speaks Farsi, he told me, but it was hard to imagine him learning a language. All he was able to hear was his own voice. I was always like, Is this guy listening to what I am saying? Or let's just say his ears were programmed to what he wanted to hear.

"I'm an asshole," he said once. "That is the way people know me, and I have no problem with it."

For the next month I had to deal with Sergeant Shally and his small gang. "We are not the FBI; we don't let lying detainees go unpunished. Just maybe not physical torture," he said. I had been witnessing for the last months how detainees were consistently being tortured under the orders of the JTF command. Abdul Rahman Shalabi was taken to interrogation every single night, exposed to loud music and scary pictures, and molested sexually. I would see Abdul Rahman when the guards took him in the evening and brought him back in the morning. He was forbidden to pray during his interrogation. I remember asking the brothers what to do in that case. "You just pray in your heart since it's not your fault," said the Algerian Sheikh in the block. I profited from this fatwa since I would be exposed to the same situation for about a year. Abdul Rahman was not spared the cold room. Mohammed al-Qahtani suffered the same; moreover his interrogator smashed the Koran against the floor to break him, and had the guards push his face down against the rough floor.* Not to speak of the poor young Yemenis and Saudis who were grossly tortured the same way. But since I'm speaking in this book about my own experience, which reflects an example of the evil practices that took place in the name of the War Against Terrorism, I don't need to talk about every single case I witnessed. Maybe on another occasion, if God so wills.†

---

* Abdul Rahman Shalabi was released and transferred to Saudi Arabia on September 22, 2015. Mohammed al-Qahtani remains in Guantánamo. His "Special Projects" interrogation has been documented extensively in the Senate Armed Services Committee and Department of Justice Inspector General reports, and in March 2006 *Time* published the interrogation log of a forty-nine-day stretch of that interrogation. The log is available at http://content.time.com/time/2006/log/log.pdf.

† Military interrogators in Guantánamo were under the command of the Joint Task Force Guantánamo (JTF-GTMO), which was led at this time by General Geoffrey Miller. Their interrogation methods were sanctioned first by the "Counter Resistance Techniques" memorandum that Secretary of Defense Donald Rumsfeld signed on December 22, 2002; then by a March 13, 2003, legal opinion written by John Yoo of the Office of Legal Counsel; and finally by another authorization memo that Rumsfeld signed on April 16, 2003. The Senate Armed Services Committee found that

When SFC Shally informed me about the intentions of his team, I was terrified. My mouth dried up, I started to sweat, my heart started to pound (a couple weeks later I developed hypertension) and I started to get nausea, a headache, a stomachache. I dropped into my chair. I knew that Sergeant Shally was not kidding, and I also knew that he was lying about physical pain-free torture. But I held myself together.

"I don't care," I said.

Things went more quickly than I thought. SFC Shally sent me back to the block, and I told my fellow detainees about being overtaken by the torture squad.

"You are not a kid. Those torturers are not worth thinking about. Have faith in Allah," said my next-door neighbor, Abu Walid from Yemen.* I really must have acted like a child all

---

General Miller sought official Pentagon approval for, and Rumsfeld personally signed off on, MOS's "Special Interrogation Plan." SASC, 135–38.

The Schmidt-Furlow report, the DOJ IG report, the Senate Armed Services Committee report, and several other sources all document the sexual humiliation and sexual assault of Guantánamo prisoners, often carried out by female military interrogators. After the release of the Schmidt-Furlow report in 2005, a *New York Times* op-ed titled "The Women of GTMO" decried the "exploitation and debasement of women in the military," noting that the report "contained page after page of appalling descriptions of the use of women soldiers as sexual foils in interrogations." See http://www.nytimes.com/2005/07/15/opinion/15fri1.html.

* Walid Said Bin Said Zaid, ISN 550, was one of several Yemeni prisoners in Guantánamo who remained imprisoned long after they were cleared for release. He was brought to Guantánamo on May 3, 2002. As early as 2006, the Guantánamo Task Force recommended that he be transferred out of the facility, and he was one of seventeen Yemeni prisoners approved for release in 2010. Their releases were stalled, however, when Congress banned the transfer of Yemeni prisoners following the attempt by twenty-three-year-old Nigerian Umar Farouk Abdulmutallab to detonate a bomb aboard a U.S.-bound flight on December 25, 2009. Walid Said Bin Said Zaid was one of a group of ten Yemeni prisoners who were transferred to Oman on January 14, 2017, less than a week before the end of Barack Obama's presidency. No prisoners have been released from Guantánamo since that transfer.

day long before the guards pried me from the cellblock later that day. You don't know how terrorizing it is for a human being to be threatened with torture. One literally becomes a child.

The Escort team showed up at my cell.

"You got to move."

"Where?"

"Not your problem," said the hateful escorting guard. But he was not very smart, for he had my destination written on his glove.

"Brothers pray for me, I am being transferred to India!" I called. The isolation India Block was reserved by then for the worst detainees in the camp; if one got transferred to India Block, many signatures must have been provided, maybe even the president of the U.S. The only people I know to have spent some time in India Block since it was designed for torture were a Kuwaiti detainee and another fellow detainee from Yemen.*

When I entered the block, it was completely empty of any signs of life. I was put at the end of the block and the Yemeni fellow was at the beginning, so there was no interaction whatsoever between us. The Kuwaiti man was put in the middle but with no contact with either. Later on both were transferred somewhere else, and the whole block was reserved for me, only me, ALLAH, my interrogation team, and the guards who

---

* Other former detainees who were held for a time in India Block describe windowless solitary confinement cells that were often kept at frigid temperatures. See, e.g., James Meek, "People the Law Forgot," *Guardian*, December 2, 2003. http://www.theguardian.com/world/2003/dec/03/guantanamo.usa1.

worked for them. I was completely exposed to the total mercy of the interrogation team, and there was little mercy.

In the block the recipe started. I was deprived of my comfort items, except for a thin iso-mat and a very thin, small, worn-out blanket. I was deprived of my books, which I owned, I was deprived of my Koran, I was deprived of my soap. I was deprived of my toothpaste and of the roll of toilet paper I had. The cell — better, the box — was cooled down to the point that I was shaking most of the time. I was forbidden from seeing the light of the day; every once in a while they gave me a rec-time at night to keep me from seeing or interacting with any detainees. I was living literally in terror. For the next seventy days I wouldn't know the sweetness of sleeping: interrogation 24 hours a day, three and sometimes four shifts a day. I rarely got a day off. I don't remember sleeping one night quietly. "If you start to cooperate you'll have some sleep and hot meals," Sergeant Shally used to tell me repeatedly.

Within a couple of days of my transfer, a young Swiss woman from the International Committee of the Red Cross showed up at my cell and asked me whether I wanted to write a letter. "Yes!" I said. Natalie handed me a paper and I wrote, "Mama, I love you, I just wanted to tell you that I love you!" After that visit I wouldn't see the ICRC for more than a year. They tried to see me, but in vain.★

"You're starting to torture me, but you don't know how

★ An October 9, 2003, JTF-GTMO Memorandum for the Record recounts a contentious meeting between a visiting delegation of the International Committee of the Red Cross and Guantánamo commander General Geoffrey Miller. During the meeting, General Miller "informed [ICRC team leader Vincent] Cassard that ISN 760, 558, and 990 were off limits during this visit due to military necessity." MOS is ISN 760. The minutes of the ICRC meeting are available at http://www.washingtonpost.com/wp-srv/nation/documents/GitmoMemo10-09-03.pdf.

much I can take. You might end up killing me," I said when Lieutenant Ronica and Sergeant Shally pulled me for interrogation.

"We do recommend things, but we don't have the final decision," Lieutenant Ronica said.

"I just want to warn you: I'm suffering because of the harsh conditions you expose me to. I've already had a sciatic nerve attack. And torture will not make me more cooperative."

"According to my experience, you will cooperate. We are stronger than you, and have more resources," Lieutenant Ronica said. SFC Shally never wanted me to know his name, but he got busted when one of his colleagues mistakenly called him by his name. He doesn't know that I know it, but, well, I do.

Sergeant Shally grew worse with every day passing by. He started to lay out my case. He began with the story of Ramzi bin al-Shibh, and me having recruited him for September 11 attack.

"Why should he lie to us," SFC Shally said.

"I don't know."

"All you have to say is, 'I don't remember, I don't know, I've done nothing.' You think you're going to impress an American jury with these words? In the eyes of the Americans, you're doomed. Just looking at you in an orange suit, chains, and being Muslim and Arabic is enough to convict you," Sergeant Shally said.

"That is unjust!"

"We know that you are criminal."

"What have I done?"

"You tell me, and we'll reduce your sentence to thirty years, after which you'll have a chance to lead a life again. Otherwise you'll never see the light of day. If you don't cooperate, we're going to put you in a hole and wipe your name out of our detainee database." I was so terrified because I knew that even though he couldn't make such a decision on his own, he had the complete back-up of a high government level. He didn't speak from thin air.

"I don't care where you take me, just do it."

In another session when he was talking to me, he seemed particularly angry. He brought up the transcripts of my phone calls in Canada. "What the fuck do you mean, tea or sugar?"

"I just meant what I said, I was not talking in code."

"Fuck you!" SFC Shally said. I figured I wouldn't degrade myself and lower myself to his level, so I didn't answer him. When I failed to give him the answer he wanted to hear, he made me stand up, with my back bent because my hands were shackled to my feet and waist and locked to the floor. Sergeant Shally turned the temperature control all the way down, and made sure that the guards maintained me in that situation until he decided otherwise. He used to start a fuss before going to lunch, so he could keep me hurt during his lunch, which took at least two to three hours. Sergeant Shally likes his food; he never missed his lunch. I always wondered how he could possibly have passed the Army's fitness test. But I realized he was in the Army for a reason: he was good at being inhumane.

"Why are you in jail?" he asked me.

"Because your country is unjust, and my country isn't defending me?"

"Now you're saying that we Americans are just looking for skinny Arabs," he said.

Lieutenant Ronica came with him occasionally, and it was kind of a blessing for me. I grew tired of dealing with a lifeless face like Sergeant Shally's. When the Navy Lieutenant came I felt like I was meeting with a human being. She offered me the appropriate chair for my back pain, while SFC Shally always insisted on the metal chair or the dirty floor.

"Do you know that Ahmed Laabidi is dealing such and such?" Lieutenant Ronica asked me, naming some kind of drug.★

"What the hell do you mean?" I asked.

"You know what she means," SFC Shally said. Lieutenant Ronica smiled because she knew that I wasn't lying. I really could have been anything but a drug dealer, and SFC Shally was dying to link me to any crime no matter what.

"It's a type of narcotic," Lieutenant Ronica replied.

"I'm sorry, I am not familiar at all with that circle."

SFC Shally and his bosses realized that it took more than just isolation, threats, and intimidation to break me. And so they decided to bring another interrogator into play. Sometime in mid-July I was taken by the Golf escort team to Brown Building to reservation. The escorting team was confused.

"They said Brown Building? That's weird!" said one of the guards.

When we entered the building there were no monitoring guards. "Call the D.O.C.!" said the other.† After the radio call, the two guards were ordered to stay with me in the room until my interrogators showed up.

"Something's wrong," said the first one.

The escort team didn't realize that I understood what they were

---

★ Ahmed Laabidi, a Tunisian national, lived in Montreal in 2000, where he and MOS were friends. Laabidi was later detained in the United States on an immigration violation. Laabidi was held in U.S. immigration custody and then deported to Tunisia in September 2003. See footnote on page 290 for more on Laabidi.

† DOC is the acronym for the Detention Operations Center, which directs all movements within Guantánamo.

talking about; they always assume that detainees don't speak English, which they typically don't. The leadership in the camp always tried to warn the guards; signs like "DO NOT HELP THE ENEMY," and "CARELESS TALK GIVES SECRETS AWAY," were not rare, but the guards talked to each other anyway.

Brown Building was at one point a regular interrogation booth, then a building for torture, then an administrative building. My heart was pounding; I was losing my mind. I hate torture so much. A slim, small female entered the room followed by Mr. Tough Guy, SFC Shally. Staff Sergeant Mary was a young woman in her early thirties, about five and a half feet tall, with long, light brown hair, of which she was very proud. She was with the National Guard, and had been called to duty after 9/11, I later learned. Neither greeted me, nor released my hands from the shackles.

"What is this?" SSG Mary asked, showing me a plastic bag with a small welding stick inside.

"It's Indian incense," I replied. That was the first thing that came to my mind. I thought she wanted to give me a treat by burning the incense during the interrogation, which was a good idea.

"No, you're wrong!" She almost stuck it in my face.

"I don't know," I said.

"Now we have found evidence against you; we don't need anymore," said SSG Mary. I was like, What the hell is going on, is that a part of a bomb they want to pull on me?

"This is a welding stick you were hiding in your bathroom," SSG Mary said.

"How can I possibly have such a thing in my cell, unless you or my guards gave it to me? I have no contact whatsoever with any detainees."

"You're smart, you could have smuggled it," said SSG Mary.

"How?"

"Take him to the bathroom," she said. SSG Mary called the Golf team that was waiting outside the door to unhook me. The guards grabbed me to the bathroom. I was thinking, "Are these people so desperate to pull shit on me, I mean any shit?" In the meantime, a senior NCO guard was explaining to SSG Mary how these welding sticks end up in the cells; I caught his last words when the guards were leading me back from the restroom. "It's common. The contractors keep throwing them in the toilets after finishing with them." As soon as I entered, everybody suddenly shut up. SSG Mary put the welding stick back in a yellow envelope. SSG Mary never introduced herself, nor did I expect her to do so. The worse an interrogator's intention is, the more he or she covers his or her identity. But those people get busted the most, and so did SSG Mary, when one of her colleagues mistakenly called her by her name.

"How does your new situation look?" SSG Mary asked me.

"I'm just doing great!" I answered. I was really suffering, but I didn't want to give them the satisfaction of having reached their evil goal.

"I think he's too comfortable," SFC Shally said.

"Get off the chair!" SSG Mary said, pulling the chair from beneath me. "I'd rather have a dirty farmer sitting on the chair than a smart ass like you," she continued, when my whole body dropped on the dirty floor. My back pain from my sciatic nerve condition was killing me. Since June 20th I never got relief from them. SFC Shally obviously was getting tired of dealing with me, so his boss offered him fresh blood, manifesting in the person of SSG Mary. SSG Mary started the session. She spread the pictures of some September 11 suspects in front of me, namely Mohamed Atta, Ziad Jarrah, Marwan al-Shehhi, Ramzi bin al-Shibh, Khalid Sheikh Mohammed, and others.

"Look at these motherfuckers," said SSG Mary. "OK, now tell us what you know about those motherfuckers!" she said.

"I swear to God, I will not tell you one word, no matter what."

"Stand up! *Guards!* If you don't stand up, it'll be ugly," SSG Mary said. And before the torture squad entered the room I stood up, with my back bent because the heavy chains bound my hands to my feet so I was tied hands and feet to the floor. This type of restraints didn't allow me to stand up straight.* I had to suffer every-inch-of-my-body pain the rest of the day. I dealt with the pain silently; I kept praying until my assailants got tired and sent me back to my cell at the end of the day, after exhausting their resources of humiliations for that day. I didn't say a single word, as if I had not been there. You, Dear Reader, said more words to them than I did.

"If you want to go to the bathroom, ask politely to use the restroom, say 'Please, may I?' Otherwise, do it in your pants," SSG Mary said.

Before lunch SSG Mary and SFC Shally dedicated the time to speaking ill about my family, and describing my wife with the worst adjective you can imagine. For the sake of my family, I dismiss their degrading quotations. The whole time the two sergeants offered me just water and a cold meal; "You are not entitled to a warm meal unless you cooperate," SFC Shally said once. Whenever they started to torture me I refused to drink or eat. SSG Mary brought her lunch from outside to frustrate me.

"Yummy, ham is tasty," she said, eating her meal.

That afternoon was dedicated to sexual molestation. SFC

---

* The Senate Armed Services Committee found that shackling MOS to the floor was prescribed in his "Special Interrogation Plan." SASC, 137.

Shally left the interrogation booth to watch from next door. SSG Mary started to press her body against me, all over, and said that if I refused to talk, she would rape me; a "fair warning," one could say. She started shyly to perform the lamest strip you could imagine.

"You know, it's not against the law to have sex with detainees," she said, as she was taking off her uniform blouse and was whispering in my ear, "You know how good I am in bed," and "American men like me to whisper in their ears," she said, slowly removing her uniform piece by piece, hoping I would crack and relieve her from the pain of humiliation she was inflicting upon herself. I could tell it wasn't her first choice to act in this way. But I couldn't help her, and said nothing. She kept talking about what American men like, and self-consciously praising herself, saying things like "I have a great body."

Every once in a while SSG Mary offered me the other side of the coin. "If you start to cooperate, I'm gonna stop harassing you. Otherwise I'll be doing the same with you and worse every day. I am very good at this kind of work and that's why my government designated me to this job. I've always been successful. Having sex with somebody is not considered torture."*

SSG Mary was leading the monologue, while SFC Shally watched from next door. Every now and then he entered and tried to make me speak, "You cannot defeat us: we have too many people, and we'll keep humiliating you with American sex."

"I have a big-boobed friend I'm gonna bring tomorrow to

---

* This incident is well documented in the Schmidt-Furlow report, the DOJ IG's report, and elsewhere. Lt. Gen. Randall Schmidt and Lt. Gen. John Furlow, *Army Regulation 15-6: Final Report, Investigation into FBI Allegations of Detainee Abuse at Guantanamo Bay, Cuba Detention Facility* (hereinafter cited as Schmidt-Furlow). Schmidt-Furlow, 22–23; DOJ IG, 124. The Schmidt-Furlow Report is available at https://www.thetorturedatabas e.org/files/foia_subsite/pdfs/schmidt_furlow_report.pdf.

help me," she said. "At least she'll cooperate," said SSG Mary wryly. SSG Mary didn't undress me, but she was touching my private parts with her body.

In the late afternoon, another torture squad started with another poor detainee. I could hear loud music playing. "Do you want me to send you to that team, or are you gonna cooperate?" SSG Mary asked. I didn't answer. The guards used to call Brown Building "The Party House" because most of the torture took place in those buildings, and at night, when darkness started to cover the sorry camp.

SSG Mary sent me back to my cell, warning me, "Today is just the beginning, what's coming is worse."

But in order for this special JTF team to know how much torture a detainee can take, they need medical assistance. I was sent to a doctor, an officer in the Navy. I would describe him as a decent and humane person.*

"Are you going to remove the chains? I don't examine people with that shit on them," he said to the escorting Golf team.

"The gentleman has a pretty serious case of sciatic nerve," he said.

"I cannot take the conditions I am in anymore," I told him. I am being stopped from taking my pain medication and my Ensure, which were necessary to maintain my head above water," I said.

_____

* Court papers filed in MOS's habeas appeal reference records that seem to be from this exam: "The medical records document increased low back pain 'for the past 5 days while in isolation and under more intense interrogation'" and note that the pain medication prescribed for him could not be administered throughout July 2003 because he was at the "reservation." The June 9, 2010, Brief for Appellee is available at https://www.aclu.org/sites/default/files/assets/brief_for_appellee_-_july_8_2010.pdf.

The interrogators would organize the sessions so that they would cover the time when you are supposed to take your medication. I had two prescriptions, tabs for the sciatic nerve back pain and Ensure to compensate the loss of weight I had been suffering since my arrest. I usually got my meds between 4 and 5 p.m., and so the interrogators made sure that I was with them and missed my medication. But look at it, what sense does it make, if the interrogators work on hurting my back and then give me back pain medication, or to give me a bad diet and want me to gain weight?

"I don't have much power. I can write a recommendation, but it's the decision of other people. Your case is very serious!" he told me. I left the clinic with some hope, but my situation only worsened.

"Look, the doctor said I've developed high blood pressure. That's serious; you know that I was a hypotensive person before," I said the next time SSG Mary called me to interrogation.

"You're alright, we spoke with the doctor," the interrogators replied. I knew then that my recipe was going to continue.

The torture was growing day by day. The guards on the block actively participated in the process. The interrogators tell them what to do with the detainees when they came back to the block. I had guards banging on my cell to prevent me from sleeping. They cursed me for no reason. They repeatedly woke me, unless my interrogators decided to give me a break. I never complained to my interrogators about the issue because I knew they planned everything with the guards.

As promised, SSG Mary pulled me early in the day. Lonely in my cell, I was terrified when I heard the guards carrying the heavy chains and shouting at my door "Reservation!" My heart started to pound heavily because I always expected the worst. But the fact that I wasn't allowed to see the light made me "enjoy" the short trip between my freakin' cold cell and the interrogation room. It was just a blessing when the warm GTMO sun hit me. I felt life sneaking back into every inch of my body. I would always get this fake happiness, though only for a very short time. It's like taking narcotics.

"How you been?" said one of the Puerto Rican escorting guards in his weak English.

"I'm OK, thanks, and you?"

"No worry, you gonna back to your family," he said. When he said that I couldn't help breaking in tears. Lately, I'd become so vulnerable. What was wrong with me? Just one soothing word in this ocean of agony was enough to make me cry. Around this time in Delta Camp we had a complete Puerto Rican division. They were different than other Americans; they were not as vigilant and unfriendly. Sometimes, they took detainees to shower outside the prescribed time. Everybody liked them. But they got in trouble with those responsible for the camps because of their friendly and humane approach to detainees. I can't objectively speak about the people from Puerto Rico because I haven't met enough; however, if you ask me, Have you ever seen a bad Puerto Rican guy? My answer would be no. But if you ask, Is there one? I just don't know. It's the same way with the Sudanese people.

"Keep the shackles on and give him no chair," said the D.O.C. worker on the radio when the escort team dropped me in Brown Building. SSG Mary and the promised big-breasted woman entered the room. They brought a picture of an American black man named Christopher Paul, who I met one time many years before in Afghanistan. "We're gonna talk today about this guy, 'Abdulmalek,'" SSG Mary said, after bribing me with a weathered metal chair.*

---

* Christopher Paul is an American who received al Qaeda training in Afghanistan in the early 1990s. He was indicted in 2007 on terrorism-

"I have told you what I know about Abdulmalek."

"No, that's bullshit. Are you gonna tell us more?"

"No, I have no more to tell."

The new female interrogator pulled the metal chair away and left me on the floor. "Now, tell us about Christopher Paul, a.k.a. Abdulmalek!"

"No, that's passé," I said.

"Yes, you're right. So if it is passé, talk about it, it won't hurt," the new female interrogator said.

"No."

"Then today, we're gonna teach you about great American sex. Get up!" said SSG Mary. I stood up in the same painful position as I had every day for about seventy days. I would rather follow the orders and reduce the pain that would be caused when the guards come to play; the guards used every contact opportunity to beat the hell out of the detainee. "Detainee tried to resist," was the "Gospel truth" they came up with, and guess who was going to be believed? "You're very smart, because if you don't stand up it's gonna be ugly," SSG Mary said.

As soon as I stood up, the two women took off their blouses, and started to talk all kind of dirty stuff you can imagine, which I minded less. What hurt me most was them forcing me to take part in a sexual threesome in the most degrading manner. What many women don't realize is that men get hurt the same as women if they're forced to have sex, maybe more due to the traditional position of the man. Both women stuck on me, literally one on the front and the other older woman stuck on my back rubbing her whole body on mine. At the same time they

---

related charges and pled guilty in a plea agreement that resulted in a fifteen-year sentence.

were talking dirty to me, and playing with my sexual parts. I am saving you here from quoting the disgusting and degrading talk I had to listen to from noon or before until 10 p.m. when they turned me over to Mr. X, the new character you'll soon meet.

To be fair and honest, the two women didn't deprive me of my clothes at any time; everything happened with my uniform on. The senior interrogator SFC Shally was watching everything through the one-way mirror from the next room. I kept praying all the time.

"Stop the fuck praying! You're having sex with American whores and you're praying? What a hypocrite you are!" said SFC Shally angrily, entering the room. I refused to stop speaking my prayers, and after that, I was forbidden to perform my ritual prayers for about one year to come. I also was forbidden to fast during the sacred month of Ramadan October 2003, and fed by force. During this session I also refused to eat or to drink, although they offered me water every once in a while. "We must give you food and water; if you don't eat it's fine." They also offered me the nastiest MRE they had in the camp. We detainees knew that JTF interrogators gathered Intels about what food a detainee likes or dislikes, when he prays, and many other things that are just ridiculous.

I was just wishing to pass out so I didn't have to suffer, and that was really the main reason for my hunger strike; I knew people like these don't get impressed by hunger strikes. Of course they didn't want me to die, but they understand there are many steps before one dies. "You're not gonna die, we're gonna feed you up your ass," said SSG Mary.

I have never felt as violated in myself as I had since the DOD Team started to torture me to get me to admit to things I haven't done. You, Dear Reader, could never understand the extent of the physical, and much more the psychological pain people in my situation suffered, no matter how hard you try to put yourself in another's shoes. Had I done what they accused me of, I would have relieved myself on day one. But the problem is that you cannot just admit to something you haven't done; you need to deliver the details, which you can't when you hadn't done anything. It's not just, "Yes, I did!" No, it doesn't work that way: you have to make up a complete story that makes sense to the dumbest dummies. One of the hardest things to do is to tell an untruthful story and maintain it, and that is exactly where I was stuck. Of course I didn't want to involve myself in devastating crimes I hadn't done — especially under the present circumstances, where the U.S. government was jumping on every Muslim and trying to pin any crime on him.

"We are going to do this with you every single day, day in, day out, unless you speak about Abdulmalek and admit to your crimes," said SSG Mary.

"You have to provide us a smoking gun about another friend of yours. Something like that would really help you," SFC Shally said in a later session. "Why should you take all of this, if you can stop it?"

I decided to remain silent during torture and to speak whenever they relieved me. I realized that even asking my interrogators politely to use the bathroom, which was a dead basic right of mine, I gave my interrogators some kind of control they don't deserve. I knew it was not just about asking for the bathroom: it was more about humiliating me and getting me to tell them what they wanted to hear. Ultimately an interrogator is interested in gathering Intels, and typically the end justifies the means in that regard. And that was another reason why I refused both to drink and to eat: so I didn't have to use the rest room. And it worked.

The extravagance of the moment gave me more strength. My statement was that I was going to fight to the last drop of my blood.

"We're stronger than you, we have more people, we have more resources, and we're going to defeat you. But if you start to cooperate with us, you'll start to have some sleep and hot meals," said SFC Shally numerous times. "You cooperate not, you eat not, you get remedy not."

Humiliation, sexual harassment, fear, and starvation was the order of the day until around 10 p.m. Interrogators made sure that I had no clue about the time, but nobody is perfect; their watches always revealed it. I would be using this mistake later, when they put me in dark isolation.

"I'm gonna send you to your cell now, and tomorrow you'll experience even worse," said SSG Mary after consulting with her colleagues. I was happy to be relieved; I just wanted to have a break and be left alone. I was so worn out, and only God knew how I looked. But SSG Mary lied to me; she just organized a psychological trick to hurt me more. I was far from being relieved. The D.O.C., which was fully cooperating when it came to torture, sent another escort team. As soon as I reached the doorstep leading out of Brown Building I fell face down, my legs refused to carry me, and every inch in my body was conspiring against me. The guards failed to make me stand up, so they had to drag me on the tips of my toes.

"Bring the motherfucker back!" shouted Mr. X, a celebrity among the torture squad.* He was about my age and about six feet tall, athletically built, and had special clothes for his work.

---

* "Mr. X" appears in the Schmidt-Furlow, DOJ IG, and Senate Armed Services Committee reports. At his 2005 Administrative Review Board hearing, with characteristic wit, MOS said this interrogator was always covered "like in Saudi Arabia, how the women are covered," with "open-

He wore dark blue coveralls, not like an Air Force pilot's but like meat locker workers wear, and a black mask covering his face. Mr. X was aware that he was committing heavy war crimes, and so he was ordered by his bosses to cover himself. But if there is any kind of basic justice, he will get busted through his bosses; we know their names and their ranks.

When I got to know Mr. X more and heard him speaking I wondered, How could a man as smart as he was possibly accept such a degrading job, which surely is going to haunt him the rest of his life? For the sake of fairness and honesty, I must say that Mr. X spoke convincingly to me, although he had no information and was completely misled. Maybe he had few choices, because many people in the Army come from poor families, and that's why the Army sometimes gives them the dirtiest job. I mean theoretically Mr. X could have refused to commit crimes of war, and he might even get away with it. Later on I discussed with some of my guards why they executed the order to stop me from praying, since it's an unlawful order. "I could have refused, but my boss would have given me a shitty job or transferred me to a bad place. I know I can go to hell for what I have done to you," one of them told me. History repeats itself: during World War II, German soldiers were not excused when they argued that they received orders.

"You've been giving the female sergeant a hard time," continued Mr. X, dragging me into a dark room with the help of the guards. He dropped me on the dirty floor. The room was as dark as ebony. Mr. X started playing a track very loudly—I mean *very* loudly. The song was, "Let the bodies hit the floor." I might never forget that song. At the same time, Mr. X turned

---

ings for his eyes" and "O.J. Simpson gloves on his hands." ARB transcript, 25–26.

on some colored blinkers that hurt the eyes. "If you fucking fall asleep, I'm gonna hurt you," he said. I had to listen to the song over and over until next morning. I started praying.*

"Stop the fuck praying," he said loudly. I was by this time both really tired and terrified, and so I decided to pray in my heart. Every once in a while Mr. X gave me water. I drank the water because I was only scared of being hurt. I really had no real feeling for time.

To the best of my knowledge, M. X sent me back to my cell around 5 a.m. in the morning.

"Welcome to hell," said the female BNCO guard when I stepped inside the block. I didn't answer, and she wasn't worth it.† But I was like, "I think you deserve hell more than I do because you're working dutifully to get there!"

When Mr. X joined the team, they organized a 24-hour shift regime. The morning shift with SFC Shally started between 7 and 9 a.m. and ended between 3 and 4 p.m.; the dayshift with SSG Mary ran between 4:30 and 10 or 11 p.m.; and the night-shift was with Mr. X. He always took over when SSG Mary left; she would literally hand me over to him. This went on until August 24, 2003; I rarely got a break or relief from even one of the shifts.

---

* The Senate Armed Services Committee, which reviewed JTF-GTMO interrogation records, dates what appears to be this interrogation session as July 8, 2003. On that day, the committee found, "Slahi was interrogated by Mr. X and was 'exposed to variable lighting patterns and rock music, to the tune of *Drowning Pool's* 'Let the Bodies Hit [the] Floor.'" SASC, 139.

† The BNCO is the Block Non-Commissioned Officer, the senior member of the guard unit.

"Three shifts! Is it not too much for a human being to be interrogated 24 hours a day, day after day?" I asked. SSG Mary was the least of many evils, so I just tried to talk to her as a human being. You might be surprised if I tell you that she possesses good qualities as a person. As much as I hated what she was doing, I must be just, fair, and honest.

"We could put on more personnel and make four shifts. We have more people," SSG Mary answered. And that's exactly what happened. The team was reinforced with another young male army sergeant, and instead of a three-shift team I had to deal with four fresh people during a 24-hour period.

"You fucked up!" said an escorting guard who by accident had to escort me twice in one day from one building to another. "What are you doing here? You've been in reservation already!"

"I get interrogated for 24 hours."

The guard laughed loudly and evilly repeated, "You fucked up!" I just looked at him and smiled.

On day three of the shifts the escorting team showed up at my door in the early morning, as soon as I fell asleep after a rough, 20-hour interrogation. You know, when you just fall asleep and the saliva starts to come out of your mouth?

"Reservation!" shouted one of the guards. My feet barely carried me. "Hurry up!" I quickly washed my face and my mouth. I tried to use every opportunity to keep myself clean, although I was deprived from the right to take a shower like other detainees. The team wanted to humiliate me.

"What a smell!" SFC Shally used to say when he entered the room where he interrogated me.

"Man, you smell like shit!" said one of the guards more than once. I only got the opportunity to shower and change my clothes when his lowness SFC Shally couldn't bear my smell anymore; "Take the guy, give him a shower, he smells like shit," he would say. Only then would I get a shower, for months to come.

"Hurry up!" the guards kept saying. I was taken out of India Block, a block I hated less only than the interrogation room. I had a headache, nausea, and heartburn from the sleeplessness of the last several days. My eyes were playing games on me. I hated the place where I was going.

The guards dropped me in Brown Building. Nobody was in the room. I kept dozing off while waiting on SFC Shally. Oh, my neck really hurt. I badly wanted him to show up, because I hated to sleep like that: at least he would enjoy depriving me of sleeping. SFC Shally is one of the laziest people I ever knew. He didn't take time to read reports, and so he always mistook me for other suspects. Most of the time he came late, but he reserved me early anyway, so I couldn't sleep.

There really was not a lot of news: SFC Shally and I facing each other with the same topics, like the movie *Groundhog Day*. But I had grown very nervous now that they were depriving me of the sweetness of sleep.

The order of the day always went as follows. SFC Shally started to read some paper crap he brought with him and asked me questions.

"Why the fuck did you go to Canada?"

"I wanted to find a job and have a nice life."

"Fuck you! Stand up!"

"I'd rather stand up like this until death than talk to your ugly face!" When SFC Shally made me stand up, he made sure that the guards maintained his orders while he was stuffing his big stomach during lunch; whenever I tried to change my inconvenient position, the guards surged from nowhere and forced me to stay as straight as I could. Every interrogator I knew missed a meal sometimes, for whatever reason. SFC Shally never missed his meal no matter what.

"If you stop denying what you've done, we'll start to give you hot meals and some sleep. We are stronger than you."

"I don't need what I don't have."

"We're gonna put you in a hole the rest of your life. You're already convicted. You will never see your family."

"It's not in your hands, but if it is, just do it, the sooner the better!"

Sometimes SFC Shally went through the propaganda posters of detainees who were supposedly released. "Look at this guy, he's a criminal but he admitted to everything, and now he's able to lead a normal life." I mean, all interrogators lie, but SFC Shally's lies were more than obvious. Though if another interrogator lies, his appearance changes, but SFC Shally recounts a lie as well as the truth: his face always had the same hateful look.

When the pain became unbearable, I became smooth for negotiation, and he agreed to let me sit on the uncomfortable chair. But he soon got shocked when I didn't give him the answers he wanted to hear.

"I am going to do everything I am allowed to to break you!" SFC Shally said angrily. He threatened me with all kind of horrible scenarios. "You're gonna spend the rest of your life in jail." "We will wipe you out of the database and put you in a hole where nobody knows about you." "You will never see your family again." My answer was always, "Do what you got to do! I have done nothing!" and as soon as I spit my words SFC Shally went wildly crazy, as if he wanted to devour me alive. So I avoided answering him and let him for the most part do the talking. As I say, SFC Shally likes to talk and hates to listen. I sometimes doubted that his ears functioned. He spoke as if he were reading some Gospels.

I was just wondering how he was so sure I was a criminal. "Sergeant, what if you are wrong in what you're suspecting me of?" I asked him.

"I would be wasting my time," he answered.

"Fair enough."

"If you provide incriminating information about somebody, say about Karim Mehdi or Ahmed Laabidi, that leads to his conviction, your life would change to a better one." I didn't answer him, because I didn't have what he was looking for. SFC Shally's view of justice was very rough: even if I provided him everything he wanted, he would reduce my sentence from the electric chair to life, and then maybe thirty years in prison. I honestly was not interested in his offer.

During his shift, SFC Shally would be reporting to his boss during the breaks. I was not sure who his boss was at that point, probably Richard Zuley. But I'm sure that the highest authority in his chain of command in GTMO was General Geoffrey Miller, and that he was briefed regularly about my case and always gave the orders for what to do next with "that bastard." According to Mary, President Bush was regularly briefed about my case, and so was Donald Rumsfeld. Donald Rumsfeld even sent his secretary, a large dark gentleman the guards told me was named Butler, to check on me in summer 2004. He asked me some Intel questions. By that time, though, the tension was already relieved.*

---

* As these July 2003 sessions were happening, General Miller was submitting Slahi's "Special Interrogation Plan" to SOUTHCOM commander General James Hill for approval. On July 18, 2003, Hill forwarded the plan to Secretary of Defense Donald Rumsfeld. The plan was approved by Deputy Secretary of Defense Paul Wolfowitz on July 28, 2003, and signed by Rumsfeld on August 13, 2003. In July 2003, Richard Zuley, a retired Chicago police officer and navy reserve lieutenant, was appointed chief of MOS's "special projects" interrogation team. Zuley's identity was first revealed in

I spent the afternoon shift with SSG Mary. Like I mentioned before, she was the least evil of all. Her order of day went as follows. When she pulled me to interrogation, she informed the D.O.C. not to give me a chair, so I had to settle for the dirty floor—but I didn't even get that, because the D.O.C. always asked the guards to make me stand up until SSG Mary arrived. Then she decided whether to allow me to sit or make me stand up during her whole shift, and after that Mr. X made me stand up for the rest of the 24 hours.*

---

an unredacted footnote of the Senate Armed Services Committee report, and has been corroborated by court documents in MOS's habeas corpus case and in numerous press reports. See, e.g., https://www.theguardian.com/us-news/2015/feb/18/american-police-brutality-chicago-guantanamo In his book *The Terror Courts: Rough Justice at Guantanamo Bay* (New Haven: Yale University Press, 2013), *Wall Street Journal* reporter Jess Bravin writes that Zuley took over MOS's interrogation on July 1, 2003, the same day General Miller approved his "Special Interrogation Plan" (Bravin, *The Terror Courts,* 105). Zuley publicly acknowledged his role as a lead interrogator in Guantánamo in an episode of the Blog Talk Radio *Dave and Chris Show* in January 2009. Audio of that podcast is available at http://www.blogtalkradio .com/perfectly-harmless/2009/01/31/the-dave-and-chris-show. For a detailed account of the development and authorization of MOS's "Special Interrogation Plan," see SASC, 135–41.

    * When Defense Secretary Rumsfeld issued his original authorization to use interrogation techniques beyond those included in the Army Field Manual, including forced standing, he famously appended the note "I stand for 8–10 hours a day. Why is standing limited to four hours?" But as Albert Biderman found in his study of coercive interrogation techniques employed by North Korean interrogators during the Korean War, "Returnees who underwent long periods of standing and sitting...report no other experience could be more excruciating." Biderman explained, "Where the individual is told to stand at attention for long periods an intervening factor is introduced. The immediate source of pain is not the interrogator but the victim himself. The contest becomes, in a way, one of the individual against himself. The motivational strength of the individual is likely to exhaust itself in this internal encounter. Bringing the subject to act 'against himself' in this manner has additional advantages for the interrogator. It leads the prisoner to exaggerate the power of the interrogator. As long as the subject remains standing, he is attributing to his captor the power to do something worse to

I started to recite the Koran quietly, for prayer was forbidden. Once, back in Gold Building, she said, "Why don't you pray? go ahead and pray!" I was like, How friendly! But as soon as I started to pray, she started to make fun of my religion, and so I settled for praying in my heart so I didn't give her the opportunity to commit blasphemy. Making fun of somebody else's religion is one of the most barbaric acts. President Bush described his holy war against the so-called terrorism as a war between the civilized and barbaric world. But his government committed more barbaric acts than the terrorists themselves. I can name tons of war crimes that Bush's government is involved in.

This particular day was one of the roughest days in my interrogation before the day around end of August that was my "Birthday Party" as SSG Mary called it. She brought someone who was apparently a Marine; he wore a woodland camouflage combat uniform. He was small and very loud for his size, and even brought his own boom box into the room.

SSG Mary offered me a metal chair. "I told you, I'm gonna bring some people to help me interrogate you," she said, sitting inches away in front of me. The guest sat almost sticking on my knee. The Marine started to ask me some questions I don't remember,

"Yes or no?" the guest shouted, loud beyond belief, in a show to scare me, and maybe to impress SSG Mary, who knows? I found his method very childish and silly.

I looked at him, smiled, and said, "Neither!" The guest threw the chair from beneath me violently. I fell on the chains. Oh, it hurt.

"Stand up, motherfucker," they both shouted, almost syn-

---

him, but there is actually no showdown of the ability of the interrogator to do so." See http://www2.gwu.edu/~nsarchiv/torturingdemocracy/documents/19570900.pdf.

chronous. Then a session of torture and humiliation started. They started to ask me the questions again after they made me stand up, but it was too late, because I told them a million times, "Whenever you start to torture me, I'm not gonna say a single word." And that was always accurate; for the rest of the day, they exclusively talked.

The Marine turned the air conditioner all the way down to bring me to freezing. This method had been practiced in the camp at least since August 2002. I had seen people who were exposed to the frozen room day after day; by then, the list was long. The consequences of the cold room are devastating, such as rheumatism, but they show up only at a later age because it takes time until they work their way through the bones. The torture squad was so well trained that they were performing almost perfect crimes, avoiding leaving any obvious evidence. Nothing was left to chance. They hit in predefined places. They practiced horrible methods, the aftermath of which would only manifest later. The interrogators turned the A/C all the way down trying to reach 0°, but obviously air conditioners are not designed to kill, so in the well insulated room the A/C fought its way to 49°F, which, if you are interested in math like me, is 9.4°C—in other words, very, very cold, especially for some-body who had to stay in it more than twelve hours, had no underwear and just a very thin uniform, and who comes from a hot country. Somebody from Saudi Arabia cannot take as much cold as somebody from Sweden; and vice versa, when it comes to hot weather. Interrogators took these factors in con-sideration and used them effectively.

You may ask, Where were the interrogators after installing the detainee in the frozen room? Actually, it's a good question. First, the interrogators didn't stay in the room; they would just come for the humiliation, degradation, discouragement, or other factor of torture, and after that they left the room and went to the monitoring room next door. Second, interrogators were adequately dressed; for instance Mr. X was dressed like somebody entering a meat locker. In spite of that, they didn't stay long with the detainee. Third, there's a big psychological difference when you are exposed to a cold place for purpose of torture, and when you just go there for fun and challenge. And lastly, the interrogators kept moving in the room, which meant blood circulation, which meant keeping themselves warm while the detainee was shackled the whole time to the floor, standing for the most part. All I could do was move my feet and rub my hands. But the Marine guy stopped me from rubbing my hands by ordering a special chain that shackled my hands on my opposite hips. When I get nervous I always start to rub my hands together and write on my body, and that drove my interrogators crazy.

"What are you writing?" the Marine shouted. "Either you tell me or you stop the fuck doing that." But I couldn't stop; it was unintentional. The Marine guy started to throw chairs around, hit me with his forehead, and describe me with all kind of adjectives I didn't deserve, for no reason.

"You joined the wrong team, boy. You fought for a lost cause," he said, alongside a bunch of trash talk degrading my family, my religion, and myself, not to mention all kinds of threats against my family to pay for "my crimes," which goes against any common sense. I knew that he had no power, but I knew that he was speaking on behalf of the most powerful country in the world, and obviously enjoyed the full support of his government. However, I would rather save you, Dear Reader, from quoting his garbage. The guy was nuts. He asked me about things I have no clue about, and names I never heard.

"I have been in Mauritania," he said, "and do you know who

was our host? The President! We had a good time in the palace." The Marine guy asked questions and answered them himself.

When the man failed to impress me with all the talk and humiliation, and with the threat to arrest my family since the Mauritanian president was an obedient servant of the U.S., he started to hurt me more. He brought ice-cold water and soaked me all over my body, with my clothes still on me. It was so awful; I kept shaking like a Parkinson's patient. Technically I wasn't able to talk anymore. The guy was stupid: he was literally executing me but in a slow way. SSG Mary gestured to him to stop pouring water on me. Another detainee had told me a "good" interrogator suggested he eat in order to reduce the pain, but I refused to eat anything; I couldn't open my mouth anyway.

The guy was very hot when Mary stopped him because she was afraid of the paperwork that would result in case of my death. So he found another technique, namely he brought a CD player with a booster and started to play some rap music. I didn't really mind the music because it made me forget my pain. Actually, the music was a blessing in disguise; I was trying to make sense of the words. All I understood was that the music was about love. Can you believe it? Love! All I had experienced lately was hatred, or the consequences thereof.

"Listen to that, Motherfucker!" said the guest, while closing the door violently behind him. "You're gonna get the same shit day after day, and guess what? It's getting worse. What you're seeing is only the beginning," said the Marine. I kept praying and ignoring what they were doing.

"Oh, ALLAH help me.... Oh Allah have mercy on me" SSG Mary kept mimicking my prayers, "ALLAH, ALLAH.... There is no Allah. He let you down!" I smiled at how ignorant she was, talking about the Lord like that. But the Lord is very patient, and doesn't need to rush to punishment, because there is no escaping him.

Detainees knew the policy in the camp: if the MI believes that you're hiding crucial information, they torture you in Camp Delta, in India Block, but if that doesn't work, they kidnap you to a secret place and nobody knows what they're doing with you. During my time in Delta Camp two individuals were kidnapped and disappeared for good, namely Abdullah Tabarak Ahmad from Morocco and Mohammed al-Qahtani from Saudi Arabia.* I started to get the feeling that I was going to be kidnapped because I really got stuck with my interrogators, and so I started to gather Intels.

"The camp out there is the worst one," said a young MP.

"They don't get food?" I wondered.

"Something like that," he replied.

Between 10 and 11 p.m., SSG Mary handed me over to Mr. X, who gave orders to the guards to move me to his specially

---

* Like MOS and Mohammed al-Qahtani, Abdullah Tabarak was held in isolation and inaccessible to the International Committee of the Red Cross. In 2006, the *Washington Post* reported, "Maj. Gen. Geoffrey Miller told Red Cross inspectors on Oct. 9, 2003, that they could not visit Tabarak or three other detainees 'because of military necessity,' according to the memos. On a follow-up visit Feb. 2, 2004, Miller informed Red Cross officials that they could see anyone at the base, except Tabarak. Miller once again cited 'military necessity.' A Defense Department spokesman declined to comment on the memos.

"Tabarak has told his attorney and other detainees that he was kept in an isolation cell during most of his stay at Guantanamo. For about one year, he said, he was interrogated only while blindfolded, so he could not see his captors or even know for certain if he was in Cuba or another country."

Tabarak was transferred to Morocco in August 2004, held for four months in the custody of Moroccan police, and then released. See http://www.washingtonpost.com/wp-dyn/content/article/2006/01/29/AR2006012901044_pf.html.

prepared room. It was freezing cold and full of pictures showing the glories of the U.S.: weapons arsenals, planes, and pictures of George Bush. "Don't pray! You'll insult my country if you pray during my national anthem. We're the greatest country in the free world, and we have the smartest president in the world," he said. For the whole night I had to listen to the U.S. anthem. I hate anthems anyway. All I can remember was the beginning, "Oh say can you see..." over and over. I was happy that no ice-cold water was poured over me. I tried at the beginning to steal some prayers, but Mr. X was watching closely by means of cameras and the one-way mirror. "Stop the fuck praying, you're insulting my country!" I was really tired and worn out, and I was anything but looking for trouble, and so I decided to pray in my heart. I was shaking all night long.

Between 4 and 5 a.m., Mr. X released me, just to be taken a couple of hours later by SFC Shally to start the same routine over. But the hardest step is the first step; the hardest days were the first days, and with every day going by I grew stronger. Meanwhile I was the main subject of talk in the camp. Although many other detainees were suffering similar fates, I was "Criminal Number One," and I was being treated that way. Sometimes when I was in the rec yard, detainees shouted, "Be patient. Remember Allah tests the people he loves the most." Comments like that were my only solace beside my faith in the Lord.

Nothing really interesting changed in my routine: cold room, standing up for hours, interrogators repeating the same threats about me being kidnapped and locked up forever.* Mr. X made

---

* Military, Department of Justice, and Senate investigators have described in more detail several of these threats. According to a footnote in the Schmidt-Furlow report, "On 17 Jul 03 the masked interrogator told that he had a dream about the subject of the second interrogation dying. Specifically he told the subject of the second special interrogation that in the dream

me write tons of pages about my life, but I never satisfied him. One night he undressed me with the help of a blond female and a male guard. Expecting the cold room, I had put shorts on over my pants to reduce the cold that was penetrating through my bones, but he was extremely mad, which led him to make a female guard undress me. I never felt so violated. I stood up all the night in the ice-cold room praying, ignoring all his barking and ordering me to stop praying. I couldn't have cared less about whatever he was going to do.*

---

he 'saw four detainees that were chained together at the feet. They dug a hole that was six-feet long, six-feet deep, and four-feet wide. Then he observed the detainees throw a plain, pine casket with the detainee's identification number painted in orange lowered into the ground.' The masked interrogator told the detainee that his dream meant that he was never going to leave GTMO unless he started to talk, that he would indeed die here from old age and be buried on 'Christian...sovereign American soil.' On 20 Jul 03 the masked interrogator, 'Mr. X,' told the subject of the second Special Interrogation Plan that his family was 'incarcerated.' "

The report continues, "The MFR dated 02 Aug 03 indicates that the subject of the second special interrogation had a messenger that day there to 'deliver a message to him.' The MFR goes on to state: 'That message was simple: Interrogator's colleagues are sick of hearing the same lies over and over and over and are seriously considering washing their hands of him. Once they do so, he will disappear and never be heard from again. Interrogator assured detainee again to use his imagination to think of the worst possible scenario he could end up in. He told Detainee that beatings and physical pain are not the worst thing in the world. After all, after being beaten for a while, humans tend to disconnect the mind from the body and make it through. However, there are worse things than physical pain. Interrogator assured Detainee that, eventually, he will talk, because everyone does. But until then, he will very soon disappear down a very dark hole. His very existence will become erased. His electronic files will be deleted from the computer, his paper files will be packed up and filed away, and his existence will be forgotten by all. No one will know what happened to him, and eventually, no one will care.' " Schmidt-Furlow, 24–25.

* An incident in which MOS was "deprived of clothing by a female interrogator" is recorded in the DOJ IG report; the report suggests the date of that session was July 17, 2003. DOJ IG, 124.

The boss of the group, Mr. Richard Zuley, crawled from behind the scene. SSG Mary told me a couple of times before his visit about a very high level government person who was going to visit me and talk to me about my family. I didn't take the information negatively; I thought he was going to bring me some messages from my family. But I was wrong, it was about hurting my family. Mr. Zuley was escalating the situation with me relentlessly.

Mr. Zuley came around 11 a.m., escorted by SSG Mary and the new male sergeant. He was brief and direct. "My name is Captain Collins. I work for the Department of Defense. My government is desperate to get information out of you. Do you understand?"*

"Yes."

"Can you read English?"

"Yes."

"Captain Collins" handed me a letter that he had obviously forged. The letter was from DoD, and it said, basically, "Ould Slahi is involved in the Millennium attack and recruited three of September 11 hijackers. Since Slahi has refused to cooperate,

---

* The date, according to the DOJ Inspector General, is now August 2, 2003. The IG reported, "On August 2, 2003, a different military interrogator posing as a Navy Captain from the White House" appeared to MOS. Both the Senate Armed Services Committee report and the DOJ IG report describe the letter he delivered. According to the Senate Armed Services Committee, the letter stated "that his mother had been detained, would be interrogated, and if she were uncooperative she might be transferred to GTMO." The DOJ IG reported that "the letter referred to 'the administrative and logistical difficulties her presence would present in this previously all-male environment,'" and "The interrogator told Slahi that his family was 'in danger if he (760) did not cooperate.'" The DOJ IG and SASC reports and the army's Schmidt-Furlow report all make clear that this interrogator was in fact the chief of MOS's "Special Projects Team," and the Schmidt-Furlow report indicates he presented himself to MOS as "Captain Collins." DOJ IG, 123; SASC, 140; Schmidt-Furlow, 25.

the U.S. government is going to arrest his mother and put her in a special facility."

I read the letter. "Is that not harsh and unfair?" I said.

"I am not here to maintain justice. I'm here to stop people from crashing planes into buildings in my country."

"Then go and stop them. I've done nothing to your country," I said.

"You have two options: either being a defendant or a witness,"

"I want neither."

"You have no choice, or your life is going to change decidedly," he said.

"Just do it, the sooner, the better!" I said. Richard Zuley put the forged letter back in his bag, closed it angrily, and left the room. Mr. Zuley would lead the team working on my case until August or September 2004. He always tried to make me believe that his real name was Captain Collins, but what he didn't know was that I knew his name even before I met him.

After that meeting I had no doubt about the intentions of "Captain Collins"; he was just seeking the required formalities to kidnap me from the camp to an unknown place. "Your being here required many signatures. We've been trying for some time to get you here," one of my guards would tell me later. Captain Collins was also putting together a complete team which would execute the Abduction. All of this was carried out in secrecy; participants knew only as much as they needed to. I know for instance that SSG Mary didn't know about the details of the plan.

On Monday August 25, 2003, around 4 p.m., SSG Mary

reserved me for interrogation in Gold Building. By then I had spent the weekend on Romeo Block, which was entirely emptied of any other detainees, in order to keep me isolated from the rest of the community. But I saw it as a positive thing: the cell was warmer and I could see daylight, while in India Block I was locked in a frozen box.

"Now I have overall control. I can do anything I want with you; I can even move you to Camp Four," said SSG Mary.*

"I know why you moved me to Romeo Block," I said. "It's because you don't want me to see anybody." SSG Mary didn't comment; she just smiled. It was more of a friendly talk. Around 5:30 p.m., she brought me my cold MRE. I had gotten used to my cold portions; I didn't savor them, but I had been suffering weight loss like never before, and I knew in order to survive I had to eat.

I started to eat my meal. SSG Mary was going in and out, but there was nothing suspicious about that, she had always been that way. I barely finished my meal, when all of a sudden Mary and I heard a commotion, guards cursing loudly ("I told you motherfucker...!"), people banging the floor violently with heavy boots, dogs barking, doors closing loudly. I froze in my seat. Mary went speechless. We were staring at each other, not knowing what was going on. My heart was pounding because

---

* Guantánamo's Camp IV opened in February 2003. Globalsecurity.org describes Camp Four as a "medium security facility built inside the limits of Camp Delta." "With dormitories able to hold up to 20 detainees in each unit, Camp 4 is aimed at enabling a limited number of captives the opportunity to interact with one another. There, detainees are able to eat, sleep and pray together," the site reports. It was the first time Guantánamo's prisoners were allowed to live communally, and photographs of prisoners in Camp Four were displayed in other blocks and in interrogations rooms as an incentive to encourage cooperation. The Camp was emptied when Camp V and Camp VI were opened. See http://www.globalsecurity.org/military/facility/guantanamo-bay_delta.htm.

I knew a detainee was going to be hurt. Yes, and that detainee was me.

Suddenly a commando team consisting of three soldiers and a German shepherd broke into our interrogation room. Everything happened quicker than you could think about it. Mr. X and a masked guard punched me violently, which made me fall face down on the floor.

"Motherfucker, I told you, you're gone!" said Mr. X. His partner kept punching me everywhere, mainly on my face and my ribs. He, too, was masked from head to toe; he punched me the whole time without saying a word, because he didn't want to be recognized. The third man was not masked; he stayed at the door holding the dog's collar, ready to release it on me.

"Who told you to do that? You're hurting the detainee!" screamed SSG Mary, who was no less terrified than I was. Mr. X was the leader of the assailing guards, and he was executing Captain Collins's orders. As to me, I couldn't digest the situation. My first thought was, They mistook me for somebody else. My second thought was to try to recognize my environment by looking around while one of the guards was squeezing my face against the floor. I saw the dog fighting to get loose. I saw SSG Mary standing up, looking helplessly at the guards working on me.

"Blindfold the Motherfucker, if he tries to look—"

One of them hit me hard across the face, and quickly put the goggles on my eyes, ear muffs on my ears, and a small bag over my head. I couldn't tell who did what. They tightened the chains around my ankles and my wrists; afterwards, I started to bleed. All I could hear was Mr. X cursing, "F-this and F-that!" I didn't say a word, I was overwhelmingly surprised, I thought they were going to execute me.

Thanks to the beating I wasn't able to stand, so Mr. X and the other guard dragged me out with my toes tracing the way and threw me in a truck, which immediately took off. The beating party would go on for the next three or four hours before they turned me over to another team that was going to use different torture techniques.

"Stop praying, Motherfucker, you're killing people," Mr. X said, and punched me hard on my mouth. My mouth and nose started to bleed, and my lips grew so big that I technically could not speak anymore. The colleague of Mr. X turned out to be one of my guards, a tall white sergeant in his late twenties who I called Big Boss. Mr. X and Big Boss each took a side and started to punch me and smash me against the metal of the truck. One of the guys hit me so hard that my breath stopped and I was choking; I felt like I was breathing through my ribs. I almost suffocated without their knowledge. I was having a hard time breathing due to the head cover anyway, plus they hit me so many times on my ribs that I stopped breathing for a moment.

Did I pass out? Maybe not; all I know is that I kept noticing Mr. X several times spraying Ammonia in my nose. The funny thing was that Mr. X was at the same time my "lifesaver," as were all the guards I would be dealing with for the next year, or most of them. All of them were allowed to give me medication and first aid.

After ten to fifteen minutes, the truck stopped at the beach, and my escorting team dragged me out of the truck and put me in a high-speed boat. Mr. X and Big Boss never gave me a break; they kept hitting me, Mr. X while talking, Big Boss silently, and jerking on my shackles in order to make them stab me. "You're killing people," said Mr. X. I believe he was thinking out loud: he knew his was the most cowardly crime in the world, torturing a helpless detainee who completely went to submission and turned himself in. What a brave operation! Mr. X was trying to convince himself that he was doing the right thing.

Inside the boat, Mr. X made me drink salt water, I believe it was directly from the ocean. It was so nasty I threw up. They would put any object in my mouth and shout, "Swallow, Motherfucker!", but I decided inside not to swallow the organ-damaging salt water, which choked me when they kept pouring it in my mouth. "Swallow, you idiot!" I contemplated quickly, and decided for the nasty, damaging water rather than death.

Mr. X and Sergeant Big Boss escorted me for about three hours in the high-speed boat. The goal of such a trip was, first, to torture the detainee and claim that "the detainee hurt himself during transport," and second, to make the detainee believe he was being transferred to some far, faraway secret prison. We detainees knew all of that; we had detainees reporting they had been flown around for four hours and found themselves in the same jail where they started. I knew from the beginning that I was going to be transferred to Camp Echo, about a five-minute ride. Camp Echo had a very bad reputation: just hearing the name gave me nausea.* I knew the whole long trip I was going

---

* The Senate Armed Services Committee found that the military's "Special Interrogation Plan" for MOS included a staged scene in which "military in full riot gear take him from his cell, place him on a watercraft, and drive him around to make him think he had been taken off the island." Afterward, the committee reported, "Slahi would be taken to Camp Echo," where his cell and interrogation room—self-contained in a single trailerlike isolation hut—had been "modified in such a way as to reduce as much outside stimuli as possible." The plan directed that "the doors will be sealed to a point that allows no light to enter the room. The walls may be covered with white paint or paper to further eliminate objects the detainee may concentrate on. The room will contain an eyebolt in the floor and speakers for sound." The SASC also recorded that an August 21, 2003,

to take was meant to terrorize me. But what difference does it make? I cared less about the place, and more about the people who were detaining me. No matter where I got transferred, I would still be a detainee of the U.S. Armed Forces; and as for rendition to a third country, I thought I was through with that because I was already sent to Jordan for eight months. The politics of the DoD toward me was to take care of me on their own; "September 11 didn't happen in Jordan; we don't expect other countries to pry Intels off detainees as we do," Mr. X said once. The Americans obviously were not satisfied with the results achieved by their "torture allies."

But I think when torture comes into play, things get out of control. Torture doesn't guarantee that the detainee cooperates. In order to stop torture, the detainee has to please his assailant, even with untruthful, and sometimes misleading, Intels; sorting information out is time-consuming. And experience shows that torture doesn't stop or even reduce terrorist attacks: Egypt, Algeria, Turkey are good examples. On the other hand, discus-

---

e-mail from a JTF-GTMO intelligence specialist to Lt. Richard Zuley reported on the final preparations to the Camp Echo hut: "The email described sealing Slahi's cell at Camp Echo to 'prevent light from shining' in and covering the entire exterior of his cell with [a] tarp to 'prevent him from making visual contact with guards.' "

According to the DOJ Inspector General, the original Special Interrogation Plan that General Miller signed on July 1, 2003, "stated that Slahi would be hooded and flown around Guantanamo Bay for one or two hours in a helicopter to persuade him that he had been moved out of GTMO to a location where 'the rules have changed.'" However, the IG reported, military interrogators told investigators that in the end "they did not use a helicopter because General Miller decided that it was too difficult logistically to pull off, and that too many people on the base would have to know about it to get this done." Instead, "on August 25, 2003, Slahi was removed from his cell in Camp Delta, fitted with blackout goggles, and taken on a disorienting boat ride during which he was permitted to hear pre-planned deceptive conversations among other passengers." SASC, 137–38, 140; DOJ IG 122–123, 127.

sion has brought tremendously good results. After the unsuc-cessful attack on the Egyptian president in Addis Ababa, the government reached a cease-fire with Al Gawaa al-Islamiyah, and the latter opted later on for a political fight. Nevertheless, the Americans had learned a lot from their torture-practicing allies, and they were working closely together.

When the boat reached the coast, Mr. X and his colleague dragged me out and made me sit, crossing my legs. I was moan-ing from the unbearable pain.

"Uh...Uh...ALLAH...ALLAH....I told you not to fuck with us, didn't I?" said Mr. X, mimicking me. I hoped I could stop moaning, because the gentleman kept mimicking me and blaspheming the Lord. However, the moaning was necessary so I could breathe. My feet were numb, for the chains stopped the blood circulation to my hands and my feet; I was happy for every kick I got so I could alter my position. "Do not move Motherfucker!" said Mr. X, but sometimes I couldn't help changing position; it was worth the kick.

"We appreciate everybody who works with us, thanks gen-tlemen," said Captain Collins. I recognized his voice; although he was addressing his Arab guests, the message was addressed to me more than anybody. It was nighttime. My blindfold didn't keep me from feeling the bright lighting from some kind of high-watt projectors.

"We happy for zat. Maybe we take him to Egypt, he say everything," said an Arab guy whose voice I had never heard, with a thick Egyptian accent. I could tell the guy was in his late twenties or early thirties based on his voice, his speech, and later on his actions. I could also tell that his English was both poor and decidedly mispronounced. Then I heard indis-tinct conversations here and there, after which the Egyptian and another guy approached. Now they're talking directly to me in Arabic:

"What a coward! You guys ask for civil rights? Guess you get none," said the Egyptian.

"Somebody like this coward takes us only one hour in Jordan to spit everything," said the Jordanian. Obviously, he didn't know that I had already spent eight months in Jordan and that no miracle took place.

"We take him to EEEgypt," said the Egyptian, addressing Captain Collins.

"Maybe later," Captain Collins said.

"How poor are these Americans! They really are spoiling these fuckers. But now we're working with them," said the Egyptian guy, now addressing me directly in Arabic. When I heard Egypt, and a new rendition, my heart was pounding. I hated the endless world tour I was forcibly taking. I seriously thought rendition to Egypt on the spot was possible, because I knew how irritated and desperate the Americans were when it came to my case. The government was and still is misled about my case.

"But you know we're working with Americans in the field," said the Egyptian. He was right: Yemeni detainees had told me that they were interrogated by Jordanians and Americans at the same table when they were captured in Karachi and afterward transferred to a secret place on September 11, 2002.*

After all kinds of threats and degrading statements, I started to miss a lot of the trash talk between the Arabs and their American accomplices, and at one point I drowned in my thoughts. I felt ashamed that my people were being used for this

---

* MOS is referring here to detainees who were captured along with Ramzi bin al-Shibh on September 11, 2002, and also held for a time in CIA custody before being transferred to Guantánamo. See footnote on page 54.

horrible job by a government that claims to be the leader of the democratic free world, a government that preaches against dictatorship and "fights" for human rights and sends its children to die for that purpose: What a joke this government makes of its own people!

What would the dead average American think if he or she could see what his or her government is doing to someone who has done no crimes against anybody? As much as I was ashamed for the Arabic fellows, I knew that they definitely didn't represent the average Arab. Arabic people are among the greatest on the planet, sensitive, emotional, loving, generous, sacrificial, religious, charitable, and light-hearted. No one deserves to be used for such a dirty job, no matter how poor he is. No, we are better than that! If people in the Arab world knew what was happening in this place, the hatred against the U.S. would be heavily watered, and the accusation that the U.S. is helping and working together with dictators in our countries would be cemented. I had a feeling, or rather a hope, that these people would not go unpunished for their crimes. The situation didn't make me hate either Arabs or Americans; I just felt bad for the Arabs, and how poor we are!

All these thoughts were sliding through my head, and distracted me from hearing the nonsense conversations. After about forty minutes, I couldn't really tell, Captain Collins instructed the Arabic team to take over. The two guys grabbed me roughly, and since I couldn't walk on my own, they dragged me on the tips of my toes to the boat. I must have been very near the water, because the trip to the boat was short. I don't know, they either they put me in another boat or in a different seat. This seat was both hard and straight.

"Move!"

"I can't move!"

"Move, Fucker!" They gave this order knowing that I was too hurt to be able to move. After all I was bleeding from my mouth, my ankles, my wrists, and maybe my nose, I couldn't tell for sure. But the team wanted to keep the factor of fear and terror maintained.

"Sit!" said the Egyptian guy, who did most of the talking while both were pulling me down until I hit the metal. The Egyptian sat on my right side, and the Jordanian on my left.

"What's your fucking name?" asked the Egyptian.

"M-O-O-H-H-M-M-EE-D-D-O-O-O-U!" I answered. Technically I couldn't speak because of the swollen lips and hurting mouth. You could tell I was completely scared. Usually I wouldn't talk if somebody starts to hurt me. In Jordan, when the interrogator smashed me in the face, I refused to talk, ignoring all his threats. This was a milestone in my interrogation history. You can tell I was hurt like never before; it wasn't me anymore, and I would never be the same as before. A thick line was drawn between my past and my future with the first hit Mr. X delivered to me.

"He is like a kid!" said the Egyptian accurately, addressing his Jordanian colleague. I felt warm between them both, though not for long. With the cooperation of the Americans, a long torture trip was being prepared.

I couldn't sit straight in the chair. They put me in a kind of thick jacket which fastened me to the seat. It was a good feeling. However, there was a destroying drawback to it: my chest was so tightened that I couldn't breathe properly. Plus, the air circulation was worse than the first trip. I didn't know why, exactly, but something was definitely going wrong.

"I c....a...a...n't br...e...a...the!"

"Suck the air!" said the Egyptian wryly. I was literally suffocating inside the bag around my head. All my pleas and my begging for some free air ended in a cul-de-sac.

I heard indistinct conversations in English, I think it was Mr. X and his colleague, and probably Captain Collins. Whoever it was, they were supplying the Arab team with torture materials during the three- or four-hour trip. The order went as follows: They stuffed the air between my clothes and me with ice cubes from my neck to my ankles, and whenever the ice melted, they put in new, hard ice cubes. Moreover, every once in a while, one of the guards smashed me, most of the time in the face. The ice served both for the pain and for wiping out the bruises I had from that afternoon. Everything seemed to be perfectly prepared. People from cold regions might not understand the extent of the pain when ice cubes get stuck on your body. Historically, kings during medieval and pre-medieval times used this method to let the victim slowly die. The other method, of hitting the victim while blindfolded in inconsistent intervals, was used by the Nazis during World War II. There is nothing more terrorizing than making somebody expect a smash every single heartbeat.

"I am from Hasi Matruh, where are you from?" said the Egyptian, addressing his Jordanian colleague. He was speaking as if nothing was happening. You could tell he was used to torturing people.

"I am from the south" answered the Jordanian. I tried to keep my prayers in my heart. I could hardly remember a prayer, but I did know I needed the Lord's help, as I always do, and in that direction went my prayers. Whenever I was conscious, I drowned in my thoughts. I finally had gotten used to the routine, ice cubes until melted, smashing. But what would it be like if I landed in Egypt after about twenty-five hours of torture? What would the interrogation there look like? Mamdouh Habib, an Australian detainee who was born in Egypt, once described his unlucky trip from Pakistan to Egypt to me; so far everything I was experiencing, like the ice cubes and smashing, was consistent with Mamdouh's story. So I expected electric shocks in the pool. How much power can my body, especially my heart, handle? I know something about electricity and its devastating, irreversible damage: I saw Mamdouh collapsing in the blocks a couple of times every week with blood gushing out of his nose until it soaked his clothes. Mamdouh Habib was a Martial art trainer and athletically built.*

I was constructing the whole interrogation over and over, their questions, my answers. But what if they don't believe me? No, they would believe me, because they understand the recipe of terrorism more than the Americans, and have more experience. The cultural barrier between the Christian and the Muslim world still irritates the approach of Americans to the whole issue considerably; Americans tend to widen the circle of involvement to catch the largest possible numbers of Muslims. They always speak about the Big Conspiracy against the U.S. I personally had been interrogated about people who just practiced the basics of the religion and sympathized with Islamic movements; I was asked to provide every detail about Islamic movements, no matter how moderate. That's amazing in a country like the U.S., where Christian terrorist organizations such as Nazis and White Supremacists have the freedom to express themselves and recruit people openly and nobody can

---

* Mamdouh Habib, held as ISN 661 in Guantánamo, was released and transferred to Australia on January 28, 2005.

bother them. But as a Muslim, if you sympathize with the political views of an Islamic organization you're in big trouble. Even attending the same mosque as a suspect is big trouble. I mean this fact is clear for everybody who understands the ABCs of American policy toward so-called Islamic Terrorism.

The Arabo-American party was over, and the Arabs turned me over once more to the same U.S. team. They dragged me out of the boat and threw me, I would say, in the same truck as the one that afternoon. We were obviously riding on a dirt road.

"Do not move!" said Mr. X, but I didn't recognize any words anymore. I don't think that anybody beat me, but I was not conscious. When the truck stopped, Mr. X and his strong associate towed me from the truck, and dragged me over some steps. The cool air of the room hit me, and boom, they threw me face down on the metal floor of my new home.

"Do not move, I told you not to fuck with me, Mother-fucker!" said Mr. X, his voice trailing off. He was obviously tired. He left right away with a promise of more actions, and so did the Arab team.

A short time after my arrival, I felt somebody taking the heavy headgear with the earmuffs and goggles off my head. Removing these things was both painful and relieving, painful because they had started to penetrate my skin and stick, leaving scars, and relieving because I started to breathe normally and the pressure around my head went away. When the blindfold was taken off I saw a masked male who seemed to be both a medical professional and part of the torture team. He wore an Army uniform but I couldn't see his rank. His way of speaking suggested he was in his early thirties. I figured he was a Doctor, but why the heck is he hiding behind a mask, and why is he

U.S. Army, when the Navy is in charge of the medical care of detainees?

"If you fuckin' move, I'm gonna hurt you!" I was wondering how could I possibly move, and what possible damage I could do. I was in chains, and every inch in my body was hurting. That is not a Doctor, that is a human butcher!

When the young man checked on me, he realized he needed more stuff. He left and soon came back with some medical gear. I glimpsed his watch: it was about 1:30 a.m., which meant about eight hours since I was kidnapped from ▆▆▆▆ Camp. The Doctor started to wash the blood off my face with a soaked bandage. After that, he put me on a mattress—the only item in the stark cell—with the help of the guards.

"Do not move," said the guard who was standing over me. The Doctor wrapped many elastic belts around my chest and ribs. After that, they made me sit. "If you try to bite me, I'm gonna fuckin' hurt you!" said the Doctor while stuffing me with a whole bunch of tablets. I didn't respond; they were moving me around like an object. Sometime later they took off the chains, and later still one of the guards threw a thin, small, worn-out blanket onto me through the bin hole, and that was everything I would have in the room. No soap, no toothbrush, no iso mat, no Koran, nothing.

I tried to sleep, but I was kidding myself; my body was conspiring against me. It took some time until the medications started to work, then I trailed off, and only woke up when one of the guards hit my cell violently with his boot.

"Get up, piece of shit!" The Doctor once more gave me a bunch of medication and checked on my ribs. "Done with the motherfucker," he said, showing me his back as he headed toward the door. I was so shocked seeing a Doctor act like that, because I knew that at least 50 percent of medical treatment is psychological. I was like, This is an evil place, since my only solace is this bastard Doctor.*

I soon was knocked out. To be honest I can report very little about the next couple of weeks because I was not in the right state of mind. I was lying on my bed the whole time, and I was not able to realize my surroundings. I tried to find out the *Kibla,* the direction of Mecca, but there was no clue.

---

* MOS's habeas appeal brief refers to medical records from what could be this exam, describing a corpsman "who treated his injuries while cursing him" and citing "medical records confirming the trauma to Salahi's chest and face, as '1) Fracture ?? 7–8 ribs, 2) Edema of the lower lip.'" Brief for Appellee, 26.

SIX

GTMO

September 2003-December 2003

First Visit in the Secret Place... My Conversation with
My Interrogators, and How I Found a Way to Quench
Their Thirst... Chain Reaction of Confessions... Good-
ness Comes Gradually... The Big Confession... A Big
Milestone

Back in Camp Delta the *Kibla* was indicated with an arrow
in every cell. Even the call to prayer could be heard five
times a day in Camp Delta.★ The U.S. has always repeated
that the war is not against the Islamic religion—which is very
prudent because it is strategically impossible to fight against a
religion as big as Islam—and back there the U.S. was showing the rest of the world how religious freedom ought to be
maintained.

But in the secret camps, the war against the Islamic religion

---

★ Defense Department publicity materials for Guantánamo indeed
emphasize protections for religious expression in Guantánamo; see, e.g.,
"Ten Facts about Guantanamo," which states, "The Muslim call to prayer
sounds five times a day. Arrows point detainees toward the holy city of
Mecca." See http://archive.defense.gov/home/dodupdate/For-the-record/
documents/20060914.html.

was more than obvious. Not only was there no sign to Mecca, but the ritual prayers were also forbidden. Reciting the Koran was forbidden. Possessing the Koran was forbidden. Fasting was forbidden. Practically any Islamic-related ritual was strictly forbidden. I am not talking here about hearsay; I am talking about something I experienced myself. I don't believe that the average American is paying taxes to wage war against Islam, but I do believe that there are people in the government who have a big problem with the Islamic religion.

For the first couple of weeks after my "Birthday Party" I had no clue about time, whether it was day or night, let alone the time of day. I could only pray in my heart lying down, because I could not stand straight or bend. When I woke up from my semi-coma, I tried to make out the difference between day and night. In fact it was a relatively easy job: I used to look down the toilet, and when the drain was very bright to lightish dark, that was the daytime in my life. I succeeded in illegally stealing some prayers, but Sergeant Big Boss busted me.

"He's praying!" Big Boss yelled, and called his colleague. "Come on!" They put on their masks. "Stop praying." I don't recall whether I finished my prayer sitting, or if I finished at all. As a punishment Sergeant Big Boss forbade me to use the bathroom for some time.

As soon as the assessing doctor reported that I was relieved from my pain, it was time to hit again before the injuries healed, following the motto "Strike While the Iron's Hot." When I heard the melee behind the door, and recognized the voices of both Captain Collins and his Egyptian colleague, I drowned in sweat, got dizzy, and my feet failed to carry me.* My heart

---

* MOS's habeas appeal brief describes this same scene: "After Salahi had been in isolation for a few days, Zuley told him he had to 'stop denying' the government's accusations. While Zuley was talking, the [redacted] man

pounded so hard that I thought it was going to choke me and fly off through my mouth. Indistinct conversations involving Captain Collins and the guards took place.

"Meester Cooleens, let mee geet him," said the Egyptian guy in his stretched-out out English to Captain Collins. "I wish Meester Cooleens let me in to have a little conversation with you," said the Egyptian in Arabic, addressing me.

"Stand back now; let me see him alone," Captain Collins said. I was shaking, listening to the bargaining between the Americans and the Egyptians about who was going to get me. I looked like somebody who was going through an autopsy while still alive and helpless.

"You are going to cooperate, whether you choose to or not. You can choose between the civilized way, which I personally prefer, or the other way," said Captain Collins when the guards dragged me out of my cell to him. In the background the Egyptian guy was barking and threatening me with all kinds of painful revenge.

"I am cooperating," I said in a weak voice. It had been a while since I had talked the last time, and my mouth was not used to talking anymore. My muscles were very sore. I was scared beyond belief. The Halloween-masked guard, Big Boss, was literally stuck on me, moving around and ready to strike at an eye's wink.

"No, quit denying. We are not interested in your denials. Don't fuck with me," Captain Collins said.

"I'm not."

"I am going to appoint some interrogators to question you. You know some of them, and some you don't."

---

was behind the tarp, cursing and shouting for Zuley to let him in." Brief for Appellee, 26–27.

"OK!" I said. The conversation was closed. Captain Collins ordered the guards to put me back in my cell, and he disappeared.

Then nothing short of a "miracle" happened: SFC Shally made it to the "far faraway secret place."

"You've been causing me so much trouble—nah, well, in Paris it wasn't that bad but in Mauritania the weather was terrible. I sat at the table across from Karim Mehdi, and when I asked him, 'Who recruited you for al Qaeda?' his answer was you. And the same with Christian Ganczarski. Both of them are working with us now. You know, you are a part of an organization which the free world wants to wipe out of the face of the earth," said SFC Shally.

I was listening carefully, and wondering, Free world? I was saying to myself, Do I really have to listen to this crap? SFC Shally was accompanied by the same female sergeant that SSG Mary had brought about two months ago to molest me sexually.

"You know, in jail the one who talks first wins. You lost and Karim Mehdi won. He said everything about you," said the female sergeant. "The good thing is, we don't have to dirty our hands with you; we have Israelis and Egyptians doing the job for us," she continued, while taunting me sexually by touching me everywhere. I neither talked nor showed any resistance. I was sitting there like a stone.*

"Why is he shaking so much?" asked the female sergeant.

---

* Threatening prisoners with the specter of abusive interrogations by Israeli or Egyptian agents apparently was commonplace. In 2010 a former Guantánamo military interrogator named Damien Corsetti testified at the military commissions trial of Omar Khadr that during his time at the Bagram air base, "interrogations included threats of sending detainees to Israel and Egypt." See http://www.thestar.com/news/canada/omarkhadr/2010/05/05/interrogator_nicknamed_the_monster_remembers_omar_khadr_as_a_child.html.

"I don't know," SFC Shally answered.

"But his hands are sweating like crazy!"

"If I were him, the same would be happening to me," said SFC Shally. "You think this place is like Camp Delta, where you survived every attempt to break you, but you won't survive here if you keep playing games with us," he said.

"Like what?" I wondered.

"Like your trip to Slovenia. You only told me about it because you knew I knew about it. Now: are you going to cooperate with us?" he asked.

"I *was* cooperating," I said.

"No, you weren't, and guess what? I am going to write in my report that you're full of shit, and other people are going to take care of you. The Egyptian is very interested in you!"

Meanwhile the female sergeant stopped molesting me since I showed no resistance. "What's wrong with him?" she wondered once more.

"I don't know. But maybe he is too relaxed in this place. We should maybe take away some of his sleep," said SFC Shally. He took the sergeant of the guards aside and whispered something that I figured was the recipe I would be receiving next. Whenever he took a guard aside to talk, I knew it wasn't going to work out to my benefit. I've never seen a human being as emotionless as he was. He spoke about keeping me from sleeping without a single change in his voice, face, or composure. I mean, regardless of our religion or the race, we human beings always feel more or less bad for somebody who is suffering. I personally can never help breaking into tears when I read a sad story or watch a sad movie. I have no problem admitting this. Some people may say that I am a weak person; well, then, let me be!

"You should ask Captain Collins to forgive you the lies, and start everything over," said the female sergeant. I didn't say anything. "Start small. Give us a piece of information you never said before!" she continued. I had no response to that malicious, nonsense suggestion either.

"Your mom is an old lady. I don't know how long she can withstand the conditions in the detention facility," SFC Shally said. I knew that he was talking out of his tail. But I also knew that the government was ready to take any measures to pry information out of me, even if it would take injury to my family members, especially when you know that the Mauritanian government is cooperating blindly with the U.S. I mean the U.S. government has more power over Mauritanians than over U.S. nationals, that's how far the cooperation goes. A U.S. citizen cannot be arrested without due process of law, but Mauritanian citizens can—and by the U.S. government! I always said to my interrogators, "Let's say I am criminal. Is an American criminal holier than a non-American?" And most of them had no answer. But I am sure that Americans are not much luckier. I've heard of many of them getting persecuted and wrongly arrested, especially Muslims and Arabs, in the name of the War Against Terror. Americans, non-Americans: it is as the German proverb puts it, Heute die! Morgen du! Today Them, Tomorrow You!

It was very hard to start a conversation with SFC Shally; even the guards hated him. Today I couldn't get anywhere with him; I just couldn't find a handrail in the train of his speech. And as to the other female sergeant, she was only sent to harass me sexually, but I was at a stage where I had no feeling toward any female at all that way. Thus, her mission was dead before it was born.

"You know how it looks when you feel our wrath," SFC Shally said, and left me with many other threats including sleep deprivation and starvation, which I believed to be true and serious. The guards put me roughly back in my cell.

Over the next several days, I almost lost my mind. Their recipe for me went like this: I must be kidnapped from Camp Delta and put in a secret place. I must be made to believe I was on a far, faraway island. I must be informed by Captain Collins that my mom was captured and put in a special facility.

In the secret place, the physical and psychological suffering must be at their highest extremes. I must not know the difference between day and night. I couldn't tell a thing about days going by or time passing; my time consisted of a crazy darkness all the time. My diet times were deliberately messed up. I was starved for long periods and then given food but not given time to eat.

"You have three minutes: Eat!" a guard would yell at me, and then after about half a minute he would grab the plate. "You're done!" And then it was the opposite extreme: I was given too much food and a guard came into my cell and forced me to eat all of it. When I said "I need water" because the food got stuck in my throat, he punished me by making me drink two 25-ounce water bottles.

"I can't drink," I said when my abdomen felt as if it was going to explode. But Sergeant Big Boss screamed and threatened me, pushing me against the wall and raising his hand to hit me. I figured drinking would be better, and drank until I vomited.

All the guards were masked with Halloween-like masks, and so were the Medics, and the guards were briefed that I was a high-level, smart-beyond-belief terrorist. They made me call them by the names of *Star Wars* characters, with the lead guard called Master Yoda.

"You know who you are?" said Yoda's friend. "You're a terrorist who helped killed 3,000 people!"

"Indeed I am!" I answered. I realized it was futile to discuss my case with a guard, especially when he knew nothing about me. The guards were all very hostile. They cursed, shouted, and constantly put me through rough Military-like basic training. "Get up," "Walk to the bin hole." "Stop!" "Grab the shit!" "Eat." "You got two minutes!" "You're done!" "Give the shit back!" "Drink!" "You better drink the whole water bottle!" "Hurry up!" "Sit down!" "Don't sit down unless I say it!" "Search the piece of shit!" Most of the guards rarely attacked me physically, but Sergeant Big Boss hit me once until I fell face-down on the floor, and whenever he and his associate grabbed me they held me very tight and made me run in the heavy chains: "Move!"

No sleep was allowed. In order to enforce this, I was given 25-ounce water bottles in intervals of one to two hours, depending on the mood of the guards, 24 hours a day. The consequences were devastating. I couldn't close my eyes for ten minutes because I was sitting most of the time on the bathroom. Later on, after the tension was relieved, I asked one of the guards, "Why the water diet? Why don't you just make me stay awake by standing up, like in Camp Delta?"

"Psychologically it's devastating to make somebody stay awake on his own, without ordering him," said Master Yoda. "Believe me, you haven't seen anything. We have put detainees naked under the shower for days, eating, pissing, and shitting in the shower!" he continued. Other guards told me about other torture methods that I wasn't really eager to know about.

I was allowed to say three sentences: "Yes, sir!" "Need my interrogator!" and "Need the medics." Every once in a while the whole guard team stormed my cell, dragged me out, put me facing the wall, and threw out whatever was in my cell, shouting and cursing in order to humiliate me. It wasn't much: I was deprived from all comfort items that a detainee needs except for a mattress and a small, thin, worn-out blanket. For the first weeks I also had no shower, no laundry, no brushing. I almost developed bugs. I hated my smell.

No sleep. Water diet. Every move behind my door made me stand up in a military-like position with my heart pounding like boiling water. My appetite was non-existent. I was waiting every minute on the next session of torture. I hoped I would die and go to heaven; no matter how sinful I am, these people can never be more merciful than God. Ultimately we all are going to face the Lord and beg for his mercy, admitting our weaknesses and our sinfulness. I could hardly remember any prayers, all I could say was, "Please, God, relieve my pain..."

I started to hallucinate and hear voices as clear as crystal. I heard my family in a casual familial conversation that I couldn't join. I heard Koran readings in a heavenly voice.★ I heard music from my country. Later on the guards used these hallucinations and started talking with funny voices through the plumbing, encouraging me to hurt the guards and plot an escape. But I wasn't misled by them, even though I played along.

"We heard somebody—maybe a genie!" they used to say.

"Yeah, but I ain't listening to him," I responded. I just realized I was on the edge of losing my mind. I started to talk to

---

★ This is corroborated chillingly in government documents. According to the Senate Armed Services Committee, on October 17, 2003, a JTF-GTMO interrogator sent an e-mail to a GTMO Behavioral Science Consultation Team (BSCT) psychologist that read, "Slahi told me he is 'hearing voices' now....He is worried as he knows this is not normal....By the way...is this something that happens to people who have little external stimulus such as daylight, human interaction, etc???? seems a little creepy." The psychologist responded, "Sensory deprivation can cause hallucinations, usually visual rather than auditory, but you never know....In the dark you create things of what little you have." SASC, 140–41.

myself. Although I tried as hard as I could to convince myself that I was not in Mauritania, I was not near my family, so I could not possibly hear them speaking, I kept hearing the voices constantly, day and night. Psychological assistance was out of the question, or really any medical assistance, besides the asshole I didn't want to see.

I couldn't find a way on my own. At that moment I didn't know if it was day or night, but I assumed it was night because the toilet drain was rather dark. I gathered my strength, guessed the *Kibla,* kneeled, and started to pray to God. "Please guide me. I know not what to do. I am surrounded by merciless wolves, who fear not thee." When I was praying I burst into tears, though I suppressed my voice lest the guards hear me. You know there are always serious prayers and lazy prayers. My experience has taught me that God always responds to your serious prayers.

"Sir," I said, when I finished my prayers. One of the guards showed up in his Halloween mask.

"What?" asked the guard with a dry, cold emotion.

"I want to see Captain Collins. Not the sergeant; I want the guy in charge," I said.

"You mean Mr. Zuley?" Oops, the guard just made a big mistake by revealing the real name of Captain Collins. In fact I was already familiar with the name, because I saw it a long time before on a file SFC Shally carried, and if you can put two and two together the puzzle is solved.*

---

* The Schmidt-Furlow report places the date of this session as September 8, 2003, noting that interrogation records show that on that date "the subject of the second special interrogation wanted to see 'Captain Collins'" and that the interrogation team "understood that detainee had made an important decision and that the interrogator was anxious to hear what Detainee had to say." Schmidt-Furlow, 25.

"Yes, I mean the one who decides things, not the sergeant."
I really wanted to speak to somebody who was likely to understand me, rather than SFC Shally, who hardly had an understanding for anything. But Mr. Zuley didn't show up, SFC
Shally did.

"You asked for Captain Collins?"

"I did."

"And you asked not to see me?"

"I did."

"Well, I work for Captain Collins, and he sent me!" said SFC
Shally dryly.

"OK, I have no problem with cooperating with you just as I
would with Captain Collins. However, I would also like the
female Staff Sergeant to take part in the interviews," I said.

"I am not the one who decides about that, but I guess it
would be no problem," he said.

"I am starving, I want you to tell the guards to give me some
food."

"If you start to cooperate, you'll get more food. I am going
to come later today to interview you. I just want to tell you that
you made the right decision."

Confessions are like the beads of a necklace: if the first bead
falls, the rest follow.

To be honest and truthful, I am telling many things here that
I had been holding back merely because of fear. I just couldn't
find any common ground to discuss my case comfortably in a
relaxed environment. I had no crimes to confess to, and that is
exactly where I got stuck with my interrogators, who were not
looking for innocent undertakings. They were looking for evil

enterprises. But through my conversations with the FBI and the DoD, I had a good idea as to what wild theories the government had about me.

"We know you came to Canada to plot to harm the U.S.," said SFC Shally.

"And what was my evil plan?"

"Maybe not exactly to harm the U.S., but to attack the CN Tower in Toronto?" he said. I was thinking, Is the guy crazy? I've never heard of such a tower.

"You realize if I admit to such a thing I have to involve other people! What if it turns out I was lying?" I said.

"So what? We know your friends are bad, so if they get arrested, even if you lie about Ahmed Laabidi it doesn't matter, because they're bad." I thought, "What an asshole! he wants to lock up innocent people just because they're Muslim Arabs! That's Nuts!" So SFC Shally very much told me a precise crime I could admit to which would comply with the Intel theory.

"Back in the states, if I recommend somebody to a good school and he ended up shooting and killing people, is that my fault?" Shally asked me once.

"No!"

"So, if you have recruited people for al Qaeda, it's not your fault if they become terrorists!" he said.

"The only problem is that I haven't, regardless of the consequences."

SFC Shally made it clearer. "We don't give a shit if you helped bin al-Shibh and two other hijackers go to Chechnya. We only give a shit if you sent them to your brother-in-law Abu Hafs." So, according to SFC Shally, I could stop the torture if I said I recruited bin al-Shibh and two hijackers. To be honest with you, they made me believe I recruited Ramzi bin-al-Shibh;

I thought, God, I might have recruited the guy before I was born!

"Looks like a dog, walks like a dog, smells like a dog, barks like a dog, must be a dog," Agent Robert used to say repeatedly during his sessions with me. It sounded awful, I know I am not a dog, and yet I must be one. The whole police theory of doing every trick to keep people in jail by pinning things on them doesn't make sense to me. I believe simply that an innocent suspect should be released. As the just, legendary Arabic King Omar put it, "I would rather release a criminal than imprison an innocent man."

Agent Michael explained the recruitment scenario the most: "Bin al-Shibh said that you helped him go to Chechnya by suggesting that he and his friends transit through Afghanistan, because Georgia was sending Mujahideen back. Furthermore, when I asked bin al-Shibh what he thinks you do for al Qaeda, he said that you're an al Qaeda recruiter."

"I believe that without you September 11 would never have happened," Michael concluded. According to his theory I was the guy; all I needed to do was to admit it. Many interrogators asked me, "What do you know about al Qaeda cells in Germany and Canada?" To be honest with you, I'd never heard of such a thing; I know al Qaeda organizations, but I don't know about al Qaeda cells in other countries, though that doesn't necessarily mean there aren't.

Robert pushed the issue even more into the light. "You are a leader, people like you, respect you, and follow you," he said to me multiple times. As you can see, my recipe was already cooked for me. I am not only a part of an al Qaeda cell in both Germany and Canada, but I am the leader.

I argued the case of bin al-Shibh with Robert many times.

274 • MOHAMEDOU OULD SLAHI

"According to you, I recruited Ramzi and his two friends for al Qaeda," I said.

"Yes."

"Okay, but that allegation requires many other things and coincidences."

"Like what?" he said.

First, I explained, I supposedly knew bin al-Shibh, and Ramzi himself said he has seen me only once, and that is not enough for knowing somebody, let alone recruiting him. Second, I must have recruited bin al-Shibh without his knowledge, because all he claims is that I told him how to get to Chechnya. "According to you," I told him, "And maybe to him, too, I told him to travel through Afghanistan, so what guaranteed that he was going to stay in Afghanistan? And if he miraculously stayed in Afghanistan, what guaranteed that he was going to train? And if he decided to train, what guaranteed that he was going to meet al Qaeda's criteria? And if by chance he met al Qaeda's criteria, what told me that he was ready to be suicide bomber, and was ready to learn how to fly? This is just ridiculous!"

"But you are very smart," Agent Robert said.

"Under these circumstances, I agree with you that I'm beyond smart: I am a psychic! But what makes you guys think that I'm so evil?"

"We just don't know, but smart people don't leave any traces. For instance, we had an FBI Agent who had been working for Russia for 20 years without being noticed," said Robert.*

"We have people who still believe that you conspired with Ressam," said SSG Mary when I told her not to ask me about

---

* The reference here is likely to Robert Hanssen, an FBI agent who spied for Soviet and then Russian intelligence services from 1979 until his arrest and conviction in 2001.

Ahmed Ressam because the FBI had settled his case since he had started cooperating.

"Obviously there is no way out with you guys," I addressed SSG Mary.

"I'm telling you how!" she responded.

Now, thanks to the unbearable pain I was suffering, I had nothing to lose, and I allowed myself to say anything to satisfy my assailants. Session followed session since I called Captain Collins.

"People are very happy with what you're saying," said SFC Shally after the first session. I answered all the questions he asked me with incriminating answers. I tried my best to make myself look as bad as I could, which is exactly the way you can make your interrogator happy. I made my mind up to spend the rest of my life in jail. You see most people can put up with being imprisoned unjustly, but nobody can bear agony day in and day out for the rest of his life.

SFC Shally started to take the shape of a human being, though a bad one. "I write my report like newspaper articles, and the members of the community submit their comments. They're really happy," Sergeant Shally said.

"So am I," I said. I was wondering about the new, half-happy face of SFC Shally. Normally Shally is an angry person; if he talks to you he always looks at the roof, he hardly ever looks anybody in the eyes. He can barely lead a dialogue, but he's very good when it comes to monologues. "I divorced my wife because she was just so annoying," he once said to me.

"Your request to see SSG Mary is not approved, in the meantime I am working on your case," he said.

"Alright!" I knew that SFC Shally was a trial, and that the DoD still wanted me to deal with the "bad guy."

"I told you I'm good at breaking detainees," he said.

"But since you don't know my limit, you drove me beyond it," I responded. When I started to talk generously to SFC Shally, Richard Zuley brought SSG Mary back into the picture; for some reason the team wanted her back, too.

"Thank you very much for getting the sergeant back," I said.

SSG Mary looked both sad and happy. "I enjoy talking to you, you're easy to talk to, and you have pretty teeth," she told me before I was kidnapped from Camp Delta. Mary was the closest person to me; she was the only one I could relate to.

"I can never do what Captain Collins is doing; all he's worried about is getting his job done," said SSG Mary, commenting on Zuley's methods when Shally was absent. Mary and Shally were now interrogating me in turn. They dedicated the whole time until around November 10, 2003 to questioning me about Canada and September 11; they didn't ask me a single question about Germany, where I really had the center of gravity of my life. Whenever they asked me about somebody in Canada I had some incriminating information about that person, even if I didn't know him. Whenever I thought about the words, "I don't know," I got nauseous, because I remembered the words of SFC Shally, "All you have to say is, 'I don't know, I don't remember, and we'll fuck you!' Or Captain Collins saying, "We don't want to hear your denials anymore!" And so I erased these words from my dictionary.

"We would like you to write your answers on paper; it's too much work to keep up with your talk, and you might forget things when you talk to us," said SFC Shally.

"Of course!" I was really happy with the idea because I would rather talk to a paper than talk to him; at least the paper wouldn't shout in my face or threaten me. SFC Shally drowned me in a pile of papers, which I duly filled with writings. It was a good outlet for my frustration and my depression.

"You're very generous in your written answers; you even wrote a whole bunch about Abu Mohammed al-Kanadi, whom you really don't know," SFC Shally accurately said, forgetting that he forbade me to use the words "I don't know."

"Captain Collins reads your writing with a lot of interest," said SFC Shally. I was extremely frightened, because this statement was ambiguous. "We're gonna give you an assignment about Ahmed Laabidi. He is detained in Florida and they cannot make him talk; he keeps denying everything. You better provide us a Smoking Gun against him," said SFC Shally. I was so sad: how rude was this guy, to ask me to provide a smoking gun about somebody I hardly know?

"All I can say is that Ahmed L. is a criminal and should be locked up the rest of his life. I'm ready to testify against him in court," I said, though I was not ready to lie in court to burn an innocent soul.

"Ahmed Laabidi is facing the death penalty if we can make him guilty of drug smuggling," SSG Mary said once, showing me his picture. I burst out laughing as soon as I saw the expression on his face and the Bob Barker–Calvin Klein prison uniform.*

"What are you laughing at?" Mary asked me.

"It's just funny!"

"How can you laugh at your friend?" I felt guilty right away, even though I knew I was not laughing at him. After all, my situation was worse than his. I was laughing at the situation: I could read everything that was going on in his head just from

---

* Bob Barker Company, Incorporated, which identifies itself as "America's Leading Detention Supplier," is a major supplier of prison uniforms for the U.S. Department of Defense. See http://news.google.com/newspapers?nid=1454&dat=20020112&id=6gJPAAAAIBAJ&sjid=Ux8EAAAAIBAJ&pg=5765,3098702.

the expression on his face. I'd been made to take that same picture many times, in Senegal, in Mauritania, in Germany, in Jordan, in Bagram, and in GTMO. I hate the pose, I hate the look, I hate the height measure. Let me tell you something, whenever you see that bleak-looking face in a jail uniform, posing in front of a height measure scaled on a wall, you can be sure that is not a happy person.

In fact, I really felt bad for that poor guy. He had sought asylum in Canada for a certain time but the Canadians refused his petition, partly because they considered him as Islamist. Ahmed Laabidi was willing to try his chances in the U.S., where he faced the harsh reality of the highly electrified environment against Muslims and Arabs, and where the U.S. gave him asylum in a high-level security prison and now was trying to link him to any crime. When I saw his face, I knew he was like, "Screw these Americans. How much I hate them! What do they want from me? How did I end up in jail when I came here seeking protection?"

"I talked today with the Canadians and they told me they don't believe your story about Ahmed Laabidi being involved in drug smuggling into the U.S., but we know he is," he told me once.

"I can only tell you what I know," I said.

"But we want you to give an evidence linking Ahmed Laabidi to the Millennium Plot. Things like, he supports the Mujs or believes in Jihad are good, but not good enough to lock him up the rest of his life," he told me.

"Oh, yes, I will," I said. He handed me a bunch of papers and I went back in my cell. Oh, my God, I am being so unjust to myself and my brothers, I kept thinking, and then repeating "Nothing's gonna happen to us.... *They'll* go to hell.... Nothing's gonna happen to us.... *They'll....*" I kept praying in my heart, and repeating my prayers. I took the pen and paper and wrote all kinds of incriminating lies about a poor person who was just seeking refuge in Canada and trying to make some money so he could start a family. Moreover, he is handicapped. I felt so bad, and kept praying silently, "Nothing's gonna happen to you dear brother..." and blowing on the papers as I finished. Of course it was out of the question to tell them what I knew about him truthfully, because SFC Shally already gave me the guidelines: "Captain Collins is awaiting your testimony against Ahmed Laabidi with extreme interest!" I gave the assignment to SFC Shally, and after evaluation, I saw Captain Collins smiling for the first time.

"Your writing about Ahmed was very interesting, but we want you to provide more detailed information," he said. I thought, What information does the idiot want from me? I don't even remember what I've just written.

"Yes, no problem," I said. I was very happy that God answered my prayers for Ahmed Laabidi when I learned in 2005 that he was unconditionally released from custody and sent back to his country. "He's facing the death penalty," SSG Mary used to tell me! I was really in no better situation.

"Since I am cooperating, what are you going to do with me?" I asked SFC Shally.

"It depends. If you provide us a great deal of information we didn't know, it's going to be weighed against your sentence. For instance, the death penalty could be reduced to life, and life to thirty years," he responded. Lord have mercy on me! What harsh justice!

"Oh, that's great," I replied. I felt bad for everybody I hurt with my false testimonies. My only solaces were, one, that I didn't hurt anybody as much as I did myself; two, that I had no choice; and three, I was confident that injustice will be defeated, it's only a matter of time. Moreover, I would not blame anybody for lying about me when he gets tortured. Ahmed was just an example. During this period I wrote more than a thousand pages about my friends with false information. I had to wear the suit the U.S. Intel tailored for me, and that is exactly what I did.

At the beginning of this phase of cooperation the pressure hardly relieved. I was interrogated day and night, and I also had visits from interrogators from the FBI and other agencies who were using my vulnerability. It was so rude to question a human being like that, especially somebody who is cooperating. They made me write names and places and addresses in Germany, Canada, and Mauritania. They showed me military maps, pointing out places of interest. I was shown thousands of pictures. I knew them all by heart because I had seen them so many times; everything was deja-vu. I was like, What ruthless people!

The whole time, the guards were driven madly against me. "Show him no mercy. Increase the pressure. Drive the hell out of him crazy," said Captain Collins. And that was exactly what the guards did. Banging on my cell to keep me awake and scared. Taking me violently out of my cell at least twice a day for cell search. Taking me outside in the middle of the night and making me do PT I couldn't due to my health situation. Putting me facing the wall several times a day and threatening me directly and indirectly. Sometimes they even interrogated me, but I never said a word to my interrogators because I knew the interrogators were behind everything.

"You know who you are?" said Yoda's associate.

"Uh..."

"You are a terrorist," he continued.

"Yes, Sir!"

"If we kill you once it wouldn't do. We must kill you three thousand times. But instead we feed you!"

"Yes, Sir."

The water diet kept working on me harshly. "You haven't seen nothing yet," they kept telling me.

"I am not looking forward to see that. I'm just fine without further measures."

The guards were working in a two-shift routine, day shift and night shift. Whenever the new shift showed up, they made their presence known by banging heavily on the door of my cell to scare me. Whenever the new shift appeared my heart started to pound because they always came up with new ideas to make my life a living hell, like giving me very little food by allowing me about 30 seconds to one minute to eat it, or forcing me to eat every bit of food I got in a very short time. "You better be done!" they would shout. Or they made me clean the shower excessively, or made me fold my towels and my blanket in an impossible way again and again until they were satisfied. To forbidding me any kind of comfort items, they added new rules. One: I should never be lying down; whenever a guard showed up at my bin hole, I always had to be awake, or wake up as soon as a guard walked into my area. There was no sleeping in the terms that we know. Two: My toilet should always be dry! And how, if I am always urinating and flushing? In order to meet the order, I had to use my only uniform to dry up the toilet and stay soaked in shit. Three: My cell should be in a predefined order, including having a folded blanket, so I could never use my blanket.

That was the guards' recipe. I always showed more fear than I felt as self-defense technique. Not that I would like to play the hero; I'm not, but I wasn't scared of the guards because I just knew they had orders from above. If they reported back that "detainee wasn't scared!" the doses would have been increased.

Meanwhile, I had my own recipe. First of all, I knew that I was really just a stone's throw away from Camp Delta. The interrogators and the guards always hinted at the "God-forsaken nowhere" I was in, but I ignored them completely, and when the guards asked me "Where do you think you are?" I just responded, "I'm not sure, but I am not worried about it; since I am far from my family, it doesn't really matter to me where I am." And so I always closed the door whenever they referred to the place. I was afraid that I would be tortured if they knew I knew where I was, but it was kind of solacing, knowing that you are not far from your fellow detainees.

Once I figured out how to tell day from night, I kept count of the days by reciting 10 pages of the Koran every day. In 60 days I would finish and start over, and so I could keep track of the days. "Shut the fuck up! There is nothing to sing about," said Sergeant Big Boss when he heard me reciting the Koran. After that I recited quietly so nobody could hear me. But my days of the week were still messed up; I failed to keep track of them until I glimpsed SFC Shally's watch when he pulled it out of his pocket to check the time. He was very vigilant and careful but it was too late, I saw it was a little past 10 a.m., Friday, October, 17, 2003, but he didn't notice. Friday is a very important Muslim holiday, and that was the reason I wanted to keep track of the weekdays. Besides, I just hated the fact that they deprived me of one of my basic freedoms.

I tried to find out everybody's name who was involved in my torture—not for retaliation or anything like that; I just didn't

want those people to have the upper hand over any of my brothers, or anybody, no matter who he is. I believe they should not
only be deprived of their powers, but they should also be locked
up. I succeeded in knowing the names of the boss himself,
Richard Zuley, two of my interrogators, two of the guards, and
other interrogators who weren't involved directly in my torture
but could serve as witnesses.

When I first met Americans I hated their language because
of the pain they made me suffer without a single reason; I didn't
want to learn it. But that was emotion; the call of wisdom was
stronger, and so I decided to learn the language. Even though
I already knew how to conjugate "to be" and "to have," my
luggage of English was very light. Since I wasn't allowed to have
books, I had to pick up the language mostly from the guards
and sometimes my interrogators, and after a short time I could
speak like common folk: "He don't care, she don't care, I ain't
done nothin', me and my friend did so and so, F—this and
F—that, damn x and damn y..."

I also studied the people around me. My observations resulted
in knowing that only white Americans were appointed to deal
with me, both guards and interrogators. There was only one
black guard, but he had no say. His associate was a younger,
white Army specialist but the latter was always in charge. You
might say, "How do you know the ranks of the guards, when
they were covered?" I wasn't supposed to know who was in
charge, nor should they have given me a hint as to who the boss
was, but in America it's very easy to notice who the boss is:
there's just no mistaking him.

My suspicion of me being near Camp Delta was cemented
when one day I got some of the diet I was used to back in Delta
Three. "Why did they give me a hot meal?" I asked the sarcastic
head guard. "Doctor said we had to." I really looked like a ghost,

just bones, no meat. In a matter of weeks I had developed gray hair on the lower half of the sides of my head, a phenomenon people in my culture refer to as the extreme result of depression. Keeping up the pressure was vital in the process of my interrogation. The plan worked: the more pressure, the more stories I produced and the better my interrogators felt toward me.

And then, slowly but surely, the guards were advised to give me the opportunity to brush my teeth, to give me more warm meals, and to give me more showers. The interrogators started to interrogate me without torture or threats; instead, they started using a reward system that included candies and cookies. From what I could see, SSG Mary was the one who took the first steps, but I am sure there had been a meeting about it. Everybody in the team realized that I was about to lose my mind due to my psychological and physical situation. I had been so long in segregation.

"Please, get me out of this living hell!" I said.

"You will not go back to the population anytime soon." SSG Mary told me. Her answer was harsh but true: there was no plan to get me back. The focus was on holding me segregated as long as they could and gathering information from me.

I still had nothing in my cell. Most of the time I recited the Koran silently. The rest of the time I was talking to myself and thinking over and over about my life and the worst-case scenarios that could happen to me. I kept counting the holes of the cage I was in. There are about four thousand one hundred holes.

Maybe because of this, SSG Mary happily started to give me some puzzles that I could spend my time solving. "If we discover that you lied to us, you're gonna feel our wrath, and we're gonna take everything back. This can all go back to the old days, you know that," SFC Shally used to tell me whenever he gave me a puzzle. My heart would pound, but I was like, What a jackass! Why can't he let me enjoy my "reward" for the time being? Tomorrow is another day.

I started to enrich my vocabulary. I took a paper and started to write words I didn't understand, and SFC Shally and SSG Mary explained them to me. If there is anything positive about SFC Shally, it is his rich vocabulary. I don't remember asking him about a word he couldn't explain to me. English was his only real language, though he claimed to be able to speak Farsi. "I wanted to learn French, but I hated the way they speak and I quit," he said.

Captain Collins wants to see you in a couple of days," SSG Mary said. I was so terrified; at this point I was just fine without his visit.

"He is welcome," I said. I started to go to the toilet relentlessly. My blood pressure went crazily high. I was wondering what the visit would be like. But thank God the visit was much easier than what I thought. Captain Collins came, escorted by SFC Shally. He was, as always, practical and brief.

"I am very happy with your cooperation. Remember when I told you that I preferred civilized conversations? I think you have provided 85% of what you know, but I am sure you're gonna provide the rest," he said, opening an ice bag with some juice.

"Oh, yeah, I'm also happy!" I said, forcing myself to drink the juice just to act as if I were normal. But I wasn't: I was like, 85% is a big step coming out of his mouth. Captain Collins advised me to keep cooperating.

"I brought you this present," he said, handing me a pillow. Yes, a pillow. I received the present with a fake overwhelming happiness, and not because I was dying to get a pillow. No, I took the pillow as a sign of the end of the physical torture. We have a joke back home about a man who stood bare naked on the street. When someone asked him, "How can I help you?" He replied, "Give me shoes." And that was exactly what happened to me. All I needed was a pillow! But it was something: alone in my cell, I kept reading the tag over and over.

"Remember when Captain Collins told you about the 15% you're holding back," said SFC Shally a couple of days after Mr. Zuley's visit. "I believe that your story about Canada doesn't make sense. You know what we have against you, and you know what the FBI has against you," he continued.

"So what would make sense?" I asked.

"You know exactly what makes sense," he said sardonically.

"You're right, I was wrong about Canada. What I did exactly was...."

"I want you to write down what you've just said. It made perfect sense and I understood, but I want it on paper."

"My pleasure, Sir!" I said.

I came to Canada with a plan to blow up the CN Tower in Toronto. My accomplices were Ahmed, Mohamed, Hasni, and Raouf. Hasni went to Russia to get us the supply of explosives. Mohamed wrote an explosives simulation software that I picked up, tested myself, and handed in a data medium to Raouf. The latter was supposed to send it with the whole plan to Sheikh Abu Qatada in London so we could get the final fatwa from the Sheikh. Raouf was supposed to buy a lot of sugar to mix with the explosives in order to increase the damage. Ahmed provided the financing. Thanks to Canadian Intel, the plan was discovered and sentenced to failure. I admit that I am as guilty as any other participants and am so sorry and ashamed for what I have done. Signed, M.O. Slahi.

When I handed the paper to SFC Shally, he read it happily.

"This statement makes perfect sense."

"If you're ready to buy, I am selling," I said. SFC Shally could hardly hold himself on the chair; he wanted to leave immediately. I guess the prey was big, and SFC Shally was overwhelmed because he reached a breakthrough where no other interrogators had, in spite of almost four years of uninterrupted interrogation from all kinds of agencies from more than six countries. What a success! SFC Shally almost had a heart attack from happiness.

"I'll go see him!"

I think the only unhappy person in the team was SSG Mary, because she doubted the truthfulness of the story.

Indeed the next day Captain Collins came to see me, escorted as always by two uniformed men he wanted people to think were his bodyguards. "Remember when I told about the 15% you were holding back?"

"Yes, I do."

"I think this confession covered that 15%!" I was like, Hell, yes!

"I am happy that it did," I said.

"Who provided the money?"

"Ahmed did."

"And you, too?" Captain Collins asked.

"No, I took care of the electrical part." I don't really know why I denied the financial part. Did it really make a difference? Maybe I just wanted to maintain the consistency.

"What if we tell you that we found your signature on a fake

credit card?" said Captain Collins. I knew he was bullshitting me because I knew I never dealt with such dubious things. But I was not going to argue with him.

"Just tell me the right answer. Is it good to say yes or to say no?" I asked. At that point I hoped I was involved in something so I could admit to it and relieve myself of writing about every practicing Muslim I ever met, and every Islamic organization I ever heard of. It would have been much easier to admit to a true crime and say that's that. "This confession is consistent with the Intels we and other agencies possess," Captain Collins said.

"I am happy."

"Is the story true?" asked Captain Collins.

"Look, these people I was involved with are bad people anyway, and should be put under lock and key. And as to myself, I don't care as long as you are pleased. So if you want to buy, I am selling."

"But we have to check with the other agencies, and if the story is incorrect, they're gonna find out," Captain Collins said.

"If you want the truth, this story didn't happen," I said sadly. Captain Collins had brought some drinks and candies that I forced myself to swallow. They tasted like dirt because I was so nervous. Captain Collins took his henchman outside and pitted him on me. SFC Shally came back harassing me and threatening me with all kinds of suffering and agony. It was amazing how much control Captain Collins had over this man who was way over forty years old. Now Shally was telling me I was going to be put back to intensive torture, and for what? Because my false confession wasn't tight enough.

"You know how it feels when you experience our wrath," SFC Shally said. I was like, what the heck does this asshole want from me? If he wants a confession, I already provided one. Does he want me to resurrect the dead? Does he want me to heal his blindness? I am not a prophet, nor does he believe in them. "The Bible is just the history of the Jewish people, nothing more," he used to say. If he wants the truth, I told him I have done nothing! I couldn't see a way out. "Yes!...Yes!...Yes!" After SFC Shally made me sweat to the last drop in my body, Captain Collins called him and gave him advice about the next tactics. Captain Collins left and SFC Shally continued.

"Captain Collins has overall control. If he is happy everybody is. And if he isn't, nobody is." SFC Shally started to ask me other questions about other things, and I used every opportunity to make myself look as bad as I could. "I'm going to leave you alone with papers and pen, and I want you to write everything you remember about your plan in Canada!"

"Yes, Sir."

Two days later they were back at my door.

"Get up! Get your hands through the bin hole!" said an unfriendly-sounding guard. I didn't welcome the visit: I hadn't missed my interrogators' faces over the weekend, and they scared the hell out of me. The guards shackled me and took me outside the building where Captain Collins and SFC Shally were waiting for me. It was my first time seeing the daylight. Many people take daylight for granted, but if you are forbidden to see it, you'll appreciate it. The brightness of the sun made my eyes squint until they adjusted. The sun hit me mercifully with its warmth. I was terrified and shaking.

"What's wrong with you?" one of guards asked me.

"I am not used to this place."

"We brought you outside so you can see the sun. We will have more rewards like this."

"Thank you very much," I managed to say, though my mouth was dry and my tongue was heavy as steel.

"Nothing is gonna happen to you if you tell us about the bad things. I know you're afraid that we will change our opinion toward you," said Captain Collins while SFC Shally was taking notes.

"I know."

"Let's talk hypothetically. You understand hypothetical?" Captain Collins said.

"Yes, I do."

"Let's assume you've done what you confessed to."

"But I haven't."

"Just let's assume."

"Okay," I said. As high-ranking as Captain Collins was, he was the worst interrogator I've ever met. I mean professionally. He just jumps back and forth without focusing on any specific thing. If I had to guess, I would say his job was anything but interrogating people.

"Between you and Raouf Hannachi, who was in charge?"

"It depends: in the mosque I was in charge, and outside he was in charge," I answered. The questions assumed that Hannachi and I are members of a gang, but I didn't even know Mr. Hannachi, let alone conspire with him as part of a corps that never existed.* But anyway I could not tell something like that

---

* It appears from MOS's 2008 Detainee Assessment and from MOS's habeas corpus decision that confessions like those MOS is describing here became part of the government's allegations against him. Both Raouf Hannachi and Ahmed Laabidi appear in both the 2008 Detainee Assessment and Judge James Robertson's 2010 habeas memorandum order; in both documents the government portrays MOS, Hannachi, and Laabidi as members of a Montreal cell of al-Qaeda, with Hannachi as the cell's leader and Laabidi as the cell's financier. A footnote to Judge Robertson's opinion specifically notes that MOS's statement under interrogation that "Laabidi [is] a terrorist who supported use of suicide bombers" came in an interrogation session dated September 16, 2003—right around the time of the scene

to Captain Collins; I had to tell him something that made me look bad.

"Have or haven't you conspired with those individuals as you admitted?"

"You want the truth?"

"Yes!"

"No, I haven't," I said. Captain Collins and SFC Shally tried to play all kinds of tricks on me, but first of all I knew all the tricks, and second I had already told them the truth. So it was futile to play tricks on me. But they drove me into the infamous Catch-22: if I lie to them, "You'll feel our wrath." And if I tell the truth, it will make me look good, which would make them believe I am withholding information because in their eyes I AM A CRIMINAL and I wasn't yet able to change that opinion.

Captain Collins handed me a printed version of the so-called Witness Protection Program. He obviously forgot to disable the date printout footnote, so I could read it. I wasn't supposed to know the date, but nobody is perfect.

"Oh, thank you very much," I said.

"If you help us, you'll see how generous our government is," Captain Collins said.

"I'll read it."

"I think this is something for you."

"Sure." Captain Collins gestured to the guards to take me back in my cell. They were still holding me all this time in Camp Echo Special.*

MOS describes here. The 2008 Detainee Assessment is available at http://projects.nytimes.com/guantanamo/detainees/760-mohamedou-ould-slahi. Detainee Assessment, 10; Memorandum Order, 26–28.

* MOS indicates later in the manuscript that he remained in the same cell he was delivered into at the end of his staged abduction through the

As soon as the interrogation team left, one of the guards was opening my cell and shouting, "Get up Motherfucker." I was like, Oh my God, again? Master Yoda and his friend took me out of the cell and made me face the wall.

"You fucking pussy. Why don't you admit?"

"I've been telling the truth."

"You ain't. Interrogators never ask if they don't have proof. They just wanted to test you. And guess what? You failed. You blew your chance," he continued. I was sweating and shaking, and I showed even more fear than I really felt. "It's so easy: we just want you to tell us what you've done, how you've done it, and who else was involved with you. We use this information to stop other attacks. Is that not easy?"

"Yeah, it is."

"So why do you keep being a pussy?"

"Because he's gay!" said Yoda's colleague.

"You think the Captain just gave you the Witness Protection information for fun? Hell, we should kill you, but we don't; instead, we're gonna give you money, a house, and a nice car, how frustrating is that? In the end, you are a terrorist," he continued. "You better tell them everything the next time they come. Take a pen and paper and write everything down."

The interrogators and guards believed the Witness Protection Program is a U.S. specialty, but it isn't. It's practiced all over the world; even in the darkest dictatorship countries, criminals can profit from such a program. Captain Collins provided me stories

---

time of the manuscript's creation. A 2010 *Washington Post* report described a "little fenced in compound at the military prison" that matches the description of his living situation in Camp Echo at the time the manuscript was written. See Peter Finn, "For Two Detainees Who Told What They Knew, Guantánamo Becomes a Gilded Cage," *Washington Post*, March 24, 2010, http://www.washingtonpost.com/wp-dyn/content/article/2010/03/24/AR2010032403135.html. MOS manuscript, 233.

about other criminals who became friends of the U.S. government, such as Wernher von Braun and Viktor Belenko, who fled the Soviets during the Cold War. I was really not enlightened by any of this, but I took the papers anyway: something to read beside the pillow tag. I kept reading and reading and reading it again because I just like to read and I had nothing to read.

"You remember what you told Captain Collins, when he told you you're hiding 15%," SSG Mary said in our next session.

"Yeah, but you see I can't argue with Captain Collins. Otherwise he gets mad." SSG Mary took a printed version of my confession and started to read it, smiling.

"But you're not only hurting yourself. You're hurting other innocent people."

"That's correct. But what else should I do?"

"You said you guys wanted to mix sugar with explosives?"

"Yes, I did." SSG Mary smiled.

"But that's not what we wanted to hear when we asked you what you meant by 'sugar.' As a matter of fact," she said, "it's obvious you have no clue about this stuff."

"Sergeant, I really don't know," I said.

"You cannot possibly lie about something as big as that," SSG Mary said. "We have a highly qualified expert who could come and question you. What do you think about a polygraph test?"

"Polygraph? I'm dying to take one!" I said, though my heart was pounding because I knew I might fail the test even if was telling the truth.

"I'm gonna organize one for you as soon as possible."★

★ At his 2005 Administrative Review Board hearing, after recounting the boat trip and its aftermath, MOS stated, "Because they said to me either I am going to talk or they will continue to do this, I said I am going to tell them everything they wanted....I told them I was on my own trying to

"I know you want to make yourself look good," I said.

"No, I care about you. I would like to see you out of jail, leading a normal life. There are some detainees I want to see stay here the rest of their lives. But you, no!" SSG Mary said genuinely.

"Thank you very much." Mary left with that promise and I retreated back to my cell, completely depressed.

"Remember that the polygraph is decidedly important in your life," said Captain Collins shortly before he left one of his sessions, trying with the help of his executioner SFC Shally to pry nonexistent information out of my mouth. He scared the hell out of me, because my whole life was now hanging on a polygraph machine.

"Yes, Sir, I know."

"Who would you like to have with you during the polygraph," asked Captain Collins a couple of days before the test.

"I think the male sergeant wouldn't be a good idea, but I would be just fine if you would be here!"

"Or the other male sergeant?" he said, pointing to SFC Shally.

"Yeah," I said reluctantly. "But why don't you just come?"

"I'll try, but if not me, it will be the sergeant."

"I am very scared because of what your boss Captain Collins said," I told SSG Mary the day before the test.

"Look, I've taken the test several times and passed. All you need to do is clear your mind and be honest and truthful," SSG Mary answered.

---

do things and they said write it down and I wrote it and I signed it. I brought a lot of people, innocent people with me because I got to make a story that makes sense. They thought my story was wrong so they put me on polygraph." ARB transcript, 27.

"I will."

On November 12, 2003, SSG Mary showed up. "Guess what?" she asked, looking at me through the cage of my cell. I quickly stood up at the bin hole.

"Yes, Sir!" I thought she was one of the guards. She got me startled, and she looked at me, smiling.

"Oh, it's you! I am sorry, I thought you were one of the guards. You came for the polygraph, didn't you?"

"Yes, in a couple of hours I'll be back with the guy with the equipment. I just want you to be prepared."

"OK, thank you very much." SSG Mary left. I performed a ritual wash and managed to steal a prayer off the guards, I don't remember whether I performed it formally or informally. "Oh, God! I need your help more than ever. Please show them that I am telling the truth. Please give not these merciless people any reason to hurt me. Please. Please!" After the prayer I exercised a kind of yoga. I never really practiced that meditation technique before, but now I sat on my bed, put my hands on my thighs, and imagined my body connected to the poly.

"Have you done any crimes against the U.S.?" I asked myself.

"No." Would I really pass? Screw them! I've done no crimes; why should I be worried? They're evil! And then I thought, No, they're not evil: it's their right to defend their own country. They're good people. They really are! And then again, Screw them, I don't owe them anything. They tortured me, they owe me! I did the yoga with all the possible questions.

"Did you tell the truth about Ahmed Laabidi?"

"No." Oh, that's a big problem, because SFC Shally said, "When we catch you lying you're gonna feel our wrath." Screw him and Captain Collins; I'm not gonna lie to please him and destroy my own life. No way. I'm gonna tell the truth no matter what. But what if I fail the test, even after answering truthfully? OK! No problem, I'm gonna lie. But what if the polygraph shows my new lies? Then I'm really gonna be stuck in a cul-de-sac. Only God can help me: my situation is serious and the Americans are crazy. Don't worry about that, just take the test and you're gonna be alright. I was going to the bathroom so often that I thought I was going to urinate my kidneys.

The doorbell rang and SSG Mary surged through with the polygraph tester. He was a small white male in his early forties, with hair that was sprinkled gray, the perfect candidate for a DOD contractor.

"My name is John Smith. Nice to meet you."

"Nice to meet you," I said, shaking his hand. I knew he was dishonest about his name. He unluckily chose the wrong name, John Smith, which I knew to be a generic name. But I really didn't care. After all, what interrogator is honest about any-thing? He could as well have introduced himself as Joe Dirt with the same effect. "You will be working with me today. How are you?"

"I am very nervous," I answered.

"Perfect. That is the way you should be. I don't like relaxed detainees. Give me a minute, I am going to install the equip-ment." In fact, SSG Mary and I helped him in setting up his equipment. He was complaining that the building wasn't steady enough and he was worried about the vibrations, and it took a long time for him to decide where to set up the machine. We ended up in a corner outside my cell. A firm plastic chair was placed next to the table, and I was told to sit facing a thick white wooden wall, so close it almost kissed my nose.

"Now, I want you to sit and look at me the whole time while I am speaking to you." John Smith was not exactly the evil-looking interrogator. He was, I think, skeptical but fair.

"Have you taken a polygraph test before?

"Yes, I have!"

"So you understand the process and how the test works?"

"I guess I do."

But John started a long explanation anyway. I noticed an ant walking up the wall, and then many more leading and following her. I learned to follow ants in the Mauritanian secret prison, watching them until they left the cell and me behind. I watched this one climb, going about her daily business and not realizing the drama that was unfolding before her very eyes. I drowned myself in her world, and I missed a lot of what the tester was saying. I was so nervous, but I took this as the first good omen of the morning. I was wondering if I should just concentrate on the ant and answer the questions without thinking.

John warned me that if I was planning to lie to him, I should just forget it and tell him the truth so I could pass the test. He was aware of my fear and anxiety. He knew that I was afraid of Captain Collins and his henchmen, including the Egyptian and the Jordanian, and he used that, saying he would report back to Captain Collins with his findings. SSG Mary told me that Captain Collins decided not to show up because he didn't want to ruin the test results with his presence; he saw himself as a man who "exudes authority," according to Mary. I had the feeling that his colleagues, who were aware of his past practices, decided he shouldn't come to the test. But as a matter of fact, he followed the whole thing through a hole he poked in the thick black plastic screen that separated the detainee's area from the guards' area, and he was really clumsy; I kept hearing the rustling of the plastic during the test. I learned later that Master Jedi and Master Luke were watching, too.

John told me his questions would be in a random order, and that his laptop spat them out as it pleased. In reality, programmers talk about pseudorandom numbers, because producing true randomness is not as easy as one would think. But his questions really weren't very random at all. I was asked to answer two types of questions, relevant and non-relevant; the sole purpose of the non-relevant questions was to "calibrate" me and the equipment.

"Are you wearing shoes?"

"Is your name Mohamedou?"

"Are you sitting on a chair?"

"Are you an astronaut?"

"Have you ever cheated on a test?" I answered yes. I remembered a time that I was frustrated with a teacher and his subject and decided to attend exactly zero classes. I ended up having to study the subject in a hurry, and I brought his textbook with me to the test for when I couldn't answer a question on my own.

John took some time to scold me. He told me that he never cheated in his life, and that he hated people who cheat to get where they don't deserve. I tried to explain that in most subjects at the university we were allowed to look things up during tests, because that is what we would do in real life, but some teachers denied that opportunity. But no amount of whitewashing myself would make him have sympathy for me or give me a break. SSG Mary was looking at me and smiling; she told me later on that she had cheated in college, too.

The real meat for John was in some direct, straightforward questions, like, "When you were in Canada, did you plan to attack the United States?" When he asked me this, I asked him to add Canada to the question because the U.S. government was trying to link me to terrorist plots there, too.

"Let's worry about the U.S. for now," he told me. But he must have changed his mind, maybe when he saw conclusively that I had done nothing against the United States, because he later started adding Canada to his questions automatically.

"Do you know any al Qaeda members in the U.S. or Canada you haven't told us about?"

"No," I answered.

"Do you know about future attacks in the U.S. or Canada?"

"No."

"Have you said anything about Ahmed Laabidi that isn't true?"

"Yes," I said. I told him Ahmed was basically an innocent man as far as I knew. When I said that, both he and Mary told me that they both had that feeling, and more importantly, that the leadership thought so, too. John went behind the screen to consult with Captain Collins and others who were watching. I knew this was a bitter pill for Captain Collins, who was watching two people being cleared before his eyes. He was obsessed with getting people convicted and sent to jail, not only in GTMO and the U.S., but even in Germany. One day he came to me upset and said he badly needed my help because a Moroccan on trial in Germany named Abdelghani Mzoudi was acquitted. My job was to provide information that would change the mind of a German federal judge, to convict a person whose name I never heard before. Looking at a picture Captain Collins must have printed from the internet, I was speechless. "I don't know this man," I said reluctantly. To Captain Collins, anyone who is arrested is a criminal; there are no innocent suspects.

Captain Collins must have advised the team to learn from me what information I had provided about Laabidi that was false, which was everything except that Ahmed Laabidi was a Muslim man from Tunisia. John amended the questions and posed them again. Until now my physiological responses were all over the place, John said, and I was just hoping he could tell the difference between a lie and a person who is simply a nervous wreck. But I felt more comfortable talking about Laabidi with Mary, because she and I were on the same wavelength. John asked me if I was now giving any false information about Laabidi.

"No."

"Have you withheld any information about Laabidi?" he asked.

"No."

John kept asking these questions until he was satisfied with my physiological responses. He also repeated the questions about whether I planned to attack the U.S. or Canada. He kept trying to reassure me because he could see on the machine my extreme fear and anxiety. At one point, he wondered how I could be a terrorist, and I told him I was "a clumsy one," which he found very funny.

"You did good," he said to me when the test was over. He didn't mean that I passed, only that I calmed down enough for him to be able to evaluate me; the evaluation had to wait until the next day. I spent a long, sleepless night, expecting the worst.

SSG Mary came to see me the next day with the broadest smile I'd seen so far.

"I always believed in you," she told me. "You passed with flying colors, and this time there was no 'inconclusive' stuff." She brought me some cookies. If I told you that I wasn't more excited about passing the exam than Mary, I would hardly be overstating her satisfaction. I realized that Captain Collins had gone too far in his quest to get me convicted, and all of a sudden I wasn't afraid of the polygraph anymore. I told her I was ready to take another one over any other statements I had made in the past.

I soon had my chance. Some in the team couldn't believe the results, and I was asked to take the same test again a week later. The tester claimed that he just wanted to make sure everything was OK, and that I was too nervous the first time. I really don't think he doubted his judgment, but there were others who had a lot to lose if I passed. The most obvious person was Captain Collins, but I think it was more than just him, and that there was a real interagency fight going on over my case.

The equipment was installed again next to my cell. This time I had a level of confidence that I didn't have the last time. I was more frustrated than scared, and I figured if I passed the first one, why shouldn't I pass this one? I also had the feeling the tester was pissed that others were doubting his expertise, and I figured he must be on my side now, if only to save his own reputation.

He didn't speak to me as much this time. The first time, it seemed like every second word he said was "for instance"; on this day, I don't remember hearing it from him once. I sat like a stone on that hard chair, looking for an ant to accompany me, but I had to settle for the stark white wooden wall.

The tester asked the same questions. After a couple of runs, he wrapped it up and off he went. The verdict did not change; the tester stuck to his guns, and one more time I passed the test. Master Jedi kept making fun of me for days, asking why I was so nervous during the first test. I told him it was because I'm "sensible," but that wasn't what I meant; I was using the wrong word. He laughed, and we agreed that I should say "sensitive" instead.*

---

* An official Report of Examination of two polygraph tests administered on November 12 and November 20, 2003 was included in the exhibits entered into the record in MOS's habeas corpus appeal proceedings. The report describes the following questions and results:

On 12 Nov 03, ISN 760 was interviewed and consented to a polygraph examination concerning his participation in plans to harm the United States or Canada and if he had provided false information in regard to a known terrorist.

On 12 Nov 03 and 20 Nov 03, ISN 760 was interviewed and consented to a Polygraph examination to verify the veracity of his statements as reflected above. . . .

Based on the above information ISN 760 was provided a Polygraph examination in which the below questions were asked and answered as indicated:

a. While in Canada, did you plan with anyone to harm the U.S. or Canada? . . . No

b. Do you know of any Al Qaida members that have lived in the U.S. or Canada that you have not told us about? . . . No

c. Do you have any knowledge regarding future plans to harm the U.S. or Canada? . . . No

After analysis of the polygrams collected during SERIES I, no opinion could be rendered due to ISN 760s physiological responses to the relevant questions. A SERIES II was conducted with the following relevant questions asked and the responses with the ISN 760's answer:

d. Have you provided any false information regarding Laabidi? . . . No

e. Have you withheld any information regarding Laabidi? . . . No

After analysis of the polygrams collected during SERIES II, no opinion could be rendered due to ISN 760's answer:

f. Have you provided any false information regarding Laabidi? . . . No

g. Have you withheld any information regarding Laabidi? . . . No

After analysis of the polygrams collected during SERIES III, the Examiner determined that ISN 760's physiological responses were not indicative of deception and is being reported as No Deception Indicated. . . .

h. While in Canada, did you ever plan with anyone to harm the U.S. or Canada? . . . No

i. Do you have any knowledge regarding future plans to harm the U.S. or Canada? . . . No

After analysis of the polygrams collected during SERIES I, no opinion could be rendered due to ISN 760's physiological responses to the relevant questions. A SERIES II was conducted with the following relevant questions asked and the responses with the ISN 760's answer:

j. While in Canada, did you make plans with anyone to harm the U.S. or Canada? . . . No

k. Do you know of any future plans to harm the U.S. or Canada? . . . No

---

After analysis of the information collected during the Polygraph, it was the opinion of the examiner that ISN 760 responses resulted in a **no deception indicated** *test result.*

(Report of Examination, ISN 760, entered into the record in the habeas corpus appeal *Mohammedou Ould Salahi v. Barack Obama*, United States Court of Appeals for the District of Columbia).

SEVEN

GTMO

2004-2005

The Good News...Goodbye Like Family Members...
The TV and the Laptop...The First Unofficial Laughter in the Ocean of Tears...The Present Situation...
The Dilemma of the Cuban Detainees

I am happy and Captain Collins is very pleased," said SSG Mary when she showed up the day after the polygraph, accompanied by another sergeant, a white female in her late twenties.

"What does 'pleased' mean?" I asked SSG Mary. I had an idea, but I wanted to be clear since the word was a quotation from Captain Collins.

"Pleased means very happy."

"Ah, OK. Didn't I tell you that I wasn't lying?"

"Yes, I'm glad," said SSG Mary, smiling. Her happiness was obvious and honest. I was hardly happier about my success than SSG Mary. Now I could tell that the resented torture was heading the other direction, slowly but surely. And yet I was extremely skeptical, since I was still surrounded by the same people as I had been since day one.

"Look at your uniform and ours. You are not one of us. You are our enemy!" Master Yoda used to say.

"I know."

"I don't want you to forget. If I speak to you, I speak to my enemy."

"I know!"

"Don't forget."

"I won't!" Such talk left no doubt that the animosity of the guards had been driven to its extreme. Most of the time I had the feeling that they were trained to devour me alive.

SSG Mary introduced her company to me. "This is another interrogator, you can call her Sergeant like me."

The new interrogator was quiet and polite. I can't really say anything negative about her. She was a workaholic, and not really open to other people. She literally followed the orders of her boss, Captain Collins, and sometimes even worked like a computer.

"Do you know about your friend Falah's travel to Iraq in 2003?" she asked me once.

"Come on, Sergeant, you know that I turned myself in in 2001. How am I supposed to know what went on in 2003? It doesn't make sense, does it?" I said.

The sergeant smiled. "I have the question in my request."

"But you know that I've been in detention since 2001!" I said. The sergeant was very careful, too careful: she used to cover her rank and her name all the time, and she never made any reference to her beliefs. I personally was content with that, as long as she didn't give me a hard time.

"I like the way you make connections," she said, smiling at me in that session. Interrogators have a tendency to enter the house through the window and not the door; instead of asking a direct question, they ask all kinds of questions around it. I took it as a challenge, and for the most part I would search out the direct question and answer that. "Your question is whether or not...," I would say. And the sergeant seemed to like that shortcut.

But has there ever, in all of recorded human history, been an interrogation that has gone on, day in and day out, for more than six years? There is nothing an interrogator could say to me that would be new; I've heard every variation. Each new interrogator would come up with the most ridiculous theories and lies, but you could tell they were all graduates of the same school: before an interrogator's mouth opened I knew what he or she was going to say and why he or she was saying it.

"I am your new interrogator. I have very long experience doing this job. I was sent especially from Washington D.C. to assess your case."

"You are the most important detainee in this camp. If you cooperate with me, I am personally going to escort you to the airport. If you don't cooperate, you're gonna spend the rest of your life on this island."

"You're very smart. We don't want to keep you in jail. We would rather capture the big fish and release the small fish, such as yourself."

"You haven't driven a plane into a building; your involvement can be forgiven with just a five-minute talk. The U.S. is the greatest country in the world; we would rather forgive than punish."

"Many detainees have talked about you being the bad person. I personally don't believe them; however, I would like to hear your side of the story, so I can defend you appropriately."

"I have nothing against Islam, I even have many Muslim friends."

"I have helped many detainees to get out of this place; just by writing a positive report stating that you told the whole truth....."

And so on, in an endless recitation that all the interrogators recited when they met with their detainees. Most detainees couldn't help laughing when they had to hear this *Groundhog Day* nonsense; in fact, it was the only entertainment we got in the interrogation booth. When his interrogator told him, "I know you are innocent," one of my fellow detainees laughed hard and responded, "I'd rather be a criminal and sitting home with my kids." I believe anything loses its influence the more we repeat it. If you hear an expression like, "You are the worst criminal on the face the earth" for the first time, you'll most likely get the hell scared out of you. But the fear diminishes the more times you hear it, and at some point it will have no effect at all. It may even sound like a daily compliment.

And yet let's look at it from the interrogator's perspective. They were literally taught to hate us detainees. "Those people are the most evil creatures on earth...Do not help the enemy... Keep in mind they are enemies...Look out, the Arabs are the worst, especially the Saudis and the Yemenis. They're hardcore, they're savages....Watch out, don't approach or talk to them unless you secure everything..." In GTMO, interrogators are taught more about the potential behavior of detainees than about their actual intelligence value, and so the U.S. interrogators consistently succeeded in missing the most trivial information about their own detainees. I'm not speaking about second hand information; I'm speaking about my own experience.

"KSM spoke about you!" SSG Mary said to me once.

"KSM doesn't know me, how could he possibly have spoken about me? Just read my file again."*

---

* KSM is Khalid Sheikh Mohammed. He remains imprisoned in Guantánamo and is on trial before a military commission as the alleged mastermind of the September 11, 2001, terrorist attacks.

"I am sure that he did. I'm gonna show you!" SSG Mary said. But she never did because she was wrong. I had heard of such and worse examples depicting the ignorance of interrogators about their detainees. The government would hold back basic information from its interrogators for tactical reasons, and then tell them, "The detainee you are assigned to is deeply involved in terrorism and has vital information about coming and already performed attacks; your job is to get everything he knows." In fact, I hardly met a detainee who was involved in a crime against the United States.

So you have interrogators who are prepared, schooled, trained, and pitted to meet their worst enemies. And you have detainees who typically were captured and turned over to U.S forces without any proper judicial process. After that, they experienced heavy mistreatment and found themselves incarcerated in another hemisphere, in GTMO Bay, by a country that claims to safeguard human rights all over the world—but a country that many Muslims suspect is conspiring with other evil forces to wipe the Islamic religion off the face of the earth. All in all, the environment is not likely to be a place of love and reconciliation. The hatred here is heavily watered.

But believe it or not, I have seen guards crying because they had to leave their duties in GTMO.

"I am your friend, I don't care what anybody says," said one guard to me before he left.

"I was taught bad things about you, but my judgment tells me something else. I like you very much, and I like speaking with you. You are a great person," said another.

"I hope you get released," said SSG Mary genuinely.

"You guys are my brothers, all of you," another whispered to me.

"I love you!" said a white female corpsman once to my neighbor, a funny young guy I personally enjoyed talking to. He was shocked.

"What...Here no love...I am Mouslim!" I just laughed about that "forbidden" love.

But I couldn't help crying myself one day when I saw a German-descendent female guard crying because she got just a little bit hurt. The funny thing was I hid my feelings because I didn't want them to be misinterpreted by my brethren, or understood as a weakness or a betrayal. At one point I hated myself and confused the hell out of myself. I started to ask myself questions about the humane emotions I was having toward my enemies. How could you cry for somebody who caused you so much pain and destroyed your life? How could you possibly like somebody who ignorantly hates your religion? How could you put up with these evil people who keep hurting your brothers? How could you like somebody who works day and night to pull shit on you? I was in a worse situation than a slave: at least a slave is not always shackled in chains, has some limited freedom, and doesn't have to listen to some interrogator's bullshit every day.

I often compared myself with a slave. Slaves were taken forcibly from Africa, and so was I. Slaves were sold a couple of times on their way to their final destination, and so was I. Slaves suddenly were assigned to somebody they didn't choose, and so was I. And when I looked at the history of slaves, I noticed that slaves sometimes ended up an integral part of the master's house.

I have been through several phases during my captivity. The first phase was the worst: I almost lost my mind fighting to get back to my family and the life I was used to. My torture was in my rest; as soon as closed my eyes, I found myself complaining to them about what has happened to me.

"Am I with you for real, or is it a mere dream?"

"No, you're really at home!"

"Please hold me, don't let me go back!" But the reality always hit me as soon as I woke up to the dark bleak cell, looking around just long enough to fall asleep and experience it all again. It was several weeks before I realized that I'm in jail and not going home anytime soon. As harsh as it was, this step was necessary to make me realize my situation and work objectively to avoid the worst, instead of wasting my time with my mind playing games on me. Many people don't pass this step; they lose their minds. I saw many detainees who ended up going crazy.

Phase two is when you realize for real that you're in jail and you possess nothing but all the time in the world to think about your life — although in GTMO detainees also have to worry about daily interrogations. You realize you have control over nothing, you don't decide when you eat, when you sleep, when you take a shower, when you wake up, when you see the doctor, when you see the interrogator. You have no privacy; you cannot even squeeze a drop of urine without being watched. In the beginning it is a horrible thing to lose all those privileges in the blink of an eye, but believe me, people get used to it. I personally did.

Phase three is discovering your new home and family.

Your family comprises the guards and your interrogators. True, you didn't choose this family, nor did you grow up with it, but it's a family all the same, whether you like it or not, with all the advantages and disadvantages. I personally love my family and wouldn't trade it for the world, but I have developed a family in jail that I also care about. Every time a good member of my present family leaves it feels as if a piece of my heart is being chopped off. But I am so happy if a bad member has to leave.★

"I'm going to leave soon," SSG Mary said a couple of days before she left.

"Really? Why?"

"It's about time. But the other sergeant is going to stay with you. That was not exactly comforting, but it would have been futile to argue: the transfer of MI agents is not a subject of discussion. "We're gonna watch a movie together before I leave," SSG Mary added.

"Oh, good!" I said. I hadn't digested the news yet.

SSG Mary most likely studied psychology, and came from the west coast, maybe California. She once told me that after joining the U.S. Army in her early twenties, she was deployed to Bosnia in the late 1990s. I think that Mary comes from a rather poor family. The U.S. Army provides a great deal of opportunity for people from the lower classes, and most of the military people I've seen are from the lower class. She looked at Richard Zuley and his ideas very highly, but she had a rather shaky relationship with the rest of the team. She has a very strong personality. At the same time, she likes her job, and might have been forced to step over the red line of her principles sometimes. "I know what we are doing is not healthy for our country," she used to tell me.

SSG Mary was my first real encounter with an American female soldier. "Sergeant, you are so foul-mouthed! I feel ashamed for you," I wondered once. She smiled.

"It's because I've been most of the time around guys." At first

---

★ MOS adds a note here in the margin of the handwritten original: "Phase four: getting used to the prison, and being afraid of the outside world."

I had a problem starting a conversation with a foul-mouthed female, but later I learned that there was no way to speak colloquial English without F—ing this and F—ing that. English accepts more curses than any other language, and I soon learned to curse with the commoners. Sometimes guards would ask me to translate certain words into Arabic, German, or French, but the translation spun around in my head and I could not spit it out; it just sounded so gross. On the other hand, when I curse in English I really have no bad feeling whatsoever, because that's the way I learned the language from day one. I had a problem when it comes to blasphemy, but everything else was tolerable. The curses are just so much more harmless when everybody uses them recklessly.

SSG Mary was one of my main teachers of the dictionary of curse words, alongside Yoda and the rest of the guards. SSG Mary had been through some bad relationships; she had been cheated on and some bad things like that.

"Did you cry when you knew?" I asked her.

"No, I didn't want to give my boyfriend the satisfaction he was important to me. I have a problem when it comes to crying."

"I see." But I personally don't see the problem: I cry whenever if I feel like it and it makes me stronger to admit my weakness.

SSG Mary was misused by SFC Shally and his colleague and boss Richard Zuley and some other behind-the-scenes guys. I know that I am looking for excuses to acquit SSG Mary; she was old enough to know that what she was doing was wrong, and she could have both saved her job and had the other higher-ranking officers fired. She certainly contributed to the pressure to which I had been subjected. But I do also know that SSG Mary doesn't believe in torture.

I used to make fun of the signs they put up for the interrogators and the guards to raise their morale, "Honor bound to defend freedom." I once cited that big sign to SSG Mary.

"I hate that sign," she said.

"How could you possibly be defending freedom, if you're taking it away?" I would say.

The bosses had noticed the close relationship developing between SSG Mary and me, and so they separated her from me when I was kidnapped. The last words I heard were, "You're hurting him! Who gave you the orders?" her shouts fading away as Mr. X and Big Boss dragged me out of the room in Gold Building. And when they decided to give me a chance at a halfway humane interrogation, SSG Mary appeared in the picture again. But this time she was somewhat unfriendly to me, and used any opportunity to make my statements look stupid. I couldn't understand her behavior. Was it in my favor, or was she just pissed off at everybody? I'm not going to judge anybody; I'm leaving that part to Allah. I am just providing the facts as I have seen and experienced them, and I don't leave anything out to make somebody look good or bad. I understand that nobody is perfect, and everybody does both good and bad things. The only question is, How much of each?

"Do you hate my government?" SSG Mary asked me once while sifting through a map.

"No, I hate nobody."

"I would hate the U.S. if I were you!" she said. "You know, nobody really knows what we're doing here. Only a few people in the government know about it."

"Really?"

"Yes. The President reads the files of some detainees. He reads your case."

"Really?"

SSG Mary enjoyed rewarding rather than punishing detainees. I can say without a doubt that she didn't enjoy harassing me, although she tried to keep her "professional" face; on the other hand, she very much enjoyed giving some stuff back. SSG Mary was even the one who came with most of the ideas related to literature that I was given to read.

"This book is from Captain Collins," Mary said one day, handing me a thick novel that was called something like *Life in the Forest*.* It was historical fiction, written by a British writer, and it covered a great deal of the medieval European history and the Norman invasion. I received the book gratefully and read it hungrily, at least three times. Later on, she brought me several *Star Wars* books. Whenever I finished one, she traded it for a new one.

"Oh, thank you very much!"

"Did you like the *Star Wars*?"

"I sure do!" In truth, I didn't really like *Star Wars* books and their language, but I had to settle for any books they gave to me. In prison you have nothing but all the time in the world to think about your life and the goal thereof. I think prison is one of the oldest and greatest schools in the world: you learn about God and you learn patience. A few years in prison are equivalent to decades of experience outside it. Of course there is the devastating side of the prison, especially for innocent prisoners who, besides dealing with the daily hardship of prison, have to deal with the psychological damages that result from confinement without a crime. Many innocent people in prison contemplate suicide.

Just imagine yourself going to bed, putting all your worries

---

* The book is Edward Rutherfurd's historical novel *The Forest,* which was published in 2000.

aside, enjoying your favorite magazine to put you to sleep, you've put the kids to bed, your family is already sleeping. You are not afraid of being dragged out of your bed in the middle of the night to a place you've never seen before, deprived of sleep, and terrorized all the time. Now imagine that you have no say at all in your life—when you sleep, when you wake up, when you eat, and sometimes when you go to the toilet. Imagine that your whole world comprises, at most, a 6 by 8 foot cell. If you imagine all of that, you still won't understand what prison really means unless you experience it yourself.

SSG Mary showed up as promised a few days later with a laptop and two movies, and told me. "You can decide which one you'd like to watch!" I picked the movie *Black Hawk Down*; I don't remember the other choice.

The movie was both bloody and sad. I paid more attention to the emotions of Mary and the guards than to the movie itself. SSG Mary was rather calm; every once in a while she paused the movie to explain the historical background of certain scenes to me. The guards almost went crazy emotionally because they saw many Americans getting shot to death. But they missed that the number of U.S. casualties is negligible compared to the Somalis who were attacked in their own homes. I was just wondering at how narrow-minded human beings can be. When people look at one thing from one perspective, they certainly fail to get the whole picture, and that is the main reason for the majority of misunderstandings that sometimes lead to bloody confrontations.

After we finished watching the movie, Mary packed her computer and got ready to leave.

"Eh, by the way, you didn't tell me when you're going to leave!"

"I am done, you won't see me anymore!" I froze as if my feet were stuck on the floor. Mary didn't tell me that she was leaving *that* soon; I thought maybe in a month, three weeks, something like that—but today? In my world that was impossible. Imagine if death were devouring some friend of yours and you just were helplessly watching him fading away.

"Oh, really, that soon? I'm surprised! You didn't tell me. Good-bye," I said. "I wish everything good for you."

"I have to follow my orders, but I leave you in good hands." And off she went. I reluctantly went back to my cell and silently burst in tears, as if I'd lost a family member, and not somebody whose job was to hurt me and extract information in an end-justifies-the-means way. I both hated and felt sorry for myself for what was happening to me.

"May I see my interrogator please?" I asked the guards, hoping they could catch Mary before they reached the main gate.

"We'll try," said Yoda. I retreated back in my cell, but soon Mary showed up at the door of my cell.

"That is not fair. You know that I suffered torture and am not ready for another round."

"You haven't been tortured. You must trust my government. As long as you're telling the truth, nothing bad is gonna happen to you!" Of course she meant The Truth as it's officially defined. But I didn't want to argue with her about anything.

"I just don't want to start everything over with new interrogators," I said.

"It's not gonna happen," Mary said. "Besides, you can write me. I promise I'll answer every email of yours," she continued.

"No, I will not write you," I said.

"OK." Mary said. "Are you alright?" she asked.

"I'm not, but you may surely leave."

"I am not leaving until you assure me everything's alright," Mary said.

"I said what I had to say. Have a good trip. May Allah guide you. I'll be just fine."

"I am sure you will. It will take at most a week and you'll forget me." I didn't speak after that. Instead I went back and lay myself down. Mary stayed a couple of minutes repeating the same thing, "I am not leaving until you assure me everything is alright."

After Mary left, I never saw her again or tried to get in contact with her. And so the chapter of SSG Mary's time with me was sealed.

"I heard yesterday's goodbye was very emotional. I never thought of you this way. Would you describe yourself as a criminal?" SFC Shally said the next day.

I prudently answered, "To an extent." I didn't want to fall in any possible trap, even though I felt that he was honestly and innocently asking the question, now that he realized that his evil theories about me were null. "All the evil questions are gone," SFC Shally said.

"I won't miss them," I said.

SFC Shally had come to give me a haircut. It was about time! One of the measures of my punishment was to deprive me of any hygienic shaves, toothbrushing, or haircuts, so today was a big day. They brought a masked barber; the guy was scary looking, but he did the job. SFC Shally also brought me a book he promised me a long time ago, *Fermat's Last Theorem,* which I really enjoyed—so much so that I hungrily read it more than twice. The book is written by a British journalist and speaks about the famous De Fermat theorem that says the equation $A^n + B^n = C^n$ has no solution when *n* is greater than two. For more than three hundred years, mathematicians from all around the world were boxing against this harmless-looking theorem without succeeding in tackling it, until a British mathematician in

1993 came up with a very complicated proof, which was surely not the one De Fermat meant when he wrote, "I have a neat proof but I have no space on my paper."

I got a haircut, and later on a decent shower. SFC Shally was not a very talkative person when it came to social interactions; he asked me just one question about computers.

"Are you going to cooperate with the new sergeant?"

"Yes."

"Or anybody who's going to work with her?"

"Yes."

The guards' names were their idea; they wanted to be baptized with the names of characters in the *Star Wars* movies. "From now on we are the Jedi and that's what you call us. Your name is Pillow," "Master Jedi" said. I eventually learned from the books that the Jedi are sort of Good Guys who fight against the Forces of Evil. So for the time being I was forced to represent the Forces of Evil, and the guards the Good Guys.

" 'Master Yoda,' that's what you call me," another guard said. I also called him names in secret, like "Interrogator Junior," because he saw himself as a little above the level of a guard and a little under the level of an interrogator. He developed his own rules for dealing with me, including punishments and rewards. He was in his early forties, married with children, small but athletically built. He spent some time working in the Middle East, in Lebanon, and then ended up doing "special missions" for the U.S. Marines. "I've been working to break terrorists like you," he told me.

"Your job is done. I am broken," I answered.

"Don't ask me anything. If you want to ask for something, ask your interrogator."

"I got you," I said. It sounds confusing or even contradictory, but although Yoda was a rough guy, he was humane. That is to say his bark was worse than his bite. Yoda understood what many guards don't understand: if you talk and tell your interrogators what they want to hear, you should be relieved. Many of the other nitwits kept doubling the pressure on me, just for the sake of it.

Master Yoda was in charge of all the other guards. "My job is to make you see the light," said Yoda, addressing me for the first time when he was watching me eating my meal. Guards were not allowed to talk to me or to each other, and I couldn't talk to them. But Yoda was not a by-the-book guy. He thought more than any other guard, and his goal was to make his country victorious: the means didn't matter.

"Yes sir," I answered, without even understanding what he meant. I thought about the literal sense of the light I hadn't seen in a long time, and I believed he wanted to get me cooperating so I could see the daylight. But Yoda meant the figurative sense. Yoda always yelled at me and scared me, but he never hit me. He illegally interrogated me several times, which is why I called him names in my mind like Interrogator Junior. Master Yoda wanted me to confess to many wild theories he heard the interrogators talking about. Furthermore, he wanted to gather knowledge about terrorism and extremism. I think his dream in life was to become an interrogator. What a hell of a dream!

Yoda is an admitted Republican, and hates the Democrats, especially Bill Clinton. He doesn't believe that the U.S. should interfere in other countries' business, and instead should focus more on internal issues—but if any country or group attacks the U.S., it should be destroyed ruthlessly.

"Fair enough," I said. I just wanted him to stop talking. He is the kind of guy who never stops when he gets started. Gosh, he gave me an earache! When Yoda first started talking to me I refused to answer, because all I was allowed to say was, "Yes, sir, No Sir, Need Medics, Need Interrogators." But he wanted a conversation with me.

"You are my enemy," Yoda said.

"Yes, Sir."

"So let's talk as enemy to enemy," he said. He opened my cell and offered me a chair. Yoda did the talking for the most part. He was talking about how great the U.S. is, and how powerful; "America is this, American is that, We Americans are so and so..." I was just wondering and nodding slightly. Every once in a while I confirmed that I was paying attention, "Yes, sir...Really?...Oh, I didn't know...You're right...I know..." During our conversations, he sneakily tried to make me admit to things I hadn't really done.

"What was your role in September 11?"

"I didn't participate in September 11."

"Bullshit!" he screamed madly. I realized it would be no good for my life to look innocent, at least for the time being. So I said, "I was working for al Qaeda in Radio Telecom."

He seemed to be happier with a lie. "What was your rank?" he kept digging.

"I would be a Lieutenant."

"I know you've been in the U.S.," he tricked me. This is a big one and I couldn't possibly lie about it. I could vaguely swallow having done a lot of things in Afghanistan, because Americans cannot confirm or disconfirm it. But the Americans could check right away whether or not I had been in their own country.

"I really haven't been in the U.S.," I answered, though I was ready to change my answer when I had no options.

"You've been in Detroit," he sardonically smiled.

I smiled back. "I really haven't." Though Yoda didn't believe me, he didn't push the matter further; he was interested in a long-term dialogue with me. In return for my confessions he gave me extra food and stopped yelling at me. Meanwhile, in order to maintain the terror, the other guards kept yelling at me and banging the metal door to my cell. Every time they did, my heart started to pound, though the more they did such things, the less effect it had.

"Why are you shaking?" Yoda asked me once when he took me out for conversation. I both hated and liked when he was on duty: I hated him interrogating me, but I liked him giving me more food and new uniforms.

"I don't know," I answered.

"I am not gonna hurt you."

"OK." It took some time until I accepted talking to Yoda. He started to give me lessons and made me practice them the hard way. The lessons were proverbs and made up of phrases he wanted me to memorize and practice in my life. I still do remember the following lessons: 1) Think before you act. 2) Do not mistake kindness for weakness. 3) Keep the questions always in mind when you are asked about somebody. Whenever Yoda judged me to have broken one of the lessons, he took me out of my cell and strew my belongings all over the place, and then Yoda asked me to put everything back in no time. I always failed to organize my stuff, but he would make me do it several times, after which I miraculously put all my stuff back in time.

My relationship with Yoda developed positively with every day that went by, and so with the rest of the guards, too, because they regarded him highly.

"Fuck it! If I look at Pillow I don't think he is a terrorist, I think he's an old friend of mine, and I enjoy playing games with him," he said to the other guards. I relaxed somewhat and gained some self-confidence. Now the guards discovered the humorous guy in me, and used their time with me for entertainment. They started to make me repair their DVD players and PC's, and in return I was allowed to watch a movie. Yoda didn't exactly have the most recent PC model, and when Yoda's colleague asked me whether I had seen Yoda's PC, I answered, "You mean that museum piece?"

Yoda's colleague laughed hard. "Better hope he doesn't hear what you said."

"Don't tell him!"

We slowly but surely became a society and started to gossip about the interrogators and call them names. In the meantime, Mary's replacement taught me the rules of chess. Before prison, I didn't know the difference between a pawn and the rear end of a knight, nor was I really a big gamer. But I found in chess a very interesting game, especially the fact that a prisoner has total control over his pieces, which gives him some confidence back. When I started playing, I played very aggressively in order to let out my frustration, which was really not very good chess playing; she was my first mentor, and she beat me in my first game ever. But the next game was mine, and so were all the other games that followed. Chess is a game of strategy, art, and mathematics. It takes deep thinking, and there is no luck involved. You get rewarded or punished for your actions.

After consulting with her boss Captain Collins, she brought me a chessboard so I could play against myself. When the guards noticed my chessboard, they all wanted to play me, and when they started to play me, they always won. The strongest among the guards was Yoda. He taught me how to control the center. Moreover, the interrogator brought me some literature, which helped decidedly in honing my skills. After that the guards had no chance to defeat me.

"That is not the way I taught you to play chess," Yoda commented angrily when I won a game.

"What should I do?"

"You should build a strategy, and organize your attack! That's why the fucking Arabs never succeed."

"Why don't you just play the board?" I wondered.

"Chess is not just a game," he said.

"Just imagine you're playing against a computer!"

"Do I look like a computer to you?"

"No." The next game I tried to build a strategy in order to let him win.

"Now you understand how chess must be played," he commented. I knew Master Yoda had issues dealing with defeat, and so I didn't enjoy playing him because I didn't feel comfortable practicing my newly acquired knowledge. He believes there are two kinds of people: white Americans and the rest of the world. White Americans are smart and better than anybody. I always tried to explain things to him by saying, for instance, "If I were you," or "If you were me," but he got angry and said, "Don't you ever dare to compare me with you, or compare any American with you!" I was shocked, but I did as he said. After all, I didn't have to compare myself with anybody. Yoda hated the rest of the world, especially the Arabs, Jews, French, Cubans, and others. The only other country he mentioned positively was England.

After one game of chess with him, he flipped the board. "Fuck your Nigger chess, this is Jewish chess," he said.

"Do you have something against Black people?" I asked.

"Nigger is not black, Nigger means stupid," he argued. We had many discussions like that. At the time we had only one Black guard who had no say, and when he worked with Yoda, they never interacted. Yoda resented him. He had a very strong personality, dominant, authoritarian, patriarchal, and arrogant.

"My wife calls me asshole," he proudly told me. Yoda listened mostly to Rock-n-Roll music and some type of country. His favorite songs were "Die Terrorist Die," "The Taliban Song," and "Let the Bodies Hit the Floor." He used to bring his laptop and play videos of military songs for me. I was amazed at how beautifully directed and filmed those propaganda videos could be.

The guards also illegally brought their laptops and asked me to draw pictures of their faces as I imagined them. Until now, my whole time in Echo Special the guards hid behind masks they chose and shared; there was Uncle Sam, George W. Bush, and a wild, cat-like face. It was an easy job: I knew if I made them look ugly and they got upset, I would feel the consequences. Yoda was happy, because I picked a model that looked like Tom Cruise, and just made a few changes here and there.

I never had the chance to see his face because he left before the new rules letting the guards show their faces were put in place. But that was OK with me; I really wasn't interested in seeing anybody's face at that point. In the beginning, he was rough with me: he used to pull me hard and make me run in the shackles, screaming loudly "Move!"

"You know who you are?" he asked me.

"Yes, Sir!"

"You are a terrorist!"

"Yes, Sir!"

"So let's do some math: if you killed five thousand people by your association with al Qaeda, we should kill you five thousand times. But no, because we are Americans we feed you and are ready to give you money if you give us information."

"That's right, Sir!" But after the polygraph test, Captain Collins ordered the guards to be friendly with me, Yoda's friends started to treat me like a human being. I enjoyed discussing things with him because his English was decent, although he was always "right" in his position.

"Our job is to accommodate you!" he used to tell me sarcastically. "You need a house maid." Since guards copy each other, Master Luke tended to copy Master Yoda.

Master Yoda's partner was the Inspector: he liked to inspect my room and make sure everything was put where it belongs, the sheet was wrapped around the edge of the mattress in a 45° angle, and things like that. He also constantly inspected the shower and if he found a tiny hair left in it, he and Yoda made me clean everything again. It didn't matter how often I cleaned; everything had to be perfect.

Master Yoda's partner was especially interested in how I could keep a calendar in my head and know the days and nights in spite of the techniques the guards used to mess up my head. They once tried to make me believe Christmas was Thanksgiving, but I didn't buy it.

"It doesn't really matter, but I do believe it's Christmas," I told them.

"We want you to explain to us what mistakes we made so we can avoid them when we get our next detainee." I explained as much as necessary, but I am sure they will make plenty of mistakes with the next detainee because nobody is perfect.

Yoda's partner explained to me how my recipe could get worse. "You haven't seen nothing."

"And I assure you I am not eager to see more," I would say. He was probably right, though he missed the fact that none of the guards had witnessed everything that happened to me. The only guard who participated in the transport party was Big Boss, and he used every opportunity to hit me in the new place. You could tell he found no problem in beating me, since he did it with the blessing of the highest authority in GTMO.

Yoda's partner was the only guard who didn't sleep during his watch. He would drive me crazy pacing around all the time, and liked to surprise me in the middle of the night by banging the metal door to my cell and making me take a shower and clean everything perfectly. I should not feel rested in my cell for more than an hour: that is one of the most important methods in breaking somebody in detention, because you must hate your life, your guards, your cell, your interrogators, and even yourself. And that is exactly what Yoda's partner did until my interrogation team and Yoda ordered otherwise.

Big Boss was a white man in his twenties, very tall, lazy, non-athletic looking.

"Mr. X is my best friend," he told me once.

"How do you know Mr. X?" He didn't answer me, he just smiled, but he kept mentioning Mr. X and how he had abused me. I always changed the subject because I didn't want the other guards to know that beating me was something normal. I was glad my guards didn't know everything that happened to me; I didn't need the gang to be encouraged to do crimes.

Big Boss was the most violent guard. In Echo Special's Building Three the guards performed regular assaults on me in order to maintain the terror. They came in a big masked team, screaming and giving contradictory orders so I wouldn't know what to do. They would drag me out of my cell and throw my belongings all over the place.

"Get up...Face the wall...You've been resting lately too much...You have a Pillow...Ha Ha!...Look inside his cell... The piece of shit might be hiding something...We found two kernels of rice hidden beneath his mattress...You have twenty seconds to put everything where it belongs!" The game was over when they made me sweat. I knew the guards didn't have the order to beat me, but this guard used every opportunity to hit me and claw me deeply. I don't think that he is the smartest guy, but he was well trained in how to beat somebody without leaving irreparable injuries. "Hitting in the ribs is painful and doesn't leave permanent scars, especially when treated right away with ice cubes" one of the guards told me. Big Boss was both violent and loud, but thank God, he was very lazy; he only barked at the beginning of the shift and after a short time he disappeared from the stage to watch a movie or go to sleep.

Big Boss didn't have any bad feelings about his job; on the contrary, he was rather proud of what he was doing, and he was mad at the fact that he was taking care of the dirty part of the job and he wanted to be rewarded adequately. "Fuck the inter-rogators: we do the work and they take the credit," Big Boss told me once.

He also didn't get along with Master Yoda, the only guy that outranked him. "Yoda is a pussy!" he described him once. But Big Boss was not a social person anyway. He could not lead a normal conversation like everybody else. He rarely spoke, and when he did, it was about his wild sex experiences. One common thing among the guards is that most of them never understood the fact that some people don't have sex outside marriage.

"You're gay," was the usual response.

"That is OK with me, but I cannot have sex outside marriage. You may consider me an idiot, but that's OK!"

"How can you buy a car without test-driving it?"

"First of all, a woman is not a car. And I am doing it because of my religion." Even my female interrogator Mary shocked me once when she said, "I wouldn't marry anybody before test-driving him." But I still do believe that some Americans don't believe in premarital sex.

The one who came up with the idea of the guards taking *Star Wars* characters' names was a specialist who called himself Master Jedi. He saw everything he was doing to me as just part of his job; no hard feelings, really. But he also would bring me cookies and even the newspaper. Every once in a while he made me clean the guards' area, but I really enjoyed that; I would get to see what the guards had there, and also got a soda as a reward.

When we interacted, Master Jedi liked to talk about himself. He told me he had been tasked to gather Intels about me before my kidnapping from Gold Building, and gave evidence of this by accurately recounting details of my special situation. I had never noticed him in the blocks at Camp Delta, nor was I supposed to. Master Jedi was mostly partnered with Master Luke; at the beginning, and in the decisive period, Jedi was in charge. Jedi was in good physical shape, unlike his friend Luke.

Master Jedi moderately and dutifully followed the rules he was given by Captain Collins and the rest of the interrogators, and he and his associate delivered my water diet, gave me PTs, forbade me to pray or fast, and kept giving me a "Party-shower." Master Jedi was even the one who came up with that annoying, never-ending, basic-training-like drill, where I had to have every piece in a defined place, toilet and sink always dry, so I ended up having to use my uniform because I had no towel. He hardly ever gave me a break except when he and Luke started to play Call of Duty and forgot about me. Nonetheless,

I can tell you truthfully that Master Jedi didn't enjoy bothering me or torturing me.

"Why did you forbid me to pray when you knew it's an illegal order?" I asked him when we became friends.

"I could have but they would have given me some shitty job." He also told me that Captain Collins gave him the order preventing me from practicing any religious activities. Jedi said, "I'm going to hell because I forbade you to pray."

Master Jedi was so happy when he was ordered to treat me nicely. "I really enjoyed being here with you more than being at home," he genuinely said. He was a very generous guy; he used to give me muffins, movies, and PS2 games. Before he left he asked me to choose between two games, Madden 2004 and Nascar 2004 I chose Nascar 2004, which I still have. Above all, Jedi was a hell of an entertainer. He tended to stretch the truth, and he would tell me all kinds of stuff. Sometimes he gave me too much information, things I didn't want to know, nor was I supposed to know.

He was a big gamer. He used to play video games all the time. I'm terrible when it comes to video games; it's just not for me. I always told the guards, "Americans are just big babies. In my country it's not appropriate for somebody my age to sit in front of a console and waste his time playing games." Indeed, one of the punishments of their civilization is that Americans are addicted to video games.

And Americans worship their bodies. They eat well. When I was delivered to Bagram Air Base, I was like, What the heck is going on, these soldiers never stop chewing on something. And yet, though God blessed Americans with a huge amount of healthy food, they are the biggest food wasters I ever knew: if every country lived as Americans do, our planet could not absorb the amount of waste we produce.

They also work out. I have a big variety of friends who come from all backgrounds, and I really had never heard any other group of mortals speaking about the next workout plan.

"Is that a homosexual magazine?" I asked one of the guards who was holding a man fitness magazine with those oversized guys. You know, those guys who keep working until their necks disappear, and their heads barely fit between their overgrown shoulders.

"What the fuck are you talking about? This is a workout magazine," he responded. American men are more intolerant toward male homosexuals compared to German men, and they work out as if they're preparing for a fight.

"When I hug my wife, she feels secure," Master Yoda told me once.

"My wife always feels secure; she doesn't need a hug to be calmed," I answered.

Master Jedi was like anybody else: he bought more food than he needed, worked out even during duty, planned to enlarge his member, played video and computer games, and was very confused when it comes to his religion.

"Pillow, I am telling you, I really don't know. But I am Christian and my parents celebrate Christmas every year," he told me, adding, "My girlfriend wants to convert to Islam but I said no."

"Come on, Jedi, you should let her choose. Don't you guys believe in freedom of religion?" I replied. The Specialist had all the qualities of a human being; I liked conversing with him because he always had something to say. He liked to impress the females on the island. And he especially resented the one guard who wouldn't take a *Star Wars* name; I really can't blame him!

Everyone resented him. He was lazy and on the slower side.

Nobody wanted to work with him, and they talked ill about him all the time. This skinny white guy didn't have any initiative or personality of his own, and he used to copy every other guard. When he started working on the team he was quiet; he just served me my food and dutifully made me drink water ever hour. And that was cool. But he quickly learned that I could be yelled at, have food taken from, and made to do harsh PTs I didn't want to do. He couldn't believe that he was entitled to so much power. He almost went wild making me stand up for hours during the night, even though he knew I suffered from sciatic nerve. He made me clean my cell over and over. He made me clean the shower over and over.

"I wish you'd make a mistake, any mistake, so I can strike," he used to say while performing some corny fake martial arts he must have learned for purposes of his mission. Even after Captain Collins ordered the guards to be nice to me, he became worse, as if trying to catch up on something he missed.

"You call me Master, OK?" he said.

"Oh, yes," I answered, thinking, Who the heck does he think he is? He has no qualification besides his luck of having been born a white guy in the U.S. His partner was the only black guard on the team, but even though his partner outranked him, he was in charge all the time. When he saw the other guards playing chess with me, he wanted to play, too, but I soon discovered how weak a person can be in chess. Moreover, he had his own rules, which he always enforced, him being the Master, and me the detainee. In his chess world the king belonged to his own color, breaking the basic rule in chess that states that the king sits on the opposite color when the game begins. I knew he was wrong, but there was no correcting him, so with him I had to play his version of chess.

*   *   *

Around March 15, 2004, the JTF interrogation team gave me a TV with an integrated VCR to watch the movies they would give me. Captain Collins himself gave me the movie *Gladiator* from his personal collection. I like that movie because it vividly depicts how the forces of evil get defeated at the end, no matter how strong they seem. On advice and approval, the sergeant and her colleague got me many interesting movies.

In my real life I was not a big fan of movies; I don't remember watching a single movie all the way through since I turned eighteen. I do like documentaries and movies based on true stories, but I have a problem giving up my mind and going with the flow of the acting when I know that everything that happens in the movie is fake. But in prison, I'm different: I appreciate everything that shows regular human beings wearing casual clothes and talking about something besides terrorism and interrogation. I just want to see some mammals I can relate to.

The Americans I met watch movies a lot. In America it's like, "Tell me how many movies you've seen, and I'll tell you who you are." But if Americans can be proud of something, they have the right to be proud of their motion picture industry.

Of course, the TV had no receiver, because I was not allowed to watch TV or know anything that happened outside my cell; all I was allowed to watch were the movies that had been approved by Captain Collins. It is so evidently unjust to cut off a person from the rest of the world and forbid him to know what's going on in the outside world, regardless of whether or not he is involved in criminal activities. I noticed that the TV/VCR combo had an FM radio receiver that could receive local broadcasts, but I never touched it: although it is my basic right to listen to whatever radio I wish, I find it so dishonest to stab the hand that reaches out to help you. And regardless of what Captain Collins and his interrogators have done to me, I found it positive that they offered me this entertainment tool, and I would not use it against them. Moreover, Captain Collins got me a laptop, which I mightily enjoyed. Of course one of the main reasons for the laptop was to make me type my answers during interrogations to save both time and manpower for the JTF team, kind of like forced labor. But I had no problem with that idea; after all, I wanted to deliver my words and not their interpretation thereof.

"Look, I got some Arabic music," said the sergeant, handing me an audio CD.

"Oh, fine!" But the CD was not even close to the Arabic language: it was Bosnian. I laughed wholeheartedly. "Close enough. It's Bosnian music," I said when the CD started to play.

"Is it not the same, Bosnian and Arabic?" asked the sergeant. That is just one example of how little Americans know about Arabs and Islam. The sergeant is a member of JTF and not just anybody; she is supposedly armed with basic knowledge about Arabs and Islam. But she and the other interrogators always addressed me, "You guys from the middle east...," which is so completely wrong. For many Americans, the world comprises three places: The U.S., Europe, and the rest of the world, the Middle East. Unfortunately, the world, geographically speaking, is a little bit more than that. In my job in my country, I had to make some calls to the U.S. for professional purposes. I remember the following conversation:

"Hello, we are dealing with office materials. We are interested in representing your company."

"Where are you calling from?" asked the lady at the other end.

"Mauritania."

"What state?" asked the lady, seeking more precise information. I was negatively surprised at how small her world was.

The confusion of Captain Collins was as obvious as his ignorance about the whole terrorism issue. The man was completely terrified, as if he were drowning and looking for any straw to grasp. I guess I was one of the straws he bumped into in his flailing, and he grasped me really hard.

"I don't understand why people hate us. We help everybody in the world!" he stated once, seeking my opinion.

"Neither do I," I replied. I knew it was futile to enlighten him about the historical and objective reasons that led to where we're at, and so I opted to ignore his comment; besides, it was not exactly easy to change the opinion of a man as old as he was.

Many young men and women join the U.S. forces under the misleading propaganda of the U.S. government, which makes people believe that the Armed Forces are nothing but a big Battle of Honor: if you join the Army, you are a living martyr; you're defending not only your family, your country, and American democracy but also freedom and oppressed people all around the world. Great, there is nothing wrong with that; it may even be the dream of every young man or woman. But the reality of the U.S. forces is a little tiny bit different. To go directly to the bottom line: the rest of the world thinks of Americans as a bunch of revengeful barbarians. That may be harsh, and I don't believe the dead average American is a revengeful barbarian. But the U.S. government bets its last penny on violence as the magic solution for every problem, and so the country is losing friends every day and doesn't seem to give a damn about it.

"Look, Staff Sergeant, everybody hates you guys, even your traditional friends. The Germans hate you, the French hate you," I said once to SSG Mary.

"Fuck all of them. We would rather have them hate us, and we'll whup their asses," Mary replied. I just smiled at how easy a solution can be made.

"That's one way to look at it," I answered.

"Fuck them Terrorists."

"OK," I would say. "But you should find the terrorists first. You can't just go wild and hurt everybody in the name of terrorism." She believed that every Arab is a terrorist until proven innocent.

Weird exchanges like this happened often with her colleague, too.

"We need you to help us lock up Ahmed Laabidi for the rest of his life," he said once.

"I am. I've been providing enough Intels to convict him."

"But he keeps denying. He is dealing with other agencies that have different rules than we do. I wish I could get my hands on him: things would be different then!"

I was like, "I hope you never get your hands on anybody."

Another time, speaking of Ahmed Ressam, SFC Shally told me, "All he says is that he did the operation on his own, and that's it."

"Oh, that's very convenient!" I said wryly. Lately I had started to copy SFC Shally, using the exact same phrases as he did. He used to tell me "All you can say is I don't know, I don't remember. That's very convenient! You think you are going to impress an American jury with your charisma?" He always liked to quote the U.S. President, saying "We will not send you guys to court and let you use our justice system, since you're planning to destroy it."

"Is that part of the Big Conspiracy?" I wryly wondered.

"Al Qaeda is using our liberal justice system," he continued. I really don't know what liberal justice system he was talking about: the U.S. broke the world record for the number of people it has in prison. Its prison population is over two million, more than any other country in the world, and its rehabilitation programs are a complete failure. The United States is the "democratic" country with the most draconian punishment system; in fact, it is a good example of how draconian punishments do not help in stopping crimes. Europe is by far more just and humane, and the rehab programs there work, so the crime rate in Europe is decisively lower than the U.S. But the American proverb has it, "When the going gets rough, the rough get going." Violence naturally produces violence; the only loan you can make with a guarantee of payback is violence. It might take some time, but you will always get your loan back.

As things improved, I asked Captain Collins to transfer me to another place because I wanted to forget the bad memories I experienced where I was. He tried to meet my request; he promised me the transfer many times, but he failed to keep his promises. I don't doubt his seriousness, but I could tell there was some kind of power struggle in the small island of GTMO. Everybody wanted the biggest portion of the pie, and the most credit for the work of intelligence gathering. He genuinely promised me many other things, but couldn't hold those promises either.

One amazing thing about Captain Collins was that he never brought up the story of my torture. I always expected him to open the topic, but nothing like that happened: Taboo! Personally I was scared to talk about it; I didn't feel secure enough. Even if he had brought the topic up, I would have dodged talking about it.

But at least he finally told me where I was.

"I have to inform you, against the will of many members in our team, that you are in GTMO," he said. "You've been honest with us and we owe you the same." Although the rest of the world didn't have a clue as to where the U.S. government was incarcerating me, I had known since day one thanks to God and the clumsiness of the JTF special team. But I acted as if this was new information, and I was happy because it meant many things to me to be told where I am. As I write these lines, I am still sitting in that same cell, but at least now I don't have to act ignorant about where I am, and that is a good thing.

In early 2004, the U.S. Army released the first letter from my family.* It was sent through the International Committee of the Red Cross. My family wrote it months before, in July 2003. It had been 815 days since I was kidnapped from my house and had all contacts with my family forcibly broken. I had been sending many letters to my family since I arrived in Cuba, but to no avail. In Jordan I was forbidden even to send a letter.

Captain Collins was the one who handed me that historical piece of paper, which read:

Nouakchott, July 2003
    In the Name of God the most Merciful.
    Peace be with you and God's mercy.
    From your mom Maryem Mint El Wadia
    After my greeting I inform you of my wellbeing and that of the rest of your family. We hope you are the same way. My health situation is OK. I still keep up with my schedule with the Doctors. I feel I am getting better. And the family is OK.

---

* Earlier in the manuscript, MOS indicates that he received the first letter from his family on February 14, 2004.

As I mentioned everybody sends his greeting to you. Beloved son! As of now we have received three letters from you. And this is our second reply. The neighbors are well and they send their greetings. At the end of this letter I renew my greeting. Peace be with you.

Your Mom, Maryem

I couldn't believe that after all I had been through I was holding a letter from my mom. I smelled the odor of a letter that had touched the hand of my mom and other members of my beloved family. The emotions in my heart were mixed: I didn't know what to do, laugh or cry. I ultimately ended up doing both. I kept reading the short message over and over. I knew it was for real, not like the fake one I got one year ago. But I couldn't respond to the letter because I was still not allowed to see the ICRC.

Meanwhile, I kept getting books in English that I enjoyed reading, most of them Western literature. I still remember one book called *The Catcher in the Rye* that made me laugh until my stomach hurt. It was such a funny book. I tried to keep my laughter as low as possible, pushing it down, but the guards felt something.

"Are you crying?" one of them asked.

"No, I'm alright," I responded. It was my first unofficial laughter in the ocean of tears. Since interrogators are not professional comedians, most of the humor they came up with was a bunch of lame jokes that really didn't make me laugh, but I would always force an official smile.

During this period, after months in the Echo Special hut, the JTF geniuses decided I should be allowed to see both my guards and the out of doors. The female sergeant came one Sunday morning and waited outside the building. Master Luke appeared before my cell and announced the plan. I didn't recognize him, of course; I thought he was a new interrogator. But when he spoke I knew it was him.

"Are you Master Luke?"

"Don't worry. Your interrogator is waiting on you outside." I was overwhelmed and terrified at the same time; it was too much for me. Master Jedi led me outside the building; I saw him looking away from me, shy that I see his face. If you deal with somebody for so long behind a face cover, that is how you know him or her. But now if he or she takes off the face cover you have to deal with his features, and that is a completely different story for both sides. I could tell the guards were uncomfortable to show me their faces.

Big Boss put it bluntly. "If I catch you looking at me, I'm gonna hurt you."

"Don't you worry, I'm not dying to see your face." Through time I had built a perception about the way everybody looked, but imagination was far from the reality.

The sergeant prepared a small table with a modest breakfast. I was scared as hell; for one, she never took me outside the building, and for two, I was not used to my guards' "new" faces. I tried to act casually but my shaking gave me away.

"What's wrong with you," she asked.

"I am very nervous. I am not used to this environment."

"But I meant it for your good," she said. The sergeant was a very official person; if she interrogates you, she does it officially, and if she eats with you, she does it as part of her job, and that was cool. I was just waiting for the breakfast to be done so I could go back to my cell, because the sergeant had brought me the movie *King Henry V* by Shakespeare.

"Sergeant, may I watch the movie more than once?" I asked. "I am afraid I am not going to understand it right away."

When the sergeant first brought the TV she briefed the

guards to let me watch a movie only once, and then the party is over. "You're allowed to watch your movie only once, but as far as we're concerned you can watch it as many times as you wish, as long as you don't tell your interrogator about it. We really don't care," Yoda told me later.

"No, if the sergeant said so, I am going to stick with it. I am not gonna cheat," I told him. I really didn't want to mess with a comfort item I had just gotten, so I chose to treat everything carefully. This time, though, the sergeant answered positively. "Yes, you can watch it as many times as you wish," she said.

I asked for one more thing.

"Sergeant, can I keep my water bottle in my cell, and drink whenever I choose?" I was just tired of the lack of sleep; as soon as I closed my eyes, the heavy metal door opened and I had to drink another bottle of water. I knew the sergeant was not the right person to ask to take the initiative; she had literally been following the orders of Captain Collins. But to my surprise, she came the next day and briefed the guards that the water bottle now belonged in my cell. You cannot imagine how happy I was to be able to decide the time and the amount of water I could drink. People who have never been in such a situation cannot really appreciate the freedom of drinking water whenever they want, however much they want.

Then, in July 2004, I found a copy of the Holy Koran in my box of laundry. When I saw the Holy Koran beneath the clothes I felt bad, thinking I had to steal it in order to save it. But I took the Koran to my cell, and nobody ever asked me why I did so. Nor did I bring it up on my own. I had been forbidden all kinds of religious rituals, so I figured a copy of the Koran in my cell would not have made my interrogators too happy. More than that, lately the religious issue had become very delicate. The Muslim chaplain of GTMO was arrested and another Mus-

lim soldier was charged with treason—oh, yes, *treason*.* Many
Arabic and religious books were banned, and books teaching
the English language were also banned. I sort of understood
religious books being banned. "But why English learning
books?" I asked the female sergeant.

"Because detainees pick up the language quickly and understand the guards."

"That's so communist, Sergeant!" I said. To this date I have
never received any Islamic books, though I keep asking for them;
all I can get are novels and animal books. After the removal of
the guards' face masks, my prayers started to be tolerated. I had
been gauging the tolerance toward the practice of my religion;
every once in a while I put the tolerance of the guards and interrogators to the test, and they kept stopping me from praying. So
I would pray secretly. But on this day at the very end of July 2004,
I performed my prayer under the surveillance of some new guards
and nobody made a comment. A new era in my detention had
emerged.

Around April of 2004, the JTF commander turned the leadership of the team over to a U.S. Marine Colonel named Forest,
and later on to an Army Major who went by Anderson, I don't

---

* Three Guantánamo-based personnel who were practicing Muslims were
arrested in September 2003 and accused of carrying classified information
out of the prison. MOS may be referring here specifically to army chaplain
Captain James Yee, who was charged with five offenses including sedition
and espionage, and Senior Airman Ahmad al-Halabi, an Arabic-language
translator who was charged with thirty-two counts ranging from espionage
and aiding the enemy to delivering unauthorized food, including the dessert
baklava, to detainees. The sedition and spying cases collapsed. All charges
against Yee were eventually dropped, and he received an honorable discharge;
al-Halabi pled guilty to four counts, including lying to investigators and
disobeying orders, and received a "bad conduct" discharge. See, e.g., http://
usatoday30.usatoday.com/news/nation/2004-05-16-yee-cover_x.htm; and
http://usatoday30.usatoday.com/news/washington/2004-09-23-gitmo
-airman_x.htm.

know his real name. Many people in the special team tried to make me think that Richard Zuley was still in charge, in order to maintain the fear factor; in fact, Zuley was sent to Iraq with General Miller. Richard Zuley came back from there once and paid me a visit in Echo Special, assuring me he was still in charge.*

"You see, I have a lot of work to do in D.C. and overseas.

---

* In April 2004, General Miller left Guantánamo to assume command of prison and interrogation operations in Iraq.

The previous year, at the end of August 2003, Miller had traveled to Iraq with a team charged with assessing intelligence operations in the wake of the American invasion. The Senate Armed Services Committee reported that during that tour, Miller told an officer of the Iraq Survey Group (ISG), the unit charged with gathering intelligence on weapons of mass destruction, that the ISG "was 'running a country club' and suggested that they were too lenient with detainees." The committee reported that another officer "said that the GTMO Commander had told him about techniques like temperature manipulation and sleep deprivation." After the trip, Miller submitted a report recommending an approach similar to the one he was presiding over in Guantánamo, which concluded: "To achieve rapid exploitation of internees it is necessary to integrate detention operations, interrogation operations, and collection management under one command authority." Several officers, including Janis Karpinski, commandant of prison operations in Iraq in 2003 and 2004, reported that Miller described this approach as "GTMO-izing" interrogation operations in Iraq.

Numerous reports, including the Senate Armed Services Committee report and the report by Major General Antonio Taguba on the abuses of prisoners at Abu Ghraib in late 2003 and early 2004, trace the Abu Ghraib abuses to these recommendations. Nevertheless, when Karpinski was suspended after the publication of the Abu Ghraib photos, Miller was appointed deputy commanding general for detainee operations in Iraq, a position he held from April to November 2004. SASC 190-223. The Taguba report, "Article 15-6 Investigation of the 800th Military Police Brigade," is available at https://fas.org/irp/agency/dod/taguba.pdf. A *Frontline* interview with Janis Karpinski is available at http://www.pbs.org/wgbh/pages/frontline/torture/interviews/karpinski.html.

You might not see me as often as you used to. But you know what makes me happy, and what makes me mad," he said.

"I sure do!" I told him. Zuley fixed some differences I had with the new team in my favor, and he gave me a desert camouflage hat as a souvenir. I still have the hat. I never saw him again after that session.

Finally, in September 2004, the ICRC was allowed to visit after a long fight with the government. It was very odd to the ICRC that I had all of sudden disappeared from the camp, as if the earth had swallowed me. All attempts by ICRC representatives to see me or just to know where I was were thoroughly flushed down the tube.

The ICRC had been very worried about my situation, but they couldn't come to me when I needed them the most. I cannot blame them; they certainly tried. In GTMO, the interrogator is integrally responsible for both detainees' happiness and their agony, in order to have total control over the detainees. General Miller and his colleague Richard Zuley categorically refused to give the ICRC access to me. Only after General Miller left was it possible for the ICRC to visit me.

"You are the last detainee we had to fight to see. We have been able to see all other detainees," said Beatrice, the ICRC delegate. Beatrice was a petite white lady in her late forties who had curly hair and a very serious expression, as if she was honestly upset about something. She and her colleagues tried to get me talking about what happened to me during the time they couldn't have access to me. "We have an idea because we have talked to other detainees who were subject to abuse, but we need you to talk so we can help in stopping further acts of abuse." But I always hid the ill-treatment when the ICRC asked me about it because I was afraid of retaliation. That and the fact that the ICRC has no real pressure on the U.S. government: the ICRC tried, but the U.S. government didn't change its path, even an inch. If they let the Red Cross see a detainee, it meant that the operation against that detainee was over.

"We cannot act if you don't tell us what happened to you," they would urge me.

"I am sorry! I am only interested in sending and receiving mail, and I am grateful that you're helping me to do so." Beatrice was a very high level ICRC delegate from Switzerland who had been working on my case. Her colleagues in Washington sent her to me to convince me to report what had happened to me; she, too, tried to get me talking, but to no avail. I was simply too afraid. Beatrice was visibly upset with me when she left, but she also tried to reassure me.

"We understand your worries," she told me. "All we're worried about is your well-being, and we respect your decision."

Although sessions with the ICRC are supposedly private, I was interrogated about the conversations I had during that first session, and I truthfully told the interrogators what we had said. Later on I told the ICRC about this practice, and after that nobody asked me what happened in our sessions. We detainees knew that the meetings with ICRC were monitored; some detainees had been confronted with statements they made to the ICRC and there was no way for the JFT interrogators to know them unless the meeting was monitored. Many detainees refused to talk to the ICRC, and suspected them to be interrogators disguised in ICRC clothes. I even know some interrogators who presented themselves as private journalists. But to me that was very naïve: for a detainee to mistake an interrogator for a journalist he would have to be an idiot, and there are better methods to get an idiot talking. Such mischievous practices led to tensions between detainees and the ICRC. Some ICRC people were even cursed and spit on.

Around this same time, I was asked to talk to real journalist. General Miller's time had been a hard time for everybody; he was a very violent person, and he decidedly hurt the already damaged image of the U.S. government. Now many people in the government were trying to polish the reputation it had earned from its mischief toward detainees. "You know many people are lying about this place and claiming that detainees get tortured. We'd like you to talk to a moderate journalist from the *Wall Street Journal* and refute the wrong things we're suspected of."

"Well, I got tortured, and I am going to tell the journalist the truth, the naked truth, without exaggeration or understatement. I'm not polishing anybody's reputation," I said. After that the interview was completely canceled, which was good because I didn't want to talk to anybody anyway.

Gradually I was introduced to the "secret" new boss. I don't exactly know why the team kept him secret from me and tried to make me believe that Richard Zuley was still in charge, but most likely they thought that I would be less cooperative when somebody other than Zuley took over. But they were wrong: I was interested more than anybody in the Intel community in bringing my case into the light. Colonel Forest had been counseled to work on my case from behind the scenes, which he did for a certain time, and then he came and introduced himself. I don't know his real name, but he introduced himself as a Marine. He was a white gentleman in his early forties, around six feet tall, with dark blondish hair. He was rather intellectual and thoughtful, and seemed to place value on his military job as an intelligence gatherer, not a torturer. In our conversations I found him rather humble. He tried everything in the realm of his power to make my life in custody as easy as possible.

I asked him to end my segregation and let me see other

detainees, and he successfully organized several meetings between me and an Egyptian detainee by the name of Tariq al-Sawah, mainly to eat together and play chess. Tariq was not my first choice, but it was not up to me who I could meet, and in any case, I was just dying to see some other detainee I could relate to.

In early summer of 2005 they moved Tariq next to my hut, and we were allowed to see each other during recreation.* Mr. al-Sawah was on the older side, about forty-eight years old. He did not seem to have passed detention's shock sanely; He suffered from paranoia, amnesia, depression, and other mental problems. Some interrogators claimed that he was playing a game, but to me he was completely out of his mind. I really didn't know what to believe, but I didn't care too much; I was dying to have company, and he was sort of company.

There is a drawback to detainees being together, though, especially if you know the detainee only from the camp: We detainees tend to be skeptical about each other. But I was very relaxed in that regard because I really didn't have anything to hide.

"Did they tell you to gather Intels from me?" he asked me once. I wasn't shocked, because I assumed the same about him.

---

* A 2010 *Washington Post* article indicated that MOS and Tariq al-Sawah occupied "a little fenced-in compound at the military prison, where they live a life of relative privilege—gardening, writing and painting." In a 2013 interview with *Slate,* Col. Morris Davis, who served as chief prosecutor of the Guantánamo military commissions in 2005 and 2006, described meetings with both MOS and Sawah in the summer of 2006. "They're in a unique environment: They're inside the detention perimeter, there's a big fence around the facility, and then they're inside what they call the wire, which is another layer within that, so it's a manpower-intensive effort to deal with two guys," he said. See http://www.washingtonpost.com/wp-dyn/content/article/2010/03/24/AR2010032403135_pf.html; and http://www.slate.com/articles/news_and_politics/foreigners/2013/04/mohamedou_ould_slahi_s_guant_namo_memoirs_an_interview_with_colonel_morris.html.

"Tariq, relax and just assume that I am only here to spy on you. Just keep your mouth shut and don't speak about anything you're not comfortable speaking about," I told him.

"You have no secrets?" he wondered.

"No, I don't, and I allow you to provide anything you may learn about me," I said.

I do remember the first day in August when an Army Specialist who called herself Amy surged through the door smiling and greeted me, "Salamu Alaikum."

"Waalaikum As-Salam! Tetkallami Arabi?" I answered her greeting, asking if she spoke Arabic.

"I don't." In fact Amy had already used all the Arabic she knew, namely the greeting, Peace upon you. Amy and I started to talk as if we had known each other for years. She studied biology and joined the U.S. Army recently as an enlisted person, most likely to pay her college tuition. Many Americans do; college education in the U.S. is sinfully high.

"I am going to help you start your garden," Amy said. A long time before, I had asked the interrogators to get me some seeds in order to experiment around, and maybe succeed in growing something in the aggressive soil of GTMO. "I have experience in gardening," she continued. And indeed Amy seemed to have experience: she helped me to grow sunflowers, basil, sage, parsley, cilantro, and things of that nature. But as helpful as she was, I kept giving her a hard time about one single bad experience she made me do.

"I have a problem with crickets that keep destroying my garden," I complained.

"Take some soap and put it in water and keep spraying it

lightly on the plants every day," Amy suggested. And I blindly followed her advice. However, I noticed that my plants were growing unhappy and sort of sick. So I decided to spray only half of the plants with the diluted soap and watch the results. It didn't take long to see the soap was responsible for the bad effects, and so I completely stopped the story of soap.

After that I kept telling Amy, "I know what you studied: You studied how to kill plants with diluted soap!"

"Shut up! You just didn't do it right."

"Whatever."

Colonel Forest had introduced Amy to me, and from then on she took my case in hand entirely. For some reason the special team thought that I would disrespect her, and were skeptical as to whether Specialist Amy was the right choice. But they had no reason to worry: Amy treated me as if I were her brother, and I as if she were my sister. Of course some might say that all that interrogators' stuff is a trick to lure detainees to provide them information; they can be friendly, sociable, humane, generous, and sensitive but still they are evil and ungenuine about everything. I mean, there is a good reason to doubt the integrity of interrogators, if only due to the nature of the interrogators' job. The ultimate goal of an interrogator is to get intel from his target, the nastier the better. But interrogators are human beings, with feelings and emotions; I have been uninterruptedly interrogated since January 2000, and I have seen all kinds of interrogators, good, bad, and in between. Besides, here in GTMO Bay everything is different. In GTMO, the U.S. government assigns a team of interrogators who stick with you almost on a daily basis for some time, after which they leave and get replaced with a new team, in a never ending routine. So whether you like it or not, you have to live with your interrogators and try to make the best out of your life. Furthermore,

I deal with everybody according to what he shows me, and not what he could be hiding. With this motto I approach everybody, including my interrogators.

Since I have not had a formal education in the English language, I needed and still do a lot of help honing my language skills. SPC Amy worked hard on that, especially on my pronunciation and spelling. When it comes to spelling, English is a terrible language: I don't know any other language that writes *Colonel* and pronounces it *Kernel*. Even natives of the language have a tremendous problem with the inconsistency of the sounds and the corresponding letter combinations.

On top of that, prepositions in English don't make any sense; you just have to memorize them. I remember I kept saying "I am afraid from...," and Amy jumping and correcting me: "afraid *of.*" I am sure I was driving her crazy. My problem is that I had been picking the language from the "wrong" people—namely, U.S. Forces recruits who speak grammatically incorrectly. So I needed somebody to take away the incorrect language from me and replace it with the correct one. Maybe you *can* teach an old dog new tricks, and that is exactly what SPC Amy duly tried to do with me. I think she was successful, even though I gave her a hard time sometimes. Amy once forgot that she was around me and said something like, "Amana use the bathroom," and I went, "Oh, is 'Amana' one of the words I missed?"

"Don't even go there!" she would say.

Amy taught me the way Americans speak English. "But British people say so and so," I would say.

"You're not British," she would say.

"I am just saying that there are different ways to pronounce it," I would answer. But she failed to give me the Grammar Rules to follow, which is the only way I can really learn. Being a native speaker, SPC Amy has a feel for the language, which I don't. Besides her mother-tongue, she also spoke Russian and proposed to teach me; I was eager but she didn't have enough time, and with time I lost the passion. A person as lazy as me won't learn a new language unless he has to. Amy was dying to learn Arabic but she didn't have time for that either. Her job kept her busy day and night

By this time, my health situation was way better than in Jordan, but I was still underweight, vulnerable, and sick most of the time, and as days went by, my situation decidedly worsened. Sometimes when the escorting team led me past the wall mirror I would get terrorized when I saw my face. It was a very pitiful sight. Although the diet kept getting better and better in the camp, I couldn't profit from it.

"Why don't you eat?" the guards always asked.

"I am not hungry," I used to reply. Then one day my interrogator SPC Amy just happened to witness one time when I got my lunch served.

"May I check your meal?"

"Yeah, sure."

"What the hell do you they serve you? That is garbage!" said Amy.

"No, it's okay. I don't like speaking about food," I said. And I really don't.

"Look it may be OK for you, but it's not OK by my standards. We've got to change your diet," she said. And nothing short of a miracle, SPC Amy managed in a relatively short time to organize an adequate diet, which decidedly improved my health situation.

Amy also turned out to be a religious person when measured at American standards. I was very excited to have somebody I could learn from.

"Amy, can you get me a Bible?"

"I'll see if I can," she said, and indeed, Amy brought me her own Bible, a Special Edition.

"According to your religion, what is the way to heaven?" I asked her.

"You take Christ as your Savior, and believe that he died for your sins."

"I do believe Christ was one of the greatest prophets, but I don't believe that he died for my sins. It doesn't make sense to me. I should save my tail on my own, by doing the right things," I replied.

"That is not enough to be saved."

"So where am I going after death?" I wondered.

"According to my religion, you go to hell." I laughed whole-heartedly. I told Amy, "That is very sad. I pray every day and ask God for forgiveness. Honestly, I worship God much more than you do. As a matter of fact, as you see, I am not very successful in this worldly life, so my only hope is in the afterlife."

Amy was both angry and ashamed—angry because I laughed at her statement, and ashamed because she couldn't find a way to save me. "I am not gonna lie to you: that's what my religion says," she said.

"No, I really don't have any problem with that. You can cook your soup as you please. I am not angry that you sent me to hell."

"What about the Islamic belief? Do I go to heaven?"

"That's a completely different story. In Islam, in order to go to heaven, you have to accept Mohamed, the natural successor of Christ, and be a good Muslim. And since you reject Mohamed you don't go to heaven," I honestly answered.

Amy was relieved because I also sent her to hell. "So, let's both of us go to hell and meet over there!" Amy said.

"I'm not willing to go to hell. Although I am an admitted sinner, I ask God for forgiveness." Whenever we had time, we discussed religion and took out the Bible and the Koran to show each other what the Books say.

"Would you marry a Muslim?"

"Never," she replied.

I smiled. "I personally wouldn't have a problem marrying a Christian woman as long as she doesn't have anything against my religion."

"Are you trying to convert me?" Amy asked emotionally.

"Yes, I am."

"I will never, never, never be a Muslim."

I laughed. "Why are you so offended about? You're sort of trying to convert me, and I don't feel offended, since that's what you believe in."

I continued. "Would you marry a Catholic, Amy?"

"Yes, I would."

"But I don't understand. It says in the Bible that you cannot marry after a divorce. So you are a potential sinner." Amy was completely offended when I showed her the verses in the Bible.

"Don't even go there, and if you don't mind, let's change the topic." I was shocked, and smiled a dry smile.

"Oh, OK! I'm sorry about talking about that." We stopped discussing religion for the day and took a break for the next few days, and then we resumed the dialogue.

"Amy, I really don't understand the Trinity doctrine. The more I look into it, the more I get confused."

"We have the Father, the Son, and the Holy Spirit, three things that represent the Being God."

"Hold on! Break it down for me. God is the father of Christ, isn't he?"

"Yes!"

"Biological Father?" I asked.

"No."

"Then why do you call him Father? I mean if you're saying that God is our father in the sense that he takes care of us, I have no problem with that," I commented.

"Yes, that's correct," she said.

"So there is no point in calling Jesus 'the Son of God.'"

"But he said so in the Bible," she said.

"But Amy, I don't believe in the 100 percent accuracy of the Bible."

"Anyway, Jesus is God," she said.

"Oh, is Jesus God, or Son of God?"

"Both!"

"You don't make any sense, Amy, do you?"

"Look, I really don't understand the Trinity. I have to research and ask an expert."

"Fair enough," I said. "But how can you believe in something you don't understand?" I continued.

"I understand but I cannot explain it," Amy replied.

"Let's move on and hit another topic." I suggested. "According to your religion I seem to be doomed anyway. But what about the bushmen in Africa who never got the chance to know Jesus Christ?" I asked.

"They are not saved."

"But what did they do wrong?"

"I don't agree that they should suffer, but that's what my religion says."

"Fair enough."

"But how about Islam?" Amy asked.

"In the Koran it says that God doesn't punish unless he sends a messenger to teach the people."

Amy introduced me to her friend SSG Charles, who was one

of those guys who you like the first time you meet. SSG Charles was a small, skinny white man in his late twenties or early thirties. He was more religious and less tolerant than Amy; he was a Baptist, he told me. He didn't like any questioning of his beliefs, even from Amy. But he was a happy person and genuinely enjoyed hanging out with me. He wasn't my interrogator; he was working with Tariq and came to me because he liked talking to me. He is more of a lover than a hater. SSG Charles and Amy are good friends, and he was fighting for the betterment of our condition.

Amy introduced him to me as a friend and someone to help her quench my thirst for information about Christianity. Although I enjoyed getting to know Charles, he didn't help me understanding the Trinity. He confused me even more, and my lot with him was no better: he, too, sent me to hell. SSG Charles ended up arguing with Amy because they had some difference in their beliefs, although both were Protestant. I realized that they could not help me understand, and so I dismissed the topic for good, and we started to talk about other issues.

It's very funny how false the picture is that western people have about Arabs: savage, violent, insensitive, and cold-hearted. I can tell you with confidence that Arabs are peaceful, sensitive, civilized, and big lovers, among other qualities.

"Amy, you guys claim that we are violent, but if you listen to the Arabic music or read Arabic poetry, it is all about love. On the other hand, American music is about violence and hatred, for the most part." During my time with Amy, many poems went across the table. I haven't kept any copies; she has all the poems. Amy also gave me a small divan of her own poems. She is very surrealistic, and I am terrible when it comes to surrealism. I hardly understood any of her poems.

One of my poems took off from the German poet Kurt

Schwitters's masterpiece "An Anna Blume." I once told her about the poem, which I learned in Germany and which one of my cousins translated into Arabic. She brought me the English version that Schwitters made, that reads,

Oh thou, beloved of my twenty-seven senses, I love thine!
Thou thee
thee thine, I thine,
thou mine, we?
That (by the way) is beside the point!
Who art thou, uncounted woman, Thou art, art thou?
People say, thou werst,
Let them say, they don't know what they are talking about

And then goes on,

PRIZE QUESTION: 1. Eve Blossom is red,
2. Eve Blossom has wheels
3. What colour are the wheels?
Blue is the colour of your yellow hair
Red is the whirl of your green wheels

I was so frustrated that the English version did not do it justice that I asked her for the German version, and when I read it to her, she enjoyed it even with the few German words she knew. So I wrote my own poem to Anna Blume in that same random style, and gave it to her. She liked it so much that she nicknamed herself Anna Blume.*

---

* The original handwritten manuscript included the poem MOS composed imitating Schwitters's "An Anna Blume." It was censored in its entirety. The U.S. government still controls that manuscript, and it is not possible to reconstruct the original text of MOS's poem. In addition to the

All this time I kept refusing to talk about the way I had been treated, which Amy and her boss understood and respected. I didn't want to talk, first, because I was afraid of retaliation, and second, because I was skeptical about the readiness of the government to deal with things appropriately, and third, because the Islamic religion suggests that it is better to bring your complaints to God rather than disclosing them to human beings. But Amy kept patiently trying to persuade me; furthermore, she explained to me that she must report any misbehavior by her colleagues to her superiors.

After thoroughly contemplating the options, I decided to talk to SPC Amy. When she heard my account, she brought Colonel Forest, who interrogated me about the issue after having sent the guards away. Colonel Forest prudently wanted to avoid any possible leak and spread of the story. I have no idea what happened after that, but I think there is sort of an internal DOD investigation, because I was asked some questions about my story in a later time.*

---

complete, uncensored handwritten manuscript of *Guantánamo Diary,* several other written texts and manuscripts that MOS wrote in Guantánamo remained under the control of the United States government when MOS was released in October 2016. MOS and his attorneys continue to request that these materials be returned to him and cleared for public release.

* The Schmidt-Furlow report records that on December 11, 2004, "after months of cooperation with interrogators," "the subject of the second special interrogation notified his interrogator that he had been 'subject to torture' by past interrogators during the months of July to October 2003." A footnote elaborates: "He reported these allegations to an interrogator. The interrogator was a member of the interrogation team at the time of the report. The interrogator reported the allegations to her supervisor. Shortly after being advised of the alleged abuse, the supervisor interviewed the subject of the second special interrogation, with the interrogator present, regarding the allegations. Based on this interview, and notes taken by the interrogator, the supervisor prepared an 11 Dec 04 MFR addressed to JTF-GTMO JIG and

"You are a very courageous guy!" Amy used to tell me in relation with my story.

"I don't think so! I just enjoy peace. But I certainly know that people who torture helpless detainees are cowards." I always tried to dismiss the subject and talk about something else. But SPC Amy and her boss spent hours asking me about the mistreatment and those who were involved in it. Both were interested in the behavior of the FBI. Amy didn't approve of the FBI or of lawyers coming from the outside, and it seemed to me that she would love to have something on the FBI. But I told them that the FBI never tortured me. I told them the story as best I could, but I was very scared of possible backlash, because I knew that those who were involved in torture were for all intents and purposes still in charge.

Not long after that, Amy took a leave for three weeks. "I'm going to Montreal with a male friend of mine. Tell me about Montreal." I provided her with everything I remembered about Montreal, which wasn't much.

When SPC Amy came back, she hardly changed out of her travel clothes before she came to see me; she was genuinely excited to see me again, and so was I. Amy said that she enjoyed her time in Canada and that everything was alright, but she was probably happier to be in GTMO. She was tired from the trip, so she stayed only for a short time to check on me, and off she went.

ICE. The supervisor forwarded his MFR to the JTF-GTMO JIG. The JIG then forwarded the complaint to the JAG for processing IAW normal GTMO procedures for investigating allegations of abuse. The JAG by email on 22 Dec 04 tasked the JDOG, the JIG, and the JMG with a review of the complaint summarized in the Dec 04 MFR and directed them to provide any relevant information. The internal GTMO investigation was never completed." Schmidt-Furlow, 22.

I went back to my cell and wrote Amy the following letter.

"Hi, Amy, I know you were in Canada with your boyfriend and I understand you were just looking for a good time outside of Guantánamo. I am just a detainee whose bad luck brought him before you; I didn't choose to know you or deal with you. I'm trying to make the best of a bad situation and I confess to you, it's proving challenging to me. I am not looking for any-thing from you; I am focusing all my energy on keeping my sanity. I have no idea why you think I care about what you do outside this prison. I haven't asked you about your trip, but I don't appreciate somebody lying to me and taking me for an idiot. I really don't know what you were thinking when you made up that story to mislead me. I don't deserve to be treated like that. I chose to write and not talk to you, just to give you the opportunity to think about everything, instead of making you come up with inaccurate answers. Furthermore, you don't have to give me any answer or comment. Just destroy this letter and consider it non-existent. Yours truly Salahi."

I read the letter to the guards before I handed the sealed envelope to Amy and asked her not to read it in my presence.

"Wha' the? How the hell do you know that Amy was with her boyfriend?" the guard on duty asked me.

"Something in my heart that never lies to me!"

"You don't make any sense. Besides, why the fuck should you care?"

"If you cannot tell whether a woman had some intimacy with a man, you ain't no man," I said. "I don't care, but I don't appreciate when Amy or anyone else uses my manhood and plays games on me, especially in my situation. Amy might think I am vulnerable but I am strong."

"You're right! That's fucked up."

Amy came the next day and confessed everything to me.

"I am sorry! I just figured we had a close relationship, and I thought it would hurt you if you knew I went on vacation with my doctor boyfriend and was enjoying Montreal while you're stuck in here," she said sadly.

"First I thank you very much for being forthcoming. I'm just confused! Do you think I'm looking forward to a relationship with you? I'm not! For Pete's sake, you are a Christian woman who is engaged in a war against my religion and my people! Besides, I am stuck until who knows when inside this prison."

Amy always tried after that to tell me that she didn't think that she would continue with my interrogation team; she was afraid I wouldn't cooperate with her or Colonel Forest anymore. But I didn't make any comment about the issue. All I did was I handcrafted a bracelet and sent it to him as I did for her and for all those who I liked and who had helped me in many issues.

"We are desperate to get information from you," said Richard Zuley when he first met with me.

It was true: when I arrived in the camp in August 2002, the majority of detainees were refusing to cooperate with their interrogators.

"Look, I told you my story over and over a million times. Now either you send me to court or let me be," they were saying.

"But we have discrepancies in your story," the interrogators would say, as a gentle way of saying, "You're lying."

Like me, every detainee I know thought when he arrived in Cuba it would be a typical interrogation, and after interrogation he would be charged and sent to court, and the court would decide whether he is guilty or not. If he was found not guilty, or if the U.S. government pressed no charges, he would be sent home. It made sense to everybody: the interrogators told us this is how it would go, and we said, "Let's do it." But it turned out either the interrogators deliberately lied to encourage detainees to cooperate with them, or the government lied to the interrogators about the procedure as a tactic to coerce information from the detainees.

Weeks went by, months went by, and the interrogators' thirst for information didn't seem close to being satisfied. The more information a detainee provided, the more interrogators complicated the case and asked more questions. All detainees had, at some point, one thing in common: they were tired of uninterrupted interrogation. As a newcomer, I first was part of a small minority that was still cooperating, but I soon joined the other group. "Just tell me why you arrested me, and I'll answer every question you have," I would say.

Most of the interrogators were coming back day after day empty-handed. "No information collected from source," was what the interrogators reported every week. And exactly as Richard Zuley said, the JTF command was desperate to get the detainees talking. So the JTF built a mini "special team" inside the bigger organization. This Task Force, which included the U.S. Army, the U.S. Marines, the U.S. Navy, and civilians, had the job of coercing information from detainees. The operation was clouded with top secrecy.

Mr. X was a very distinguished character in this JTF special interrogators group. Although Mr. X was a smart person, they gave him the dirtiest job on the Island, and shockingly brainwashed him into believing he was doing the right thing. Mr.

X was always wrapped in a uniform that covered him from head to toe, because he was aware that he was committing war crimes against helpless detainees. Mr. X was The Night Owl, The Devil Worshipper, Loud Music Man, the Anti-Religion Guy, the interrogator par excellence. Every one of those nicknames had a reason.

Mr. X used to keep detainees who were not allowed to sleep "entertained." He deprived me of sleep for about two months, during which he tried to break my mental resistance, to no avail. To keep me awake, he drove the temperature of the room crazily down, made me write all kinds of things about my life, kept giving me water, and sometimes made me stand the whole night. Once he stripped me naked with the help of a female guard in order to humiliate me. Another night, he put me in a frozen room full of propaganda pictures of the U.S., including a picture of George W. Bush, and made me listen to the national anthem over and over.

Mr. X was serving several detainees at the same time; I could hear many doors slamming, loud music, and detainees coming and leaving, the sound of their heavy metal chains giving them away. He used to put detainees in a dark room with pictures that were supposed to represent devils. He made detainees listen to the music of hatred and madness, and to the song "Let the Bodies Hit the Floor" over and over for the whole night in the dark room. He was very open about his hatred toward Islam, and he categorically forbade any Islamic practices, including prayers and mumbling the Koran.

Even with all that, around the end of August 2003, the special team realized that I was not going to cooperate with them as they wished, and so the next level of torture was approved. Mr. X, my guard Big Boss, and another guy with a

German shepherd pried open the door of the interrogation room where SSG Mary and I were sitting. It was in Gold Building. Mr. X and his colleague kept hitting me, mostly on my ribs and my face, and made me drink salt water for about three hours before giving me over to an Arabic team with an Egyptian and a Jordanian interrogator. Those interrogators continued to beat me while covering me in ice cubes, one, to torture me, and two, to make the new, fresh bruises disappear.

Then, after about three hours, Mr. X and his friend took me back and threw me in my present cell. "I told you not to fuck with me, Motherfucker!" was the last thing I heard from Mr. X. Later on, SSG Mary told me that Mr. X wanted to visit me for friendly purposes, but I didn't show any eagerness, and so the visit was cancelled. I am still in that same cell, although I no longer have to pretend I don't know where I am.

They finally allowed doctors to see me around March 2004, and I was able to get psychological assistance for the first time that April. Since then I have been taking the anti-depressant Paxil and Klonopin to help me sleep. The doctors also prescribed a multi-vitamin for a condition that was due to a lack of exposure to the sun. I also got some sessions with some psychologists who were assessing me; they really helped me, though I couldn't tell them the real reason for my sickness because I was afraid of retaliation.

"My job is to help your rehabilitation," one of my guards told me in the summer of 2004. The government realized that I was deeply injured and needed some real rehab. I got a new guard team that included a Marine corporal everyone called Marine, a tall, skinny white guard we called Stretch, and an athletic-looking guard I called Big G. From the moment he started to work as my guard in July 2004, the corporal related to me right;

in fact, he hardly talked to anybody beside me. He used to put his mattress right in front of my cell door, and we started to talk about all kinds of topics like old friends. We talked about history, culture, politics, religion, women, everything but current events. The guards were taught that I was a detainee who would try to outsmart them and learn current events from them, but the guards are my witnesses, I didn't try to outsmart anybody, nor was I interested in current events at the time because they only made me sick.

Before Stretch left, he brought me a couple of souvenirs, and with Marine and Big G dedicated a copy of Steve Martin's *The Pleasure of My Company* to me.

Marine wrote, "Pill, over the past 10 months I have gotten to know you and we have become friends. I wish you good luck, and I am sure I will think of you often. Take good care of yourself. — Marine"

Stretch wrote, "Pillow, good luck with your situation. Just remember Allah always has a plan. I hope you think of us as more than just guards. I think we all became friends."

Big G wrote, "19 April 2005. Pillow: For the past 10 months I have done my damnedest to maintain a Detainee–Guard relationship. At times I have failed: it is almost impossible not to like a character like yourself. Keep your faith. I'm sure it will guide you in the right direction."

I used to debate faith with Marine. The corporal was raised as a conservative Catholic. He was not really religious, but I could tell he was his family's boy. I kept trying to convince him that the existence of God is a logical necessity.

"I don't believe in anything unless I see it," he told me.

"After you've seen something, you don't need to believe it," I responded. "For instance, if I tell you I have a cold Pepsi in my fridge, either you believe it or you don't. But after seeing it, you know, and you don't need to believe me." Personally, I do have faith. And I picture him, and these other guards, as good friends if we would meet under different circumstances. May God guide them and help them make the right choices in life.

Crisis always brings out the best and worst in people—and in countries, too. Did the Leader of the Free World, the United States, really torture detainees? Or are stories of torture part of a conspiracy to present the U.S. in a horrible way, so the rest of the world will hate it?

I don't even know how to treat this subject. I have only written what I experienced, what I saw, and what I learned first-hand. I have tried not to exaggerate, nor to understate. I have tried to be as fair as possible, to the U.S. government, to my brothers, and to myself. I don't expect people who don't know me to believe me, but I expect them, at least, to give me the benefit of the doubt. And if Americans are willing to stand for what they believe in, I also expect public opinion to compel the U.S. government to open a torture and war crimes investigation. I am more than confident that I can prove every single thing I have written in this book if I am ever given the opportunity to call witnesses in a proper judicial procedure, and if military personnel are not given the advantage of straightening their lies and destroying evidence against them.

Human beings naturally hate to torture other human beings, and Americans are no different. Many of the soldiers were doing the job reluctantly, and were very happy when they were ordered to stop. Of course there are sick people everywhere in the world who enjoy seeing other people suffering, but generally human beings make use of torture when they get chaotic and confused. And Americans certainly got chaotic, vengeful, and confused, after the September 11, 2001 terrorist attacks.

At the direction of President Bush, the U.S. began a campaign against the Taliban government in Afghanistan. On September 18, 2001, a joint resolution of Congress authorized President Bush to use force against the "nations, organizations, or persons" that "planned, authorized, committed, or aided the terrorist attacks on September 11, 2001, or harbored such organizations or persons." Then the U.S. government started a secret operation aimed at kidnapping, detaining, torturing, or killing terrorist suspects, an operation that has no legal basis.

I was the victim of such an operation, though I had done no such thing and have never been part of any such crimes. On September 29, 2001, I got a call on my cellphone and was asked to turn myself in, and I immediately did, sure I would be cleared. Instead, Americans interrogated me in my home country, and then the U.S. reached a joint agreement with the Mauritanian government to send me to Jordan to squeeze the last bits of information out of me. I was incarcerated and interrogated under horrible conditions in Jordan for eight months, and then the Americans flew me to Bagram Air Base for two weeks of interrogation, and finally on to the Guantánamo Navy Base, and to Camp Echo Special, where I still am today.★

So has the American democracy passed the test it was subjected to with the 2001 terrorist attacks? I leave this judgment to the reader. As I am writing this, though, the United States

---

★ MOS remained in the isolation hut in the classified zone of Camp Echo for nine years after the manuscript was completed. He was finally moved out of Camp Echo Special and into a nonsecret section of Camp Echo in October 2014, about three months before *Guantánamo Diary* was published in the United States, the United Kingdom, and seven other countries. On October 16, 2016, he was escorted onto a military transport jet and flown to Mauritania. He arrived in Mauritania, a free man, on October 17, 2016.

and its people are still facing the dilemma of the Cuban detainees.

In the beginning, the U.S. government was happy with its secret operations, since it thought it had managed to gather all the evils of the world in GTMO, and had circumvented U.S. law and international treaties so that it could perform its revenge. But then it realized, after a lot of painful work, that it had gathered a bunch of non-combatants. Now the U.S. government is stuck with the problem, but it is not willing to be forthcoming and disclose the truth about the whole operation.

Everybody makes mistakes. I believe the U.S. government owes it to the American people to tell them the truth about what is happening in Guantánamo. So far, I have personally cost American taxpayers at least one million dollars, and the counter is ticking higher every day. The other detainees are costing more or less the same. Under these circumstances, Americans need and have the right to know what the hell is going on.

Many of my brothers here are losing their minds, especially the younger detainees, because of the conditions of detention. As I write these words, many brothers are hunger-striking and are determined to carry on, no matter what.* I am very worried about these brothers I am helplessly watching, who are practically dying and who are sure to suffer irreparable damage even if they eventually decide to eat. It is not the first time we have had a hunger strike; I personally participated in the hunger

---

* MOS completed this manuscript in the fall of 2005; the last page is signed and dated September 28, 2005. One of the largest Guantánamo hunger strikes started in August 2005 and extended through the end of the year. See, e.g., http://www.nytimes.com/2005/09/18/politics/18gitmo .html?pagewanted=1&_r=0; and http://america.aljazeera.com/articles/ multimedia/guantanamo-hungerstriketimeline.html.

strike in September 2002, but the government did not seem to be impressed. And so the brothers keep striking, for the same old, and new, reasons. And there seems to be no solution in the air. The government expects the U.S. forces in GTMO to pull magic solutions out of their sleeves. But the U.S. forces in GTMO understand the situation here more than any bureaucrat in Washington, DC, and they know that the only solution is for the government to be forthcoming and release people.

What do the American people think? I am eager to know. I would like to believe the majority of Americans want to see justice done, and they are not interested in financing the detention of innocent people. I know there is a small extremist minority that believes that everybody in this Cuban prison is evil, and that we are treated better than we deserve. But this opinion has no basis but ignorance. I am amazed that somebody can build such an incriminating opinion about people he or she doesn't even know.

~~UNCLASSIFIED~~   ~~PROTECTED~~

331

personality, very confident, knows what he is supped to do, and doesn't respect his less comptent superiors. Before ▓ left he ~~so~~ bought me a couple of souvenirs; and dedicated to me The Pleasure of My Company by Steve Martin, with ▓▓ and ▓▓▓ wrotes " PILL, over the past 10 months I have gotten to Know you and we have become friends. I wish you good luck and I am sure I will think of you often. take good care of yourself. ▓▓ - ". ▓▓ wrote: " Pillow, Good Luck with your situation. Just remember Allah always has a plan. I hope you think of us as more than just guards. I think we all became friends. ▓▓ ". ▓▓ wrote: " Pillow 19 APRIL, 2005 For the past 10 months I have done my damnest to Detainee Guard relationship. At time I have ~~failed~~. It is almost impossible not to like a charachter like yourself. keep your ~~ferith~~ + I'm sure it will guide you in the right direction. ▓▓ " That was not exactly a bad time. ② ▓▓▓▓▓▓▓▓▓▓▓▓▓▓▓▓▓▓▓▓▓▓

Religions, Islam, Christianity, and Judaism as the Middle Eastern culture as well. He ~~faind~~ found in me the bright address as I did in him. We had been discussing all the time, without any prejudices or any taboos. We had been even hitting, some tins, Racism in the U.S when ~~the other~~ his other black colleague ▓▓ worked with him, ▓▓ is proud on him ▓▓ all he reads, watches is mostly ▓▓, and that why ▓▓ and I always startes a friendly discussion with him. ▓▓▓▓ suspecter me of hawja some tines, instigated the discussion, and

Author's Note

When this book was first published, when I was still in prison, I sent a message through my lawyers that appeared as an Author's Note in that edition. That note said:

> In a recent conversation with one of his lawyers, Mohamedou said that he holds no grudge against any of the people he mentions in this book, that he appeals to them to read it and correct it if they think it contains any errors, and that he dreams to one day sit with all of them around a cup of tea, after having learned so much from one another.

I want to repeat and affirm this message here, and to say that now that I am home, that dream is also an invitation. The doors of my house are open.

Editor's Introduction to the First Edition

In the summer and early fall of 2005, Mohamedou Ould Slahi handwrote a 466-page, 122,000-word draft of this book in his single-cell segregation hut in Camp Echo, Guantánamo.

He wrote it in installments, starting not long after he was finally allowed to meet with Nancy Hollander and Sylvia Royce, two attorneys from his pro bono legal team. Under the strict protocols of Guantánamo's sweeping censorship regime, every page he wrote was considered classified from the moment of its creation, and each new section was surrendered to the United States government for review.

On December 15, 2005, three months after he signed and dated the manuscript's last page, Mohamedou interrupted his testimony during an Administrative Review Board hearing in Guantánamo to tell the presiding officers:

> *I just want to mention here that I wrote a book recently while in jail here recently about my whole story, okay? I sent it for release to the District [of] Columbia, and when it is released I advise you guys to read it. A little advertisement. It is a very interesting book, I think.*[1]

But Mohamedou's manuscript was not released. It was stamped "SECRET," a classification level for information that could cause serious damage to national security if it becomes public, and

"NOFORN," meaning it can't be shared with any foreign nationals or intelligence services. It was deposited in a secure facility near Washington, DC, accessible only to those with a full security clearance and an official "need to know." For more than six years, Mohamedou's attorneys carried out litigation and negotiations to have the manuscript cleared for public release.

During those years, compelled largely by Freedom of Information Act litigation spearheaded by the American Civil Liberties Union, the U.S. government released thousands of secret documents that described the treatment of prisoners in U.S. custody since the September 11, 2001, terrorist attacks. Many of those documents hinted at Mohamedou's ordeal, first in the hands of the CIA, and then in the hands of the U.S. military in Guantánamo, where a "Special Projects Team" subjected him to one of the most stubborn, deliberate, and cruel interrogations in the record. A few of those documents contained something else as well: tantalizing samples of Mohamedou's voice.

One of these was in his own handwriting, in English. In a short note dated March 3, 2005, he wrote, "Hello. I, Mohamedou Ould Slahi, detained in GTMO under ISN #760, herewith apply for a writ of habeas corpus." The note concluded simply, "I have done no crimes against the U.S., nor did the U.S. charge me with crimes, thus I am filing for my immediate release. For further details about my case, I'll be happy for any future hearings."

Another handwritten document, also in English, was a letter to his attorney Sylvia Royce dated November 9, 2006, in which he joked, "You asked me to write you everything I told my interrogators. Are you out of your mind? How can I render uninterrupted interrogation that has been lasting the last 7 years? That's like asking Charlie Sheen how many women he dated." He went on:

> Yet I provided you everything (almost) in my book, which the government denies you the access to. I was going to go deeper in details, but I figured it was futile.
>
> To make a long story short, you may divide my time in two big steps.
>
> (1) Pre-torture (I mean that I couldn't resist): I told them the truth about me having done nothing against your country. It lasted until May 22, 2003.
>
> (2) Post-torture era: where my brake broke loose. I yessed every accusation my interrogators made. I even wrote the infamous confession about me planning to hit the CN Tower in Toronto, based on SSG ███████ advice. I just wanted to get the monkeys off my back. I don't care how long I stay in jail. My belief comforts me.[2]

The documents also included a pair of transcripts of Mohamedou's sworn testimony before detainee review boards in Guantánamo. The first—and the first sample of his voice anywhere in the documents—is from his Combatant Status Review Tribunal (CSRT) hearing; the date is December 8, 2004, just months after his so-called "special interrogation" ended. It includes this exchange:

> Q: Can I get your response to the very first allegation that you are a member of the Taliban or al Qaida?
>
> A: The Taliban, I have nothing to do with them whatsoever. Al Qaida, I was a member in Afghanistan in 91 and 92. After I left Afghanistan, I broke all my relations with al Qaida.
>
> Q: And you've never provided them money, or any type of support since then?
>
> A: Nothing whatsoever.

Q: *Ever recruited for them?*

A: *No, not at all; no trying to recruit for them.*

Q: *You said that you were pressured to admit you were involved in the Millennium plot, right?*

A: *Yes.*

Q: *To whom did you make that confession?*

A: *To the Americans.*

Q: *And what do you mean by pressure?*

A: *Your honor, I don't wish to talk about this nature of the pressure if I don't have to.*

Q: *Tribunal President: You don't have to; we just want to make sure that you were not tortured or coerced into saying something that wasn't true. That is the reason he is asking the question.*

A: *You just take from me I am not involved in such a horrible attack; yes I admit to being a member of al Qaida, but I am not willing to talk about this. The smart people came to me and analyzed this, and got the truth. It's good for me to tell the truth, and the information was verified. I said I didn't have anything to do with this. I took and passed the polygraph, and they said I didn't have to speak of this anymore. They said please don't speak of this topic anymore, and they haven't opened it up to this topic for a year now.*

Q: *So no U.S. authorities abused you in any way?*

A: *I'm not willing to answer this question; I don't have to, if you don't force me to.*[3]

The other transcript comes from the 2005 Administrative Review Board hearing where he announced he had written this book. A year had passed since the CSRT hearing, a year when he was finally allowed to meet with attorneys, and when he somehow found the distance and the stamina to write down his experience. This time he speaks freely of his odyssey, not in fear or in anger, but in a voice inflected with irony and wit. "He was very silly," Mohamedou says of one of his interrogator's threats, "because he said he was going to bring in black people. I don't have any problem with black people, half of my country is black people!" Another interrogator in Guantánamo known as Mr. X was covered head to toe "like in Saudi Arabia, how the women are covered," and wearing "gloves, O.J. Simpson gloves on his hands." Mohamedou's answers are richly detailed, for deliberate effect and for an earnest purpose. "Please," he tells the board, "I want you guys to understand my story okay, because it really doesn't matter if they release me or not, I just want my story understood."[4]

We do not have a complete record of Mohamedou's effort to tell his story to the review board at that hearing. Just as he begins to describe what he experienced in Guantánamo during the summer of 2003, "the recording equipment began to malfunction," notes a boldface interruption in the transcript. For the lost section, in which "the detainee discussed how he was tortured while here at GTMO by several individuals," the document offers instead "the board's recollection of that 1000 click malfunction":

The Detainee began by discussing the alleged abuse he received from a female interrogator known to him as ▓▓▓▓▓▓▓▓▓. *The Detainee attempted to explain to the Board* ▓▓▓▓▓▓▓▓▓ *actions but he became distraught and visibly upset. He explained that he was sexually harassed and although he does like women he did not like what* ▓▓▓▓▓▓▓▓ *had done to him. The Presiding Officer noticed the Detainee was upset and told him he was not required to tell the story. The Detainee was very appreciative and elected not to elaborate on the alleged abuse from* ▓▓▓▓▓▓▓▓.

The Detainee gave detailed information regarding the alleged abuse from ▓▓▓▓▓▓▓▓ *and* ▓▓▓▓▓▓▓▓. *The Detainee stated that* ▮▮▮▮▮ *and* ▮▮▮▮▮ *entered a room with their faces covered and began beating him. They beat him so badly that* ▮▮▮▮▮ *became upset.* ▮▮▮▮▮ *did not like the treatment the Detainee was receiving and started to sympathize with him. According to the Detainee,* ▮▮▮▮▮ *was crying and telling* ▮▮▮▮▮ *and* ▮▮▮▮▮ *to stop beating him. The Detainee wanted to show the Board his scars and location of injuries, but the board declined the viewing. The Board agrees that this is a fair recap of the distorted portion of the tape.*[5]

We only have these transcripts because in the spring of 2006, a federal judge presiding over a FOIA lawsuit filed by the Associated Press ordered them released. That lawsuit also finally compelled the Pentagon, four years after Guantánamo opened, to publish an official list of the men it was holding in the facility. For the first time, the prisoners had names, and the names had voices. In the transcripts of their secret hearings, many of the prisoners told stories that undercut claims that the Cuban detention camp housed "the worst of the worst," men so dangerous, as the military's presiding general famously declared as the first prisoners were landing at the camp in 2002, they would "gnaw hydraulic lines in the back of a C-17 to bring it down."[6] Several, like Mohamedou, broached the subject of their treatment in U.S. custody.

The Pentagon doubled down. "Detainees held at Guantánamo are terrorist trainers, bomb-makers, would-be suicide bombers, and other dangerous people," a military spokesman again asserted when the transcripts became public. "And we know that they're trained to lie to try to gain sympathy for their condition and to bring pressure against the U.S. government."[7] A year later, when the military released the records of Guantánamo's 2006 Administrative Review Board hearings, Mohamedou's transcript was missing completely. That transcript is still classified.

Mohamedou's manuscript was finally cleared for public release, and a member of his legal team was able to hand it to me on a disk labeled "Slahi Manuscript—Unclassified Version," in the summer of 2012. By then, Mohamedou had been in Guantánamo for a decade. A federal judge had granted his habeas corpus petition two years before and ordered him released, but the U.S government had appealed, and the appeals court sent his petition back down to the federal district court for rehearing. That case is still pending.

Mohamedou remains to this day in the same segregation cell where he wrote his Guantánamo diary. I have, I believe, read everything that has been made public about his case, and I do not understand why he was ever in Guantánamo in the first place.

Mohamedou Ould Slahi was born on December 31, 1970, in Rosso, then a small town, now a small city, on the Senegal River on Mauritania's southern border. He had eight older siblings; three more would follow. The family moved to the capital, Nouakchott, as Mohamedou was finishing primary school, and his father, a nomadic camel trader, died not long after. The timing, and Mohamedou's obvious talents, must have shaped his sense of his role in the family. His father had taught him to read the Koran, which he had memorized by the time he was a teenager, and he did well in high school, with a particular aptitude for math. A 2008 feature in *Der Spiegel* describes a popular kid with a passion for soccer, and especially for the German national team—a passion that led him to apply for, and win, a scholarship from the Carl Duisberg Society to study in Germany. It was an enormous leap for the entire family, as the magazine reported:

Slahi boarded a plane for Germany on a Friday in the late summer of 1988. He was the first family member to attend a university—abroad, no less—and the first to travel on an airplane. Distraught by the departure of her favorite son, his mother's goodbye was so tearful that Mohamedou briefly hesitated before getting on his flight. In the end, the others convinced him to go. "He was supposed to save us financially," his brother [Y]ahdih says today.[8]

In Germany, Mohamedou pursued a degree in electrical engineering, with an eye toward a career in telecom and computers, but he interrupted his studies to participate in a cause that was drawing young men from around the world: the insurgency against the communist-led government in Afghanistan. There were no restrictions or prohibitions on such activities in those days, and young men like Mohamedou made the trip openly; it was a cause that the West, and the United States in particular, actively supported. To join the fight required training, so in early 1991 Mohamedou attended the al-Farouq training camp near Khost for seven weeks and swore a loyalty oath to al-Qaeda, the camp's operators. He received light arms and mortar training, the guns mostly Soviet-made, the mortar shells, he recalled in his 2004 Combatant Status Review hearing, made in the U.S.A.

Mohamedou returned to his studies after the training, but in early 1992, with the communist government on the verge of collapsing, he went back to Afghanistan. He joined a unit commanded by Jalaluddin Haqqani that was laying siege to the city of Gardez, which fell with little resistance three weeks after Mohamedou arrived. Kabul fell soon thereafter, and as Mohamedou explained at the CSRT hearing, the cause quickly turned murky:

> *Right after the break down of [the] Communists, the Mujahiden themselves started to wage Jihad against themselves, to see who would be in power; the different factions began to fight against each other. I decided to go back because I didn't want to fight against other Muslims, and found no reason why; nor today did I see a reason to fight to see who could be president or vice-president. My goal was solely to fight against the aggressors, mainly the Communists, who forbid my brethren to practice their religion.*

That, Mohamedou has always insisted, marked the end of his commitment to al-Qaeda. As he told the presiding officer at his CSRT:

> *Ma'am, I was knowledgeable I was fighting with al Qaida, but then al Qaida didn't wage Jihad against America. They told us to fight with our brothers against the Communists. In the mid-90's they wanted to wage Jihad against America, but I personally had nothing to do with that. I didn't join them in this idea; that's their problem. I am completely out of the line between al Qaida and the U.S. They have to solve this problem themselves; I am completely independent of this problem.*[9]

Back in Germany, Mohamedou settled into the life he and his family in Nouakchott had planned. He completed his degree in electrical engineering at the University of Duisburg, his young Mauritanian wife joined him, and the couple lived and worked in Duisburg for most of the 1990s. During that time, though, he remained friends or kept in touch with companions from the Afghanistan adventure, some of whom maintained al-Qaeda ties. He also had his own direct association with a prominent al-Qaeda member, Mahfouz Ould al-Walid, also known as Abu Hafs al-Mauritani, who was a member of al-Qaeda's Shura Council and one of Osama bin Laden's senior theological advisers. Abu Hafs is a distant cousin of Mohamedou, and also a brother-in-law through his marriage to Mohamedou's wife's sister. The two were in occasional phone contact while Mohamedou was in Germany—a call from Abu Hafs, using bin Laden's satellite phone, caught the ears of German intelligence in 1999—and twice Mohamedou helped Abu Hafs transfer $4,000 to his family in Mauritania around the Ramadan holidays.

In 1998, Mohamedou and his wife traveled to Saudi Arabia to perform the hajj. That same year, unable to secure permanent residency in Germany, Mohamedou followed a college friend's recommendation and applied for landed immigrant status in Canada, and in November 1999 he moved to Montreal. He lived for a time with his former classmate and then at Montreal's large al Sunnah mosque, where, as a *hafiz*, or someone who has memorized the Koran, he was invited to lead Ramadan prayers when the imam was traveling. Less than a month after he arrived in Montreal, an Algerian immigrant and al-Qaeda member named Ahmed Ressam was arrested entering the United States with a car laden with explosives and a plan to bomb Los Angeles International Airport on New Year's Day, as part of what became known as the Millennium Plot. Ressam had been based in Montreal. He left the city before Mohamedou arrived, but he had attended the al Sunnah mosque and had connections with several of what Mohamedou, at his CSRT hearing, called his classmate's "bad friends."

Ressam's arrest sparked a major investigation of the Muslim immigrant community in Montreal, and the al Sunnah mosque community in particular, and for the first time in his life, Mohamedou was questioned about possible terrorist connections. The

Royal Canadian Mounted Police "came and interrogated me," he testified at his 2005 Administrative Review Board hearing.

> *I was scared to hell. They asked me do I know Ahmed Ressam, I said, "No," and then they asked do you know this guy and I said, "No, No." I was so scared I was shaking. . . . I was not used to this, it was the first time I had been interrogated and I just wanted to stay out of trouble and make sure I told the truth. But they were watching me in a very ugly way. It is okay to be watched, but it is not okay to see the people who are watching you. It was very clumsy, but they wanted to give the message that we are watching you.*

Back in Mauritania, Mohamedou's family was alarmed. " 'What are you doing in Canada?' " he recalled them asking. "I said nothing but look[ing] for a job. And my family decided I needed to get back to Mauritania because this guy must be in a very bad environment and we want to save him." His now ex-wife telephoned on behalf of the family to report that his mother was sick. As he described to the Review Board:

> *[She] called me and she was crying and she said, "Either you get me to Canada or you come to Mauritania." I said, "Hey, take it easy." I didn't like this life in Canada, I couldn't enjoy my freedom and being watched is not very good. I hated Canada and I said the work is very hard here. I took off on Friday, 21 January 2000; I took a flight from Montreal to Brussels, then to Dakar.[10]*

With that flight, the odyssey that will become Mohamedou's *Guantánamo Diary* begins.

It begins here because from this moment forward, a single

force determines Mohamedou's fate: the United States. Geo-graphically, what he calls his "endless world tour" of detention and interrogation will cover twenty thousand miles over the next eighteen months, starting with what is supposed to be a home-coming and ending with him marooned four thousand miles from home on a Caribbean island. He will be held and interro-gated in four countries along the way, often with the participation of Americans, and always at the behest of the United States.

Here is how the first of these detentions is described in a timeline that U.S. District Judge James Robertson included in his declassified 2010 order granting Mohamedou's habeas cor-pus petition:

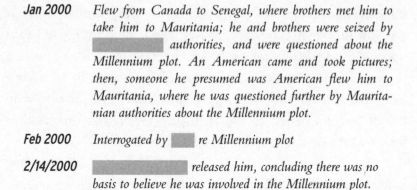

Jan 2000   *Flew from Canada to Senegal, where brothers met him to take him to Mauritania; he and brothers were seized by* ▓▓▓▓▓▓ *authorities, and were questioned about the Millennium plot. An American came and took pictures; then, someone he presumed was American flew him to Mauritania, where he was questioned further by Maurita-nian authorities about the Millennium plot.*

Feb 2000   *Interrogated by* ▓▓ *re Millennium plot*

2/14/2000   ▓▓▓▓▓▓▓▓▓ *released him, concluding there was no basis to believe he was involved in the Millennium plot.*

"The Mauritanians said, 'We don't need you, go away. We have no interest in you,'" Mohamedou recalled, describing that release at his ARB hearing. "I asked them what about the Americans? They said, 'The Americans keep saying you are a link but they don't give us any proof so what should we do?'"

But as Judge Robertson chronicled in his timeline, the Mau-ritanian government summoned Mohamedou again at the United States' request shortly after the 9/11 terrorist attacks:

9/29/2001   *Arrested in Mauritania; authorities told him* ▉▉▉▉▉
▉▉▉▉▉▉▉ *arrest because Salahi was allegedly involved in*
Millennium plot.

10/12/2001   *While he was detained, agents performed a search at his*
house, seizing tapes and documents.

10/15/2001   *Released by* ▉▉▉▉▉▉▉▉▉ *authorities.*[11]

Between those two Mauritanian arrests, both of which
included interrogations by FBI agents, Mohamedou was living
a remarkably ordinary and, by his country's standards, successful
life, doing computer and electronics work, first for a medical
supply company that also provided Internet services, and then
for a similarly diversified family-owned import business. But
now he was nervous. Although he was free and "went back to
his life," as he explained to the ARB:

I thought now I will have a problem with my employer because
my employer would not take me back because I am suspected of
terrorism, and they said they would take care of this. In front of
me while I was sitting [there] the highest intelligence guy in Mau-
ritania called my employer and said that I was a good person, we
have no problem with [him] and we arrested him for a reason. We
had to question him and we have questioned him and he is good
to go, so you can take him back.[12]

His boss did take him back, and just over a month later,
Mohamedou's work would take him to the Mauritanian Presidential Palace, where he spent a day preparing a bid to upgrade
President Maaouya Ould Sid'Ahmed Taya's telephone and computer systems. When he got home, the national police appeared
again, telling him he was needed once more for questioning.
He asked them to wait while he showered. He dressed, grabbed

his keys—he went voluntarily, driving his own car to police headquarters—and told his mother not to worry, he would be home soon. This time, though, he disappeared.

For almost a year, his family was led to believe he was in Mauritanian custody. His oldest brother, Hamoud, regularly visited the security prison to deliver clean clothes and money for Mohamedou's meals. A week after Mohamedou turned himself in, however, a CIA rendition flight had spirited him to Jordan; months later, the United States had retrieved him from Amman and delivered him to Bagram Air Base in Afghanistan and, a few weeks after that, to Guantánamo. All this time, his family was paying for his upkeep in the Nouakchott prison; all this time, the prison officials pocketed the money, saying nothing. Finally, on October 28, 2002, Mohamedou's youngest brother, Yahdih, who had assumed Mohamedou's position as the family's European breadwinner, picked up that week's edition of *Der Spiegel* and read that his brother had by then "been sitting for months in a wire cage in the U.S. prison camp in Guantánamo."

Yahdih was furious—not, he remembers, at the United States but at the local authorities who had been assuring the family they had Mohamedou and he was safe. "Those police are bad people, they're thieves!" he kept yelling when he called his family with the news. "Don't say that!" they panicked, hanging up. He called them back and started in again. They hung up again.

Yahdih still lives in Düsseldorf. He and I met last year over a series of meals in a Moroccan restaurant on Ellerstraße, a center for the city's North African community. Yahdih introduced me to several of his friends, mainly young Moroccans, many of them, like Yahdih, now German citizens. Among themselves they spoke Arabic, French, and German; with me, like Yahdih, they gamely tried English, laughing at one another's mistakes. Yahdih told a classic immigrant's joke, in Arabic for his friends and then translating for me, about an aspiring hotel worker's English test. "What do you say if you want to call someone over to you?" the applicant is quizzed. "Please come here," he answers. "What if you want him to leave?" The applicant pauses, then brightens. "I go outside and tell him, 'Please come here!'"

In Düsseldorf, Yahdih and I spent an entire meal sorting and labeling photographs of siblings, sisters- and brothers-in-law, nieces and nephews, many living in the family's multigenerational household in Nouakchott. During his 2004 CSRT hearing, Mohamedou explained his disinterest in al-Qaeda after he returned to Germany by saying, "I had a big family to feed, I had 100 mouths to feed." It was an exaggeration, but only by half, maybe. Now Yahdih bears a large share of that responsibility. Because activism can be a risky business in Mauritania, he has also assumed the family lead in advocating for Mohamedou's release. During our last meal together, we watched YouTube videos of a demonstration he helped organize in Nouakchott last year outside the Presidential Palace. The featured speaker, he pointed out, was a parliament minister.

A few days before I visited Yahdih, Mohamedou had been allowed one of his twice-yearly calls with his family. The calls are arranged under the auspices of the International Committee of the Red Cross and connect Mohamedou with the family household in Nouakchott and with Yahdih in Germany. Yahdih told me he had recently written to the Red Cross to ask if the number of calls could be increased to three a year.

The first of these calls took place in 2008, six and a half years after Mohamedou disappeared. A reporter for *Der Spiegel* witnessed the scene:

At noon on a Friday in June 2008, the Slahi family convenes at the offices of the International Red Cross (IRC) in the Mauritanian capital Nouakchott. His mother, brothers, sisters, nephews, nieces and aunts are all dressed in the flowing robes they would normally wear to a family party. They have come here to talk to Mohamedou, their lost son, by telephone. The Joint Task Force in Guantanamo has granted its approval, with the IRC acting as go-between. Thick carpets cover the stone floor and light-colored curtains billow at the windows of the IRC office.

"My son, my son, how are you feeling?" his mother asks. "I am so happy to hear you." She breaks into tears, as she hears his voice for the first time in more than six years. Mohamedou's older brother speaks with him for 40 minutes. Slahi tells his brother that he is doing well. He wants to know who has married whom, how his siblings are doing and who has had children. "That was my brother, the brother I know. He has not changed," Hamoud Ould Slahi says after the conversation.[13]

From what Yahdih tells me, the conversations remain more or less the same five years later, though two things have changed. The calls are now Skype calls, so they can see one another. And they are now missing Mohamedou's and Yahdih's mother. She died on March 27, 2013.

The lead editorial in the *New York Daily News* on March 23, 2010, was titled "Keep the Cell Door Shut: Appeal a Judge's Outrageous Ruling to Free 9/11 Thug." The editorial began:

It is shocking and true: a federal judge has ordered the release of Mohamedou Ould Slahi, one of the top recruiters for the 9/11 attacks—a man once deemed the highest-value detainee in Guantanamo.

That ruling was Judge James Robertson's then still-classified memorandum order granting Mohamedou's habeas corpus petition—the petition Mohamedou handwrote in his Camp Echo cell five years before. Without access to that order or to the legal filings or court hearing that resulted in the order, the newspaper's editorial board nevertheless conjectured that a judge was letting "a terrorist with the blood of 3,000 on his hands" go free, adding contortedly, "he possibly being a man whose guilt was certain but unprovable beyond a reasonable doubt thanks to squeamishness over evidence acquired under rough treatment." Expressing confidence that Mohamedou was "squeezed appropriately hard after 9/11" and that his treatment made the country safer, the editors urged the Obama administration to appeal the order, adding, "What was the rush to release? The judge could have waited, should have waited, for the country to understand why this had to happen before exercising his legal authority."[14]

Two weeks later, the court released a declassified, redacted version of Judge Robertson's order. A section of the opinion summarizing the government's arguments for why Mohamedou must remain in Guantánamo included a footnote that might have surprised the newspaper's readers:

> *The government also argued at first that Salahi was also detainable under the "aided in 9/11" prong of the AUMF, but it has now abandoned that theory, acknowledging that Salahi probably did not even know about the 9/11 attacks.*★[15]

That certainly would make it a stretch to call Mohamedou a "9/11 thug." It is also a stretch, by any measure, to call a

---

★ The AUMF, or Authorization for Use of Military Force, is the September 14, 2001, law under which Guantánamo operates. It authorizes the judgment ordering a man freed nine years after he was taken into custody a "rush to release." But there is a truth at the heart of that *Daily News* editorial—and much of the press coverage about Mohamedou's case—and that truth is confusion. Nine years is now thirteen, and the country seems to be no closer to understanding the U.S. government's case for holding Mohamedou than when Judge Robertson, the one judge who has thoroughly reviewed his case, ordered him released.

This much seems clear from the available record: Mohamedou's time in U.S. custody did not begin with allegations that he was a top 9/11 recruiter. When he was questioned by FBI agents on his return to Mauritania in February 2000, and again a few weeks after the 9/11 attacks, the focus was on the Millennium Plot. This appears to have been the case for his rendition to Jordan as well: "The Jordanians were investigating my part in the Millennium plot," Mohamedou told the Administrative Review Board in 2005. "They told me they are especially concerned about the Millennium plot."

By the time the CIA delivered Mohamedou to Jordan, though, Ahmed Ressam had been cooperating for months with the Justice Department in the United States, and by the time the CIA retrieved Mohamedou eight months later, Ressam had testified in two terrorism trials and provided the names of more than 150 people involved in terrorism to the U.S. government and the governments of six other countries. Some of those people were Guantánamo detainees, and the U.S. government has used Ressam's statements as evidence against them in their habeas cases.

---

president "to use all necessary and appropriate force against those nations, organizations, or persons he determines planned, authorized, committed, or aided the terrorist attacks that occurred on September 11, 2001, or harbored such organizations or persons, in order to prevent any future acts of international terrorism against the United States by such nations, organizations or persons."

Not so with Mohamedou. Ressam "conspicuously fails to implicate Salahi," Robertson noted in his habeas opinion.

The CIA would have known this. The agency would also have known if the Jordanians had uncovered anything linking Mohamedou to the Millennium Plot, the September 11 attacks, or any other terrorist plots. But the CIA apparently never provided any information from his interrogation in Amman to Guantánamo prosecutors. In a 2012 interview with the Rule of Law Oral History Project at Columbia University, Lt. Col. Stuart Couch, the Marine prosecutor assigned to build a case against Mohamedou in Guantánamo, said that the CIA showed him no intelligence reports of its own, and most of the reports the agency did share with him came from Mohamedou's Guantánamo interrogation. "He had been in their custody for six months. They knew I was the lead prosecutor. They knew we were contemplating a capital case. If we could have found his connection to 9/11, we were going to go for the death penalty."

"So something must have gone on," Stuart Couch surmised in that interview. "Slahi was in the custody of the CIA, and they must have felt like they got as much information out of him as they could, or the information they had didn't pan out to his significance, and they just kind of threw him over to U.S. military control at Bagram, Afghanistan."[16]

There is a chilling passage in the 2004 CIA inspector general's investigation report *Counterterrorism and Detention Interrogation Activities, September 2001–October 2003*, one of only two unredacted passages in a four-page blacked-out section of the report headed "Endgame." It says:

> *The number of detainees in CIA custody is relatively small by comparison with those in military custody. Nevertheless, the Agency, like the military, has an interest in the disposition of*

detainees and a particular interest in those who, if not kept in isolation, would likely have divulged information about the circumstances of their detention.[17]

In early 2002, not even Mohamedou's family knew he was in Jordan. Few people anywhere knew that the United States was operating a rendition, detention, and interrogation program, and that it was doing so not just with the assistance of long-standing allies like the Jordanian intelligence service but also with the cooperation of other, shakier friends. Mauritania was such a friend. In 2002, Mauritania's president and multi-decade ruler Ould Taya was under fire internationally for his country's human rights record, and at home for his close cooperation with the United States' antiterrorism policies. That Mohamedou had been questioned by FBI agents in his own country in 2000 had been controversial enough to attract the press. What if he had returned to the country in mid-2002 with stories that he had been turned over to the Americans without extradition proceedings, in violation of an explicit Mauritanian constitutional protection; that the CIA had delivered him in secret to Jordan; and that he had been interrogated for months in a Jordanian prison?

In any case, there is no indication that when a U.S. military C-17 carrying Mohamedou and thirty-four other prisoners landed in Guantánamo on August 5, 2002, the thirty-one-year-old Mauritanian was an especially high-value detainee. He would have stood out if so: an article published two weeks later in the *Los Angeles Times* titled "No Leaders of al Qaeda Found at Guantánamo Bay, Cuba" quoted government sources who said that there were "no big fish" in custody there, and the island's nearly six hundred detainees were not "high enough in the command and control structure to help counter-terrorism experts unravel al Qaeda's tightknit cell and security system."[18] A top secret CIA audit of the facility around the same time reportedly echoed those conclusions. When journalists visited the camp that August, the commander of Guantánamo's detention operations told them his own uniformed officers were questioning the continuing designation of detainees as "enemy combatants" as opposed to prisoners of war entitled to Geneva convention protections. The Pentagon's solution was to replace that commander and ratchet up the camp's intelligence operations.

Almost immediately a schism opened between military interrogators and the FBI and Criminal Investigation Task Force agents who had generally been leading prisoner interviews in Guantánamo. In September and October, over the fierce objections of the FBI and CITF agents, the military set up its first "Special Projects Team" and developed a written plan for the interrogation of the Saudi prisoner Mohammed al-Qahtani. That plan incorporated some of the "enhanced interrogation techniques" the CIA had been employing for several months in its own secret prison. Under the plan, which was implemented in fits and starts through the fall and finally, with the signed authorization of Defense Secretary Rumsfeld, in a harrowing fifty-day barrage starting in November, military interrogators subjected Qahtani to a round-the-clock regime of extreme sleep deprivation, loud music and white noise, frigid temperatures, stress positions, threats, and a variety of physical and sexual humiliations.

It was during this time, as the struggle over interrogation methods was playing out in the camp, that a link surfaced between Mohamedou Ould Slahi and the 9/11 hijackers. "September 11, 2002, America arrested a man by the name of Ramzi bin al-Shibh, who is said to be the key guy in the September 11th attacks," Mohamedou recounted at his 2005 ARB hearing.

> *It is exactly one year after September 11, and since his capture my life has changed drastically. The guy identified me as the guy that he saw in October 1999, which is correct, he was in my house. He said that I advised him to go to Afghanistan to train. Okay, then his interrogator* ▮▮▮▮▮▮ *from the FBI asked him to speculate who I was as a person. He said I think he is an operative of Osama bin Laden and without him I would never have been involved in September 11th.*[19]

Bin al-Shibh had been the target of an international manhunt since 9/11 for his alleged role in coordinating the "Hamburg cell" of hijackers. He was transferred to CIA custody immediately after his capture in a shoot-out in a suburb of Karachi and was held first in the CIA's "Dark Prison" in Afghanistan and then, through the fall, in a prison near Rabat, Morocco. During interrogations in one of those facilities, bin al-Shibh told of a chance meeting with a stranger on a train in Germany, where he and two friends talked of jihad and their desire to travel to Chechnya to join the fight against the Russians. The stranger suggested they contact Mohamedou in Duisburg, and when they did, Mohamedou put them up for a night. "When they arrived," the 9/11 Commission recorded in a description drawn from intelligence reports from those interrogations, "Slahi explained that it was difficult to get to Chechnya at the time because many travelers were being detained in Georgia. He recommended they go through Afghanistan instead, where they could train for jihad before traveling to Chechnya."[20]

Bin al-Shibh did not assert that Mohamedou sent him to Afghanistan to join a plot against the United States. Lt. Col. Couch, who saw the bin al-Shibh intelligence report, recalled in the 2012 interview, "I never saw any mention that it was to attack America. I never saw the fact that Ramzi Bin al-Shibh had said, 'We told him what we wanted to do, and he said, "This is where you need to go train."' It was sort of, 'This is where you can get training.'"[21] During Mohamedou's habeas proceedings, the U.S. government did not argue that he had persuaded the men to join bin Laden's plot; rather, the government alleged that in suggesting that the men seek training in Afghanistan—something Mohamedou had learned was necessary to join an earlier fight involving Russians—he was serving in general as an al-Qaeda recruiter. Judge Robertson disagreed, finding that the record showed only that "Salahi provided lodging for three men for one night in Germany, that one of these was Ramzi bin al-Shibh, and that there was discussion of jihad and Afghanistan."[22]

Stuart Couch received bin al-Shibh's intelligence reports when he was assigned Mohamedou's case in the fall of 2003. The reports, and the assignment itself, had particular significance for the former Marine pilot: his close friend Michael Horrocks, a fellow refueling tanker pilot in the Marines, was the copilot on the United Airlines flight that the 9/11 hijackers used to bring down the World Trade Center's South Tower. That event had drawn Stuart Couch back to active service. He joined the Guantánamo military commission's team of prosecutors with a purpose, hoping, as he explained in a 2007 *Wall Street Journal* profile, "to get a crack at the guys who attacked the United States."[23]

Soon he was looking at batches of intelligence reports from another source, Mohamedou himself, the fruit of what military interrogators were already touting as their most successful Guantánamo interrogation. Those reports contained no information about the circumstances of that interrogation, but Lt. Col. Couch had his suspicions. He had been told that Mohamedou was on "Special Projects." He had caught a glimpse, on his first visit to the base, of another prisoner shackled to the floor in an empty interrogation booth, rocking back and forth as a strobe light flashed and heavy metal blared. He had seen this kind of thing before: as a Marine pilot, he had endured a week of such techniques in a program that prepares U.S. airmen for the experience of capture and torture.

Those suspicions were confirmed when the lieutenant colonel's investigator, a Naval Criminal Investigative Service (NCIS) agent, gained access to military interrogators' files. Those files included the Special Projects Team's daily memoranda for the record, the interrogators' detailed accounts not only of what was said in each session but also of how the information was extracted.

Those records remain classified, but they are summarized in the U.S. Senate Armed Services Committee's 2008 *Inquiry into the Treatment of Detainees in U.S. Custody* and the Justice Department's own 2008 review of interrogations in Guantánamo, Afghanistan, and Iraq. Those reports document a "special interrogation" that followed a second painstaking, Rumsfeld-approved plan and unfolded almost exactly as Mohamedou describes it in his *Guantánamo Diary*. Among the specific documents described in those reports are two that, when Stuart Couch uncovered them in early 2004, convinced him that Mohamedou had been tortured.

The first was a fake State Department letter Mohamedou had been presented in August 2003, which was clearly meant to exploit his close relationship with his mother. In its report, the Senate Armed Services Committee describes "a fictitious letter that had been drafted by the Interrogation Team Chief stating that his mother had been detained, would be interrogated, and if she were uncooperative she might be transferred to GTMO. The letter pointed out that she would be the only female detained at 'this previously all-male prison environment.'"

The second was an October 17, 2003, e-mail exchange between

one of Mohamedou's interrogators and a U.S. military psychiatrist. In it, the committee found, the interrogator "stated that 'Slahi told me he is "hearing voices" now.... He is worried as he knows this is not normal.... By the way...is this something that happens to people who have little external stimulus such as daylight, human interaction etc???? Seems a little creepy.'" The psychologist responded, "Sensory deprivation can cause hallucinations, usually visual rather than auditory, but you never know.... In the dark you create things out of what little you have."[24]

In a 2009 interview, Lt. Col. Couch described the impact of these discoveries:

> *Right in the middle of this time, when I had received this information from the NCIS agent—the documents, the State Department letterhead—and it was at the end of this, hearing all of this information, reading all this information, months and months and months of wrangling with the issue, that I was in church this Sunday, and we had a baptism. We got to the part of the liturgy where the congregation repeats—I'm paraphrasing here, but the essence is that we respect the dignity of every human being and seek peace and justice on earth. And when we spoke those words that morning, there were a lot of people in that church, but I could have been the only one there. I just felt this incredible, alright, there it is. You can't come in here on Sunday, and as a Christian, subscribe to this belief of dignity of every human being and say I will seek justice and peace on the earth, and continue to go with the prosecution using that kind of evidence. And at that point I knew what I had to do. I had to get off the fence.*[25]

Stuart Couch withdrew from Mohamedou's case, refusing to proceed with any effort to try him before a military commission.

No charge sheet has ever been drawn up against Mohamedou

Ould Slahi in Guantánamo, no military commission defense attorney was ever appointed to his case, and it appears there have been no further attempts to prepare a case for prosecution. The *Daily News* editorial decrying Judge Robertson's habeas decision attributes this to "squeamishness" over using "evidence acquired under rough treatment," but it is not at all clear that Mohamedou's brutal Guantánamo interrogation yielded any evidence that he had a hand in any criminal or terrorist activities. At his 2005 ARB hearing, he told of manufacturing confessions under torture, but the interrogators themselves must have discounted what they knew to be induced confessions; what they passed along in their scrubbed intelligence reports consisted instead, Stuart Couch has said, of a kind of "Who's Who of al Qaeda in Germany and all of Europe."[26]

Just as his extreme treatment is often cited as an indicator of his guilt, so those intelligence reports have come to serve as a kind of after-the-fact proof that Mohamedou himself must be among the Who's Who. And yet, Stuart Couch has suggested, Mohamedou's knowledge seems to have been little better than his interrogators'. "I think, if my recollection is right, that most of them had already been known to the intelligence services when he was being questioned," Couch noted in the 2012 interview, adding:

> *I've got to be clear on something. When you read the intelligence reports given up by Slahi, he doesn't implicate himself in anything. The only way he implicates himself is by his knowledge of these people. He never implicates himself in any of what I would consider to be an overt act that was part of the al-Qaeda conspiracy to attack the United States on 9/11.*[27]

Nor, it seems, have U.S. intelligence services unearthed anything else implicating Mohamedou in other terrorist plots or attacks. In a 2013 interview, Colonel Morris Davis, who became chief prosecutor for the Guantánamo military commissions in 2005, described a last-ditch effort, almost two years after Stuart Couch withdrew from Mohamedou's case, to develop some kind of charge against Mohamedou. Colonel Davis's real target at the time was not Mohamedou, who by then hardly even registered on the prosecutorial radar, but rather the prisoner the military had moved into the hut next door to Mohamedou's to mitigate the effects of his torture and almost two years of solitary confinement. That prisoner would not accept a plea bargain, however, unless Mohamedou received a similar offer. "We had to figure some kind of similar deal for Slahi," Colonel Davis said in that interview, "which meant we had to find *something* we could charge him with, and that was where we were having real trouble."

When Slahi came in, I think the suspicion was that they'd caught a big fish. He reminded me of Forrest Gump, in the sense that there were a lot of noteworthy events in the history of al-Qaida and terrorism, and there was Slahi, lurking somewhere in the background. He was in Germany, Canada, different places that look suspicious, and that caused them to believe that he was a big fish, but then when they really invested the effort to look into it, that's not where they came out. I remember a while after I got there, in early 2007, we had a big meeting with the CIA, the FBI, the Department of Defense, and the Department of Justice, and we got a briefing from the investigators who worked on the Slahi case, and their conclusion was there's a lot of smoke and no fire.[28]

When Mohamedou's habeas corpus petition finally came before the federal court in 2009, the U.S. government did not try to argue that he was a major al-Qaeda figure or that he had a hand in any al-Qaeda plans or attacks. As the DC Circuit Court of Appeals wrote in its subsequent review of the case:

> The United States seeks to detain Mohammedou Ould Salahi on the grounds that he was "part of" al-Qaida not because he fought with al-Qaida or its allies against the United States, but rather because he swore an oath of allegiance to the organization, associated with its members, and helped it in various ways, including hosting its leaders and referring aspiring jihadists to a known al-Qaida operative.[29]

When Judge Robertson heard Mohamedou's petition in 2009, the DC district courts presiding over Guantánamo habeas cases were judging the question of whether a petitioner was part of al-Qaeda based on whether the government could show that the petitioner was an active member of the organization at the time he was detained. Mohamedou had joined al-Qaeda in 1991 and sworn a loyalty oath to the organization at that time, but that was a very different al-Qaeda, practically an ally of the United States; Mohamedou has always maintained that the fall of the communist government in Afghanistan marked the end of his participation in the organization. In his habeas proceedings, the government insisted that his occasional contacts and interactions with his brother-in-law and cousin Abu Hafs and a handful of other friends and acquaintances who had remained active in al-Qaeda proved that Mohamedou was still a part of the organization. While a few of those interactions involved possible gestures of support, none, Robertson suggested, rose to the level of criminal material support for terrorism, and overall, Mohamedou's contacts with these people were so sporadic that "they tend to support Salahi's submission that he was attempting to find the appropriate balance — avoiding close relationships with al Qaida members, but also trying to avoid making himself an enemy."

Judge Robertson's decision granting Mohamedou's habeas corpus petition and ordering his release came at a critical moment: as of April 1, 2010, the U.S. government had lost thirty-four out of forty-six habeas cases. In appeals of several of those cases, the government persuaded the DC Circuit Court of Appeals to accept a looser standard for judging whether a petitioner was "part of" al-Qaeda; now, as the appellate court explained in reversing Judge Robertson's order and remanding the case to district court for rehearing, the government no longer needed to show that a Guantánamo prisoner was carrying out al-Qaeda orders or directions at the time he was taken into custody.

In its opinion, the appeals court was careful to delineate "the precise nature of the government's case against Salahi." "The government has not criminally indicted Salahi for providing material support to terrorists or the 'foreign terrorist organization' al-Qaida," the court emphasized. "Nor," it added, "does the government seek to detain Salahi under the AUMF on the grounds that he aided the September 11 attacks or 'purposefully and materially support[ed]' forces associated with al-Qaeda 'in hostilities against U.S. Coalition partners.'" Rather, when Mohamedou's habeas corpus case is reheard in federal court, the government will likely again be arguing that his sporadic interactions with active al-Qaeda members in the 1990s mean that he too remained a member. Under the new standard, the court wrote, "Even if Salahi's connections to these individuals fail independently to prove that he was 'part of' al-Qaeda, those connections make it more likely that Salahi was a member of the organization when captured and thus remain relevant to the question of whether he is detainable."[30]

Ironically, when a district court rehears the case, the government will likely face questions about what it has always contended is the most damaging of those connections, Mohamedou's relationship with his cousin and brother-in-law Abu Hafs. As a member of bin Laden's Shura Council, Abu Hafs had a $5 million bounty on his head from the United States in the late 1990s, a figure that increased to $25 million after the September 11, 2001, terrorist attacks. For years, though, the United States has known that Abu Hafs opposed those attacks; the 9/11 Commission reported that he "even wrote Bin Laden a message basing opposition to those attacks on the Qur'an." After the attacks, Abu Hafs left Afghanistan for Iran, where Iranian authorities placed him under a soft form of house arrest for more than a decade. In April 2012, Iran repatriated Abu Hafs to Mauritania. He was held for two months in a Mauritanian prison, during which he reportedly met with an international delegation that included Americans, condemned the 9/11 attacks, and renounced his ties to al-Qaeda. He was released in July 2012 and has been living since then as a free man.

I have not met Mohamedou Ould Slahi. Other than sending him a letter introducing myself when I was asked if I would help to bring his manuscript to print—a letter I do not know if he received—I have not communicated with him in any way.

I did request to meet with him at least once before submitting the completed work to make sure my edits met with his approval. The answer from the Pentagon was brief and absolute. "Visiting or otherwise communicating with any detainee in the detention facility in Guantanamo, unless you are legal counsel representing the detainee, is not possible," a public affairs officer wrote.

"As you are aware, the detainees are held under the Law of War. Additionally, we do not subject detainees to public curiosity."

The phrase "public curiosity" comes from one of the pillars of the Law of War, the 1949 Geneva Convention Relative to the Treatment of Prisoners of War. Article 13 of the convention, "Humane Treatment of Prisoners," says:

> *Prisoners must at all times be humanely treated. Any unlawful act or omission by the Detaining Power causing death or seriously endangering the health of a prisoner of war in its custody will be prohibited, and will be regarded as a serious breach of the present Convention. . . .*
>
> *Prisoners must at all times be protected, particularly from acts of violence or intimidation and against insults and public curiosity.*
>
> *Measures of reprisal against prisoners of war are prohibited.*

I had proposed a confidential meeting, under strict security protocols, to make sure the edited version of Mohamedou's work—a work he specifically wrote for a public readership—accurately represents the original content and intent. For years that work itself was withheld, under a censorship regime that has not always served Geneva's purposes.

Censorship has been integral to the United States' post-9/11 detention operations from the start. It has been purposeful, not once but twice: first, to open a space for the abuse of prisoners, and then to conceal that those abuses happened. In Mohamedou's case, those abuses include enforced disappearance; arbitrary and incommunicado detention; cruel, inhuman, and degrading treatment; and torture. We know this thanks to a documentary record that was also, for years, rigorously suppressed.

I do not know to what extent personal and institutional

interests in covering up those abuses have contributed to Mohamedou's continuing imprisonment. I do know that in the five years I have spent reading the record about his case, I have not been persuaded by my government's vague and shifting explanations for why he is in Guantánamo, or by the assertions of those who defend his now-thirteen-year detention by saying he is almost certainly, or possibly, a this or a that. My own sense of fairness tells me the question of what this or that may be, and of why he must remain in U.S. custody, should long ago have been answered. It would have been, I believe, if his *Guantánamo Diary* had not been kept secret for so long.

When Mohamedou wrote the manuscript for this book nine years ago, in the same isolated hut where some of the book's most nightmarish scenes had very recently happened, he set himself a task. "I have only written what I experienced, what I saw, and what I learned first-hand," he explains near the end. "I have tried not to exaggerate, nor to understate. I have tried to be as fair as possible, to the U.S. government, to my brothers, and to myself."

He has, from everything I have seen, done just that. The story he tells is well corroborated by the declassified record; he proves again and again to be a reliable narrator. He certainly does not exaggerate: the record contains torments and humiliations not included in the book, and he renders several of those he does include with considerable discretion. Even when the events he recounts are at their most extreme, his narration is tempered and direct. The horrors of those events speak for themselves.

That is because his real interest is always in the human dramas of these scenes. "The law of war is harsh," Mohamedou writes early on.

If there's anything good at all in a war, it's that it brings the best and the worst out of people: some people try to use the lawlessness to hurt others, and some try to reduce the suffering to the minimum.

In chronicling his journey through the darkest regions of the United States' post-9/11 detention and interrogation program, his attention remains on his interrogators and guards, on his fellow detainees, and on himself. In his desire "to be fair," as he puts it, he recognizes the larger context of fear and confusion in which all these characters interact, and the much more local institutional and social forces that shape those interactions. But he also sees the capacity of every character to shape or mitigate the action, and he tries to understand people, regardless of stations or uniforms or conditions, as protagonists in their own right. In doing so, he transforms even the most dehumanizing situations into a series of individual, and at times harrowingly intimate, human exchanges.

This is the secret world of Guantánamo—a world of startlingly premeditated brutalities and of incidental degradations, but also a world of ameliorating gestures and kindnesses, of acknowledgments and recognitions, of mutual curiosities and risky forays across deep divides. That Mohamedou managed to experience all of this despite four years of the most arbitrary treatment imaginable and in the midst of one of Guantánamo's most horrendous interrogations says a great deal about his own character and his humanity. It says even more about his skills as a writer that he was able, so soon after the most traumatic of those experiences, to create from them a narrative that manages to be both damning and redeeming.

And yet this is not what impressed me most, as a reader and as a writer, when I first opened the file with Mohamedou's handwritten manuscript of *Guantánamo Diary*. What arrested me were characters and scenes far removed from Guantánamo: The hard-luck stowaway in a Senegalese prison. A sunset in Nouakchott after a Saharan dust storm. A heartbreaking moment of homesickness during a Ramadan call to prayer. The airport approach over Nouakchott's shantytowns. A rain-glazed runway in Cyprus. A drowsy predawn lull on a CIA rendition flight. Here is where I first recognized Mohamedou the writer, his sharp eye for character, his remarkable ear for voices, the way his recollections are infused with information recorded by all five senses, the way he accesses the full emotional register, in himself and others. He has the qualities I value most in a writer: a moving sense of beauty and a sharp sense of irony. He has a fantastic sense of humor.

He manages all of this in English, his fourth language, a language he was in the process of mastering even as he wrote the manuscript. This accomplishment testifies to a lifelong facility and fascination with words. But it also stems, it is clear, from a determination to engage, and to meet his environment on its own terms. On one level, mastering English in Guantánamo meant moving beyond translation and interpretation, beyond the necessity of a third person in the room, and opening the possibility that every contact with every one of his captors could be a personal exchange. On another, it meant decoding and understanding the language of the power that controls his fate — a power, as his twenty-thousand-mile odyssey of detention and interrogation vividly illustrates, of staggering influence and reach. Out of this engagement comes a truly remarkable work. On the one hand, it is a mirror in which, for the first time in anything I have read from Guantánamo, I have recognized aspects of myself, in both the characters of my compatriots and of those my country is holding captive. On another, it is a lens on an empire with a scope and impact few of us who live inside it fully understand.

For now, that power still controls Mohamedou's story. It is present in these pages in the form of more than 2,600 black-box redactions. These redactions do not just hide important elements of the action. They also blur Mohamedou's guiding principles and his basic purpose, undercutting the candor with which he addresses his own case, and obscuring his efforts to distinguish his characters as individuals, some culpable, some admirable, most a complex and shifting combination of both.

And it is present above all in his continuing, poorly explained imprisonment. Thirteen years ago, Mohamedou left his home in Nouakchott, Mauritania, and drove to the headquarters of his national police for questioning. He has not returned. For our collective sense of story and of justice, we must have a clearer understanding of why this has not happened yet, and what will happen next.

Guantánamo lives on unanswered questions. But now that we have *Guantánamo Diary*, how can we not at least resolve the questions in Mohamedou's case?

When we do, I believe there will be a homecoming. When that happens, the redactions will be filled in, the text will be reedited and amended and updated as Mohamedou himself would have it, and we will all be free to see *Guantánamo Diary* for what it ultimately is: an account of one man's odyssey through an increasingly borderless and anxious world, a world where the forces shaping lives are ever more distant and clandestine, where destinies are determined by powers with seemingly infinite reach, a world that threatens to dehumanize but fails to dehumanize—in short, an epic for our times.

1 Transcript, Administrative Review Board Hearing for Mohamedou Ould Slahi, December 15, 2005, 18. The ARB transcript is available at http://www.dod.mil/pubs/foi/operation_and_plans/Detainee/csrt_arb /ARB_Transcript_Set_8_20751-21016.pdf, 184–216.

EDITOR'S NOTE ON THE INTRODUCTION: None of Mohamedou Ould Slahi's attorneys holding security clearances has reviewed this introduction, contributed to it in any way, or confirmed or denied anything in it. Nor has anyone else with access to the unredacted manuscript reviewed this introduction, contributed to it in any way, or confirmed or denied anything in it.

2 Letter to attorney Sylvia Royce, November 9, 2006, http://online .wsj.com/public/resources/documents/couch-slahiletter-03312007.pdf.

3 Transcript, Combatant Status Review Tribunal Hearing for Mohamedou Ould Slahi, December 8, 2004, 7–8. The CSRT transcript is available at http://online.wsj.com/public/resources/documents/couch -slahihearing-03312007.pdf.

4 ARB transcript, 14, 18–19, 25–26.

5 ARB transcript, 26–27.

6 Department of Defense News Briefing, Secretary Rumsfeld and Gen. Myers, January 11, 2002, http://www.defense.gov/transcripts/transcript .aspx?transcriptid=2031.

7 Department of Defense Press Release, April 3, 2006, http://www .defense.gov/news/newsarticle.aspx?id=15573.

8 John Goetz, Marcel Rosenbach, Britta Sandberg, and Holger Stark, "From Germany to Guantanamo: The Career of Prisoner No. 760," *Der Spiegel*, October 9, 2008, http://www.spiegel.de/international/world/from -germany-to-guantanamo-the-career-of-prisoner-no-760-a-583193.html.

9 CSRT transcript, 3–4.

10 ARB transcript, 15–16.

11 Memorandum Order, *Mohammedou Ould Salahi v. Barack H. Obama*, No. 1:05-cv-00569-JR, 13–14. The Memorandum Order is available at https://www.aclu.org/files/assets/2010-4-9-Slahi-Order.pdf.

12 ARB transcript, 19.

13 Goetz et al., "From Germany to Guantanamo."

14 "Keep the Cell Door Shut: Appeal a Judge's Outrageous Ruling to Free 9/11 Thug," Editorial, *New York Daily News*, March 23, 2010, http:// www.nydailynews.com/opinion/cell-door-shut-appeal-judge-outrageous -ruling-free-9-11-thug-article-1.172231.

15 Memorandum Order, 4.

16 The Reminiscences of V. Stuart Couch, March 1–2, 2012, Columbia Center for Oral History Collection (hereafter cited as CCOHC), 94, 117, http://www.columbia.edu/cu/libraries/inside/ccoh_assets/ccoh_10100507 _transcript.pdf.

17 CIA Office of the Inspector General, "Counterterrorism Detention and Interrogation Activities, September 2001–October 2003," May 7, 2004, 96. The CIA OIG report is available at http://media.luxmedia.com/aclu /IG_Report.pdf.

18 Bob Drogin, "No Leaders of Al Qaeda Found at Guantanamo," *Los Angeles Times*, August 18, 2002, http://articles.latimes.com/2002/aug/18 /nation/na-gitmo18.

19 ARB transcript, 23–24.

20 The National Commission on Terrorist Attacks upon the United States, *The 9/11 Commission Report* 165–166. The 9/11 Commission report is available at http://govinfo.library.unt.edu/911/report/911Report.pdf.

21 CCOHC interview with V. Stuart Couch, 90.

22 Memorandum Order, 19.

23 Jess Bravin, "The Conscience of the Colonel," *Wall Street Journal*, March 31, 2007, http://online.wsj.com/news/articles/SB117529704337355155.

24 U.S. Senate Committee on Armed Services, "Inquiry into the Treatment of Detainees in U.S. Custody," November 20, 2008, 140–41. The committee's report is available at http://www.armed-services.senate .gov/imo/media/doc/Detainee-Report-Final_April-22-2009.pdf.

25 Transcript of interview with Lt. Col. Stuart Couch for *Torturing Democracy*, http://www2.gwu.edu/~nsarchiv/torturingdemocracy/interviews /stuart_couch.html.

26 Bravin, "The Conscience of the Colonel."

27 CCOHC interview with V. Stuart Couch, 95.

28 Colonel Morris Davis, interview by Larry Siems, *Slate*, May 1, 2013, http://www.slate.com/articles/news_and_politics/foreigners/2013/04 /mohamedou_ould_slahi_s_guant_namo_memoirs_an_interview_with _colonel_morris.html.

29 Order, *Salahi v. Obama*, 625 F.3d 745, 746 (D.C. Cir. 2010). The decision is available at http://caselaw.findlaw.com/us-dc-circuit/1543844 .html.

30 Ibid., 750, 753.

Editor's Acknowledgments to the First Edition

That we are able to read this book at all is thanks to the efforts of Mohamedou Ould Slahi's pro-bono lawyers, who fought for more than six years to have the manuscript cleared for public release. They did this quietly and respectfully, but also tenaciously, believing—and ultimately proving—that the truth is not incompatible with security. Time will only underscore what an accomplishment this has been, and how much readers everywhere owe a debt of gratitude to Nancy Hollander and Theresa M. Duncan, his lead attorneys; to their private co-counsel Linda Moreno, Sylvia Royce, and Jonathan Hafetz; and to their co-counsel Hina Shamsi, Brett Kaufman, Jonathan Manes, and Melissa Goodman of the National Security Project of the American Civil Liberties Union and Art Spitzer of the ACLU of the National Capital Area.

I owe my own profound thanks to Nancy Hollander and the rest of Mohamedou Ould Slahi's legal team, and above all to Mohamedou Ould Slahi himself, for offering me the opportunity to help bring these words to print. Every day I have spent reading, thinking about, and working with Mohamedou's manuscript has illuminated in some new way what a gift their trust and confidence has been.

Publishing material that remains subject to severe censorship restrictions is not for the faint of heart, and so I am especially grateful to all those who have championed the publication of Mohamedou's work: to Will Dobson and *Slate* for the chance to present excerpts from the manuscript and the space to put those excerpts in context; to Rachel Vogel, my literary agent, to Geoff Shandler, Michael Sand, and Allie Sommer at Little, Brown, and to Jamie Byng and Katy Follain at Canongate for their vision and patient navigation of a variety of publication challenges; and to everyone at Little, Brown/Hachette, Canongate, and all the foreign language publishers of *Guantánamo Diary* for making it possible for this once-suppressed but irrepressible work to be read around the world.

Anyone who has written about what has happened in Guantánamo owes a debt to the ACLU's National Security Project, whose Freedom of Information Act litigation unearthed the trove of secret documents that stands as the stark historical record of the United States's abusive post–9/11 detention and interrogation practices. I am grateful for that record, without which the cross-referencing, corroboration, and annotation of Mohamedou's account would not have been possible, and even more grateful for the opportunities the ACLU has given me over the last five years to explore, absorb, and write about that indispensable record.

I am indebted to many who shared their time, insights, experiences, and ideas with me as I was working with this manuscript. I cannot mention them all, but I cannot fail to mention Yahdih Ould Slahi, for helping me understand Mohamedou's experience from his family's perspective, and Jameel Jaffer, Hina Shamsi, Lara Tobin, and Eli Davis Siems, for their constant support, thoughtful counsel, and careful readings of edited versions of this book.

Finally, I am forever indebted to Mohamedou Ould Slahi, for the courage to write his manuscript, for the integrity, wit, and humanity of his writing, and for the faith he has shown in all of us, the reading public, in committing his experiences to print. May he at least, and at last, receive the same honest judgment he has afforded us.

About the Authors

Mohamedou Ould Slahi was born in a small town in Mauritania in 1970. He won a scholarship to attend college in Germany and worked there for several years as an engineer. He returned to Mauritania in 2000. The following year, at the behest of the United States, he was detained by Mauritanian authorities and rendered to a prison in Jordan; later he was rendered again, first to Bagram Air Force Base in Afghanistan, and finally, on August 5, 2002, to the U.S. prison at Guantánamo Bay, Cuba, where he was subjected to severe torture. In 2010, a federal judge ordered him immediately released, but the government appealed that decision. He was cleared and released on October 16, 2016, and repatriated to his native country of Mauritania. No charges were filed against him during or after this ordeal.

Larry Siems is a writer and human rights activist and for many years directed the Freedom to Write Program at PEN American Center. He is the author, most recently, of *The Torture Report: What the Documents Say about America's Post-9/11 Torture Program*. He lives in New York.

UNCLASSIFIED PROTECTED

372

responded the detainee in broken Arabic with his obvious Turkish accent. I right away knew the setup. This interrogation ▓▓▓ was meant for me in the first place, "Liar!" shouted ▓▓▓ "I ain't lying" responded the guy in Arabic, although ▓▓▓ kept speaking his loose English, "I don't care if you have a German or American Passport you're going to tell me the truth!" said ▓▓▓ Now, I knew that the ▓▓▓ The setup fitted perfectly, and meant to terrorize me even more. Although I knew right away it was a setup but the scaring effect was not affected." Hi ▓▓▓ said ▓▓▓ "Hi" I responded feeling his breath right in front of my face. I was so terrorized that I couldn't realize what he was saying." So your name is ▓▓▓ "he concluded "No!". "But you responded when I called you ▓▓▓ he argued. I didn't really realize that he had called me ▓▓▓ but I found it idiot to tell him that I was so terrorized that I couldn't realize what name he call me "If you look at it we all are ▓▓▓ I correctly answered. ▓▓▓ means in Arabic God's servant. However, I knew where Abu Fati How ▓▓▓ came up with the name of ▓▓▓ The Story of the Name ▓▓▓ : When I arrived in Montreal / Canada on 26 Nov 1999 my friend ▓▓▓ introduced me to his roommate ▓▓▓ with my same civilian name. When I later on met with another ▓▓▓ who happened to see a year before with me, he called me ▓▓▓ and I responded b/c I found it impolite to correct him. Since then ▓▓▓ called me ▓▓▓